SCHAUM'S OUTLINE OF

THEORY AND PROBLEMS

of

PERSONAL FINANCE

JAE K. SHIM, Ph.D.

Professor of Finance and Accounting
California State University at Long Beach

JOEL G. SIEGEL, Ph.D., CPA

Professor of Finance and Accounting
Queens College
City University of New York

SCHAUM'S OUTLINE SERIES

McGRAW-HILL, INC.

New York   St. Louis   San Francisco   Auckland   Bogotá   Caracas
Hamburg   Lisbon   London   Madrid   Mexico   Milan   Montreal
New Delhi   Paris   San Juan   São Paulo   Singapore
Sydney   Tokyo   Toronto

JAE K. SHIM, Ph.D., is Professor of Finance and Accounting at California State University, Long Beach. He received his MBA and Ph.D. degrees from the University of California at Berkeley. Dr. Shim is also a financial consultant to companies. He has 18 books to his credit including the Schaum's Outlines of Managerial Finance, Managerial Accounting, and Financial Accounting. His books have been published by McGraw-Hill, Prentice-Hall, John Wiley, Harper and Row, Barron's, and American Institute of CPAs. Dr. Shim has written over 50 articles. He was the recipient of the Credit Research Foundation Award.

JOEL G. SIEGEL, Ph.D., CPA, is Professor of Finance and Accounting at Queens College of the City University of New York. He is also an active financial consultant to several companies. Dr. Siegel coauthored the Schaum's Outlines of Managerial Finance, Managerial Accounting, and Financial Accounting. He has 24 books to his credit and approximately 175 articles. His books have been published by McGraw-Hill, Prentice-Hall, John Wiley, Harper and Row, Barron's, and American Institute of CPAs. Dr. Siegel is listed in Who's Where Among Writers and Who's Who in the World.

Schaum's Outline of Theory and Problems of
PERSONAL FINANCE

2 3 4 5 6 7 8 9 10 11 12 13 14 15 16 17 18 19 20 SHP SHP 9 2 1

0-07-057559-2

Sponsoring Editor, John Aliano
Production Supervisor, Annette Mayeski
Editing Supervisors; Meg Tobin, Maureen Walker
Cover design by Amy E. Becker.

Library of Congress Catalog-in-Publication Data
Shim, Jae K.
    Schaum's outline of personal finance / Jae K. Shim, Joel G.
    Siegel.--1st ed.
        p.   cm.--(Schaum's outline series)
    Includes index.
    ISBN 0-07-057559-2
    1. Finance, Personal.   2. Finance, Personal--Examinations,
questions, etc.   3. Finance, Personal--Outlines, syllabi, etc.
I. Siegel, Joel G.   II. Title.
HG179.S466   1991
332.024—dc20
                                                    90-42602
                                                    CIP

Preface

Personal finance is the fastest growing discipline in the academic world and one of the most demanded areas by individuals. Colleges are offering Personal Finance courses in their business programs. This book can be used at both the undergraduate and graduate levels of college education. It may also be used as a trade book for the layperson. What is more important to the "average person" than personal financial planning and money management? Our Outline is an excellent study guide and includes all the major topics covered in college texts on personal finance. Hence, our book will prove a valuable supplement to students trying to understand this difficult material.

We provide many solved problems to explain specific points. In contrast, college textbooks do not have enough problems at the end of each chapter for the student to practice with (for example, homework).

The Schaum's Outline of Personal Finance has text discussion, examples, review questions, and solved problems. Our book is oriented toward computation consistent with the Schaum approach. To clarify and supplement the discussion in each chapter, we will make use of charts, tables, illustrations, exhibits, and checklists. There is practical application of principles, concepts, and tools of personal finance. It is comprehensive in coverage and presentation. The student is provided with the following:

1. Definitions and explanations that are clear and concise
2. Examples that illustrate the concepts and techniques discussed in each chapter
3. Review questions and answers
4. Detailed solutions to representative problems covering the subject matter

Professional designations (notably, Certified Financial Planner, abbreviated as CFP, and Chartered Financial Consultant, abbreviated as ChFC) recognize competence in the field of financial planning. They are gaining popularity and prestige. This book helps students prepare for these professional examinations and is a valuable source for review and self-testing.

We would like to thank our graduate assistants Rei-Mei Tang and Chih-Chen Huang for their assistance in evaluating the clarity of the problems.

Jae K. Shim
Joel G. Siegel

Contents

CONTENTS

CONTENTS

Chapter 1

Introduction

Financial planning is the way to arrive at solutions to your financial concerns and problems and to take advantage of your earning years to become financially independent. It involves implementation of total, coordinated plans for the achievement of overall personal objectives. Financial planning can start at any age, but the sooner the better. You may want to have substantial assets during midlife to buy a businesss or just to enjoy yourself. You should define your financial goals and establish plans to accomplish them, which may involve some sacrifices. You should learn how to manage your own money including how to save and invest so that at retirement you will have adequate funds. Even with a moderate level of income, you can build substantial wealth by exercising discipline in your financial affairs.

WHAT SHOULD YOU KNOW ABOUT THE PERSONAL FINANCIAL PLANNING PROCESS?

The main causes of failing financially are procrastination and inability to formulate personal goals, ignorance of where to invest, inability to manage debt, lack of tax planning, failure to plan for retirement, insufficient insurance, taking excessive risk, and failure to keep adequate records.

SOLVED PROBLEM 1.1

What should you consider in personal financial planning?

SOLUTION

Personal financial planning involves consideration of investments, cash management and banking, savings plans, risk tolerance, insurance coverage, credit management, tax planning, retirement planning, estate planning, cost determination, where to live, planning for children's education, career choice, and specific job choice.

SOLVED PROBLEM 1.2

How does personal financial planning help you?

SOLUTION

Personal financial planning helps you to:

Obtain what you really want through each life cycle.

Preserve assets.

Use credit prudently.

Exercise good risk management including establishing risk tolerance for investing.

Provide adequate insurance protection. Protection against personal risk is needed for death, disability, income loss, medical care, property and liability, and unemployment.

Increase your wealth.

Control costs.

SOLVED PROBLEM 1.3

What are the objectives of personal financial planning?

SOLUTION

The goals of personal financial planning include: preserve financial security, have a program to meet financial requirements, evaluate and select available options, manage risk effectively, take care of records, and avoid areas where impending legislation threatens profitability or tax treatment of the investment.

Certain goals may have to be modified because of changing times.

EXAMPLE 1.1 Increasing costs may require adjusting your goal of depositing a certain amount to a savings account.

SOLVED PROBLEM 1.4

What are the key areas in personal financial planning?

SOLUTION

The major areas of personal financial planning include

Proper insurance coverage to protect against personal risk such as death, disability, and losses. For example, adequate life insurance is needed for dependents. Insurance coverage should be modified periodically, as necessary.

Capital accumulation. There should be a regular savings and investment program. A balanced investment portfolio should exist (for example, certificates of deposit, equity securities, fixed-income securities) taking into account financial goals and risk tolerance.

Investment and property management. You should manage your assets for high return without undue risk.

Tax planning. Tax saving techniques should be employed.

Debt and credit management. You should not be overextended.

Planning for retirement. Adequate retirement income should be provided for.

Estate planning. Proper estate planning is needed to assure assets are transferred to beneficiaries, as desired. Some assets may be arranged in such a way as to provide your heirs protection from creditors' claims in bankruptcy. Examples are spendthrift provisions in life insurance settlement options and personal trust agreements.

SOLVED PROBLEM 1.5

What are the steps in personal financial planning?

SOLUTION

Personal financial planning involves the following steps:

Setting objectives and goals.

Formulating a plan to meet objectives.

Obtaining needed information (for example, current investments, provisions in insurance policies, retirement benefits, tax law provisions).

Determining desired risk level.

Preparing personal financial statements.

Looking at current position and evaluating alternatives, including appraising current financial status.

Reviewing estate plan.

Reviewing performance of financial plan and making necessary revisions.

Identifying and solving personal financial planning problems.

SOLVED PROBLEM 1.6

There are many questions that need answering in personal financial planning. What are some of these questions?

SOLUTION

Relevant questions are

Have you communicated your goals to family members?

What are you most concerned with when it comes to money?

How much discretionary income do you have?

Are you spending more than you should? Where?

Do you anticipate a material change in income and if so by how much?

Are you adequately insured?

What annual income will your family need if you die, and how long will they need it?

Are insurance premiums reasonable?

What is your credit and debt situation?

What is your return-risk trade-off?

How much should you save annually?

Is your investment portfolio balanced?

Have you minimized taxes as much as legally possible?

Can you reduce living expenses? Where?

Will you have enough at retirement to live on?

Does your estate plan meet your needs and what, if any, are the tax consequences?

Do you expect to receive a significant inheritance? How much?

Do you have a will and what does it provide?

Is your personal record-keeping system adequate? Are you able to keep track of important family records and documents?

How are you affected by inflation? For example, will your earned after-tax income grow at a faster rate than inflation?

Do you have good collateral for loans? Examples of good collateral are savings accounts and quality securities. On the other hand, some types of property are not good quality such as speculative stocks and vacant real estate.

What do you earn after tax on your investments?

SOLVED PROBLEM 1.7

You earn 8 percent on a taxable savings account and are at the 28 percent marginal tax rate.

(a) How much will you net after tax on your savings?

(b) Assuming an inflation rate of 5 percent, what are you left with after taxes and inflation?

SOLUTION

(a) $.08 - .28(.08) = .08 - .0224 = .0576 = 5.76\%$

(b) $5.76\% - 5.00\% = .76\%$

SOLVED PROBLEM 1.8

You borrow $10,000 at 10 percent interest in 19X8 to buy property. After 1 year, inflation has increased the replacement cost of the property by 8 percent.

(a) How much would the property sell for in 19X9?

(b) By borrowing, how much principal and interest will you pay?

(c) What is the real cost of financing the property?

SOLUTION

(a) $10,000 \times 1.08 = $10,800

(b) $10,000 \times 1.10 = $11,000

(c) $11,000 - $10,800 = $200

SOLVED PROBLEM 1.9

What are the negative effects from inadequate planning?

SOLUTION

The adverse consequences of not planning include inadequate protection if personal catastrophe occurs (for example, death, illness, accident, unemployment); insufficient funds for children's education; inadequate retirement funds; payment of higher taxes than necessary (for example, income tax, estate tax, gift tax); excessive costs to settle the estate; and not meeting lifetime objectives.

Caution: Do not waste financial resources by planning excessively (for example, excessive insurance coverage such as insuring your house for more than it's worth).

SOLVED PROBLEM 1.10

What personal factors should be taken into account in financial planning?

SOLUTION

Personal factors to be considered in financial planning include

Present income and desired future income.

Liquidity needs.

Possible inheritances.

Standard of living (for example, level of expenses).

Net worth.

Age and health. Younger individuals are more concerned with insurance and capital accumulation. Further, younger individuals can take more risks than older ones. Older people are concerned with retirement and estate planning. They look to fixed income. Middle-aged individuals are concerned more with reducing taxes and capital accumulation.

Investment preferences. If you are risk adverse, you will favor U.S. government securities. If you desire growth, you will select stocks with capital appreciation potential.

Stability of employment.

Insurance coverage.

Family composition. If you are married, you want adequate life insurance to protect your family. If there are small children, education costs (for example, college) are ahead. A childless working couple is free to speculate with investments. A retired couple on a fixed income do not want to take undue risk.

Personal and/or retirement obligations.

Sufficiency of estate to satisfy beneficiaries.

The factors causing a change in the personal plan are change in the inflation rate, new tax laws, children, divorce, and illness.

WHAT RECORDS DO YOU NEED?

Filing and record keeping may be boring, but it is essential as part of your personal financial planning program. You must know your family's assets and where vital documents are.

SOLVED PROBLEM 1.11

What important records have to be kept?

SOLUTION

The following records should be retained: tax records; sources of income; investment records; owner-ship records to home and other real estate (for example, deeds, mortgages); ownership records of other ma-jor assets (for example, proof of ownership may be needed for fire or theft loss to obtain insurance reimbursement); pictures of property; insurance policies; credit card accounts; notes payable; banking records; pension and profit sharing plan information; health records; and will.

Bills, canceled checks, and other substantiating documentation (for example, purchase and sale of stock confirmations) are needed if there is an IRS or state audit of your tax return.

A simple or complex system of record keeping is used depending upon your needs. For some, check-book stubs, canceled checks, securities brokers' and bank statements, and sales receipts are enough. Others require a more elaborate system including an income-and-expense ledger, an investment-transaction log, and a diary for recording business expenses. *Note:* Expenses under $25 do not require receipts.

SOLVED PROBLEM 1.12

What records should be kept in a safe deposit box?

SOLUTION

Records to be retained in a safe deposit box include

Documents of properties and investments, such as bonds, real estate deeds, automobile titles and lists of insurance policies, leases, securities certificates, and contracts. Identifying numbers should be clearly presented on these. The supporting documentation should be retained until the investments or properties are sold. Dividend logs may be kept for 1 year.

Household inventory to document insurance claims and tax losses. These should be kept for the life of the item.

Personal documents, such as marriage license, birth certificates, discharge papers, citizenship docu-mentation, adoption papers, and social security record.

Copies of wills.   To avoid delays, particularly in states that seal a safe deposit box upon death of the owner (for example, New York) and do not open it until a tax agent arrives, life insurance policies and originals of wills should be kept elsewhere. The executor should retain the original will.

SOLVED PROBLEM 1.13

How long should other files and records be stored at home?

SOLUTION

A 3-year statute of limitations usually exists. Some records have to be maintained for a long-term period. An example is canceled checks and evidence of home improvements, which reduce your capital gain when you sell your home. Consult your tax advisor for specific guidelines.

SOLVED PROBLEM 1.14

The cost of your home was $90,000 and you made home improvements of $40,000. You sold the home for $150,000 and moved into an apartment. You are under 55 years old and your tax rate is 28 percent. What is the tax on the gain?

SOLUTION

Selling price		$150,000
Less: Purchase price	$90,000	
Home improvements	40,000	130,000
Gain		$ 20,000
Tax rate		× .28
Total tax		$ 5,600

SOLVED PROBLEM 1.15

You incur property taxes of $5,000 and interest of $7,000 on your home. You are in the 28 percent tax bracket. What is your after-tax cost?

SOLUTION

$$\$12,000 \times .72 = \$8,640$$

SOLVED PROBLEM 1.16

What are some "rules of thumb" for record retention?

SOLUTION

Following are some record-retention guidelines:

Insurance policies.   Retain current policies only.

Large purchases.   Keep bills and canceled checks for major purchases (for example, furniture, major appliances) as long as you own them. They may be needed to substantiate an insurance claim or tax loss.

Tax returns.   Retain copies of returns and supporting documents (for example, 1099 forms, W-2 forms, salary-check stubs, and self-employment income records). Tax records should be kept for 7 years.

Credit cards.   Keep a current list of cards and their numbers. Have available the telephone number and address of whom to contact if the cards are stolen. You may be able to use a centralized company for all your credit cards.

Documentation on valuables.   Bills, canceled checks, and appraisals of such items as jewelry, art, and antiques should be kept until you sell them, or for 3 tax years after their sale. You will need proof to substantiate insurance claims, tax losses, or capital gains.

Warranties and service contracts.   Current contracts must be kept for servicing to be honored.

Loan agreements.   Retain current contracts only.

HOW DO THE STAGES IN LIFE AFFECT YOU?

Your financial plan will vary depending on individual circumstances through life including age. The stages in the life cycle for personal financial planning are

Single-adult.   Planning includes obtaining proper insurance, savings, and paying for career training.

Young-married.   Planning involves having children. A larger family requires a house, which involves establishing a credit rating. There is a need to obtain adequate health and life insurance.

Beginning-parenthood.   Planning is required to support children and provide for their education.

Divorced-parenthood. If a divorce occurs, one individual may be required to pay alimony and child support. The financial demands are significant since one person may have to support two households.

Parenthood with older children. Planning involves preparing a will and estate planning. A more adequate insurance program may be needed. Excess savings are invested. The early stage of retirement planning is begun.

Children move out. Planning may require moving to smaller living quarters or to be closer to the children. Serious retirement planning is needed.

Retirement stage. Planning involves reviewing insurance and annuity programs. Increased travel may be undertaken.

SOLVED PROBLEM 1.17

What personal financial planning is needed if you are in your 20s?

SOLUTION

When you are in your 20s, you should

Have habits of saving and investing. Try to save 5 percent to 10 percent of gross income. Save to make a down payment on a home. Have an emergency fund of about 6 months' expenses.

Develop a favorable credit rating.

Buy or improve your home.

Invest for long-term growth.

Establish a pension fund.

Have adequate insurance.

Establish an emergency fund.

Make up a will.

SOLVED PROBLEM 1.18

A couple has an annual gross income of $40,000. Their yearly expenses are $25,000.

(*a*) What is the realistic maximum to be saved?

(*b*) How much should the emergency fund be?

SOLUTION

(*a*) $40,000 × 10% = $4,000

(*b*) $25,000 per year/2 = $12,500 (6 months)

SOLVED PROBLEM 1.19

What personal financial planning is needed if you are in your 30s?

SOLUTION

Personal financial planning in your 30s involves doing the following:

Budget and monitor discretionary expenses.

Engage in tax planning.

Contribute to a pension fund.

Save for children's education.

Start retirement planning.

Reevaluate insurance requirements.

Modify the will as the family status changes.

SOLVED PROBLEM 1.20

What personal financial planning is needed if you are in your 40s?

SOLUTION

If you are in your 40s, do the following:

Continue providing for children's graduate education.

Increase personal savings.

Continue contributing to a pension fund.

Consider the tax consequences of investments.

Invest for long-term appreciation.

Reappraise insurance needs as children get married.

Review homeowner's insurance.

Formulate estate planning including gifts and trusts, as needed.

SOLVED PROBLEM 1.21

What personal financial planning is needed if you are in your 50s?

SOLUTION

If you are in your 50s, do the following:

Increase savings to 10 to 15 percent of gross income.

Plan for retirement.

Be more conservative in investing.

Hedge against inflation.

Engage in tax saving strategies.

Adjust the estate plan, as needed.

SOLVED PROBLEM 1.22

What personal financial planning is needed if you are in your 60s or above?

SOLUTION

When you are in your 60s, you should

Update the pension plan.

Invest to generate stable retirement income.

Avoid excessive debt.

Reduce discretionary expenses if income is lacking.

Assure the adequacy of health insurance.

Plan for future cash needs.

Update the estate plan.

Table 1-1 shows the typical *major* financial goal in the life cycles.

Table 1-1   Prime Goals in the Life Cycle

Life Stage and Age	Major Financial Goal
Single and under 25	New car
Young married between 25–29	Cooperative or condominium
Beginning parenthood between 30–34	House
Parenthood of older children between 45–54	College education of children
Near retirement between 55–64	Adequacy of pension plan
Retirement from 65 on	Fixed income

WHO YOU ARE AND PERSONAL FINANCIAL PLANNING

Personal financial planning differs depending upon who you are. For example, the planning aspects are different for an owner of a closely held business, an owner of a professional practice, an executive, and a dual-career couple.

SOLVED PROBLEM 1.23

What is an owner of a closely held business interested in?

SOLUTION

An owner of a closely held business is looking toward retirement at a certain age. He or she wants to arrange financial affairs so that the value of the net assets (assets less liabilities) of the business will fund a secure retirement. In some cases, the owner may want to accumulate a sufficient value in the business to buy a new and different venture. A diversified investment base is a priority for the owner of the closely held business.

SOLVED PROBLEM 1.24

What is important to an owner of a professional practice?

SOLUTION

An owner of a professional practice is optimistic about future earnings. As a result, there is an emphasis on current consumption. This attitude detracts from long-term financial planning. While the professional typically has *personal* accumulated wealth, the value of the practice is primarily the result of the professional's personal efforts. Professionals typically have structured investments to shelter income from taxes and have a high amount of leverage. Usually, the professional saves little and borrows. Typically, they do not have a diversified, balanced portfolio. Unfortunately, many professionals are dependent upon their practice as a source of income and do not have appropriate outside investments to provide supplemental income. Professionals should spend less and better manage themselves such as through preparing budgets. Debts incurred to finance their education or set up the practice should be repaid. Sound self-employed retirement and disability plans should be established. There must also be adequate professional liability insurance.

SOLVED PROBLEM 1.25

What is important to dual-career couples?

SOLUTION

Dual-career couples are accustomed to a high standard of living based on two incomes. The emphasis is on consumption rather than saving. Usually, there is not substantial accumulated wealth in terms of investments. A home equity may or may not exist. Since the prospects for accumulating wealth are good due to increasing income, the discretionary cash flow will be adequate to accumulate wealth for retirement. The dual-career couple has to be flexible because of the possibility of curtailment or elimination of one of the two incomes. A high priority should be given to a budget and savings plan. The adequacy of employer insurance should be examined.

SOLVED PROBLEM 1.26

Bill is self-employed and his wife Roberta is a part-time teacher. Bill earns $25,000 while Roberta earns $10,000. Their total income is $37,000 that includes dividend and interest income of $2,000. Their major cash payments include

Mortgage and property taxes	$ 8,000
Income taxes	7,000
Savings in bank	3,000
Retirement savings	2,000
Whole life insurance	1,000
Entertainment	4,500
Automobile	2,000
Total	$27,500

Retirement savings are in a bank account and a life insurance policy. After speaking with his sister, Bill decided to pay an extra $2,000 on the home mortgage. The mortgage interest rate is 8 percent. The couple plans to retire in 20 years. The inflation rate is 7 percent.

What would you advise this dual-career couple?

SOLUTION

It appears the couple will not have adequate funds at retirement to enjoy their life-style as retirees. The couple should restructure their expenditures so that more money goes to the retirement fund.

The couple should not have paid the additional $2,000 toward the mortgage. It would have been better to invest that money in a high-yielding investment. Bill should get advice from a financial expert instead of his sister!

A budget should be established to better control expenditures. For example, they should reduce their high entertainment costs. In fact, the entertainment costs ($4,500) are just under their total savings ($5,000).

Since the returns earned on a bank account and insurance policy are low, money should be invested in higher-return investments such as "blue chip" stocks.

WHAT CONSIDERATIONS ARE THERE IN SELECTING A PERSONAL FINANCIAL PLANNER?

The criteria in selecting a personal financial planner include credentials, compensation arrangements, past performance, timeliness in advice, and ability to communicate properly and answer questions. Sources of personal financial planning include accounting and financial advisory firms, banks, brokerage firms, and insurance companies.

Professional financial planning organizations include The International Association for Financial Planning (IAFP) and Institute of Certified Financial Planners (ICFP).

The following are some professional certifications or designations in personal financial planning:

Certified public accountant (CPA)

Certified financial planner (CFP)

Chartered financial consultant (ChFC)

Certified life underwriter (CLU)

Chartered financial analyst (CFA)

Warning: There are no restrictions on who can call themselves financial planners.
Table 1-2 provides the areas of expertise and fee structure for personal financial planners.

Table 1-2   Areas of Expertise and Fee Structure for Personal Financial Planners

	CPA	Attorney	Commission Planner	Fee Planner	Customer Representative*
Best services provided	Taxes	Taxes and legal	Entire plan	Entire plan	Specialty (e.g., insurance investment)
Compensation based on	Hourly fee	Hourly fee	Commission	Hourly fee	Salary and/or commission

*Includes representatives from financial service companies, brokerage houses, and insurance firms.

WHAT CAN YOU REFER TO AND USE AS AN AID IN PERSONAL FINANCIAL PLANNING?

Various journals and periodicals may be read to aid you in personal financial planning including

Money Magazine.   Time Inc.

Changing Times.   The Kiplinger Washington Editors.

Sylvia Porter's Personal Finance Magazine.   Sylvia Porter's Personal Finance Company.

Institute of Certified Financial Planners Journal.   Institute of Certified Financial Planners.

Tax Management Financial Planning Journal.   The Bureau of National Affairs.

PERSONAL FINANCIAL PLANNING SOFTWARE

Software packages exist to aid you in planning. Many packages can conduct detailed analyses of financial data and formulate suitable recommendations. Some software can evaluate "what-if" scenarios to see the effect of alternative courses of action.

For a detailed listing of personal finance and money management software, see Appendix 2.

Review Questions

(1)   An older individual favors _____ investments.

(2)   Younger individuals favor _____ investments.

(3)   Older individuals are more concerned with _____ planning and _____ planning.

(4)   Middle-aged individuals are more concerned with _____ and _____ .

(5) The first stage in the life cycle for personal financial planning is _____ and the last stage is _____ .

(6) If you are in your 20s, you should try to save between _____ percent of gross income and have an emergency fund of about _____ months' expenses.

(7) If you are in your 50s, try to save _____ percent of gross income.

(8) The IRS requires you to hold documents in support of your expenses for _____ years after the tax-return filing date.

(9) CFP stands for the designation of a _____ .

(10) A good magazine to read is Time Incorporated's _____ .

(11) CPA stands for the designation of a _____ .

Answers: (1) fixed income; (2) growth; (3) retirement, estate (4) reducing taxes, capital accumulation; (5) single-adult, retirement; (6) 5%–10%, 6; (7) 10%–15%; (8) 7; (9) certified financial planner; (10) *Money Magazine*; (11) certified public accountant.

Additional Solved Problems

1.1 Of what benefit is personal financial planning?

SOLUTION

The benefits of personal financial planning include using credit wisely, accomplishing lifetime goals including wealth maximization, preserving assets, reducing risk, and obtaining proper insurance.

1.2 A personal financial plan depends upon what factors?

SOLUTION

Important factors in personal financial planning include age, current and future income, objectives, family status, tolerable risk, possible inheritances, life-style, investment preferences, current net worth, health, liquidity, stability of employment, insurance coverage, tax status, and current debt level.

1.3 What are the prime areas of personal financial planning?

SOLUTION

Prime areas of personal financial planning are tax planning, retirement planning, estate planning, managing assets, using credit wisely, accumulating net worth through proper savings, managing assets, and adequacy of insurance.

1.4 You earn 9 percent on a taxable savings account and are at the 28 percent tax rate.

(*a*) How much will you net after taxes on your savings?

(*b*) If the inflation rate is 4 percent, what is your return after taxes and inflation?

SOLUTION

(*a*) $.09 - .28(.09) = .09 - .0252 = .0648$

(*b*) $.0648 - .04 = .0248$

1.5   You borrow $30,000 at 8 percent to buy property. At the end of 1 year, inflation has increased the replacement cost of the property by 6 percent.

    (a)   How much would the property be worth in 19X6?

    (b)   By borrowing you will have to pay principal and interest of how much?

    (c)   What is the real cost of financing the property?

    SOLUTION

    (a) $30,000 × 1.06 = $31,800

    (b) $30,000 × 1.08 = $32,400

    (c) $32,400 − $31,800 = $600

1.6   You buy a home for $120,000 and make home improvements of $30,000. You then sell the home for $190,000 and move into an apartment. You are under 55 years old and your tax rate is 28 percent. What is the tax on the gain?

    SOLUTION

Selling price		$190,000
Less: Purchase price	$120,000	
Home improvements	30,000	150,000
Gain		$ 40,000
Tax rate		× .28
Tax		$ 11,200

1.7   You incur interest on your mortgage of $7,000 and property taxes of $4,000. Your tax rate is 28 percent. What is your after-tax cost?

    SOLUTION

$$\$11,000 \times .72 = \$7,920$$

1.8   What are some records that you should maintain?

    SOLUTION

    You should keep the following records: investment records, insurance policies, tax returns, ownership records to home and major assets, credit card accounts, banking records, loan agreements, pension records, will, and personal documents (for example, marriage license, birth certificate).

1.9   If you are 20 years old, what kind of personal financial plan is suggested?

    SOLUTION

    A person who is 20 years old should achieve a positive credit rating, invest for long-term growth, have proper insurance, have an attorney prepare a will, and start a pension plan.

1.10   What is important in personal financial planning to an owner of a closely held company?

    SOLUTION

    An owner of a closely held business is concerned with maximizing net worth, retirement planning, and diversifying investments.

Chapter 2

Time Value Applications

In making financial decisions, such as annual loan payments or investment accumulation, you may need to use future value and present value tables that take into account the time value of money. You may want to know how much to invest each year to have a desired balance at retirement. You may desire to calculate the interest rate being charged on an auto loan. You may have to figure out how many years it will be before you can buy a house. These are just a few of the many practical applications that the tables offer.

USING FUTURE VALUE TABLES IN DECISION MAKING

Future (compound) value of money is important to consider in making investment decisions. You can solve for different unknowns, such as accumulated amount, annual payment, interest rate, and number of periods. Here are some guidelines in using future value tables.

A future value table is used to determine the future (later) amount of cash flows paid or received.

The "Future Value of $1" table is used if there are unequal cash flows each period or a lump-sum cash flow.

The "Future Value of Annuity of $1" table is used if the cash flows are equal and occur at the end of each period.

If you want to determine a total dollar amount in the future, you have a multiplication problem.

If you want to calculate an annual payment, interest rate, or number of periods, you have a division problem. In such a case, what you put in the numerator of a fraction determines which table to use. For example, if you put a future value that involves equal year-end payments in the numerator, you have to use a "Future Value of Annuity of $1" table.

If you are solving for an annual payment, divide the numerator by the factor corresponding to the interest rate i and the number of periods n.

If you are solving for an interest rate, divide the numerator by the annual payment to get a factor. Then, to find the interest rate, find the factor on the table opposite the number of years. The interest rate will be indicated at the top of the column where the factor is located.

If you are solving for the number of years, divide the numerator by the annual payment to get the factor. Then find the factor in the appropriate interest rate column. The number of years will be indicated in the far left-hand column.

Now let us look at situations in which you may actually solve problems using the future value tables.

THE "FUTURE VALUE OF $1" TABLE

This computation indicates the increased value of a single sum of money over a certain future time period. A determination must be made of what money will be worth tomorrow (see Appendix Table 1).

SOLVED PROBLEM 2.1

You deposit $5,000 in a mutual fund to be kept for 6 years that will earn 10 percent annual return. How much will you have accumulated?

SOLUTION

$$\$5,000 \times 1.77156 = \$8,858$$

14

SOLVED PROBLEM 2.2

Your current salary is $30,000. You anticipate receiving a 4 percent pay raise each year. What will your salary be in 10 years?

SOLUTION

$$\$30,000 \times 1.48024 = \$44,407$$

SOLVED PROBLEM 2.3

You bought a house today for $150,000 that you plan to sell in 15 years. The expected annual growth rate is 12 percent. What is the expected value of the house at the end of the fifteenth year?

SOLUTION

$$\$150,000 \times 5.47357 = \$821,036$$

SOLVED PROBLEM 2.4

You invest $10,000 today in a bank account. It is to be kept in the bank for 5 years at 12 percent annual interest.

(*a*)   What is the accumulated amount?

(*b*)   If interest is compounded quarterly, what is the accumulated amount?

SOLUTION

(*a*) $\$10,000 \times 1.76234 = \$17,623$

(*b*) $n = 5 \times 4 = 20$ (number of quarterly periods)

$$i = \frac{12\%}{4} = 3\%   \text{(quarterly interest rate)}$$

$$\$10,000 \times 1.80611 = \$18,061$$

The reason that the accumulated amount with quarterly compounding is more than annual compounding is that greater compounding of interest exists.

SOLVED PROBLEM 2.5

On January 1, 1994, you deposit $10,000 to earn 10 percent compounded semiannually. Effective January 1, 1998, the interest rate increased to 12 percent compounded semiannually. At that time, you doubled the balance in your bank account. What is the balance on deposit on January 1, 2004?

SOLUTION

January 1, 1994	$10,000
Amount of $1 factor (Table 1) for	
$n = 4 \times 2 = 8, i = 10\%/2 = 5\%$	× 1.47746
January 1, 1998	$14,475
Deposit	14,475
Total	$29,550
Amount of $1 factor (Table 1) for	
$n = 6 \times 2 = 12, i = 12\%/2 = 6\%$	× 2.01220
January 1, 2004	$59,461

SOLVED PROBLEM 2.6

You want to have $1,000,000 at the end of 15 years. The interest rate is 8 percent. How much do you have to deposit today?

SOLUTION

$$\frac{\$1,000,000}{3.17217} = \$315,242$$

SOLVED PROBLEM 2.7

At an interest rate of 12 percent, how long will it take for your money to double?

SOLUTION

$$\frac{\$2}{\$1} = 2$$

$$n = 6 \text{ years (approximate)}$$

SOLVED PROBLEM 2.8

You want to have $250,000. Your initial deposit is $30,000 and the interest rate is 12 percent. How many years will it take to accomplish your objective?

SOLUTION

$$\frac{\$250,000}{\$30,000} = 8.3333$$

$$n = 18.5 \text{ years (approximate)}$$

The factor falls about midway between 18 and 19 years.

SOLVED PROBLEM 2.9

You agree to pay back $3,000 in 6 years on a $2,000 loan made today. What interest rate are you being charged?

SOLUTION

$$\frac{\$3,000}{\$2,000} = 1.5$$

$$i = 7\%$$

SOLVED PROBLEM 2.10

Your salary was $12,000 in 19X1 and 8 years later it is $36,700. What is the compounded annual growth rate?

SOLUTION

$$\frac{\$36,700}{\$12,000} = 3.05833$$

$$\text{Growth rate} = 15\% \text{ (approximate)}$$

THE "FUTURE VALUE OF ANNUITY OF $1" TABLE

You can also compute the increased value of equal payments over time (see Appendix Table 2).

SOLVED PROBLEM 2.11

You plan to put $20,000 in a savings account earning 8 percent at the end of each year for the next 15 years. What is the accumulated balance at the end of the fifteenth year?

SOLUTION

$$\$20,000 \times 27.15211 = \$543,042$$

SOLVED PROBLEM 2.12

You deposit $1,000 per month for 2 years. The annual interest rate is 24 percent. What is your accumulated balance?

SOLUTION

$$n = 2 \times 12 = 24 \qquad \text{(number of months)}$$

$$i = \frac{24\%}{12} = 2\% \qquad \text{(monthly interest rate)}$$

$$\$1,000 \times 30.42186 = \$30,422$$

SOLVED PROBLEM 2.13

You want to determine the annual year-end deposit needed to accumulate $100,000 at the end of 15 years. The interest rate is 12 percent. What is the annual deposit?

SOLUTION

$$\frac{\$100,000}{37.27972} = \$2,682$$

SOLVED PROBLEM 2.14

You want to have $500,000 accumulated in your mutual fund. You make four deposits of $100,000 per year. What interest rate must you earn?

SOLUTION

The interest rate you must earn is determined below.

Step 1: Get the factor, which is

$$\frac{\$500,000}{\$100,000} = 5$$

Step 2: Refer to Appendix Table 2 and look across four periods to get a factor closest to 5, which is 4.99338.

Step 3: Look at the interest rate that is the heading for the column 4.99338, which is 15 percent.

Step 4: The interest rate is approximately 15 percent.

SOLVED PROBLEM 2.15

You want $500,000 in the future. The interest rate is 10 percent and the annual payment is $80,000. How long will it take to achieve your goal?

SOLUTION

$$\frac{\$500,000}{\$80,000} = 6.25$$

$$n = 5 \text{ years (approximate)}$$

USING PRESENT VALUE TABLES IN DECISION MAKING

Present (discount) value of money is considered in personal finance decisions. Different unknowns may be solved for, such as present value amount, annual payment, interest rate, and number of periods. The following are guidelines for using the tables:

A present value table is used if you want to determine the *current* amount of receiving or paying future cash flows.

The "Present Value of $1" table (see Appendix Table 3) is used if you have unequal cash flows each period or a lump-sum cash flow.

The "Present Value of Annuity of $1" table (see Appendix Table 4) is used if the cash flows each period are equal.

THE "PRESENT VALUE OF $1" TABLE

Present value is the opposite of compounding. By knowing what something is worth in a later year, you can find out its value today. In effect, you are discounting a future amount to compute its current worth (see Appendix Table 3).

SOLVED PROBLEM 2.16

You have an opportunity to receive $30,000 four years from now. You earn 12 percent on your investment. What is the most you should pay for this investment?

SOLUTION

$$\$30,000 \times .63552 = \$19,066$$

SOLVED PROBLEM 2.17

You are 30 years old and plan to invest in a 25-year, zero-coupon bond yielding 10 percent. Upon retirement at age 60, you want to have accumulated $400,000. How much should be invested today to satisfy your goal?

SOLUTION

$$\$400,000 \times .03558 = \$14,232$$

SOLVED PROBLEM 2.18

You are thinking of investing $30,000. Your required rate of return is 10 percent. Your annual net cash inflows from the investment are

Year 1	$ 8,000
Year 2	15,000
Year 3	18,000

What is the net present value of this investment and should it be made?

SOLUTION

The net present value of the investment is positive and the investment should be made, as indicated in the following calculations:

YEAR	CALCULATION	NET PRESENT VALUE
0	−$30,000 × 1	−$30,000
1	8,000 × .90909	7,273
2	15,000 × .82645	12,397
3	18,000 × .75132	13,524
Net present value		$ 3,194

THE "PRESENT VALUE OF ANNUITY OF $1" TABLE

This values a series of equal future payments, such as annuities received from pension plans and insurance policies, in today's dollars. When using this table, all you need to do is multiply the annual cash payment by the factor (see Appendix Table 4).

SOLVED PROBLEM 2.19

You will receive $10,000 a year for 6 years at 10 percent. What is the present value?

SOLUTION

$$\$10,000 \times 4.35526 = \$43,553$$

SOLVED PROBLEM 2.20

The terms of the divorce settlement are that you will receive monthly payments of $600 for 3 years. The discount rate is 24%. What is the settlement worth today?

SOLUTION

$$\$600 \times 25.48884 = \$15,293$$

SOLVED PROBLEM 2.21

You are trying to determine the price you are willing to pay for a $1,000 five-year U.S. savings bond paying $50 interest semiannually, which is sold to yield 8 percent. What is the present value?

SOLUTION

$$i = \frac{8\%}{2} = 4\% \quad \text{(semiannual interest rate)}$$

$$n = 5 \times 2 = 10 \quad \text{(number of interest periods)}$$

To determine the present value of the principal use the
   "Present Value of $1" (Appendix Table 3) ($1,000 ×
   .67556) $ 676

To determine the present value of the interest payments
   use the "Present Value of an Annuity of $1"
   (Appendix Table 4) ($50 × 8.11090)   406

                                                                   $1,082

SOLVED PROBLEM 2.22

You borrow $200,000 for 5 years at an interest rate of 12 percent. What is the annual year-end payment on the loan?

SOLUTION

$$\frac{\$200,000}{3.60478} = \$55,482$$

SOLVED PROBLEM 2.23

You take out a $30,000 loan payable monthly over 3 years at 24 percent annual interest. What is the monthly payment?

SOLUTION

$$n = 3 \times 12 = 36 \qquad \text{(number of monthly payments)}$$

$$i = \frac{24\%}{2} = 2\% \qquad \text{(monthly interest rate)}$$

$$\frac{\$30,000}{25.48884} = \$1,177$$

SOLVED PROBLEM 2.24

You borrow $300,000 at 12 percent payable at $70,000 a year. How many years do you have to pay off the loan?

SOLUTION

$$\frac{\$300,000}{\$70,000} = 4.2857$$

$$n = 6 \text{ years (approximate)}$$

SOLVED PROBLEM 2.25

You borrow $20,000, to be repaid in 12 monthly payments of $1,891.20. What is the interest rate you are paying?

SOLUTION

$$\frac{\$20,000.00}{\$1,891.20} = 10.5753$$

$$i = 2\%$$

SOLVED PROBLEM 2.26

You borrow $1,000,000 and agree to make payments of $100,000 per year for 18 years. What is the interest rate you are paying?

SOLUTION

$$\frac{\$1,000,000}{\$100,000} = 10$$

$$i = 7\% \text{ (approximate)}$$

SOLVED PROBLEM 2.27

When you retire you want to receive an annuity of $80,000 at the end of each year for 10 years. The interest rate is 8 percent. How much must be in the retirement plan when you retire?

SOLUTION

$$\$80,000 \times 6.71008 = \$536,806$$

SOLVED PROBLEM 2.28

You have $300,000 in your pension plan today. You want to take an annuity for 20 years at an interest rate of 12 percent. How much will you receive each year?

SOLUTION

$$\frac{\$300,000}{7.46944} = \$40,164$$

You may have to solve a financial problem involving both the use of the "Present Value of $1" table (Appendix Table 3) and the "Present Value of Annuity of $1" table (Appendix Table 4).

SOLVED PROBLEM 2.29

You incur the following expenditures:

YEAR	AMOUNT
0	−$3,000
1	− 4,000
2	− 5,000
3–10	−12,000

What is the present value of the negative cash flows assuming a 10 percent interest rate?

SOLUTION

YEAR	COMPUTATION	PRESENT VALUE
0	−$ 3,000 × 1	−$ 3,000
1	−$ 4,000 × .90909 (Appendix Table 3)	− 3,636
2	−$ 5,000 × .82645	− 4,132
3–10	−$12,000 × 4.40903* (Appendix Table 4)	− 52,908
Present value		−$63,676

*The factor of 4.40903 is computed as follows:

Present value of ordinary annuity for $n = 10$, $i = 10\%$	6.14457
Less: Present value of ordinary annuity for $n = 2$, $i = 10\%$	1.73554
Factor	4.40903

Review Questions

(1) If you want to know how much is needed in the pension plan when you retire after making equal annual payments, you would use a _____ table.

(2) If you want to determine the current amount of receiving annual equal cash flows, you would use a _____ table.

(3) If you want to determine the accumulated amount after making unequal monthly deposits, a _____ table would be used.

(4) If you have a lump-sum cash flow in the future and want to determine the current amount, a _____ table would be used.

(5) To determine a total dollar amount, we have a _____ problem.

(6) To determine annual payment, interest rate, or number of years, we have a _____ problem.

(7) The table having the highest factors would be the _____ table.

(8) In the event you receive unequal cash flows each period and you want to determine the present worth, you would use a _____ table.

(9) The table having the lowest factors would be the _____ table.

(10) If you wanted to know what equal annual payments you had to make on an auto loan, you would use the _____ table.

(11) To determine the present value or future value amount, we have a _____ problem.

Answers: (1) future value of annuity of $1; (2) present value of annuity of $1; (3) future value of $1; (4) present value of $1; (5) multiplication; (6) division; (7) future value of annuity of $1; (8) present value of $1; (9) present value of $1; (10) present value of annuity of $1; (11) multiplication.

Additional Solved Problems

2.1 You put $4,000 in a savings account earning 10 percent interest compounded annually for 6 years. What will you have accumulated?

SOLUTION

Use Appendix Table 1.

$$\$4,000 \times 1.77156 = \$7,086$$

2.2 Your present salary is $25,000. You expect to receive a 6 percent pay raise each year. What will your salary be in 5 years?

SOLUTION

Use Appendix Table 1.

$$\$25,000 \times 1.33823 = \$33,456$$

2.3 You deposit $10,000 in an account offering an annual interest rate of 20 percent with the interest compounded quarterly. You will keep the money on deposit for 5 years. What will the accumulated amount be at the end of the fifth year?

SOLUTION

Use Appendix Table 1.

$$n = 5 \times 4 = 20 \qquad \text{(number of quarters)}$$

$$i = \frac{20\%}{4} = 5\% \qquad \text{(quarterly interest rate)}$$

$$\$10,000 \times 2.65330 = \$26,533$$

2.4 On January 1, 1990, you deposit $10,000 to earn 8 percent compounded semiannually. Effective January 1, 1993, the interest rate increases to 10 percent compounded semiannually. At that time, you deposit an additional $5,000. What is the balance on deposit on January 1, 1995?

SOLUTION

January 1, 1990	$10,000
Amount of $1 (Appendix Table 1) factor for $n = 3 \times 2 = 6$, $i = 8\%/2 = 4\%$	$\times$ 1.26532
January 1, 1993	$12,653
Deposit	5,000
Total	$17,653
Amount of $1 (Appendix Table 1) factor for $n = 2 \times 2 = 4$, $i = 10\%/2 = 5\%$	$\times$ 1.21551
January 1, 1995	$21,457

2.5 You wish to have $500,000 at the end of 10 years. The interest rate is 10 percent. How much do you have to deposit today to achieve your goal?

SOLUTION

Use Appendix Table 1.

$$\frac{\$500,000}{2.59374} = \$192,772$$

2.6 You wish to have $1,000,000. Your initial deposit is $143,000. The interest rate is 15 percent. How many years will it take to accomplish your objective?

SOLUTION

Use Appendix Table 1.

$$\frac{\$1,000,000}{\$143,000} = 6.99$$

$$n = 14 \text{ years (approximate)}$$

2.7 You agree to pay back $4,000 in 5 years on a $2,500 loan made today. What interest rate are you being charged?

SOLUTION

Use Appendix Table 1.

$$\frac{\$4,000}{\$2,500} = 1.6$$

$$i = 10\% \text{ (approximate)}$$

2.8   You expect to deposit $5,000 in a mutual fund at the end of each year for the next 12 years. The interest rate is 10 percent. What will the accumulated balance be at the end of the twelfth year?

SOLUTION

Use Appendix Table 2.

$$\$5,000 \times 21.38428 = \$106,921$$

2.9   You deposit $500 per month for 3 years. The annual interest rate is 24 percent. What will the accumulated balance be?

SOLUTION

Use Appendix Table 2.

$$n = 3 \times 12 = 36 \qquad \text{(number of months)}$$

$$i = \frac{24\%}{12} = 2\% \qquad \text{(monthly interest rate)}$$

$$\$500 \times 51.99437 = \$25,997$$

2.10   What is the annual year-end deposit required to accumulate $400,000 at the end of 20 years at 8 percent interest?

SOLUTION

Use Appendix Table 2.

$$\frac{\$400,000}{45.76196} = \$8,741$$

2.11   You desire to have $750,000 accumulated in your pension fund. You make 20 deposits of $25,000. What interest rate must you earn?

SOLUTION

Use Appendix Table 2.

$$\frac{\$750,000}{\$25,000} = 30$$

$$i = 4\% \text{ (approximate)}$$

2.12   You wish to have $600,000 at a later date. The interest rate is 12 percent. The annual payment is $60,000. How many years will it take to achieve your goal?

SOLUTION

Use Appendix Table 2.

$$\frac{\$600,000}{\$60,000} = 10$$

$$n = 7 \text{ years (approximate)}$$

2.13   You will receive a $100,000 settlement from an insurance company at the end of 7 years. The inflation rate is 9 percent. What is the present value of the settlement?

SOLUTION

Use Appendix Table 3.

$$\$100,000 \times .54703 = \$54,703$$

2.14 You are considering buying a business for $100,000. Your desired rate of return is 12 percent. The net cash earnings expected from this business are

Year 1	$20,000
Year 2	50,000
Year 3	70,000

Should you buy this business?

SOLUTION

Use Appendix Table 3.

YEAR	CALCULATION	NET PRESENT VALUE
0	$-$100,000 \times 1$	$-$100,000
1	$+\ \ \ 20,000 \times .89286$	$+\ \ \ 17,857$
2	$+\ \ \ 50,000 \times .79719$	$+\ \ \ 39,860$
3	$+\ \ \ 70,000 \times .71178$	$+\ \ \ 49,825$
Net present value		$+\ \ \ $7,542$

Since the net present value of the business is positive, it should be purchased.

2.15 You will receive $5,000 a year for 5 years at 8 percent. What is the present value?

SOLUTION

Use Appendix Table 4.

$$\$5,000 \times 3.99271 = \$19,964$$

2.16 You incur the following expenditures:

YEAR	AMOUNT
0	$-$2,000
1	$-\ \ 5,000$
2	$-\ \ 6,000$
3	$-\ \ 4,000$
4–20	$-\ \ 8,000$

What is the present value of the negative cash flows assuming an 8 percent interest rate?

SOLUTION

YEAR	COMPUTATION	PRESENT VALUE
0	$-$2,000 \times 1$	$-\$\ \ 2,000$
1	$-\ \ 5,000 \times .92593$ (Appendix Table 3)	$-\ \ \ 4,630$
2	$-\ \ 6,000 \times .85734$	$-\ \ \ 5,144$
3	$-\ \ 4,000 \times .79383$	$-\ \ \ 3,175$
4–10	$-\ \ 8,000 \times 7.24105\,^*$ (Appendix Table 4)	$-\ \ 57,928$
Present value		$-$72,877

*The factor of 7.24105 is computed as follows:

Present value of ordinary annuity for $n = 20$, $i = 8\%$	9.81815
Less: Present value of ordinary annuity for $n = 3$, $i = 8\%$	2.57710
Factor	7.24105

2.17 You will receive monthly payments of $300 for 2 years. The annual discount rate is 24 percent. What is the present value?

SOLUTION

Use Appendix Table 4.

$$n = 2 \times 12 = 24 \quad \text{(number of months)}$$

$$i = \frac{24\%}{12} = 2\% \quad \text{(monthly interest rate)}$$

$$\$300 \times 18.91393 = \$5,674$$

2.18 If you buy a car, you have to give a 10 percent down payment on the list price of $10,000 and finance the balance over 3 years at an interest rate of 12 percent. What is the annual payment required on the lease agreement?

SOLUTION

Use Appendix Table 4.

$$\frac{\$9,000}{2.40183} = \$3,747$$

2.19 You take out a loan of $10,000 from a finance company payable monthly over 3 years. The annual interest rate is 24 percent. What is the monthly payment?

SOLUTION

Use Appendix Table 4.

$$\frac{\$10,000}{25.48884} = \$392$$

2.20 You borrow $75,000 at 15 percent payable at $20,000 a year. How many years will it take to pay off the loan?

SOLUTION

Use Appendix Table 4.

$$\frac{\$75,000}{\$20,000} = 3.75$$

$$n = 6 \text{ (approximate)}$$

2.21 You borrow $50,000 and agree to make payments of $10,000 per year for 10 years. What interest rate are you paying?

SOLUTION

Use Appendix Table 4.

$$\frac{\$50,000}{\$10,000} = 5$$

$$i = 15\% \text{ (approximate)}$$

2.22 When you retire you want to receive an annuity of $60,000 at the end of each year for 20 years. The interest rate is 6 percent. What is the amount that must be in your retirement account at the date of retirement?

SOLUTION

Use Appendix Table 4.

$$\$60,000 \times 11.46992 = \$688,195$$

2.23 You have $500,000 in your pension plan today. You want to take an annuity for 10 years at an interest rate of 8 percent. What will you receive each year?

SOLUTION

Use Appendix Table 4.

$$\frac{\$500,000}{6.71008} = \$74,515$$

Chapter 3

Personal Financial Statements and Budgeting

What is your net worth? You will learn how to determine it in this chapter. The greater your net worth, the better standard of living you will enjoy and the earlier you can retire. A personal financial statement will help you in evaluating your money habits.

A personal financial statement is like a map: It shows present financial status, reveals where money is going, and guides you in later financial decisions. A personal financial statement may be prepared for an individual, a husband and a wife, or a family. Also helpful in planning finances is the preparation of a budget showing the sources of income and types of expenditures.

Personal financial statements include a personal balance sheet, statement of changes in net worth, and a personal income statement.

HOW MUCH ARE YOU WORTH?

Assets (what you own having a market value) and liabilities (what you owe) are shown in a personal balance sheet. An example of an asset is cash while an example of a liability is loans payable. By preparing a personal balance sheet, you can determine how much you are worth. Your net worth is equal to the difference between assets and liabilities. The balance sheet shows the status of your financial position and whether any changes are needed. It may help you answer many questions, such as whether to obtain additional financing, how much insurance you need, what your potential estate is for planning purposes, whether you can buy a house, how much money is available for investments, when you can retire, and what funds are available for the education of your children.

Try to maximize your net worth by building up assets and controlling liabilities. Be careful how you finance assets. For example, avoid financing long-term assets with short-term debt.

Use the same criterion every year as a basis for valuing assets and liabilities. For example, if you value your house using recent area sales, do the same next year.

You can compare your personal balance sheet with those of others in your age group or professional category to see how you stack up against your peers.

An abbreviated personal balance sheet would include the following:

ASSETS

Liquid assets (e.g., cash and marketable securities)

Loan assets (e.g., certificates of deposit, bonds)

Investment assets (e.g., stocks, stock mutual funds, real estate, gold)

Personal assets (e.g., auto, jewelry)

Deferred assets (e.g., pension plan, insurance annuities, deferred compensation, trust, and inheritances)

LIABILITIES

Short-term debt (e.g., credit cards)

Intermediate-term debt (e.g., notes, loans)

Long-term debt (e.g., mortgage)

Net worth = Assets − Liabilities

YOUR ASSETS

Assets should be listed in the order of liquidity at current market values. The most liquid assets are cash and marketable securities. Liquid assets can be sold quickly without loss of principal (for example, money market fund). Assets may be short term, intermediate term, or long term, depending on the maturity date.

Some assets have appreciation potential (for example, real estate, stocks). Personal assets often depreciate (for example, automobile, furniture). Deferred assets (for example, retirement plans, trusts, and inheritances) are inaccessible and will be reduced by taxes. Investment assets, such as stocks and bonds, provide you with additional income or increase your net worth.

If assets are jointly owned, only your interest as beneficial owner should be included. A listing of assets may take the following form:

ASSETS   DESCRIPTION   CARRYING VALUE   PERCENT OF TOTAL ASSETS

How should assets be valued? There are certain guidelines used to derive a value, depending on the type of asset.

SOLVED PROBLEM 3.1

What type of assets do you have and how should they be valued?

SOLUTION

Your assets and their valuations might include

Amount of money in bank savings and checking accounts

Cash surrender value of life insurance

United States savings bonds at current market price

Amount you could withdraw today from your profit sharing and retirement program

Annuities at accumulated current value

Market value of stocks and bonds (for example, quoted market price on the exchange, bid price for an over-the-counter security)

Net asset value of mutual fund shares

Market value of other investments (for example, mortgages given to others)

Current offering price for unit trusts

Market value of real estate owned, including your house

Price you could receive for your car or boat (for example, trade-in value)

Market value of household items (for example, furniture, appliances) determined by what you could get for them if you sold them. (*Rule of thumb:* Value household items at 5 percent of the value of the home.)

Market value of personal items (for example, jewelry, clothing). (*Rule of thumb:* Jewelry can be valued at 30 percent of the purchase price.)

Appraised value for collectibles

Price to be obtained if you sold your investment in an unincorporated business

Receivables due you from others

SOLVED PROBLEM 3.2

You agree to give a mortgage on the house you are selling. You will receive $10,000 each year for 10 years. The interest rate is 10 percent. What is the present value of the mortgage payments?

SOLUTION

The present value of the stream of mortgage payments is determined using Appendix Table 4, "Present Value of Annuity of $1," as follows:

$$\$10,000 \times 6.14457 = \$61,446$$

Business interests that represent a large part of total assets should be shown separately from other investments.

Limited business activities not conducted as a separate business entity (such as investment in real estate and related mortgages) should be presented separately.

SOLVED PROBLEM 3.3

What questions should you ask about your assets?

SOLUTION

The relevant questions are

Are most assets concentrated in one category? (This is not desirable since it lacks diversification.)

Which of the assets are not liquid, and what do they amount to?

What is the balance between liquid and nonliquid investments?

Are your investments resulting in tax benefits or problems?

What is the fair market value of your assets and how does that differ from your initial cost and book value (initial cost less accumulated depreciation)?

Which assets are most risky?

What amount of your assets can be used to meet impending obligations?

If the market values of your assets do not increase at the rate of inflation, your "real" net worth will experience a decline. In order to guard against a decline in net worth, the assets you have must appreciate to at least equal the inflation rate.

YOUR LIABILITIES

What about what you owe? Liabilities should be shown at estimated current amounts by order of maturity. Categorize liabilities by final payment date. Bills due within 1 year (for example, credit cards) are short-term debt, loans due between 1 to 5 years (for example, auto and consumer loans) are intermediate-term debt, and debts due in more than 5 years (for example, mortgage obligations) are long-term debt.

SOLVED PROBLEM 3.4

What are some of your liabilities?

SOLUTION

Liabilities include

Amounts owed on the mortgage on your house

Amounts owed for taxes that have not been withheld

Funds set aside and earmarked for college

SOLVED PROBLEM 3.5

What questions should you ask about your debt?

SOLUTION

Relevant questions include

Are you debt averse or prone?

Which assets are being financed by debt?

What is the interest rate on the debt?

What is the maturity of debt and repayment schedule?

What are the sources of repaying the debt (for example, salary, taking out new loans to pay off old loans, selling assets)?

What has been the trend in debt position?

Income taxes should be estimated on the differences between assets and liabilities and their tax bases. Disclosure should be made of the methods and assumptions used in estimating income taxes. Figure 3-1 shows an illustrative balance sheet.

MR. JACK SMITH
BALANCE SHEET
DECEMBER 31, 19X9

ASSETS
Liquid

Cash	$ 4,000		
Money market fund	25,000		
Marketable securities	30,000		
Mutual fund	14,000		
Cash surrender value of life insurance	6,000		
Total liquid assets		$ 79,000	

Nonliquid

Long-term investments	$ 50,000		
Real estate	150,000		
Automobile	10,000		
Personal property	25,000		
Retirement funds	40,000		
Total nonliquid assets		275,000	
Total assets			$354,000

LIABILITIES
Short-term

Accounts and bills due	$ 1,000		
Credit card	2,500		
Total short-term liabilities		$ 3,500	

Long-term

Mortgage payable	$ 80,000		
Auto loan	4,000		
Bank loan	3,000		
Total long-term liabilities		87,000	
Total liabilities			90,500
Net worth			$263,500

Fig. 3-1   Illustrative balance sheet.

SOLVED PROBLEM 3.6

At year-end, you have $500 in a checking account and $8,000 in a savings account. Your car is worth $7,000. You recently bought furniture for $2,000. The estimated worth of your clothing and jewelry is $2,500. You owe $1,000 on a credit card. Unpaid utility bills are $150. There is an outstanding loan on your car of $3,000. You also have a regular bank loan of $2,000. Prepare a personal balance sheet.

SOLUTION

ASSETS

Liquid Assets

Checking account	$ 500	
Savings account	8,000	
Total liquid assets		$ 8,500

Nonliquid Assets

Automobile	$7,000	
Furniture	2,000	
Clothing and jewelry	2,500	
Total nonliquid assets		11,500
Total assets		$20,000

LIABILITIES

Short-Term Liabilities

Credit card	$1,000	
Utility bills payable	150	
Total short-term liabilities		$ 1,150

Long-Term Liabilities

Auto loan	$3,000	
Bank loan	2,000	
Total long-term liabilities		5,000
Total liabilities		$ 6,150
Net worth		$13,850

SOLVED PROBLEM 3.7

You bought a house for $125,000 which now has a fair market value of $200,000. Your mortgage loan balance is $60,000. What is your equity in the house?

SOLUTION

$$\$200,000 - \$60,000 = \$140,000$$

SOLVED PROBLEM 3.8

An uncompleted personal balance sheet follows:

	19X5	19X6
ASSETS		
Liquid assets	$5,000	?
Nonliquid assets	6,000	$ 6,000
Total assets	$?	$13,000
LIABILITIES		
Short-term liabilities	$?	$ 2,000
Long-term liabilities	2,000	?
Total liabilities	$6,000	$?
Net worth	$?	$ 4,000

(*a*) Fill in the missing numbers of the personal balance sheet.

(*b*) Determine the percentage increase or decrease in net worth.

SOLUTION

(a)

	19X5	19X6
ASSETS		
Liquid assets	$ 5,000	$ 7,000
Nonliquid assets	6,000	6,000
Total assets	$11,000	$13,000
LIABILITIES		
Short-term liabilities	$ 4,000	$ 2,000
Long-term liabilities	2,000	7,000
Total liabilities	$ 6,000	$ 9,000
Net worth	$ 5,000	$ 4,000

(b)
$$\text{Decrease in net worth} = \frac{\text{Change}}{\text{Base year}} = \frac{\$1,000}{\$5,000} = 20\%$$

SOLVED PROBLEM 3.9

You have the following balances:

1. Automobile, $7,000
2. Bank loan, $5,000
3. Furniture, $6,000
4. Credit cards, $3,000
5. Savings account, $10,000
6. Checking account, $2,000
7. Personal property, $8,000
8. Appliances, $4,000
9. Auto loan, $1,000
10. Utilities payable, $2,000

(a) Classify each balance as an asset (A) or a liability (L).

(b) Determine your net worth.

SOLUTION

(a) 1. A   6. A
     2. L   7. A
     3. A   8. A
     4. L   9. L
     5. A   10. L

(b)

ASSETS	
Checking account	$ 2,000
Savings account	10,000
Automobile	7,000
Personal property	8,000
Furniture	6,000
Appliances	4,000
Total assets	$37,000

LIABILITIES

Utilities payable	$ 2,000	
Bank loan	5,000	
Auto loan	1,000	
Credit cards	3,000	
Total liabilities		11,000
Net worth		$26,000

Personal financial statements should disclose the following:

Major methods of determining the current values of assets and current amounts of liabilities

Nature of joint ownership of assets, if any

Identification of significant investments in particular companies and/or industries

For a closely held business, name of the company, the percent owned, and nature of business

Face value of life insurance

Maturities, interest rates, collateral, and other pertinent information with regard to debt

Your debt as a percentage of your total assets should generally be less than 50 percent. If, however, your job position is unstable, the debt percentage should be lower, approximating no more than 25 percent.

STATEMENT OF CHANGES IN NET WORTH

A statement of changes in net worth may also be prepared. The increases or decreases in net worth may arise as shown in Table 3-1.

Table 3-1   Statement of Changes in Net Worth

Sources of Increases in Net Worth	Sources of Decreases in Net Worth
Revenue	Expenses
Increase in carrying value of assets	Decrease in carrying value of assets
Decrease in current amounts of liabilities	Increase in current amounts of liabilities
Decrease in estimated taxes	Increase in estimated taxes

SOLVED PROBLEM 3.10

Indicate whether the following items represent increases or decreases in net worth:

(a) Taking out a loan

(b) Appreciation in market price of stock investments

(c) Payment on a mortgage

(d) Dividend income

(e) Taxes

(f) Cost of vacation

SOLUTION

(a)	Decrease	(d)	Increase
(b)	Increase	(e)	Decrease
(c)	Increase	(f)	Decrease

COMMITMENTS AND CONTINGENCIES

You must also consider any commitments and contingencies which may exist.

SOLVED PROBLEM 3.11

What are some examples of commitments and contingencies?

SOLUTION

Examples are cosigning loans, guaranteeing of a family member's debt, and financial commitments made to a relative or third party (for example, a promise to pay for the cost of a home to a daughter when she gets married).

Although commitments and contingencies are not presently reported as liabilities on your balance sheet, they represent *potential* obligations that have to be thought about and considered in appraising your financial status.

PERSONAL INCOME STATEMENT — YOUR NET SAVINGS

Net savings equals total income less total expenses. You can prepare an income statement showing your income and expenses. This reveals your economic health and indicates if there is excess discretionary income to save. Looking at the relationship between expenses and income may give you ideas on ways to readjust expenses.

Income sources have to be considered to determine future stability and recurrence possibilities. Potential for growth in income may also be revealed. Some sources of income are salaries, interest and dividends, gifts, and pensions. Living expenses are also itemized to see if any category is unusually high, and why. Are your spending habits excessive, and in what areas?

The amount you save depends on the importance of savings in your financial plan and your income level. As your income goes up, the percentage of income saved also increases. This is because at higher incomes many expenses (for example, food) do not increase at the same pace with the income. Hence, it becomes easier to save.

In general, families save about 4 percent of disposable income.

SOME EXPENSE CONSIDERATIONS

Managing expenses well has a lot to do with how much you know about your expenses.

SOLVED PROBLEM 3.12

What questions need to be answered about your expenses?

SOLUTION

The following questions require answers:

Which expenses are fixed (inflexible) and which are variable (flexible). Fixed expenses are the same each month (for example, insurance) and are typically provided by written agreement. Since fixed expenses are inflexible, you have very little control over them in the short run. Variable expenses may fluctuate each month (for example, transportation, food). Because variable expenses are flexible you have some control over them in the short run.

What amount of each expense is discretionary?

Which expenses are excessive, based on your goals?

Which expenses can be eliminated if costs have to be cut?

Recurring expenses (for example, rent) may not be easily reduced. Nonrecurring expenses (for example, entertainment and recreation) may be reduced, if necessary.

Recommendation: Use an Expense Record Book to record expenses. A loose-leaf binder may suffice.

An abbreviated income statement should include the following elements:

INCOME

Fully taxable income (for example, salaries, interest, dividends, gains on sale of securities)

Tax-sheltered income (for example, social security benefits)

Tax-exempt bond interest

Retirement plan earnings

Disability benefits

Gifts and inheritances

EXPENSES

Recurring expenses (for example, mortgage interest, rent, telephone, electric, insurance)

Nonrecurring expenses (for example, food, repairs, transportation, recreation, education, clothing)

Taxes and tax-sheltered expenses (for example, taxes, losses on sale of securities, business expenses, health insurance, medical expenses, alimony, donation, child-care costs, home improvements)

$$\text{Net savings} = \text{Total income} - \text{Total expenses}$$

A sample income statement is given in Figure 3-2.

SOLVED PROBLEM 3.13

This year you had take-home income of $18,000. You received a tax refund of $600 and sold your car for $2,000. The interest income on your savings account was $500. Your expenses for the year were rent, $3,000; clothing, $500; groceries, $2,000; transportation (commuting), $250; utilities, $900; and vacation, $300. Prepare an income statement for the current year.

SOLUTION

INCOME

Salary	$18,000	
Tax refund	600	
Sale of car	2,000	
Interest income	500	
Total income		$21,100

EXPENSES

Fixed expenses:			
Rent	$ 3,000		
Groceries	2,000		
Transportation (commuting)	250		
Utilities	900		
Total fixed expenses		$6,150	
Discretionary expenses:			
Clothing	$ 500		
Vacation	300		
Total discretionary expenses		800	
Total expenses			6,950
Net savings			$14,150

MR. AND MRS. TOM JONES
INCOME STATEMENT
FOR THE YEAR ENDING DECEMBER 31, 19X8

INCOME

Salary, commission, bonus	$75,000	
Self-employment income (net)	20,000	
Interest	2,000	
Dividends	4,000	
Gain on sale of securities	4,000	
Rental, royalty, and partnership income	5,000	
Pensions, social security	10,000	
Total income		$120,000

EXPENSES

FIXED EXPENSES

Insurance	$ 3,000	
Housing (mortgage, rent)	12,000	
Real estate taxes	4,000	
Utilities	2,000	
Medical	2,000	
Groceries	6,000	
Transportation (commuting)	1,000	
Repayment of debt	3,000	
Income taxes	5,000	
Contribution to pension plan	—	
Total fixed expenses		$38,000

DISCRETIONARY EXPENSES

Clothing and cleaning	$ 2,000	
Personal care	1,000	
Restaurants	5,000	
Entertainment/recreation	3,000	
Vacation/travel	4,000	
Education	3,000	
Charities and gifts	1,000	
Furniture and appliances	4,000	
Household expenses and repairs	3,000	
Total discretionary expenses		26,000
Total expenses		64,000
Net savings		$ 56,000

Fig. 3-2   Illustrative income statement.

ARE YOU LIQUID?

You should compare your financial performance to the inflation rate, asset liquidity, and debt posture.

If you are illiquid, you will not be able to pay your bills. On the other hand, if you have excessive liquid assets, you will earn a lower rate of return. The more liquid the asset, the lower the return. Cash, for example, is the most liquid but does not provide a return.

You should compute the following liquidity ratios:

1. *Liquid assets/take-home pay.* Typically, your current earnings are the basis to pay current bills. The rule of thumb is that your liquid assets should be 6 months of take-home pay. This enables the individual to protect himself so that he is able to pay his bills even if for some reason his monthly take-home pay stops (for example, layoffs, illness). Of course, a lower multiple would be needed if the individual had good loss-of-income protection (for example, insurance policy, union contract).

SOLVED PROBLEM 3.14

Your liquid assets are $50,000 and your monthly take-home pay is $20,000. What is the liquid assets to take-home pay ratio and what does it mean?

SOLUTION

$$\frac{\text{Liquid assets}}{\text{Take-home pay}} = \frac{\$50,000}{\$20,000} = 2.5$$

The liquid assets could cover the loss of monthly take-home pay for 2.5 months. Hence, a larger liquid balance in assets is suggested.

2. *Liquid assets/current liabilities.* Unfortunately, the ratio of liquid assets to take-home pay does not take into account existing liabilities. A useful ratio in this area is liquid assets to current liabilities.

SOLVED PROBLEM 3.15

If liquid assets are $50,000 and current liabilities are $10,000, what is the liquidity ratio and what does it mean?

SOLUTION

$$\text{Liquidity ratio} = \frac{\text{Liquid assets}}{\text{Current liabilities}} = \frac{\$50,000}{\$10,000} = 5$$

This ratio means that for every $1 of current liabilities there are $5 in liquid assets to satisfy it. The higher the ratio, the better your liquidity.

In general, liquidity ratios are designed to identify liquidity problems so an individual can take appropriate corrective action. Will you be able to meet a cash crisis?

LOOKING AT YOUR DEBT LEVEL

Excessive debt is not described in terms of total dollars but rather relative to total assets and considering the individual's monthly income. Two useful ratios relating to this are

1. *Total debt/total assets.* Compute your ratio of total debt to total assets to determine how much of the assets is financed. If debt exceeds your assets, you may have a great deal of difficulty paying your bills. This may eventually lead to personal bankruptcy and result in a devastating effect on your credit rating. The debt ratio equals

$$\frac{\text{Total debt}}{\text{Total assets}}$$

SOLVED PROBLEM 3.16

Total liabilities are $30,000 and total assets are $50,000.

(a) What is the total debt to total assets ratio and what does it mean?

(b) Are you better off with a higher or lower ratio? Why?

SOLUTION

(a) $$\frac{\text{Total liabilities}}{\text{Total assets}} = \frac{\$30,000}{\$50,000} = .6$$

The ratio means that you have $.60 of total debt for every $1 in total assets.

(b) A lower ratio is preferred since it is better not to owe too much money. A lower ratio would also be preferable if the market value of your assets fluctuate greatly?

2. *Take-home pay/debt service charges.* Your ability to handle debt not only depends on your assets but also on your take-home pay relative to debt service charges (monthly payment of principal and interest).

SOLVED PROBLEM 3.17

Your take-home pay is $40,000, and the debt-service charges (principal and interest on loans) are $10,000.

(a) What is the debt service coverage ratio and what does it mean?

(b) Are you better off with a higher or lower ratio?

SOLUTION

(a) $$\frac{\text{Take-home pay}}{\text{Debt service charges}} = \frac{\$40,000}{\$10,000} = 4$$

There is $4 in take-home pay for each $1 of necessary debt repayment and interest.

(b) A high ratio reveals better debt-carrying capacity. In general, the ratio should be at least 2.

SOLVED PROBLEM 3.18

A summary of your personal balance sheet follows:

ASSETS

Liquid assets	$ 75,000	
Nonliquid assets	300,000	
Total assets		$375,000

LIABILITIES

Short-term liabilities	$ 50,000	
Long-term liabilities	200,000	
Total liabilities		250,000
Net worth		$125,000

Additional information:

Take-home pay	$40,000
Debt service charges	$ 8,000

Compute the following ratios:

(a) Liquid assets/take-home pay

(b) Liquid assets/current liabilities

(c) Total debt/total assets

(d) Take-home pay/debt service charges

SOLUTION

(a) $70,000/$40,000 = 1.75   (c) $250,000/$375,000 = .67

(b) $70,000/$50,000 = 1.4   (d) $40,000/$8,000 = 5

You may also relate current debt to future income.

SOLVED PROBLEM 3.19

Your current income is $15,000 but your income next year is expected to be $20,000. You do not want to have current debt at more than 30 percent of future income. What is the maximum amount of debt you should have this year?

SOLUTION

$$30\% \times \$20,000 = \$6,000$$

HOW DOES YOUR BUDGET LOOK?

You should prepare a realistic budget of the different sources of income (for example, salary, investment income, pensions) and itemize expenses by category. A budget should be based on past experience taking into account the current environment. The preparation of a budget will show how you manage cash flow. A money plan enables you to direct dollars where they are needed most.

Budgeting is best done on a monthly basis, since timely figures are needed to monitor the situation and take timely action. You are able to evaluate your estimated cash balance at the end of a period (for example, month, quarter, year). You should compare actual amounts to budgeted amounts and identify the reasons for the variances. Are you spending too much in a given expense area? Are your sources of income different than expected? Why? If actual income exceeds budgeted income, variance is favorable. However, if actual expense exceeds the budgeted expense, it is unfavorable. The variance will reveal whether corrective steps need to be made to control the situation. You may find that you have to adjust your employment activities or adjust your expenses downward.

SOLVED PROBLEM 3.20

(a) Fill in the variance column for your comparison of budget to actual figures and indicate whether the variance is favorable (F) or unfavorable (U).

(b) What do the variances tell you, if anything?

SOLUTION

(a)

	BUDGET	ACTUAL	VARIANCE
Take-home pay	$16,000	$14,000	$2,000 U
Entertainment expense	4,000	9,000	5,000 U
Rent	3,000	3,100	100 U
School books and supplies	1,000	800	200 F

(b) There is a significant unfavorable variance in take-home pay indicating you may want to get a part-time job to supplement your income or change positions. You are entertaining yourself too much! You would be better off spending less on entertainment and more on your education. The rent is basically stable.

Based on the budget, you can find out what sources of income may be increased to improve your cash balance. You may decide that certain costs have to be cut because of forcasted cash problems. You can separate necessities from luxury expenditures to see which costs you can do without. You can identify which expenses are tax deductible and which are not. More emphasis should be given to tax-deductible expenses, to obtain tax savings.

An important aspect in budgeting is the control of personal credit. The use of credit should be minimized because of the high financing cost.

SOLVED PROBLEM 3.21

You incur a tax-deductible expense (for example, interest on a mortgage) of $4,000. If you are in the 28 percent tax bracket, what is the after-tax cost?

SOLUTION

The after-tax cost is $2,880 (4,000 × .72). The remaining $1,120 is in effect subsidized by the government because it represents a tax savings.

SOLVED PROBLEM 3.22

How does budgeting enhance your planning ability?

SOLUTION

The advantages of budgeting are

It aids in meeting personal goals and planning expenditures.

It allows planning for situations when increases in income are not going to keep up with increased expenses.

It shows where expenses can be selectively reduced.

It enables the paying of bills on time.

It aids in controlling expenditures.

It assures that spending (for example, credit cards) is within predetermined limits.

It enables setting timetables for major purchases (for example, buying a house).

SOLVED PROBLEM 3.23

What factors should be considered in determining your budget?

SOLUTION

Important budgetary factors include your age, children's ages, hobbies, liquidity, health, and tax status.

There are differences involved in deriving budget estimates. Income does not always come in evenly each month. Bonuses are given at year-end. Dividends are received quarterly. It is most difficult to estimate expenses for personal maintenance, such as food, clothing, and medicine. The amount may vary from month to month. *Tip:* Actual expenses should be compared to estimated expenses each month.

Be conservative in preparing a cash inflow forecast, since it is better to underestimate. If you overestimate cash inflows, you may be planning for and incurring expenses you cannot meet.

When planning your expenses, you will know some of them by heart (for example, monthly loan payment, rent). Other expense predictions will require reference to your checkbook, credit card statements, and purchase receipts when cash has been paid.

In preparing an annual budget, you should show budgeted figures for each of the 12 months and a total column. An illustrative cash budget is shown in Figure 3-3.

SOLVED PROBLEM 3.24

You receive $1,200 per month in take-home pay. Your monthly interest income and dividend income are $50 and $20, respectively. Prepare a monthly cash inflow budget.

BEGINNING CASH BALANCE		$15,000
CASH RECEIPTS		
Salary—Husband	$40,000	
Salary—Wife	20,000	
Interest income	5,000	
Dividend income	2,000	
Royalty income	3,000	
Gifts	6,000	
Tax refunds	4,000	
Sale of securities	7,000	
Sale of assets	5,000	
Total cash receipts		$92,000
CASH EXPENSES		
Rent	$ 4,000	
Mortgage	3,000	
Fuel bills	1,000	
Telephone	2,000	
Electricity	600	
Gas expense	400	
Water	1,000	
Loan payments	4,000	
Education expense	3,000	
Property taxes	4,000	
Income taxes	2,000	
Insurance payments	6,000	
Medical bills	8,000	
Food	10,000	
Household items	12,000	
Furniture	14,000	
Clothing	6,000	
Transportation costs	5,000	
Entertainment expense	2,000	
Gift payments	1,000	
Personal care	1,000	
Total cash payments		90,000
Increase in cash flow		2,000
Ending cash balance		$17,000

Fig. 3-3 Sample cash budget.

SOLUTION

SOURCE	CASH INFLOW
Wages	$1,200
Interest income	50
Dividend income	20
Total	$1,270

SOLVED PROBLEM 3.25

Your budgeted cash inflows and cash outflows for next month are $6,000 and $4,000, respectively. How much can you expect to save next month?

SOLUTION

Cash inflows	$6,000
Cash outflows	4,000
Savings	$2,000

A "Money Planner Worksheet" prepared by Bank of New York compares actual to goal figures for revenues and expenses (see Figure 3-4).

Looking at the worksheet, you should note several items. The goal may be either to limit spending or to increase it in certain areas. Is the goal realistic? Organize bills so that you know how much you owe and to whom. Is payment current or past due?

SOLVED PROBLEM 3.26

On January 1, you forecast your February expenses as rent, $400; utilities, $70; personal care, $100; and entertainment, $140. Prepare a condensed statement of forecasted expenses for February.

SOLUTION

FIXED EXPENSES

Rent	$400	
Utilities	70	
Total fixed expenses		$470

DISCRETIONARY EXPENSES

Personal care	$100	
Entertainment	140	
Total discretionary expenses		240
Total expenses		$710

SOLVED PROBLEM 3.27

You budget 8 percent of your monthly take-home pay of $1,600 for medical bills. What is your budgeted medical cost?

SOLUTION

$$\$1,600 \times .08 = \$128$$

SOLVED PROBLEM 3.28

You make installment payments of $170 per month. What percentage is this of your monthly take-home pay of $1,500?

SOLUTION

$$\frac{\$170}{\$1,500} = 11.3\%$$

SOLVED PROBLEM 3.29

Your monthly take-home income is $1,800. You want to buy a house that is expected to cost $480 a month to upkeep. Will this amount keep you within 25 percent of your budget?

Money Planner Worksheet

NET INCOME

SOURCES These could include wages, alimony, child support, pensions, and so on. For more categories, see *How to Prepare a Personal Financial Statement,* another report in this series.

	Annual	Monthly
	_____	_____
_____	_____	_____
_____	_____	_____
_____	_____	_____
TOTAL INCOME	$ _____	$ _____

EXPENSES

	Annual		Monthly	
	Now	Goal	Now	Goal
HOUSING				
Rent, home loan payment				
Property taxes, assessments*				
Property insurance (homeowner, tenant)*				
Maintenance, repairs				
Utilities				
Gas, electricity				
Other fuel				
Telephone				
Water, sewer				
Cable TV				
Garbage collection				
Home furnishings*				
Other (such as homeowner's association fees, household help other than child care)				
PERSONAL MAINTENANCE				
Food				
Clothing				
Purchases				
Laundry, dry cleaning, repairs				
Self-Improvement				
Education				
Books, magazines, newspapers				
Entertainment, recreation				
Vacations*				
Other (including movies, sports, restaurants, hobbies)				

(cont'd.)

Fig. 3-4 Money planner worksheet. (*Source:* Personal Money Planner, Bank of New York, Circular Information Report, 1986.)

	Annual		Monthly	
	Now	Goal	Now	Goal
PERSONAL MAINTENANCE (cont'd.)				
Transportation				
Gas, oil				
Repairs, maintenance*				
Parking, tolls				
Auto insurance				
License registration				
Public transportation				
Cab fare				
Gifts, holiday expenses (other than Christmas Club accounts)				
Child/dependent care (including babysitters, nursery school fees, convalescent care)				
Health care				
Health insurance				
Doctors' visits				
Prescriptions, medicine				
Personal care (including barber, hairdresser, cosmetics)*				
OBLIGATIONS				
Regular payments to others (including alimony, child support, other court-ordered payments)				
Contributions, dues (voluntary, including those deducted from your paycheck)				
Debt payments				
Installment loan payments (for vehicles, furniture, etc.)				
Credit card, charge accounts				
SAVINGS AND INVESTMENTS				
Short-term savings (including Christmas Club, emergency fund)				
Long-term savings (including company or private pension, certificates of deposit)				
Life insurance				
Investments (including stocks, bonds, real estate)				
TOTAL EXPENSE	$	$	$	$

*Set-aside account

Fig. 3-4   continued

SOLUTION

$$\$1,800 \times .25 = \$450$$

No. You are $30 ($480 − $450) over your budget.

SOLVED PROBLEM 3.30

You budget 30 percent of your take-home pay for food and 25 percent for housing. Your monthly pay is $1,700.

(a) How much is budgeted for food and housing?

(b) How much remains for other items?

SOLUTION

(a)

Food (.30 × $1,700)	$510
Housing (.25 × $1,700)	425
Total	$935

(b)
$$\$1,700 - \$935 = \$765$$

SOLVED PROBLEM 3.31

You budget 25 percent for food, 30 percent for housing, and 10 percent for clothing. The remainder is discretionary. If your monthly take-home pay is $2,000, how much can you spend on other items?

SOLUTION

$$100\% - 25\% - 30\% - 10\% = 35\% \text{ remaining}$$
$$\$2,000 \times 35\% = \$700$$

SOLVED PROBLEM 3.32

You will be purchasing a new car. You budget 14 percent of your monthly income of $2,300 for transportation. Of this amount, you spend $110 a month on automobile expenses.

(a) How much can you afford to spend on car payments?

(b) What percent are the car payments of the transportation budget?

SOLUTION

(a)

Transportation expense ($2,300 × 14%)	$322
Auto expenses	110
Car payments	$212

(b)
$$\frac{\$212}{\$322} = 65.8\%$$

SOLVED PROBLEM 3.33

Your monthly take-home pay is $1,200. You want to save 15 percent per month. Your monthly expenses except for entertainment are $750. How much can you afford to spend on entertainment?

SOLUTION

$$\$1,200 \times 15\% = \$180 \text{ savings}$$

$$\$750 + \$180 = \$930 \text{ savings and expenses (except entertainment)}$$

Monthly income	$1,200
Savings and expenses	930
Entertainment expense	$ 270

To take inflation into account, expense projections should incorporate the expected inflation rate.

SOLVED PROBLEM 3.34

If clothing is currently $1,000 and inflation is forecasted at 5 percent, what is your budgeted cost?

SOLUTION

$$\$1,000 \times 1.05 = \$1,050$$

SOLVED PROBLEM 3.35

In 19X9, an auto costs $15,000, a dinner costs $20, and an appliance is $400. The costs of autos are rising at an annual rate of 5 percent, dinners are rising at 7 percent, and appliances are rising at 4 percent. What is the expected cost of these items next year?

SOLUTION

Auto ($15,000 × 1.05)	$15,750.00
Dinner ($20 × 1.07)	21.40
Appliance ($400 × 1.04)	416.00

SOLVED PROBLEM 3.36

Your beginning cash balance on January 1, 19X8, is $50,000. Taxable sources of income (for example, salaries, interest, dividends) are $60,000. Nontaxable sources of income (for example, gifts) are $25,000. Tax-deductible expenses (for example, interest on mortgage and property taxes) are $30,000. Nondeductible expenses (for example, entertainment and clothing) are $15,000. Your tax rate is 28 percent. What is the ending cash balance on December 31, 19X8?

SOLUTION

Cash balance, January 1, 19X8		$ 50,000
Cash receipts:		
Taxable receipts ($60,000 × .72)	$43,200	
Nontaxable receipts	25,000	68,200
		$118,200
Cash payments:		
Taxable payments ($30,000 × .72)	$21,600	
Nontaxable payments	15,000	36,600
Cash balance, December 31, 19X8		$ 81,600

Some tips for the preparation of a budget are

Code your check stub with an account number for the expense. This aids in summarizing expenses by category at the end of the budget period.

Code income items as you make bank deposits.

Inquire at your bank to see if it provides computerized services to summarize checks and deposit slips.

See if you can use a budgeting software program on your personal computer.

WHAT ABOUT YOUR SAVINGS?

To be conservative and safe, you should have at least 6 months' income in a savings account. However, 3 to 6 months is more realistic for most people. Try to put a minimum of 10 percent of gross income each period into savings. If you tie up your last cent in stocks and bonds, you may have to sell them when they are down in price. You need to have a basic amount of money saved for ordinary living expenses and emergencies.

SOLVED PROBLEM 3.37

Your gross income and net income are $25,000 and $10,000, respectively.

(a) If you want to save 12 percent of gross income, what should your savings be?

(b) If you want to save 4 percent of net income, what should your savings be?

SOLUTION

(a) $25,000 \times 12\% = \$3,000$

(b) $10,000 \times 4\% = \$400$

If your income fluctuates sharply have more in a savings account. Also have a backup fund that can be tapped if needed. The backup fund should be about the same amount as that in your liquid bank account. A backup fund may be in the form of a certificate of deposit.

Take full advantage of a pension plan, since your contributions and interest earned on them are tax deferred. You are also accumulating a nest egg for old age.

Review Questions

(1) What you own is called an _____.

(2) A _____ is what you owe.

(3) Net worth equals _____ minus _____.

(4) Net savings equals total _____ less total _____.

(5) An expense that is the same each month is called _____.

(6) An expense that changes each month is called _____.

(7) An approximate value of household items is _____ percent of the value of the home.

(8) A mortgage obligation is an example of _____ debt.

(9)   As a general rule, your debt as a percentage of total assets should usually be less than _____ percent.

(10)   A pension plan that can be established by a self-employed individual is called a _____ account.

Answers: (1) asset; (2) liability; (3) assets, liabilities; (4) income, expenses; (5) fixed; (6) variable; (7) 5; (8) long-term; (9) 50; (10) Keogh.

Additional Solved Problems

3.1   You agree to give the buyer of your house a mortgage. You will receive $12,000 each year for 10 years. The interest rate is 10 percent. What is the present value of the mortgage payments?

SOLUTION

Use Appendix Table 4.

$$\$12,000 \times 6.14457 = \$73,735$$

3.2   Your total liabilities are $150,000 and your total assets are $250,000. Compute your debt ratio.

SOLUTION

$$\text{Debt ratio} = \frac{\text{Total liabilities}}{\text{Total assets}} = \frac{\$150,000}{\$250,000} = 60\%$$

3.3   You incur a tax-deductible expense of $1,200. Assuming you are in the 28 percent tax bracket, what is the after-tax cost?

SOLUTION

$$\$1,200 \times .72 = \$864$$

3.4   You plan to buy a used car. You budget 15 percent of monthly take-home pay of $2,000 for transportation. Of this budgetary figure, you spend $180 a month on automobile expenses. What can you afford to pay for the monthly car payment?

SOLUTION

Total transportation cost ($2,000 × 15%)	$300
Less: Automobile expenses	180
Car payments	$120

3.5   You have monthly take-home income of $1,500. You want to buy a house that will cost you $400 per month to maintain. Will this amount keep you within 30 percent of your budget?

SOLUTION

$$\$1,500 \times .30 = \$450$$

Yes. The $400 monthly cost is below your budgetary figure of $450.

3.6 You have take-home monthly income of $2,500. Your monthly expenses (excluding entertainment) are $1,100. If you want to save 10 percent of gross income, how much remains for entertainment?

SOLUTION

Take-home pay	$2,500
Savings percent	× .10
Desired savings	$ 250

Take-home pay		$2,500
Total expenses	$1,100	
Desired savings	250	
Total expenses and savings		1,350
Remaining for entertainment		$1,150

3.7 You receive $1,300 per month in take-home pay. Your monthly interest income is $60. Each month your parents give you $200. Prepare a monthly cash inflow budget.

SOLUTION

SOURCE	CASH INFLOW
Wages	$1,300
Interest income	60
Parent support	200
Total	$1,560

3.8 You bought a house for $100,000 which now has a fair market value of $150,000. You still owe $40,000 on your mortgage. What is your equity in the house?

SOLUTION

$$\$150,000 - \$40,000 = \$110,000$$

3.9 Your liquid assets are $80,000 and your monthly take-home pay is $10,000. What is the liquid assets to take-home pay ratio and what does it mean?

SOLUTION

$$\frac{\text{Liquid assets}}{\text{Take-home pay}} = \frac{\$80,000}{\$10,000} = 8$$

The liquid assets could cover the loss of monthly take-home pay for 8 months. This represents a good liquid balance in assets.

3.10 Your liquid assets and current liabilities are $70,000 and $20,000, respectively. What is the liquidity ratio and what does it mean?

SOLUTION

$$\frac{\text{Liquid assets}}{\text{Current liabilities}} = \frac{\$70,000}{\$20,000} = 3.5$$

The ratio means that for every $1 of current liabilities there are $3.50 in liquid assets available to meet them. This is a satisfactory situation.

3.11 Your total liabilities and total assets are $40,000 and $80,000, respectively. What is the total debt to total assets ratio and what does it mean?

SOLUTION

$$\frac{\text{Total liabilities}}{\text{Total assets}} = \frac{\$40,000}{\$80,000} = .5$$

This ratio means that you have $.50 of total debt for every $1 in total assets. You want a low ratio since it is best not to owe too much money.

3.12 Your take-home pay is $50,000 and the debt service charges are $10,000. What is the debt service coverage ratio and what does it mean?

SOLUTION

$$\frac{\text{Take-home pay}}{\text{Debt service charges}} = \frac{\$50,000}{\$10,000} = 5$$

There is $5 in take-home pay for each $1 of necessary debt repayment and interest. The ratio is favorable because it is greater than 2.

3.13 Indicate whether the following items represent increases or decreases in net worth.

(a) Interest expense

(b) Decline in market price of bond investment

(c) Interest income

(d) Payment of taxes

(e) Sales tax

SOLUTION

(a) Decrease   (d) Decrease

(b) Decrease   (e) Decrease

(c) Increase

3.14 A summary of your personal balance sheet follows:

ASSETS

Liquid assets	$ 50,000	
Nonliquid assets	200,000	
Total assets		$250,000

LIABILITIES

Short-term liabilities	$ 40,000	
Long-term liabilities	90,000	
Total liabilities		130,000
Net worth		$120,000

Additional information:

Take-home pay	$30,000
Debt service charges	5,000

Compute the following ratios:

(a)   Liquid assets/take-home pay
(b)   Liquid assets/current liabilities
(c)   Total debt/total assets
(d)   Take-home pay/debt service charges

SOLUTION

(a) $50,000/$30,000 = 1.67   (c) $130,000/$250,000 = .52
(b) $50,000/$40,000 = 1.25   (d) $30,000/$5,000 = 6

3.15   You have the following balances:

1.	Checking account	$ 1,000
2.	Bank loan	5,000
3.	Marketable securities	4,000
4.	Automobile	8,000
5.	Clothing and jewelry	3,000
6.	Credit cards	2,000
7.	Mortgage payable	80,000
8.	Utilities payable	1,000
9.	Savings account	6,000
10.	House	180,000

(a)   Classify each balance as an asset (A) or a liability (L).
(b)   Determine your net worth.

SOLUTION

(a)   1. A   6. L
      2. L   7. L
      3. A   8. L
      4. A   9. A
      5. A   10. A

(b)

ASSETS

Checking account	$ 1,000	
Savings account	6,000	
Marketable securities	4,000	
Clothing and jewelry	3,000	
Automobile	8,000	
House	180,000	
Total assets		$202,000

LIABILITIES

Utilities payable	$ 1,000	
Bank loan	5,000	
Credit cards	2,000	
Mortgage payable	80,000	
Total liabilities		88,000
Net worth		$114,000

3.16 (*a*) Fill in the missing numbers of the personal balance sheet below.

(*b*) Determine the percentage increase or decrease in net worth.

	19X5	19X6
ASSETS		
Liquid assets	$4,000	$?
Nonliquid assets	8,000	7,000
Total assets	$?	$18,000
LIABILITIES		
Short-term liabilities	$?	$ 4,000
Long-term liabilities	3,000	?
Total liabilities	$8,000	$?
Net worth	$?	$ 6,000

SOLUTION

(*a*)

	19X5	19X6
ASSETS		
Liquid assets	$ 4,000	$11,000
Nonliquid assets	8,000	7,000
Total assets	$12,000	$18,000
LIABILITIES		
Short-term liabilities	$ 5,000	$ 4,000
Long-term liabilities	3,000	8,000
Total liabilities	$ 8,000	$12,000
Net worth	$ 4,000	$ 6,000

(*b*)

$$\text{Increase} = \frac{\text{Change}}{\text{Base year}} = \frac{\$2,000}{\$4,000} = 50\%$$

3.17 On March 1, you forecast your June expenses as insurance, $30; commuting, $140; clothing, $200; and vacation, $300. Prepare a condensed statement of forecasted expenses for June.

SOLUTION

FIXED EXPENSES		
Insurance	$ 30	
Commuting	140	
Total fixed expenses		$170
DISCRETIONARY EXPENSES		
Clothing	$200	
Vacation	300	
Total discretionary expenses		500
Total expenses		$670

3.18 Your cash balance on January 1, 19X6 is $40,000. Taxable sources of income are $50,000. Nontaxable sources of income are $10,000. Tax-deductible expenses are $20,000. Nondeductible expenses are $15,000. Your tax rate is 28 percent. What will be your cash balance on December 31, 19X6?

SOLUTION

Cash balance, January 1, 19X6		$40,000
Cash receipts:		
Taxable receipts ($50,000 × .72)	$36,000	
Nontaxable receipts	10,000	46,000
Cash available		$86,000
Cash payments:		
Tax-deductible payments ($20,000 × .72)	$14,400	
Nondeductible payments	15,000	29,400
Cash balance, December 31, 19X6		$56,600

3.19 Prepare a personal balance sheet on December 31, 19X1 based on the following information: cash, $2,000; mutual fund, $35,000; marketable securities, $20,000; long-term investments, $17,000; automobile, $12,000; personal property, $9,000; credit cards, $1,000; mortgage payable, $30,000; and bank loan, $6,000.

SOLUTION

Personal Balance Sheet
December 31, 19X1

ASSETS			
Liquid:			
Cash	$ 2,000		
Marketable securities	20,000		
Mutual fund	35,000		
Total liquid assets		$57,000	
Nonliquid:			
Long-term investments	$17,000		
Automobile	12,000		
Personal property	9,000		
Total nonliquid assets		38,000	
Total assets			$95,000
LIABILITIES			
Short-term:			
Credit cards	$ 1,000		
Total short-term liabilities		$ 1,000	
Long-term:			
Mortgage payable	$30,000		
Bank loan	6,000		
Total long-term liabilities		36,000	
Total liabilities			37,000
Net worth			$58,000

3.20 Prepare a personal income statement on December 31, 19X1, based on the following information: salary income, $40,000; interest income, $2,000; dividend income, $500; insurance, $400; rent, $5,000; utilities, $600; food, $1,500; transportation, $700; clothing, $1,000; entertainment, $800; education, $2,000; household expenses, $900.

SOLUTION

Personal Income Statement
For the Year Ended December 31, 19X1

INCOME

Salary income	$40,000	
Interest income	2,000	
Dividend income	500	
Total income		$42,500

EXPENSES

Fixed expenses:

Insurance	$ 400	
Rent	5,000	
Utilities	600	
Food	1,500	
Transportation	700	
Total fixed expenses		$ 8,200

Discretionary expenses:

Clothing	$ 1,000	
Entertainment	800	
Education	2,000	
Household	900	
Total discretionary expenses		4,700
Total expenses		$12,900
Net savings		$29,600

3.21 Prepare a cash budget for the year 19X1 based on the following information: beginning cash balance, $25,000; salary income, $60,000; interest income, $5,000; gifts received, $1,000; rent expense, $12,000; utilities, $5,000; and food, $6,000.

SOLUTION

Cash Budget
December 31, 19X1

Beginning cash balance		$25,000

Cash receipts:

Salary income	$60,000	
Interest income	5,000	
Gift income	1,000	
Total cash receipts		66,000
Cash available		$91,000

Cash payments:

Rent	$12,000	
Utilities	5,000	
Food	6,000	
Total cash payments		23,000
Ending cash balance		$68,000

Chapter 4

Career Planning and Financial Success

You have to find a career that you not only feel comfortable with but also one that is financially rewarding. A quantitative evaluation can be used to select the best job considering salary, fringe benefits, and promotion. The "real earnings" involved in alternative job offers must be determined. Further, it may pay to work out of your home. A lot of money can be made in starting your own business or opening a franchise. But how do you determine the value of a prospective business? Also when starting a new business you must be willing to take the risk of losing all or part of your investment. Finally, if you hold an undergraduate college degree, you may wish to decide whether it pays to earn a graduate degree.

WHICH CAREER PATH SHOULD YOU ENTER?

There is a positive relationship between higher income and higher education. How much more does the college graduate earn? The average income of college graduates is about 1.5 times the average income of high school graduates. You can estimate future income on the basis of data that show average incomes in different occupational groups in various parts of the country. Certain occupations not only have a higher starting salary but also provide greater opportunity to achieve a higher final salary (for example, attorneys). Income varies with years of experience. Limited salary increases apply to file clerks and typists. Average salaries tend to be higher in larger companies than smaller ones.

SOLVED PROBLEM 4.1

In deciding upon a career, what should you consider?

SOLUTION

In selecting a career, consider the current and future salary levels, opportunity for advancement, working conditions, stability of employment, and personal satisfaction of the job.

SOLVED PROBLEM 4.2

What should be in your career checklist?

SOLUTION

Your career checklist should include obtaining proper education and training, selecting a growing industry and economic area, assuring your continued learning, and providing flexibility.

To help determine a career choice and job opportunities you may refer to the *Occupational Outlook Handbook* published by the U.S. Department of Labor's Bureau of Labor Statistics. It can be found in many libraries. Occupational groupings can be found in Table 4-1. In Table 4-2, you can see the fastest growing occupations. Table 4-3 provides major employment projections. A career opportunity map appears in Figure 4-1.

SOLVED PROBLEM 4.3

What are some important occupational motivators?

SOLUTION

Important occupational motivators include pay and fringe benefits, interesting work, hours, security, potential for advancement, recognition, working environment, and learning opportunities.

Table 4-1 Occupational Groupings

1. Administrative and managerial
   accountants
   bank managers
   personnel and labor relations
   purchasing agents
   school administrators
   hotel managers
2. Engineers, surveyors, and architects
   aerospace
   chemical
   civil
   nuclear
3. Natural scientists and mathematicians
   mathematical scientist
   systems analyst
   physical scientist
   life scientist
4. Social scientists, social workers, religious
   workers, lawyers
   economists
   psychologists
   social workers
   rabbis
   priests
5. Teachers, librarians, counselors
   kindergarten
   secondary school
   university faculty
   librarians
6. Health diagnosing and treating practitioners
   chiropractors
   dentists
   optometrists
   physicians
   veterinarians
7. Health technologists and technicians
   dental hygienist
   surgical technician
   radiologic technician
8. Writers, artists, entertainers
   reporters
   writers
   designers
   actors
   singers
9. Technologists, except health
   air traffic controller
   computer programmer
   legal assistant
10. Marketing and sales
    cashiers
    insurance
    real estate
    securities
    travel agents

11. Administrative support, including clerical
    bank teller
    mail carrier
    receptionist
    secretary
    typist
12. Service
    police officer
    firefighter
    bartender
    waiter/waitress
    custodian
    hairdresser
13. Agriculture and forestry
14. Mechanics and repairers
    aircraft
    automotive
    farm equipment
    appliance
    computer service
    radio/TV
    air conditioning
    millwrights
    musical instrument
    office machines
15. Construction and extraction
    bricklayer
    carpenter
    mason
    electrician
    glazier
    floor covering installer
    ironworker
    painters/paperhangers
    roofers
    sheet metal workers
16. Production
    boilermaker
    bookbinder
    butcher
    jeweler
    furniture upholsterer
    machinist
    shoe repair
    patternmakers
    welders
17. Transportation
    airline pilots
    bus drivers
    truck drivers

Source: Bureau of Labor Statistics, *Occupational Outlook Handbook* (Washington, D.C.: U.S. Government Printing Office, 1984).

Table 4-2   Fastest Growing Occupations

Occupations	Percentage Change in Employment 1984–1995
The Ten Fastest Growing	
Paralegal personnel	97.5
Computer programmers	71.7
Computer systems analysts	68.7
Medical assistants	62.0
Data processing equipment repairers	56.2
Electrical and electronics engineers	52.8
Electrical and electronic technicians and technologists	50.7
Computer operators	46.1
Peripheral EDP equipment operators	45.0
Travel agents	43.9

Source: Employment Projections to 1995. U.S. Department of Labor, Bureau of Labor Statistics. Bulletin 2253, April 1986.

SOLVED PROBLEM 4.4

Roberta is 21 years old, attending college, and majoring in journalism. She writes well and has received good grades. Roberta is an editor for the school newspaper. Unfortunately, she finds that graduates from her program are not having much luck finding suitable jobs. Roberta hears that there is a great demand for accounting majors who are starting at high salaries. Although math and arithmetic manipulation are not her strengths, she is thinking about changing majors because of the opportunities in accounting. What would you advise her?

SOLUTION

Although the demand/supply relationship is a factor in selecting a career, Roberta seems to lack the numerical abilities demanded in accounting. Thus, she will have difficulty in school and her poor grades may prevent her from getting an attractive job. Even if she finds a position, she may fail on the job. Roberta should consider other suitable career opportunities such as majoring in general business or marketing.

HOW TO APPRAISE A JOB ALTERNATIVE

There are many financial and nonfinancial factors to examine in deciding on a particular job offer.

Table 4-3   Employment Projections

Occupation	1995 Percent
Executive, administrative, and managerial workers	11.2
Professional workers	12.7
Technicians and related support workers	3.4
Salesworkers	10.9
Administrative support workers, including clerical	16.7
Total white collar	54.9
Precision production, craft, and repair workers	11.1
Operators, fabricators, and laborers	15.2
Total blue collar	26.3
Service workers	16.1
Farming, forestry, and fishing workers	2.8
Grand total	100.0

Source: Employment Projections for 1995, U.S. Department of Labor, Bureau of Labor Statistics, Bulletin 2253, April 1986, p. 42.

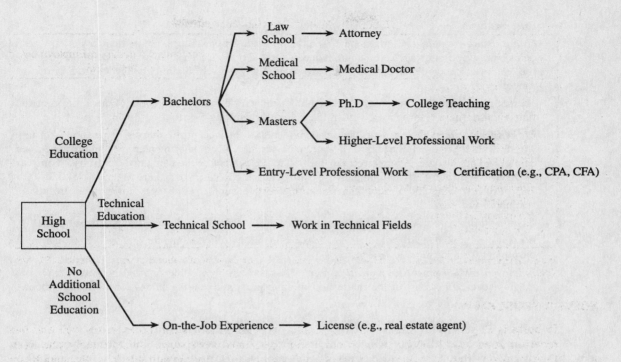

Fig. 4-1 Career opportunity map.

SOLVED PROBLEM 4.5

What are some considerations to take into account in pursuing a job option?

SOLUTION

Relevant factors in deciding upon a proper job include skills and abilities, work experience, education, health, financial position, career goal, and personal interest.

Try to seek a position that is one level higher than your present position.

SOLVED PROBLEM 4.6

What employment benefits do you need to quantify?

SOLUTION

You should quantify the following employment benefits:

Salary including overtime premium

Fringe benefits

Nontaxable compensation (for example, automobile use, use of a house, liability insurance)

Stock option plan

Low interest loans

SOLVED PROBLEM 4.7

What fringe benefits are important to consider?

SOLUTION

Important fringe benefits include

Holidays.

Paid vacations.

Group insurance policies (for example, health, life, catastrophic illness, outpatient psychiatric care, dental, prescription drugs, automobile, homeowners). Do the policies cover dependents? If you leave the employer, can you convert the group coverage to a low-cost individual policy within a prescribed time period?

Pension plan. Employer-sponsored pension plans may differ as to the amount of employee contribution. By law, the employee must vest in the plan after working 5 years.

Profit sharing plan. You pay no tax on monies in the deferred profit sharing or pension plan until withdrawals are made. For example, if your employer has a profit sharing plan, you will receive a percent of the net income. Assume you are entitled to .03 percent of the company's profit based on years of service and salary. If the company's earnings are $1,800,000, your share is $5,400 ($1,800,000 × .003). Profit sharing and pension plans require a certain number of years of employment in order to vest under the plans.

Investment programs, such as in the company's stock. Included are dividend reinvestment plans.

Employer reimbursement for education expenses, including scholarships for children. Employer reimbursement for education is taxable.

Employer reimbursement for relocation costs. Assistance may include finding the house, paying for moving costs and/or part of the interest on the mortgage, and lending money for a down payment.

Employer discounts on company products.

Paying membership fees to professional and trade associations.

What is the before-tax effect of fringe benefits? Fringe benefits are desirable because you receive something of value without having to pay tax. If the employer increased your salary so you could buy health insurance on your own, you would have to pay tax on that higher salary. Thus, it is better to get more fringe benefits from the employer so you will not have to pay additional income tax.

SOLVED PROBLEM 4.8

You are given a tax-free fringe benefit of $420 and you are in the 33 percent marginal tax bracket. What is the amount of taxable income necessary to individually purchase this same benefit?

SOLUTION

$$\text{Before-tax cost} = \frac{\text{Tax-free fringe benefit}}{1 - \text{Marginal tax rate}}$$
$$= \frac{\$420}{1 - .33} = \frac{\$420}{.67} = \$627$$

SOLVED PROBLEM 4.9

Your employer provides $1,000 of medical coverage as a fringe benefit. Assuming a tax rate of 28 percent, what does that translate to on a before-tax basis?

SOLUTION

$$\frac{\$1,000}{1 - .28} = \frac{\$1,000}{.72} = \$1,389$$

In other words, if you received extra compensation and you bought your own $1,000 policy, your salary would have to increase by $1,389 before tax. The tax on it would be $389 ($1,389 × .28).

When comparing job offers, always compute the "real pay."

SOLVED PROBLEM 4.10

You want to determine your "real" compensation. This represents your equivalent before-tax total income. Remember fringe benefits are nontaxable so your equivalent before-tax earnings are higher. Assume you are in the 28 percent tax bracket. Your annual salary is $35,000. You receive fringe benefits of medical insurance, $2,000; disability insurance, $200; life insurance, $150; employer pension plan contribution, $1,750; discounts on company products, $300; services paid by your employer (for example, parking fees, meals), $250; and tuition reimbursement, $500. What is your total real pay?

SOLUTION

Your total real pay is computed below.

Annual salary		$35,000
Fringe benefits:		
Medical insurance	$2,000	
Disability insurance	200	
Life insurance	150	
Pension plan contribution	1,750	
Company discounts	300	
Services paid by employer	250	
Tuition reimbursement	500	
Total fringe benefits	$5,150	
Value on a before-tax basis ($5,150/.72)		7,153
Real pay		$42,153

Note: The costs of searching for a new job in your *present* occupation may qualify as a miscellaneous tax deduction.

SOLVED PROBLEM 4.11

You are a stockbroker who has been laid off. The cost of looking for a new position as a stockbroker includes putting an ad in the newspaper costing $125 and paying a placement service $600.

(*a*)　How much of these costs can you deduct on your tax return?

(*b*)　If you decide to switch careers and go into teaching, how much of these job-seeking costs are tax deductible?

SOLUTION

(*a*)　$725　(*b*)　$0

SHOULD YOU WORK OUT OF YOUR HOME?

There are many tax breaks for running a business at home. Business income and related business expenses are reported on Schedule C of Form 1040. Business deductions include interest on mortgage and real estate taxes.

The percentage of business use of the home is determined by dividing the total number of rooms by the number of rooms used for the business. This percentage is multiplied by your costs to determine the business-related part of that expense. For example, multiply the percentage based on rooms by mortgage interest and real estate taxes to determine the business portion. The percentage use for business of other expenses, including utilities, housecleaning, and repairs, are also taken off on Schedule C. Also, you should have a separate telephone number for business calls. Do not forget to deduct depreciation on the home and office furniture.

SOLVED PROBLEM 4.12

Your house consists of eight rooms, of which one room is used as an office. The mortgage interest and real estate taxes are $3,500. How much can you deduct as a business expense?

SOLUTION

$$\$3,500 \times \tfrac{1}{8} = \$437.50$$

SOLVED PROBLEM 4.13

What cost savings are there to working at home?

SOLUTION

The cost savings of working at home include commuting costs, personal expenses associated with the job (for example, cost of lunch at a restaurant), expensive clothing, and child-care fees.

SOLVED PROBLEM 4.14

What are the dollar disadvantages of self-employment versus working for an employer?

SOLUTION

The drawbacks of self-employment are

Employer's share of FICA tax (social security) (for example, in 1990 7.65 percent of annual wages up to $51,300

Higher-rate premiums for individual insurance policies compared to group insurance policies (for example, medical, dental, life insurance)

The comparative dollar difference between self-employment and working for an employer may be determined.

SOLVED PROBLEM 4.15

If you worked for a company, your salary would be $30,000. The employer contributes $3,000 to your pension plan and pays your health insurance of $1,000. Assume you contribute to your social security at the rate of 7.15 percent of earned wages. The employer matches this.

If you were self-employed, cash revenue would be $46,000 and the related business expenses would be $10,000. You would contribute 20 percent of your earnings to a Keogh pension plan. You would have to pay for your own health insurance amounting to $1,200. In addition, you would have to contribute to social security the full 14.3 percent of your wages since you do not have an employer.

While it is usually true that some of your business expenses allow you to deduct items you normally could not if working for an employer (for example, auto expense, computer costs, room in a house), we will not take this into account because of the difficulty in determination and possible abuse of deducting personal items as business expenses.

(a) What is the net dollar income of working for the employer?

(b) What is the net dollar income of self-employment?

(c) Are you financially better off working for the employer or yourself?

SOLUTION

(a) Net dollar income of working for an employer:

Salary	$30,000
Pension plan	3,000
Health insurance	1,000
Employer social security payment	
(7.15% × $30,000)	2,145
Net employment income	$36,145

(b)   Net dollar income of self-employment:

Cash revenue less cash expenses from business		$36,000
Less: Health insurance	$1,200	
Your extra contribution to social security (7.15% × $36,000)	2,574	3,774
Net self-employment income		$32,226

Note that the Keogh pension contribution comes out of your net income amounting to $7,200 ($36,000 × .20). Thus, this $7,200 pension savings is included in your income figure of $36,000.

(c)   There is a net advantage of $3,919 ($36,145 − $32,226) to working for an employer rather than being self-employed.

SHOULD YOU START YOUR OWN BUSINESS?

There is a great risk in starting your own business but the potential rewards are exceptional. To determine the value of a prospective business, numerous methods can be used including capitalization of earnings, multiple of earnings, capitalization of excess earnings, gross revenue multiplier, and market comparison. If the company's financial statements are not audited, you should insist on an audit to assure accurate reporting of financial figures.

CAPITALIZATION OF EARNINGS

You may capitalize earnings as follows:

$$\frac{\text{Net income}}{\text{Capitalization rate}}$$

The capitalization rate is the multiplier of earnings to obtain the market value of the business.

SOLVED PROBLEM 4.16

A business you are looking at generates a net income of $120,000. A satisfactory return rate used as the capitalization rate is 10 percent. What is the business worth?

SOLUTION

$$\frac{\text{Net income}}{\text{Capitalization rate}} = \frac{\$120,000}{.10} = \$1,200,000$$

This business is worth 10 times earnings.

MULTIPLE OF SIMPLE AVERAGE EARNINGS

The value of a business may be based on the average earnings over 5 years times a multiplier. The multiplier may be based on many factors including what other companies are selling for, the risk of the business, the firm's earning potential, liquidity, competition, and stability. Often, the multiplier is the one prevalent in the industry. The valuation equals

Average earnings over 5 years × Multiplier = Value

SOLVED PROBLEM 4.17

The earnings of a business for a 5-year period are 19X9, $120,000; 19X8, $100,000; 19X7, $110,000; 19X6, $90,000; and 19X5, $115,000.

You estimate, based on industry norms and the company's past history, that the business is worth 3 times earnings. What is the value of the business?

SOLUTION

$$\text{Average earnings} = \frac{\$120{,}000 + \$100{,}000 + \$110{,}000 + \$90{,}000 + \$115{,}000}{5}$$

$$= \frac{\$535{,}000}{5} = \$107{,}000$$

Average earnings over 5 years	$107,000
× Multiplier	× 3
Value of business	$321,000

MULTIPLE OF WEIGHTED-AVERAGE EARNINGS

Instead of a simple average, a weighted-average earnings figure is usually recommended. This gives more weight to the most recent years, which reflect higher current prices and recent business performance. If a 5-year weighted average is used, the current year is given a weight of 5 while the first year is assigned a weight of 1. The multiplier is then applied to the weighted-average 5-year earnings to get the value of the business.

SOLVED PROBLEM 4.18

Assume the same facts as in Solved Problem 4.17 except that a weighted-average earnings figure is to be used. What is the value of the business under this method?

SOLUTION

YEAR	NET INCOME	×	WEIGHT	=	TOTAL
19X9	$120,000	×	5		$ 600,000
19X8	100,000	×	4		400,000
19X7	110,000	×	3		330,000
19X6	90,000	×	2		180,000
19X5	115,000	×	1		115,000
			15		$1,625,000

$$\text{Weighted-average 5-year earnings} = \frac{\$1{,}625{,}000}{15} = \$108{,}333$$

Weighted-average 5-year earnings	$108,333
× Multiplier	× 3
Valuation	$324,999

CAPITALIZATION OF EXCESS EARNINGS

The best method is to capitalize excess earnings. The normal rate of return on the weighted-average net tangible assets is subtracted from the weighted-average earnings to determine excess earnings. The net tangible assets are defined as those assets having physical substance, such as property, plant, and equipment. It is suggested that the weighting be based on a 5-year period. The excess earnings are then capitalized to determine the value of goodwill. Goodwill is defined as the *superior* earning potential of a business relative to other similar businesses in the industry. Goodwill applies to the good name of a business that attracts customers to it. The addition of the value of the intangibles and the fair market value of the net tangible assets equals the total valuation. Note that according to IRS Revenue Ruling 68-609, 1968-2 C.B. 327 the IRS recommends this method to value a business for tax purposes.

SOLVED PROBLEM 4.19

The net tangible assets of a business are 19X1, $950,000; 19X2, $1,000,000; 19X3, $1,200,000; 19X4, $1,400,000; and 19X5, $1,500,000. The weighted-average earnings for the 5-year period are $400,000. A reasonable rate of return on assets is 10 percent. The multiplier is 5 times excess earnings. The fair market value of net tangible assets is $3,000,000. What is the value of the business?

SOLUTION

Weighted-average net tangible assets is computed below:

YEAR	AMOUNT	×	WEIGHT	=	TOTAL
19X1	$ 950,000	×	1		$ 950,000
19X2	1,000,000	×	2		2,000,000
19X3	1,200,000	×	3		3,600,000
19X4	1,400,000	×	4		5,600,000
19X5	1,500,000	×	5		7,500,000
			15		$19,650,000

$$\text{Weighted-average net tangible assets} = \frac{\$19,650,000}{15} = \$1,310,000$$

Weighted-average earnings (5 years)	$ 400,000
Reasonable rate of return on weighted-average tangible net assets ($1,310,000 × 10%)	131,000
Excess earnings	$ 269,000
× Multiplier	× 5
Value of intangibles	$1,345,000
Fair market value of net tangible assets	3,000,000
Capitalization-of-excess-earnings valuation	$4,345,000

The business may also be valued based on the book value or fair market value of the net assets at the *most* recent balance sheet date. The latter approach is preferred since it takes into account current prices.

GROSS REVENUE MULTIPLIER

The value of the business may be determined by multiplying the revenue by the gross revenue multiplier common in the industry. To obtain an appropriate multiplier, refer to *Financial Studies of the Small Business* published annually by Financial Research Associates. This approach may be used when earnings are questionable.

SOLVED PROBLEM 4.20

Revenue is $14,000,000 and the multiplier in the industry is .2. What is the value of the business?

SOLUTION

$$\$14,000,000 \times .2 = \$2,800,000$$

You may also look at the comparative values of similar going concerns. Under this approach, you obtain the market price of a company in the industry similar to the one being examined. That is, recent sales prices of similar businesses may be determined and an average derived.

Upward and downward adjustments to the average price of similar businesses being sold may be made depending on the particular circumstances of the company being valued. While a perfect match is not possible, the companies should be reasonably similar (for example, size, product, structure, geographic location).

The value of the business may be approximated by determining the average value of two or more methods. This may be a sound approach because it looks at several methods in deriving a valuation.

SOLVED PROBLEM 4.21

The fair market value of net assets approach gives a value of $2,100,000 while the capitalization of excess earnings method provides a value of $2,500,000. Using a simple average, what is the value of the business?

SOLUTION

$$\frac{\$2,100,000 + \$2,500,000}{2} = \$2,300,000$$

A combination of methods may give greater weight to the earnings approach and less weight to the asset approach.

SOLVED PROBLEM 4.22

Using the same information as in Solved Problem 4.21, if a weight of 2 was assigned to the earnings approach and a weight of 1 was assigned to the fair market value of net assets method, what would the valuation be?

SOLUTION

METHOD	AMOUNT	×	WEIGHT	=	TOTAL
Fair market value of net assets	$2,100,000	×	1		$2,100,000
Capitalization of excess earnings	2,500,000	×	2		5,000,000
			3		$7,100,000

$$\text{Valuation} = \frac{\$7,100,000}{3} = \$2,366,667$$

Opening a franchise (for example, Burger King) offers fast but not always stable and permanent growth. Most franchisors require a substantial initial fee.

To learn about the possibilities of starting your own business, you may want to visit the library of the nearest branch office of the U.S. Small Business Association. For a listing of franchises and related information, refer to *The Franchise Annual Handbook and Directory* published by Info Press Inc., 736 Center Street, Lewiston, N.Y. 14092.

REASONS FOR BUSINESS FAILURE

Will the business fail? Young (5 years old or less), small companies have high failure rates. The probability of failing in the first 2 years is about 50 percent. The prime reason for a new business failing is management inability. Watch out for excessive fixed costs that you may be unable to meet.

SOLVED PROBLEM 4.23

What are some reasons for business failure?

SOLUTION

A business may fail due to lack of experience and/or education, lack of money, wrong location, mismanagement of inventory, deficient internal control structure, poor credit granting practices, unplanned expansion, and a bad attitude.

SHOULD YOU GO FOR A GRADUATE DEGREE?

If you decide *not* to start your own business, you might want to consider obtaining a higher degree. An advanced degree will enable you to pursue a stable or satisfying salaried job.

You may be unsure whether it pays financially to go for a graduate degree. A present value (discounted cash flow) analysis will be helpful.

SOLVED PROBLEM 4.24

A graduate degree will take you 2 years to complete. The initial application fee is $100. The cost of tuition and books will be $4,000 in the first year and $4,800 in the second year. The salary at your job will be the same while you are in school. However, after you receive your degree your salary will be $5,000, $7,000 and $12,000 more in years 3, 4, and 5. If you did not go to graduate school, you could earn an extra $3,000 and $4,500 in years 1 and 2. Your discount rate is 10 percent. Should you undertake the graduate degree?

SOLUTION

You should go for the graduate degree as indicated below. Appendix Table 3, "Present Value of $1," is used to obtain the appropriate discount factors.

Schedule 1

	Present Value	Year 0	Year 1	Year 2	Year 3	Year 4	Year 5
MBA		−$100 × 1	− $4,000 × .90909	− $4,800 × .82645	+ $5,000 × .75132	+ $7,000 × .68301	+$12,000 × .62092
	$8,286	−$100	− $3,636	− $3,967	+ $3,757	+ $4,781	+$ 7,451
No MBA			+ $3,000 × .90909	+ $4,500 × .82645			
	$6,446		+ $2,727	+ $3,719			

The present value is higher with the graduate degree than without it.

Although the graduate degree will benefit you for more than 5 years, we cut off our analysis at 5 years to avoid making too many calculations which do not add further to our knowledge.

Of course, money is not the only reason to go for a graduate degree. Other motivating factors include promotion, personal satisfaction, mobility, and interest in particular subjects.

You may want to work for a company that will pay for your graduate education.

As far as taxes are concerned, educational costs are deductible as miscellaneous expenses provided you are currently employed and the educational program either

1. Maintains or improves skills required in your occupation

2. Is required by your employer

3. Is a current regulation for your occupation

However, you cannot deduct educational expenses if the objective of the program is to aid in satisfying the minimum educational level for your occupation.

SOLVED PROBLEM 4.25

You are attending a graduate program that will enhance your professional skills in your job. The tuition is $2,000 for the year with books costing another $300. If your adjusted gross income (AGI) is $30,000 and miscellaneous expenses must be in excess of 2 percent of AGI, how much of these educational expenses are tax deductible? (Assume there are already $250 in other miscellaneous expenses.)

SOLUTION

Tuition		$2,000
Books		300
		$2,300
2% of AGI (2% × $30,000)	$600	
Other miscellaneous expenses	250	
Balance		350
Deductible educational costs		$1,950

EXECUTIVE JOB LOSS INSURANCE

You can take out an executive job loss insurance policy. In return for paying a specified percentage of salary as a premium you will be compensated if you are laid off. The policy not only includes coverage for after-tax earnings but also for fringe benefits and typical bonuses.

Review Questions

(1) In general, a college graduate earns _____ times the average income of a high school graduate.

(2) Average salaries tend to be _____ in larger companies than in smaller ones.

(3) Information about careers and job opportunities may be found in the _____ published by the U.S. Department of Labor's Bureau of Labor Statistics.

(4) A self-employed individual files Schedule _____ of Form 1040.

(5) A self-employed individual can have a _____ pension plan.

(6) A listing of franchises and relevant information about them may be found in _____ published by Info Press.

(7) The probability of a new business failing within the first 2 years is about _____ percent.

(8) The best way to value a business is based on _____.

(9) The _____ multiplier method may be used to value a business when _____ are questionable.

Answers: (1) 1.5; (2) higher; (3) *Occupational Outlook Handbook*; (4) C; (5) Keogh; (6) *The Franchise Annual Handbook and Directory*; (7) 50; (8) earnings; (9) gross revenue, earnings.

Additional Solved Problems

4.1 You are employed by a company that has a profit sharing plan. You are entitled to .01 percent of the earnings. If the company's net income for the year is $1,600,000, what will your share be?

SOLUTION

$$\$1,600,000 \times .001 = \$1,600$$

4.2 Your employer provides $4,000 of medical coverage. If you are in the 28 percent tax bracket, what is the extra compensation you are receiving since you do not have to pay tax on the $4,000 of medical coverage?

SOLUTION

$$\text{Before-tax cost} = \frac{\text{Tax-free fringe benefit}}{1 - \text{Marginal tax rate}}$$
$$= \frac{\$4,000}{1 - .28} = \frac{\$4,000}{.72} = \$5,556$$

4.3 You are comparing two job offers. One employer offers medical insurance of $1,200 while the other does not. Assuming a 28 percent tax rate, how much extra should the salary offer without the medical insurance coverage be?

SOLUTION

$$\frac{\$1,200}{1 - .28} = \frac{\$1,200}{.72} = \$1,667$$

4.4 You want to know your "real" compensation. You are in the 28 percent tax bracket. Your annual salary is $40,000 and the fringe benefits you receive are worth $7,000. What are you really receiving?

SOLUTION

Annual salary	$40,000
Value on a before-tax basis of fringe benefits ($7,000/.72)	9,722
Real pay	$49,722

4.5 Your home has six rooms, of which one room is used as an office. The real estate taxes and mortgage interest are $4,000. What dollar portion of the expenses is allowed as a business deduction?

SOLUTION

$$\$4,000 \times \tfrac{1}{6} = \$667$$

4.6 Assume a typical college graduate can earn $40,000 in annual income while a high school graduate can only earn $25,000 per year. If the individual's rate of return is 10 percent, what is the implied incremental asset value of the college education?

SOLUTION

$$\$40,000 - \$25,000 = \$15,000 \text{ excess income}$$

$$\frac{\$15,000}{.10} = \$150,000 \text{ implied asset value}$$

4.7   A business you are thinking of buying has a net income of $80,000. A satisfactory rate of return is 12 percent. What is the business worth?

SOLUTION

$$\frac{\$80,000}{.12} = \$666,667$$

4.8   You are attending an MBA program that is required by your employer. The tuition and books are $2,900. If your adjusted gross income is $40,000 and miscellaneous expenses must exceed 2 percent of AGI to be deductible, how much of the educational expenses are tax deductible? (Assume there are already $500 in other miscellaneous expenses.)

SOLUTION

Tuition and books		$2,900
2% of AGI (2% × $40,000)	$800	
Other miscellaneous expenses	500	
Balance		300
Deductible educational costs		$2,600

4.9   Revenue is $1,000,000 and the multiplier in the industry is .15. What is the value of the business?

SOLUTION

$$\$1,000,000 \times .15 = \$150,000$$

4.10   The earnings of a business for 5 years were 19X9, $80,000; 19X8, $60,000; 19X7, $70,000; 19X6, $85,000; and 19X5, $90,000. The business is worth 2 times earnings. What is the value of the business based on a simple average of earnings?

SOLUTION

$$\text{Average earnings} = \frac{\$80,000 + \$60,000 + \$70,000 + \$85,000 + \$90,000}{5}$$

$$= \frac{\$385,000}{5} = \$77,000$$

Average earnings over 5 years	$ 77,000
× Multiplier	× 2
Value of business	$154,000

4.11   Assume the same facts as in Solved Problem 4.10 except that a weighted-average earnings figure is to be used. The weights are 19X9 = 5, 19X8 = 4, 19X7 = 3, 19X6 = 2, and 19X5 = 1. The multiplier is 2. What is the value of the business?

SOLUTION

YEAR	NET INCOME	×	WEIGHT	=	TOTAL
19X9	$80,000	×	5	=	$ 400,000
19X8	60,000	×	4	=	240,000
19X7	70,000	×	3	=	210,000
19X6	85,000	×	2	=	170,000
19X5	90,000	×	1	=	90,000
			15		$1,110,000

$$\text{Weighted-average 5-year earnings} = \frac{\$1,110,000}{15} = \$74,000$$

Weighted-average 5-year earnings	$ 74,000
× Multiplier	× 2
Value of the business	$148,000

4.12 The net tangible assets of a business are 19X1, $500,000; 19X2, $480,000; 19X3, $520,000; 19X4, $530,000; and 19X5, $540,000. The weighted-average earnings for the 5-year period are $80,000. The reasonable rate of return on assets is 8 percent. The multiplier is 4 times excess earnings. The fair market value of net tangible assets is $300,000. What is the value of the business using the capitalization-of-excess-earnings method?

SOLUTION

YEAR	AMOUNT	×	WEIGHT	=	TOTAL
19X1	$500,000	×	1		$ 500,000
19X2	480,000	×	2		960,000
19X3	520,000	×	3		1,560,000
19X4	530,000	×	4		2,120,000
19X5	540,000	×	5		2,700,000
			15		$7,840,000

$$\text{Weighted-average net tangible assets} = \frac{\$7,840,000}{15} = \$522,667$$

Weighted-average earnings (5 years)	$ 80,000
Less: Reasonable rate of return on weighted-average net tangible assets ($522,667 × .08)	−41,813
Excess earnings	$ 38,187
× Multiplier	× 4
Value of intangibles	$152,748
Fair market value of net tangible assets	300,000
Capitalization-of-excess-earnings valuation	$452,748

4.13 You are valuing a business. The fair market value of net assets approach gives a value of $600,000 while the earnings approach gives a value of $700,000. Using a simple average, what is the value of the business?

SOLUTION

$$\frac{\$600,000 + \$700,000}{2} = \$650,000$$

4.14 Assume the same facts as in Solved Problem 4.13 except a weight of 2 is assigned to the earnings approach while a weight of 1 is assigned to the asset-based method. What is the value of the business?

SOLUTION

METHOD	AMOUNT	×	WEIGHT	=	TOTAL
Fair market value of net assets	$600,000	×	1		$ 600,000
Earnings approach	700,000	×	2		1,400,000
			3		$2,000,000

$$\text{Valuation} = \frac{\$2,000,000}{3} = \$666,667$$

4.15   You are considering going for an MBA that will take 2 years. The initial application fee is $75. The cost of tuition and books will be $5,000 in the first year and $5,800 in the second year. Your salary will be the same while you are attending school. After you receive the MBA, your salary will increase by $6,000, $8,000, and $11,000 in years 3, 4, and 5. If you did not have to attend classes for the MBA, you would have earned an extra $2,000 and $3,000 in years 1 and 2. You earn 10 percent on your money. Should you go for the MBA?

SOLUTION

Schedule 2

	Present Value	Year 0	Year 1	Year 2	Year 3	Year 4	Year 5
MBA		−$75	− $5,000	− $5,800	+ $6,000	+ $8,000	+$11,000
		× 1	× .90909	× .82645	× .75132	× .68301	× .62092
	$7,389	−$75	− $4,545	− $4,793	+ $4,508	+ $5,464	+$ 6,830
No MBA			+ $2,000	+ $3,000			
			× .09090	× .82645			
	$4,297		+ $1,818	+ $2,479			

You should go for the MBA since the present value is higher with a graduate degree than without it.

Chapter 5

Planning for Your Children's College Education

This chapter deals with providing for your child's college education. It discusses how to save to meet future educational costs; what types and amounts of costs will be incurred; and how to make the future value calculations necessary to determine annual savings, interest rate required on funds, etc. Various sources of financial aid are identified. Information on career opportunities is also provided.

SAVING FOR YOUR CHILD'S COLLEGE EDUCATION

Gifts are a simple way to build a college fund for your child while saving on income taxes. Obtain a social security number for your child and start an account under the Uniform Gifts to Minors Act. Encourage relatives to give gifts to the child's college fund. The gifts earn interest taxed to the child, whose tax bracket is usually much lower than the parents. Under present law, a child under the age of 14 pays tax at the child's tax rate on the first $1,000 of interest or dividend income from gift money. Any interest or dividend income in excess of $1,000 is taxed at the parent's rate. However, after the age of 14 the child's tax rate is used on all taxable income.

SOLVED PROBLEM 5.1

A child age 10 earns interest and dividend income of $3,600 on gift monies. The parent's tax bracket is 28 percent. What is the tax?

SOLUTION

The tax is $728 computed as follows:

First $1,000 of income taxed at child's rate	$ 0
Balance of $2,600 of income taxed at parent's rate ($2,600 × .28)	728
Tax	$728

SOLVED PROBLEM 5.2

Assume the same facts as in Solved Problem 5.1 except that the child is 16 years old. The child's tax rate is 15 percent. What rate would be used to compute the tax?

SOLUTION

15 percent

WAYS TO FINANCE A COLLEGE EDUCATION

There are many ways to put money aside to finance a college education including buying zero-coupon bonds (preferably with distant maturity dates), home equity loans, and hiring children in your business.

One way to finance your child's education is by taking out a home equity loan. Interest is deductible on a mortgage to finance the child's education. (In contrast, with a regular loan you *cannot* deduct the interest starting in 1991.)

SOLVED PROBLEM 5.3

You take out a home equity loan of $30,000 to finance the education of two children. The interest rate is 12 percent. If you are in the 28 percent tax bracket, how much of the interest is tax deductible?

SOLUTION

$$\$30,000 \times 12\% \times 28\% = \$1,008$$

You can buy your child shares in a growth mutual fund, automatically reinvesting the dividends and capital gain distributions. The dividends and distributions do not amount to much; most of the money is earned from the growth in the value of the shares. Therefore, the annual yield might not exceed the $1,000 limit. However, 10 years down the line there should be a significant increase in the share value. For example, for the year ended December 31, 1989, Fidelity Magellan mutual fund had an astonishing 10-year cumulative return in excess of 1100 percent. If the shares are sold after the child's fourteenth birthday, the capital gain is taxed at the child's lower tax rate.

If you have a business, you can hire your children. Their wages, if reasonable, are tax deductible. Place the money in an account for the child's future education. Further, if you have an unincorporated business, you do not have to pay social security tax on wages paid to children.

WHAT DOES EDUCATION COST AND HOW MUCH MONEY WILL YOU NEED?

The cost of higher education has increased significantly and therefore you must begin saving well in advance. In fact, college costs are expected to more than double within the next 10 years.

SOLVED PROBLEM 5.4

What are some examples of college-related costs?

SOLUTION

College-related costs include tuition, fees, room and board, books, supplies, transportation, and personal expenses.

College costs vary, depending on whether a state school or private university is chosen. The private alternative is more costly. A 4-year education at a private school may cost anywhere between $20,000 to $80,000, depending on the academic standing of the institution.

SOLVED PROBLEM 5.5

What are some financial planning ways to meet college costs?

SOLUTION

Some financial planning ways to meet college costs are to use long-term savings plans, take advantage of financial assistance programs, and to shift income to your lower-tax-bracket child.

According to *Newsday* (August 10, 1989), college costs are increasing by 7 to 9 percent at the 4-year colleges. The average tuition and fees at private colleges was $8,737 in 1989. According to the College Board of Manhattan, this is the ninth consecutive year that college costs have outpaced inflation. The average annual cost at public 4-year and 2-year colleges are up 7 and 5 percent, to $1,694 and $842, respectively.

SOLVED PROBLEM 5.6

Your child wants to go to college for the next 4 years. The annual cost is $4,500 and will increase at the rate of 8 percent per year. What is the cost of the education?

SOLUTION

The educational cost is

$4,500 × future value factor (see Appendix Table 2, "Future Value of Annuity of $1" for $n = 4$, $i = 8\%$)

$$\$4,500 \times 4.50611 = \$20,278$$

Education costs at private and public colleges at the 4-year and 2-year levels are available in a publication entitled *Student Expenses at Post Secondary Institutions*. You can obtain a copy by writing to The College Board, P.O. Box 2815, Princeton, NJ 08541. Also available is the *College Cost Book* published by the College Entrance Examination Board.

You should estimate the total college cost for the first year. Be careful not to underestimate costs because you want a well-prepared figure. To take into account inflation and other increased price factors, add 7 percent to the first year's cost for the second year, 15 percent for the third year, and 23 percent for the fourth year.

SOLVED PROBLEM 5.7

Your child's estimated expenses at ABC College in the first year are $6,000. Using the percents above, determine the projected costs for the remaining years?

SOLUTION

The projected costs for years 2, 3, and 4 are

Year 2	$6,000 × 1.07 = $6,420
Year 3	$6,000 × 1.15 = $6,900
Year 4	$6,000 × 1.23 = $7,380

Obtain and use a worksheet included in *Meeting College Costs* to estimate educational costs. It is a free booklet published by the College Scholarship Service.

Why not prepare a budget for your child's estimated costs at the various colleges being considered? Table 5-1 provides an illustrative budget format.

Table 5-1   Budget Comparison of College Costs

	X College	Y College
Tuition		
Fees (admission, library, activity)		
Room and board		
Books and supplies		
Travel to and from school		
Organizational dues (e.g., fraternity)		
Health costs		
Clothing		
Entertainment and recreation		
Total budgeted cost		

SOLVED PROBLEM 5.8

What ways are available to reduce college costs?

SOLUTION

College costs may be decreased by doing the following:

Try to obtain credit by examination.

See if the college offers a special payment plan.

Pick a low-cost college.

Attend a 3-year degree program, thus reducing tuition fees and living costs.

SOLVED PROBLEM 5.9

Can you list college types in ascending order from less costly to more costly?

SOLUTION

Public 2-year college

State college in your own state

State college outside of your home state

Private 2-year college

Private 4-year college

DETERMINING NEED — FUTURE VALUE CALCULATIONS CAN HELP

How much money will you need to have accumulated when your child is ready for college?

SOLVED PROBLEM 5.10

Your income is $54,000. You expect to save 12 percent of your income each year for the college education of your child, which amounts to $6,480 ($54,000 × 12 percent). Therefore, each month you save $540 ($6,480/12). You expect to earn 8 percent on your savings. Your child will be going to college 10 years from now. How much will be accumulated after 10 years for your child's education?

SOLUTION

The future value factor (see Appendix Table 2, "Future Value of Annuity of $1") for $n = 10$, $i = 8\%$ is 14.48656.

$$\$6,480 \times 14.48656 = \$93,873$$

An interest-sensitive life insurance policy on the life of the parent may aid in education funding. Single premium life, universal life, and other interest-sensitive insurance policies sometimes allow the withdrawal of cash from the policies, instead of a loan. If the policy is taken out when the child is young, a withdrawal could be taken later to fund his or her education. Cash up to the amount paid into the policy can be withdrawn tax-free.

SOLVED PROBLEM 5.11

Your child is 5 years old and you buy, in your name, a $20,000 single-premium whole life policy and let the earnings accumulate for the child's education. If the rate of return is 10 percent, how much will the policy be worth in 12 years?

SOLUTION

The factor from the future value of $1 table (see Appendix Table 1) for $n = 12$, $i = 10\%$ is 3.13843.

$$\$20,000 \times 3.13843 = \$62,769$$

The annual deposits in a bank account necessary to provide for your child's education can be computed.

SOLVED PROBLEM 5.12

You want to send your child to college 10 years from now and will need $40,000 at that time. Assuming an 8 percent interest rate, you will have to make annual deposits of how much?

SOLUTION

The annual deposit is $2,761.18, as computed below [future value factor (see Appendix Table 2) for $n = 10$, $i = 8\%$ is 14.48656]:

$$\frac{\$40,000}{14.48656} = \$2,761.18$$

You may have to determine the monthly savings required to have sufficient funds for your child's education.

SOLVED PROBLEM 5.13

In today's dollars, you will need $30,000 to provide for a college education for your child. Your child will be going to college 10 years from now. You anticipate earning a net rate of return (after considering the inflation rate) of 8 percent. At present, you have $5,000 saved for your child's education.

(a) How much will your $5,000 of savings be worth in 10 years?

(b) What additional savings is needed?

(c) What is the annual savings required each year to accomplish your goal?

(d) What is the monthly savings?

SOLUTION

(a) The factor for $n = 10$, $i = 8\%$ from Appendix Table 1, "Future Value of $1," is 2.15892.

$$\$5,000 \times 2.15892 = \$10,795$$

(b) $$\$30,000 - \$10,795 = \$19,205$$

(c) The savings factor for $n = 10$, $i = 8\%$ (see Appendix Table 2, "Future Value of Annuity of $1") is 14.48656.

$$\frac{\$19,205}{14.48656} = \$1,326$$

(d) $$\frac{\$1,326}{12} = \$111$$

You may need to know the interest rate that has to be earned on your money to have adequate funds available for your child's education.

SOLVED PROBLEM 5.14

You want to have $28,000 saved in 12 years when your child will be ready for college. What is the annual rate of return you must earn on your money if you invest $1,500 annually?

SOLUTION

The rate of return is about 8 percent as computed below:

$$\frac{\$28,000}{\$1,500} = 18.6667 \qquad \text{Factor}$$

As per Appendix Table 2, "Future Value of Annuity of $1," the interest rate for $n = 12$ and a factor of 18.6667 (18.97713 exactly) is about 8 percent.

SOURCES OF FINANCIAL AID

It is important to know sources that are available for financial aid.

SOLVED PROBLEM 5.15

What are some sources of financial aid?

SOLUTION

In examining financial aid, do the following:

Check out federal and state government programs first, since they represent the most funding available. *Note:* You can use one form to apply for various federal, state, and college programs.

Consider specialized programs directed toward certain types of people (for example, based on race or religion).

Find out about funds available from the college itself.

You may obtain assistance to determine the sources of financial aid by contacting Scholarship Search, 1775 Broadway, New York NY 10019.

You also may obtain information on scholarships and student college aid by contacting Student College Aid, 3641 Deal Street, Houston, TX 77025.

A publication discussing college aid offerings is *Don't Miss Out: The Ambitious Student's Guide to Financial Aid,* published by Octameron Associates, P.O. Box 3437, Alexandria, VA 22302.

The Early Financial Aid Planning Service provides a computerized estimate of your eligibility for financial aid from various sources, in addition to a comprehensive analysis of your family's financial status relative to college costs and potential aid. Information can be obtained from Early Financial Aid Planning, Box 2843, Princeton, NJ 08541.

To obtain financial aid, your child must be attending an *accredited* college (one approved by a recognized accrediting agency).

Scholarships and grants do *not* have to be repaid. However, they are taxable to the degree they exceed tuition and course fees.

SOLVED PROBLEM 5.16

You receive a scholarship for $18,000. Tuition and course fees are $11,000. You are in the 15 percent tax bracket.

(*a*) How much of the scholarship is taxable?

(*b*) How much tax will you have to pay?

SOLUTION

(*a*) $7,000

(*b*) $7,000 × 15% = $1,050

Eligibility for scholarships may be based on merit (academic or athletic) or financial need.

SOLVED PROBLEM 5.17

What are some bases for scholarships?

SOLUTION

Scholarships may be based on religion, nationality, race, and occupation.

SOLVED PROBLEM 5.18

What are some private scholarship sources?

SOLUTION

Private scholarship sources include your company; labor union, trade, or professional associations; advocacy groups for minorities; National Merit Scholarship Corporation (NMSC) for students who earn a high grade on an NMSC examination; civic or fraternal organization (for example, American Legion); State Department of Vocational Rehabilitation (for handicapped students); ROTC (for students who pursue careers in the military as officers); and other sponsors (for example, Boy Scouts).

Information on opportunities for minorities and women can be obtained from the *Selected List of Post Secondary Education Opportunities for Minorities and Women,* available from the Department of Health, Education and Welfare, Office of Education, Regional Office Building 3, Room 4082, Washington, DC 20202.

Social security benefits may be available for unmarried full-time students who are children of disabled or retired individuals. Inquiry may be made at any social security office. Veterans' educational benefits may be available to veterans and their immediate family.

The amount of financial aid equals the difference between college costs and the amount you can afford.

SOLVED PROBLEM 5.19

You expect to incur the following costs to educate your child: tuition and fees, $25,000; room and board, $20,000; books and supplies, $2,500; travel expenses, $1,800; and personal expenses, $500. You can afford to spend $15,000. How much financial aid will you need?

SOLUTION

The costs for your child's education and the amount of financial aid needed follows:

Tuition and fees	$25,000
Room and board	20,000
Books and supplies	2,500
Travel expenses	1,800
Personal expenses	500
Total cost	$49,800
Less: Amount you can afford to pay	15,000
Amount of financial aid required	$34,800

SOLVED PROBLEM 5.20

In estimating the financial aid required, what should be considered?

SOLUTION

To estimate financial aid you should

Determine all educational costs.

Determine your share of the educational costs.

Determine the amount of financial aid needed; it equals

Total education costs − your share of total costs

Typically, you are eligible for financial aid equal to the amount you need.

SOLVED PROBLEM 5.21

What is financial need?

SOLUTION

Financial need is the difference between the cost of attending college and the amount the parents and student are capable of contributing.

Financial aid officials expect parents to use 5 percent of their assets each year and all their "available income" to provide for their child's education.

SOLVED PROBLEM 5.22

What is available income?

SOLUTION

Available income equals

Taxable and nontaxable income − basic expenses   (for example, housing, food, clothing)

To get financial aid, you have to prove that you cannot pay the total educational costs on your own. It is a mistake to think that financial aid is just for poor people.

Many middle-income families do not qualify for guaranteed student loans and other assistance programs. For these families, regular loans may be the answer.

SOLVED PROBLEM 5.23

What regular loans are available for college from the least to the most expensive?

SOLUTION

Available loans include

College loan with low interest, repayable after graduation

Low-interest loan through a civic organization

Deferred-tuition plan, if offered by the college

Loan from a credit union

Bank loan

Finance company loan

Some colleges offer their own long-term loans. Usually, they are at low interest and have convenient repayment schedules.

You will have to contribute some aid toward your child's education, since financial aid sponsors require some participation on your part. The amount *you* have to contribute depends on a "need analysis" conducted by a national organization, for example, the College Scholarship Service (CSS) of the College Board. The confidential Financial Aid Form requires you to state your income, expenses, assets (home equity, stock owned), obligations, and number of children (including those now in college). Note unusual costs, such as those incurred by a handicapped child. The results of the "need analysis" are sent to the financial aid directors of the colleges.

From your total assets, an asset protection allowance will be subtracted (for example, $10,000 to $40,000) depending on your circumstances (for example, age). Only 12 percent of the balance is considered in computing your ability to meet college costs.

SOLVED PROBLEM 5.24

Your total assets are $150,000. The asset protection allowance is $20,000. What is the remaining assets figure considered in determining ability to pay for college?

SOLUTION

The remaining assets are computed below:

Total assets	$150,000
Less: Asset protection plan	20,000
	$130,000
	× 12%
Remaining assets	$ 15,600

"Needs analysis" for college aid determines your eligible assets. *Tip:* Try to lower your eligible assets so as to obtain more college aid. Since the asset formula does not consider retirement accounts—IRAs, 401(k)s, and Keoghs—put more of your money into those accounts.

The asset formula does not deduct consumer debt from total assets, but it does count mortgage debt. Therefore, obtain funds from a home equity loan to pay off your other debts.

Business assets do not count as much as personal assets in the aid formula. Thus, try to shift some personal assets to business assets.

In determining your ability to pay for your child's college education, the assets figure is divided by the number of children.

SOLVED PROBLEM 5.25

Your eligible assets for your four children's college education is $80,000. What is your ability to pay for each child?

SOLUTION

$$\frac{\$80,000}{4} = \$20,000$$

If your family is richer in assets than income, you can figure the ability to pay with a different formula, based on income only. If you use that formula, you have to renounce all forms of federal aid except guaranteed student loans.

FEDERAL GOVERNMENT PROGRAMS

The federal government has several programs for helping families defray the costs of college education.

SOLVED PROBLEM 5.26

What are some federal aid programs?

SOLUTION

The federal aid programs include

Basic Educational Opportunity Grants (BEOG). This program has the most funds of all federal programs. Eligibility depends on a family's financial condition. Full-time and part-time students are eligible. The grants can be used for 4-year and 2-year public and private colleges as well as for vocational and technical schools. To obtain information, write to P.O. Box 84, Washington, DC 20004.

Supplemental Educational Opportunity Grant (SEOG). The grant cannot be greater than 50 percent of the total cost of college, or 50 percent of the total aid provided. Colleges match the SEOG amount with grants from their own funds, loans, or jobs.

College work-study program. Part-time and summer jobs are subsidized by the federal government for students in need. The government will pay up to 80 percent of the salaries.

National Direct Student Loans (NDSL). These loans are made by the college, but 90 percent of the money comes from the federal government. Eligibility and loan amount are determined by financial aid directors. Half-time students are also eligible to apply. Repayment of principal and interest (at a very low rate) does not start until 9 months after studies end. All or a portion of the loan may be canceled if the graduate enters specified fields or the armed forces.

Guaranteed Student Loan Program (GSLP). These loans are available without an income ceiling. Full-time or part-time students may receive loans through financial institutions (for example, banks). The interest rate is low and repayment commences 9 to 12 months after leaving college. Students at business, trade, vocational, and technical schools are also eligible. Guaranteed student loans do have dollar limits.

You can also apply to the state for aid. The State Student Incentive Grant Program (SSIG) involves the federal government matching funds for state grants to students. Eligibility, funding, application requirements, etc., vary depending upon the state.

WHAT ARE THE CAREER OPPORTUNITIES FOR YOUR CHILDREN?

Occupational Outlook for College Graduates, published by the Bureau of Labor Statistics, contains supply and demand information for various careers, as well as job descriptions. Another source of information on jobs is the *College Placement Annual.* Abilities and skills tests can be taken to determine your child's aptitude for a particular career.

Review Questions

(1) College tuition has risen _____ than the inflation rate.

(2) The tuition at public colleges has risen _____ than at private colleges.

(3) A helpful worksheet in estimating education costs can be found in _____ .

(4) The _____ will help you in finding sources of financial aid for college.

(5) A federal loan for college that is available without an income ceiling is the _____ .

(6) The publication _____ lists the education costs at private and public colleges.

(7) A child under the age of _____ pays tax at the child's tax rate on the first $1,000 of income.

(8) Scholarships are taxable only to the extent they exceed _____ and course fees.

(9) *College Placement Annual* is a source of information on _____ .

Answers: (1) faster; (2) slower; (3) *Meeting College Costs*; (4) Scholarship Search; (5) Guaranteed Student Loan Program; (6) *Student Expenses at Post-Secondary Institutions*; (7) 14; (8) tuition; (9) jobs.

Additional Solved Problems

5.1 A child earns dividend and interest income of $2,700 on gift monies. The parent's tax rate is 28 percent. What is the tax due?

SOLUTION

The tax is $476 computed as follows:

First $1,000 of income taxed at child's rate	$ 0
Balance of $1,700 of income taxed at	
parent's rate ($1,700 × .28)	476
Total tax	$476

5.2 Your total assets are $130,000. The asset protection allowance is $10,000. Use a 12 percent rate to determine remaining assets. What is the amount you are able to pay to meet college costs?

SOLUTION

Total assets	$130,000
Less: Asset protection plan	10,000
	$120,000
	× 12%
Remaining assets	$ 14,400

5.3 You anticipate incurring the following costs to educate your child: tuition and fees, $16,000; room and board, $12,000; books and supplies, $3,000; travel expenses, $1,500; and personal expenses, $700. You can afford to spend $20,000. How much financial aid will you require?

SOLUTION

Tuition and fees	$16,000
Room and board	12,000
Books and supplies	3,000
Travel expenses	1,500
Personal expenses	700
Total cost	$33,200
Less: Amount you can afford to pay	20,000
Amount of financial aid needed	$13,200

5.4 Your child wants to go to college for the next 4 years. The annual cost is $5,000 and will increase at the rate of 6 percent per year. What is the cost of the education?

SOLUTION

Using Appendix Table 2 ("Future Value of an Annuity of $1"), the factor for $n = 4$, $i = 6\%$ is 4.37462.

$$\$5,000 \times 4.37462 = \$21,873$$

5.5 Your child is 8 years old and you buy, in your name, a $10,000 single-premium whole life insurance policy and let the earnings accumulate. Assuming an interest rate of 8 percent, how much money will you have for your child's education when he or she reaches the age of 17?

SOLUTION

The future value of $1 factor from Appendix Table 1 for $n = 9$, $i = 8\%$ is 1.99900.

$$\$10,000 \times 1.99900 = \$19,990$$

5.6 Your child's estimated expenses at X College in the first year are $4,000. The projected costs for the remaining years are expected to rise by 7 percent of the first year's cost in the second year, by 15 percent in the third year, and by 23 percent in the fourth year. What are the projected costs for the remaining years?

SOLUTION

$$
\begin{array}{lr}
\text{Year 2 (\$4,000} \times \text{1.07)} & \$\ 4,280 \\
\text{Year 3 (\$4,000} \times \text{1.15)} & 4,600 \\
\text{Year 4 (\$4,000} \times \text{1.23)} & \underline{4,920} \\
& \underline{\underline{\$13,800}}
\end{array}
$$

5.7 You want to send your child to college 15 years from now and will need $50,000 at that time. The interest rate is 10 percent. How much will the annual deposit need to be to your savings account?

SOLUTION

The factor for $n = 15$, $i = 10\%$ from the "Future Value of Annuity" table (see Appendix Table 2) is 31.77248.

$$\frac{\$50,000}{31.77248} = \$1,574$$

5.8 You want to have $35,000 saved in 21 years when your child will be ready for college. You invest $1,000 annually. What annual rate of return must you earn on this money?

SOLUTION

$$\frac{\$35,000}{\$1,000} = 35 \quad \text{factor} \quad n = 18$$

Looking at Appendix Table 2 for $n = 18$ and a factor of 35 gives an approximate interest rate of 5 percent.

5.9 Your income is $48,000. You anticipate saving 10 percent of your income each year for the college education of your child. You expect to earn 9 percent on your savings. Your child will be going to college 12 years from now.

(a) How much will you save each month?

(b) After 12 years, how much will you have accumulated in savings?

SOLUTION

(a) $\qquad\qquad\qquad$ $\$48,000 \times 10\% = \$4,800$ savings per year

$$\frac{\$4,800}{12} = \$400 \text{ savings per month}$$

(b) The future value of annuity of $1 factor from Appendix Table 2 for $n = 12$, $i = 9\%$ is 20.14072.

$$\$4,800 \times 20.14072 = \$96,675$$

5.10 In today's dollars you will need to provide $25,000 for your child's college education. Your child will be going to college 8 years from now. You expect to earn a net rate of return of 6 percent (after taking into account inflation). At the current time, you have $8,000 saved for your child's education.

(a) How much will your $8,000 of savings be worth in 8 years?

(b) What is the additional savings needed?

(c) What is the annual savings required each year to accomplish your goal?

(d) What is the monthly savings?

SOLUTION

(*a*)   The future value of $1 factor (see Appendix Table 1) for $n = 8$, $i = 6\%$ is 1.59385.

$$\$8,000 \times 1.59385 = \$12,751$$

(*b*) $$\$25,000 - \$12,751 = \$12,249$$

(*c*)   The savings factor for an annuity for $n = 8$, $i = 6\%$ (see Appendix Table 2) is 9.89747.

$$\frac{\$12,249}{9.89747} = \$1,238$$

(*d*) $$\frac{\$1,238}{12} = \$103$$

Chapter 6

Return and Risk

To be successful as an investor, you need an understanding of investment risk and realistic expectations of reward. Also, an understanding of the trade-off between the return you are expecting from an investment and the degree of risk you must assume to earn it is perhaps the most important key to successful investing. This chapter discusses

Return and how it is measured

Types of risk and how to reduce them

How to manage uncontrollable risk using the concept of *beta*

Investment alternatives and their relationship to risk

WHAT IS RETURN?

Return is the reward for investing. You must compare the expected return for a given investment with the risk involved. The *return on an investment* consists of the following sources of income:

1. Periodic cash payments, called current income
2. Appreciation (or depreciation) in market value, called capital gains (or losses)

Current income, which is received on a periodic basis, may take the form of interest, dividends, rent, and the like. *Capital gains* or *losses* represent changes in market value. A capital gain is the amount by which the proceeds from the sale of an investment exceed the original purchase price. If the investment is sold for less than its purchase price, then the difference is a capital loss.

The way you measure the return on a given investment depends primarily on how you define the relevant period over which you hold the investment, called the holding period. We use the term *holding period return (HPR)*, which is the total return earned from holding an investment for that period of time. It is computed as follows:

$$HPR = \frac{Current\ income + Capital\ gain\ (or\ loss)}{Purchase\ price}$$

SOLVED PROBLEM 6.1

Consider the investment in stocks A and B over one period of ownership:

	Stock A	Stock B
Purchase price (beginning of year)	$100	$100
Cash dividend received (during the year)	10	15
Sales price (end of year)	108	98

(a) What is the current income from the investments?

(b) What is the capital gain or loss from the investments?

(c) What is the total return on the investments?

(d) What is the holding period return (HPR) on the investments?

86

SOLUTION

(a) The current income from the investment in stocks A and B over the 1-year period are $10 and $15, respectively.

(b) For stock A, a capital gain of $8 ($108 sales price − $100 purchase price) is realized over the period. In the case of stock B, a $2 capital loss ($98 sales price − $100 purchase price) results.

(c) Combining the capital gain return (or loss) with the current income, the total return on each investment is summarized below:

	Stock A	Stock B
Return		
Cash dividend	$10	$15
Capital gain (loss)	8	(2)
Total return	$18	$13

(d)

$$\text{HPR (stock A)} = \frac{\$10 + (\$108 - \$100)}{\$100} = \frac{\$10 + \$8}{\$100}$$

$$= \frac{\$18}{\$100} = 18\%$$

$$\text{HPR (stock B)} = \frac{\$15 + (\$98 - \$100)}{\$100} = \frac{\$15 - \$2}{\$100}$$

$$= \frac{\$13}{\$100} = 13\%$$

MEASURING THE RETURN OVER TIME

It is one thing to measure the return over a single holding period and quite another to describe a series of returns over time. When an investor holds an investment for more than one period, it is important to understand how to compute the average of the successive rates of return. There are two types of multiperiod average (mean) returns. They are the arithmetic average return and the geometric average return. The *arithmetic average return* is simply the arithmetic average of successive one-period rates of return. It is defined as

$$\text{Arithmetic average return} = \frac{1}{n} \sum_{t=1}^{n} r_t$$

where n = the number of time periods and r_t = the single holding period return in time t. The arithmetic average return, however, can be quite misleading in multiperiod return calculations.

A more accurate measure of the actual return generated by an investment over multiple periods is the *geometric average return*. The geometric return over n periods is computed as follows:

$$\text{Geometric average return} = \sqrt[n]{(1 + r_1)(1 + r_2) \cdots (1 + r_n)} - 1$$

SOLVED PROBLEM 6.2

Consider the following data where the price of a stock doubles in one period and then depreciates back to the original price. Dividend income (current income) is zero.

| | Time Periods |||
	$t = 0$	$t = 1$	$t = 2$
Price (end of period)	$80	$160	$80
HPR	—	100%	−50%

(a) Compute the arithmetic average return.

(b) Compute the average geometric return.

SOLUTION

(a) The arithmetic average return is the average of 100 percent and −50 percent, which is 25 percent, as shown below:

$$\frac{100\% + (-50\%)}{2} = 25\%$$

(b) The stock was purchased for $80 and was sold for the same price two periods later. Therefore, it did not earn 25 percent; it clearly earned zero return. This can be shown by computing the geometric average return.

Note that $n = 2$, $r_1 = 100\% = 1$, and $r_2 = -50\% = -0.5$. Then,

$$\text{Geometric return} = 2\sqrt{(1 + 1)(1 - 0.5)} - 1$$
$$= 2\sqrt{(2)(0.5)} - 1$$
$$= 2\sqrt{1} - 1 = 0$$

WHAT IS THE EFFECTIVE ANNUAL YIELD?

Different types of investments use different compounding periods. For example, most bonds pay interest semiannually; some banks pay interest quarterly. If you wish to compare investments with different compounding periods, you need to put them on a common basis. The effective annual yield, commonly referred to as *annual percentage rate (APR)*, is used for this purpose and is computed as follows:

$$APR = \left(1 + \frac{r}{m}\right)^m - 1.0$$

where r = the stated, nominal, or quoted rated

m = the number of compounding periods per year

SOLVED PROBLEM 6.3

If a bank offers 6 percent interest, compounded quarterly, what is the annual percentage rate (APR)?

SOLUTION

$$APR = \left(1 + \frac{.06}{4}\right)^4 - 1.0 = (1.015)^4 - 1.0 = 1.0614 - 1.0$$
$$= .0614 = 6.14\%$$

This means that if one bank offered 6 percent with quarterly compounding, while another offered 6.14 percent with annual compounding, they would both be paying the same effective rate of interest.

A comprehensive table showing the nominal and effective interest rates for different compounding periods is provided in Table 7.1.

Annual percentage rate (APR) is also a measure of the cost of credit, expressed as a yearly rate. It includes interest as well as other financial charges such as loan origination and certain closing fees. The lender is required to tell you the APR. It provides you with a good basis for comparing the cost of loans, including mortgage plans. (For more information, see Chapter 8, "Consumer Credit and Loans").

WHAT IS THE EXPECTED RATE OF RETURN?

You are primarily concerned with predicting future returns from an investment in a security. No one can state precisely what these future returns will be. At best you can state the most likely expected outcome, referred to as the *expected rate of return.*

Of course, historical (actual) rates of return could provide a useful basis for formulating these future expectations. Probabilities may be used to evaluate the expected return. Using probabilities, expected rate of return ($\bar{r}$) is the weighted average of possible returns from a given investment, weights being probabilities. Mathematically,

$$\bar{r} = \sum_{i}^{n} r_i p_i$$

where r_i is the ith possible return, p_i is the probability of the ith return, and n is the number of possible returns.

SOLVED PROBLEM 6.4

Consider the possible rate of return, depending upon the states of the economy, that is, recession, normal, and prosperity, that you might earn next year on a $50,000 investment in stock A or on a $50,000 investment in stock B:

State of Economy	Return (r_i)	Probability (p_i)
Stock A		
Recession	−5%	.2
Normal	20	.6
Prosperity	40	.2
Stock B		
Recession	10%	.2
Normal	15	.6
Prosperity	20	.2

What are the expected rates of return?

SOLUTION

For stock A,

$$\bar{r} = (-5\%)\,(.2) + (20\%)\,(.6) + (40\%)\,(.2) = 19\%$$

For stock B,

$$\bar{r} = (10\%)\,(.2) + (15\%)\,(.6) + (20\%)\,(.2) = 15\%$$

RISK AND THE RISK-RETURN TRADE-OFF

Risk refers to the variability of possible returns associated with a given investment. Risk, along with the return, is a major consideration in investment decisions. You must compare the expected return from a given investment with the risk associated with it (see Fig. 6-1). Higher levels of return are required to compensate for increased levels of risk. In general, there is a wide belief in the risk-return trade-off. In other words, the higher the risk undertaken, the more ample the return, and conversely, the lower the risk, the more modest the return. The start-up phase of a high-tech company, for example, may involve high business risk. You would, therefore, require a high return on your investment in the company. In contrast, U.S. Treasury bills have very low business, interest rate, purchasing power, or market risk, which means a modest return to the investor. In fact, their average yield in the past 60 years has been .3 percent over the average inflation rate for the same period.

Fig. 6-1 Return vs. risk.

HOW IS RISK MEASURED?

As a measure of risk, we use the *standard deviation,* which is a statistical measure of dispersion of the probability distribution of possible returns. The smaller the deviation, the tighter the distribution, and thus, the lower the riskiness of the investment. Mathematically,

$$\sigma = \sqrt{(r - \bar{r})^2 p}$$

To calculate σ, we proceed as follows:

Step 1: First compute the expected rate of return ($\bar{r}$).

Step 2: Subtract each possible return from r to obtain a set of deviations ($r - \bar{r}$).

Step 3: Square each deviation, multiply the squared deviation by the probability of occurrence for its respective return, and sum these products to obtain the variance (σ^2):

$$\sigma^2 = \sqrt{(r - \bar{r})^2 p}$$

Step 4: Finally, take the square root of the variance to obtain the standard deviation (σ).

SOLVED PROBLEM 6.5

Using the same data as in Solved Problem 6.4, compute the standard deviations.

SOLUTION

To follow this step-by-step approach, it is convenient to set up a table, as follows:

Return (r)	Probability (p)	(Step 1) rp	(Step 2) $(r - \bar{r})$	(Step 3) $(r - \bar{r})^2$	$(r - \bar{r})^2 p$
Stock A					
−5%	.2	−1%	−24%	576	115.2
20	.6	12	1	1	.6
40	.2	8	21	441	88.2
		$\bar{r} = 19\%$			$\sigma^2 = 204$
					(Step 4)　$\sigma = \sqrt{204}$
					$\sigma = 14.28\%$
Stock B					
10%	.2	2%	−5%	25	5
15	.6	9	0	0	0
20	.2	4	5	25	5
		$\bar{r} = 15\%$			$\sigma^2 = 10$
					(Step 4)　$\sigma = \sqrt{10}$
					$\sigma = 3.16\%$

One must be careful in using the standard deviation to compare risk since it is only an absolute measure of dispersion (risk) and does not consider the dispersion of outcomes in relationship to an expected return. In comparisons of securities with differing expected returns, we commonly use the coefficient of variation. The *coefficient of variation (CV)* is computed simply by dividing the standard deviation for a security by its expected value, that is, $\sigma/\bar{r}$.

The higher the coefficient, the more risky the security.

SOLVED PROBLEM 6.6

(a) Based on the following data, compute the coefficient of variation for each stock.

(b) Which stock is more risky?

	STOCK A	STOCK B
$\bar{r}$	19%	15%
σ	14.28%	3.16%

SOLUTION

(a) For stock A,

$$\frac{\sigma}{\bar{r}} = \frac{14.18}{19} = .75$$

For stock B,

$$\frac{\sigma}{\bar{r}} = \frac{3.16}{15} = .21$$

(b) Although, stock A produces a considerably higher return than stock B, stock A is overall more risky than stock B, based on the computed coefficient of variation.

Selected rates of return and standard deviations appear in Table 6-1.

Table 6-1   Risk and Return 1960–1984

Series	Geometric Average	Arithmetic Average	Standard Deviation
Common stocks	8.81%	10.20%	16.89%
Long-term corporate bonds	5.03	5.58	11.26
Long-term government bonds	4.70	5.11	9.70
U.S. Treasury bills	6.25	6.29	3.10

Source: R. Ibbotson and Gary P. Brinson, *Investment Markets* (New York: McGraw-Hill Book Company, 1987), p. 31.

As can be seen from Table 6-1, the highest rates of return and risk are associated with common stock.

HOW MANY YEARS DOES IT TAKE TO GET YOUR MONEY BACK OR DOUBLE YOUR MONEY?

To determine the number of years necessary to recover your initial investment, you can compute the payback period:

$$\text{Payback period} = \frac{\text{Initial investment}}{\text{Annual cash inflow}}$$

SOLVED PROBLEM 6.7

You invest $10,000 in a security that will pay $2,000 a year for 8 years. What is the payback period?

SOLUTION

$$\frac{\$10,000}{\$2,000} = 5 \text{ years}$$

The shorter the payback period the better, since by recouping your money faster you can invest it for a return. Also, a shorter payback period means less risk associated with getting your money back. Two limitations of the payback method are that it ignores the time value of money as well as cash flows received after the payback period.

To determine how many years it takes to double your money, we employ the *rule of 72*. Under it, dividing the number 72 by the fixed rate of return equals the number of years it takes for annual earnings from the security to double the original investment.

SOLVED PROBLEM 6.8

You bought a piece of property yielding an annual return of 25%. How many years will it take before the investment doubles?

SOLUTION

$$\frac{72}{25} = 2.88 \text{ years}$$

WHAT ARE THE TYPES OF RISK?

Risk refers to the variation in earnings. It includes the chance of losing money on an investment. There are different types of risk that affect various investment alternatives, such as stocks, bonds, and real estate. All investments are subject to risk. The major risks are

1. *Business risk.*   Business risk is the risk that the company will have general business problems. It depends on changes in demand, input prices, and obsolescence due to technological advances.

2. *Liquidity risk.*   It represents the possibility that an asset cannot be sold on short notice for its market value. If an investment must be sold at a high discount, then it is said to have a substantial amount of liquidity risk.

3. *Default risk.*   It is the risk that the issuing company is unable to make interest payments or principal repayments on debt. For example, there is a great amount of default risk inherent in the bonds of a company experiencing financial difficulty.

4. *Market risk.*   Prices of all stocks are correlated to some degree with broad swings in the stock market. Market risk refers to changes in the price of a stock that result from changes in the stock market as a whole, regardless of the fundamental change in a firm's earning power. For example, the prices of many stocks are affected by trends such as bull or bear markets.

5. *Interest rate risk.*   It refers to the fluctuations in the value of an asset as the interest rates and conditions of the money and capital markets change. Interest rate risk relates to fixed-income securities such as bonds and real estate. For example, if interest rates rise (fall), bond prices fall (rise).

6. *Purchasing power risk.*   This risk relates to the possibility that you will receive a lesser amount of purchasing power than was originally invested. Bonds are most affected by this risk since the issuer will be paying back in cheaper dollars during an inflationary period.

7. *Financial risk.*   This risk refers to financial problems the company may have. It occurs when the firm's debt level is too high.

8. *Industry risk.*   This risk is the uncertainty associated with the inherent nature of the industry. Examples include high-technological industries such as computers and cyclical industries such as automobiles.

9. *Political risk.*   This risk results from the problems a company may have because of foreign operations in politically and economically unstable foreign countries. An example is banks that are experiencing loan defaults in third world countries.

10. *Economic risk.*   This risk relates to adverse effects on the company from downturns of the economy. An example is the impact of recession on hotels.

11. *Social risk.*   Social risks are difficulties for the company that may result because of social concerns. An example is a boycott of a company's products because of the firm's position on important issues, for example, a U.S. company having operations in South Africa.

CONSIDERATIONS IN DECIDING THE AMOUNT OF RISK TO TAKE

You have to consider the following factors in deciding the amount of risk to take:

Your age.   If you are young, you can take more risk than if you are old. When approaching retirement age, you cannot take the chance of high-risk investments unless you already have a significant amount of safe earnings. If you are young and making a good salary, you can afford to take more risk to obtain significant wealth.

Your occupation.   You should invest conservatively if you have uncertain or fluctuating earnings.

Family status.   If you are single, you can take more risk than if you have a wife and child to support.

Personality.   If you feel uncomfortable and will stay up nights thinking about your investments, do not invest in stock. However, others find a thrill in investing in stock.

Tax-bracket.   If you are in a high tax bracket, you can afford to take more risk when investing in securities since the loss for the year (up to $3,000) is tax deductible.

Financial position.   If you have good net worth and liquidity, you can take greater investment risk.

Business sophistication. If you are knowledgeable about the investment markets, you may undertake more risk.

The return-risk relationship for an individual depends partly upon the person's utility preferences.

HOW CAN YOU REDUCE RISK?

Diversification is usually an answer to reduction of risk. In diversification of a portfolio (for example, stocks, bonds, real estate, savings accounts), the value of all these investments do not increase or decrease at the same time or in the same magnitude. Thus, you can protect yourself against fluctuations. One popular way of diversification is to own a share of a mutual fund, which is a portfolio of securities professionally managed by investment companies.

You can diversify in terms of maturity. For example, with securities of fixed maturity dates (for example, bonds, 1-year certificate of deposit), you can have maturities spaced so the securities do not all come due at once. Thus, new principal is available to invest periodically during times of high or low interest rates.

WHAT DOES BETA MEAN?

Many investors hold more than one financial asset. A portion of a security's risk (called unsystematic risk) can be controlled through diversification. This type of risk is unique to a given security. Business, liquidity, and default risks, which were discussed earlier, fall into this category. Nondiversifiable risk, more commonly referred to as systematic risk, results from forces outside of the firm's control and is therefore not unique to the given security. Purchasing power, interest rate, and market risks fall into this category. This type of risk is measured by *beta*.

Beta is useful in predicting how much the security will go up or down, provided that you know which way the market will go. It does help you to figure out risk and expected return.

In general, there is a relationship between a security's expected (or required return) and its beta. The following formula is helpful in determining a security's expected return:

$$r_i = r_f + b(r_m - r_f)$$

where r_i = a security's expected (required) return, r_f = risk-free rate, and r_m = market return.

Thus, in words,

Expected return = risk-free rate + beta (market return − risk-free rate)

= risk-free rate + beta × market risk premium

where the risk-free rate is the rate on a security such as a Treasury bill and the risk-free rate *minus* expected market return (such as Standard & Poor's 500 Stock Composite Index or Dow-Jones 30 Industrials) is called the *market risk premium*.

Note that the market risk premium is the additional return above that which you could earn on, say, a Treasury bill, to compensate for assuming a given level of risk (as measured by beta). Remember that the relevant measure of risk is the risk of the individual security, or its beta. The higher the beta for a security, the greater the return expected (or demanded) by the investor.

SOLVED PROBLEM 6.9

Assume that the risk-free rate is 6 percent, and the expected return for the market is 10 percent. If a stock has a beta of 2.0,

(*a*) What should be the risk premium?

(*b*) What should be the total expected (required) return?

SOLUTION

(*a*) $2.0 \times (10\% - 6\%) = 2.0 \times 4\% = 8\%$

This means that you would expect (or demand) an extra 8 percent (risk premium) on this stock in addition to the risk-free return of 6 percent.

(*b*) $6\% + 8\% = 14\%$

HOW TO READ BETA

Beta measures a security's volatility relative to an average security. Put another way, it is the ratio of a security's return over time to the return of the overall market. For example, if Paine Webber's beta is 2.0, it means that if the stock market goes up 10 percent, Paine Webber's common stock goes up 20 percent; if the market goes down 10 percent, Paine Webber goes down 20 percent. Here is a tip for how to read betas:

BETA	WHAT IT MEANS
0	The security's return is independent of the market. An example is a risk-free security such as a Treasury bill.
0.5	The security is only half as responsive as the market.
1.0	The security has the same response or risk as the market (that is, average risk). This is the beta value of the market portfolio such as Standard & Poor's 500 or Dow Jones 30 Industrials.
2.0	The security is twice as responsive, or risky, as the market.

Table 6-2 shows examples of betas for selected stocks.

Table 6-2   Beta Values for Selected Companies

Stock	Beta
Intel Corp.	1.55
International Paper	1.30
Johnson & Johnson	1.05
Boeing	.95
Proctor & Gamble	.90

Source: Value Line Investment Survey (October and November issues, 1989), published by Value Line, Inc., 711 3d Avenue, New York, NY 10017.

INVESTMENT ALTERNATIVES AND RISK-RETURN

You have a wide variety of investment alternatives available. These alternatives vary in terms of both returns they provide and the risks they carry. Table 6-3 summarizes major types of investments and their return/risk characteristics. The rankings assigned to each (none or low to very high) reflect the authors' opinions. It should not be construed as an absolute guideline. *Note:* The ranking is for a typical investment within the class, but there are many variations within each class.

Table 6-3   Investment Alternatives and Their Return-Risk Characteristics

Type of Investment	Total Return	Business Risk	Liquidity Risk	Purchasing Power Risk	Interest Rate Risk	Market Risk
Savings bonds, savings accounts, money market accounts, CDs	Low	Very low or none	None	High	High	None
High-grade bonds	Medium	Low	Low	Medium	Medium	Medium
Speculative bonds	High	High	Medium	Medium	High	High
Blue-chip common stocks	High	Very low	Very low	Low	Medium	Medium
Common stock mutual funds	High	Low	Very low	Low	Medium	Medium
Options and futures	Very high	Very high	Very high	High	Low–high	Very high
Real estate	High–very high	Low–medium	High	Low	High	Low
Collectibles	High–very high	Medium or high	Medium	Low–medium	Medium	Medium

SOLVED PROBLEM 6.10

For each of the following investments, rank them in the order of risk with 1 being the least risk and 5 being the highest risk.

(a)   Precious metals

(b)   Bonds

(c)   Preferred stock

(d)   Common stock

(e)   Certificates of deposit

SOLUTION

(a)   5

(b)   2

(c)   3

(d)   4

(e)   1

Review Questions

(1)   _____ is a key consideration in the investment decision.

(2)   The return on an investment consists of _____ and _____ .

(3)   The relevant period over which you hold the investment is called the _____ .

(4)   Current income may take the form of interest, _____ , rent, and the like.

(5) There are two types of multiperiod average returns: _____ and _____ .

(6) If you wish to compare investments with different compounding periods, you need to put them on _____ .

(7) _____ may be used to evaluate the expected return.

(8) Using probabilities, _____ is the weighted average of possible returns from a given investment, weights being probabilities.

(9) The _____ the risk undertaken, the more ample should be the return.

(10) The _____ is a statistical measure of dispersion of the probability distribution of possible returns.

(11) The smaller the deviation, the tighter the distribution, and thus, the _____ the riskiness of the investment.

(12) In comparing securities with differing expected returns, we commonly use the _____ .

(13) _____ is the risk that the issuing company is unable to make interest or principal payments on debt.

(14) _____ is usually an answer to reduction of risk.

(15) _____ is useful in predicting how much the security will go up or down, provided that you know which way the market will go.

(16) _____ risk arises from an inflationary period.

Answers: (1) Return; (2) current income, capital gains (or losses); (3) holding period; (4) dividends; (5) arithmetic average, geometric average; (6) a common basis; (7) Probabilities; (8) expected rate of return; (9) higher; (10) standard deviation; (11) lower; (12) coefficient of variation; (13) Default risk; (14) Diversification; (15) Beta; (16) Purchasing power.

Additional Solved Problems

6.1 You purchased a share of stock for $40 one year ago and sold it today for $50, and during the year received three dividend payments totaling $1.70. Calculate

(a) Current income

(b) Capital gain (loss)

(c) Total return (in dollars)

SOLUTION

(a) Current income is the dividend income, which is $1.70.

(b) Capital gain = sales price − purchase price = $50 − $40 = $10

(c) Total return = $1.70 + $10 = $11.70

6.2 You invest $100 in a security, sell it for $107, and earn a cash dividend of $13. What is the holding period return?

SOLUTION

The holding period return (HPR) is

$$HPR = \frac{\text{Current income + Capital gain (or loss)}}{\text{Purchase price}}$$

$$= \frac{\$13 + \$7}{\$100} = \frac{\$20}{\$100} = 20\%$$

6.3 Consider the investments in stocks A and B over one period of ownership:

	STOCK A	STOCK B
Purchase price (beginning of year)	$100	$100
Cash dividend received (during the year)	13	18
Sales price (end of year)	107	97

The current income from the investment in stocks A and B over the 1-year period are $13 and $18, respectively.

(*a*) What is the capital gain (or loss) from stocks A and B?

(*b*) What is the total return on each investment?

(*c*) What is the holding period return on the investments?

SOLUTION

(*a*) For stock A, a capital gain of $7 ($107 sales price − $100 purchase price) is realized over the period. In the case of stock B, a $3 capital loss ($97 sales price − $100 purchase price) results.

(*b*) Combining the capital gain return (or loss) with the current income, the total return on each investment is summarized below:

	Stock A	Stock B
Current income	$13	$18
Capital gain (loss)	7	(3)
Total return	$20	$15

(*c*)

$$HPR \text{ (stock A)} = \frac{\$13 + (\$107 - \$100)}{\$100} = \frac{\$13 + \$7}{\$100}$$

$$= \frac{\$20}{\$100} = 20\%$$

$$HPR \text{ (stock B)} = \frac{\$18 + (\$97 - \$100)}{\$100} = \frac{\$18 - \$3}{\$100}$$

$$= \frac{\$15}{\$100} = 15\%$$

6.4 You purchased a share of stock for $60 a year ago and sold it for $65, and during the year received four dividend payments totaling $3.60. Compute the following:

(*a*) Current income

(*b*) Capital gain (or loss)

(*c*) Total return

(*d*) Holding period return (HPR)

SOLUTION

(a) Current income = $3.60 dividend payments received

(b) Capital gain = Sales price − Purchase price = $65 − $60 = $5

(c) Total return = Current income + Capital gain = $3.60 + $5 = $8.60

(d) Holding period return $= \dfrac{\text{Current income + Capital gain}}{\text{Purchase price}}$

$$= \frac{\$3.60 + \$5}{\$60} = \frac{\$8.60}{\$60} = 14.33\%$$

6.5 Consider the following data where the price of a stock doubles in one period and depreciates back to the original price in the next period. Dividend income (current income) is zero.

	Time Periods		
	$t = 0$	$t = 1$	$t = 2$
Price (end of period)	$50	$100	$50
HPR	—	100%	−50%

What is the arithmetic average return over the two periods?

SOLUTION

The arithmetic average return is the average of 100 percent and −50 percent, which is 25 percent, as shown below:

$$\frac{100\% + (-50\%)}{2} = 25\%$$

6.6 In Problem 6.5, the stock purchased for $50 and sold for the same price two periods later did not earn 25 percent; it clearly earned a zero return. Show this by computing the geometric average return.

SOLUTION

Note that $n = 2$, $r_1 = 100\% = 1$, and $r_2 = -50\% = -0.5$. Then,

$$\text{Geometric return} = 2\sqrt{(1 + 1)(1 - 0.5)} - 1$$
$$= 2\sqrt{(2)(0.5)} - 1$$
$$= 2\sqrt{1} - 1 = 1 - 1 = 0\%$$

6.7 You are trying to evaluate a stock investment you paid $20 per share for 2 years ago. Its price was $16 at the end of the first year. Today it is worth $24. Dividend income each year was $1.00.

	Time Periods		
	$t = 0$	$t = 1$	$t = 2$
Price (end of period)	$20	$16	$24
Dividend	—	1	1

(a) Calculate the HPR for each period.

(b) Calculate the arithmetic average return over the two periods.

(c) Calculate the geometric average return over the two periods.

SOLUTION

(a)

	Time Periods		
	$t = 0$	$t = 1$	$t = 2$
Price (end of period)	$20	$10	$24
Dividend	—	1	1
Capital gain (loss)	—	−10 ($10 − $20)	14 ($24 − $10)

$$\text{Holding period rate of return (HPR)} = \frac{\text{Current income} + \text{Capital gain}}{\text{Purchase price}}$$

For $t = 1$

$$\text{HPR} = \frac{\$1 - \$10}{\$20} = \frac{-\$9}{\$20} = -.45 = -45\%$$

For $t = 2$

$$\text{HPR} = \frac{\$1 + \$14}{\$20} = \frac{\$15}{\$10} = 1.5 = 150\%$$

(b) The arithmetic average return is the average of −.45 and 1.5, which is 52.5 percent, as shown below:

$$\frac{-.45 + 1.5}{2} = .525 = 52.5\%$$

(c) Note that $n = 2$, $r_1 = -.45$, and $r_2 = 1.5$. Then,

$$\begin{aligned}
\text{Geometric return} &= 2\sqrt{(1 - .45)(1 + 1.5)} - 1 \\
&= 2\sqrt{(.55)(2.5)} - 1 \\
&= 2\sqrt{1.375} - 1 = 1.173 - 1 = .173 = 17.3\%
\end{aligned}$$

6.8 An investment has the following range of returns and probabilities:

RETURNS (%)	PROBABILITY
6	.20
9	.60
12	.20

Calculate (a) the expected return and (b) the standard deviation.

SOLUTION

Return (r)	Probability (p)	(Step 1) rp	(Step 2) $r - \bar{r}$	(Step 3) $(r - \bar{r})^2$	$(r - \bar{r})^2 p$
6%	.2	1.2	−3%	9	1.8
9	.6	5.4	0	0	0
12	.2	2.4	3	9	1.8
		(a) $\bar{r} = 9.0\%$			$\sigma^2 = 3.6$
				(Step 4) $\sigma = \sqrt{3.6}$	
				(b) $\sigma = 1.9\%$	

The expected return and the standard deviation are 9 percent and 1.9 percent, respectively.

6.9   Stocks A and B have the following probability distributions of possible future returns that you might earn next year on a $50,000 investment in stock A or on a $50,000 investment in stock B, depending upon the state of the economy: recession, normal, and prosperity.

PROBABILITY (p)	A (%)	B (%)
.1	−15	−20
.2	0	10
.4	5	20
.2	10	30
.1	25	50

Calculate (a) the expected rates of return for each stock and (b) the standard deviation for each stock.

SOLUTION

It is convenient to set up the following table to calculate both the expected return and standard deviation:

Return (r)	Probability (p)	(Step 1) rp	(Step 2) $r - \bar{r}$	(Step 3) $(r - \bar{r})^2$	$(r - \bar{r})^2 p$
		Stock A			
−15%	.1	−1.5	−20%	400	40
0	.2	0	−5	25	5
5	.4	2	0	0	0
10	.2	2	5	25	5
25	.1	2.5	20	400	40
		(a) $\bar{r} = 5.0$			$\sigma^2 = 90$
				(Step 4)	$\sigma = \sqrt{90}$
				(b)	$\sigma = 9.5\%$
		Stock B			
−20%	.1	−2	−39%	1521	152.1
10	.2	2	−9	81	16.2
20	.4	8	1	1	0.4
30	.2	6	11	121	24.2
50	.1	5	31	961	96.1
		(a) $\bar{r} = 19$			$\sigma^2 = 289$
				(Step 4)	$\sigma = \sqrt{289}$
				(b)	$\sigma = 17\%$

To summarize,

(a) The expected rates of return for stocks A and B are 5 percent and 19 percent, respectively.

(b) The standard deviations for stocks A and B are 9.5 percent and 17 percent, respectively.

6.10   Based on the results in Problem 6.9, compute the coefficient of variation for each stock. Which stock is less risky?

SOLUTION

The results in Problem 6.9 are summarized below.

	Stock A	Stock B
$\bar{r}$	5%	19%
σ	9.5	17

The coefficient of variation is computed as follows:
For stock A,

$$\frac{\sigma}{\bar{r}} = \frac{9.5}{5} = 1.9$$

For stock B,

$$\frac{\sigma}{\bar{r}} = \frac{17}{19} = .89$$

Stock B is less risky than stock A since the coefficient of variation (a measure of relative risk) is smaller for stock B.

6.11 Stock X has a standard deviation of 14.28 percent and an expected return of 19 percent. What is the coefficient of variation?

SOLUTION

The coefficient of variation equals

$$\frac{\sigma}{\bar{r}} = \frac{\text{Standard deviation}}{\text{Expected return}} = \frac{14.28\%}{19\%} = 0.75$$

6.12 You are thinking of investing in a security with the following possible returns and probabilities associated with them:

RETURNS (%)	PROBABILITY
0	.30
20	.40
30	.30

(a) Calculate:

    (1) The expected return ($\bar{r}$)

    (2) The standard deviation (σ)

    (3) The coefficient of variation (CV)

(b) Compare this security with another you are considering. Its statistics are $\bar{r} = 12$ percent, $\sigma = 4$ percent, and CV = .33. Which security should you choose?

SOLUTION

(a)

Return (r)	Probability (p)	(Step 1) rp	(Step 2) $(r - \bar{r})$	(Step 3) $(r - \bar{r})^2$	$(r - \bar{r})^2 p$
0%	.3	0	−17%	289	87
20	.4	8	−9	81	32
30	.3	9	−8	64	19
		$\bar{r} = 17\%$			$\sigma^2 = 138$
				(Step 4)	$\sigma = \sqrt{138}$
					$\sigma = 12\%$

$$CV = \frac{12\%}{17\%} = .706$$

The expected return, the standard deviation, and the coefficient of variation are 17 percent, 12 percent, and .706, respectively.

(b) Based on the coefficient of variation, which is a measure of relative risk, you should choose the other investment. In other words, the other investment has a lower risk (.33 versus .706).

6.13 You bought a piece of property yielding an annual return of 20 percent. How long will it take to double your investment?

SOLUTION

Using the rule of 72, it will take $3\frac{1}{2}$ years for annual earnings from the investment to double:

$$\frac{72}{20\%} = 3.6 \text{ years}$$

6.14 If Treasury bills yield 7.5 percent, the market's expected return is 12 percent, and Alpha Company's beta is 2, what is Alpha's expected return?

SOLUTION

$$r = 7.5\% + 2(12\% - 7.5\%) = 7.5\% + 9\% = 16.5\%$$

6.15 Assume that the risk-free rate of return is 8 percent, the required rate of return on the market is 13 percent, and stock X has a beta coefficient of 1.5.

(a) What is stock X's required rate of return?

(b) What if the beta increases to 2.0?

(c) What if the risk-free rate decreases to 6 percent, assuming the beta is still 1.5?

SOLUTION

Recall that $r = r_f + b(r_m - r_f)$.

(a) $r = 8\% + 1.5(13\% - 8\%) = 15.5\%$

(b) $r = 8\% + 2.0(13\% - 8\%) = 18\%$

(c) $r = 6\% + 1.5(13\% - 6\%) = 16.5\%$

6.16   Assume that the risk-free rate (r_f) is 8 percent, and the expected return for the market (r_m) is 12 percent. Calculate the required (expected) rate of return on a security if

(a) $b = 0$

(b) $b = .5$

(c) $b = 1.0$

(d) $b = 2.0$

SOLUTION

(a)   If $b = 0$ (risk-free security), $r = 8\% + 0(12\% - 8\%) = 8\%$

(b)   If $b = .5$, $r = 8\% + .5(12\% - 8\%) = 10\%$

(c)   If $b = 1.0$ (market portfolio), $r = 8\% + 1.0(12\% - 8\%) = 12\%$

(d)   If $b = 2.0$, $r = 8\% + 2.0(12\% - 8\%) = 16\%$

6.17   You are considering the purchase of one or more of the following three stocks:

	Alpha	Gamma	Sigma
Beta	.5	1.2	2.0
Expected return	8.75%	18.5%	17.5%

Assume a market return of 15 percent and a risk-free return of 8 percent. Which of the stocks should you buy, if any?

SOLUTION

Using the formula $r = r_f + b(r_m - r_f)$, which will give you the required rate of return:

	Required Return	Expected Return
Alpha	$r = 8\% + .5(15\% - 8\%) = 11.5\%$	8.75%
Gamma	$r = 8\% + 1.2(15\% - 8\%) = 16.4\%$	18.50
Sigma	$r = 8\% + 2.0(15\% - 8\%) = 22.0\%$	17.50

Only Gamma's expected return exceeds its required return. You should buy only Gamma stock.

Chapter 7

Banking and Cash Management

The bank is the one institution that has the facilities and services to handle your day-to-day financial transactions. Selecting a place to do your banking is an important decision. So is selecting the type of bank account. Some important issues are discussed in this chapter, including

How to select a bank

How to get the most out of your bank

The major offerings of today's banking institutions

How to reconcile bank balances

Method of determining savings account balance

Investing in certificates of deposit and U.S. savings bonds

Endorsing checks

Other services offered by the bank and how to take advantage of them.

HOW DO YOU SELECT A BANK?

Selecting a place to do banking should be considered a long-term decision, since once you choose a bank, chances are either you stick to the bank selected or it is increasingly difficult to switch to another bank for all the resulting inconveniences. So be aware: When you are shopping for a bank, consider the following elements in terms of quality of service and convenience:

1. *Comparison of rates and fees.* Compare rates on savings and checking accounts and fees (such as service charges, the cost of cashier's checks, and money order fees).

2. *Clarity of information.* Can you understand the bank's handouts and applications? They should describe in readable fashion the account rules and the way rates and fees change as your balance rises and falls?

3. *Convenient hours and services.* Sometimes convenience is probably the most important factor in your decision. Can the bank accommodate direct deposit of your paycheck? Does it offer evening and weekend hours? Does it have a link to a statewide or national network of automatic teller machines (ATMs) and drive-in windows? Which would you prefer? Do they open more teller windows whenever there is a long line?

4. *Quick crediting of deposits.* In this age of electronic transactions and check clearing, you should have access to routine deposits almost immediately. Can the bank give you a quick credit on your deposit for immediate use?

5. *Good deals on loans.* Many banks provide preference on credit applications or lower loan rates to regular customers or to those with large accounts. This sort of treatment can be invaluable, since once you go beyond credit cards and installment loans, the lending process is highly subjective. Does the bank offer an automatic increase in overdraft privileges without your asking for them?

6. *Extra free services.* Some banks offer extra services free of charge to regular or special customers, such as free notary services, no-charge money orders, etc.

7. *Easy access to problem solvers.* If you have ever had an emergency—a deposit that was not posted, a stolen checkbook, a missing loan payment, a bungled automatic teller transaction— did somebody resolve the problem quickly and courteously? A good bank anticipates these kinds of problems and trains its staff to handle them.

HOW DO YOU GET THE MOST FROM YOUR BANK?

It is ironic that the banks you are dealing with make money off your lack of information about banking services. For example, if you do not read the fine print regarding the number of checks you can write on your money market account in a month, you will probably be tapped with a $5 to $10 service charge. You may also find your interest for that month has dwindled to the savings passbook rate of, say, 6 percent. Here are two questions you should ask to get the most out of your bank.

1. *Are you paying too much in check charges?* Fee structures vary drastically between banks. Before opening a checking account, ask for bank service charge brochures. Comparison shopping could make the difference. Investigate savings and loan, brokerage house, and credit union alternatives. Next, assess your checkwriting habits. If you are a frequent checkwriter, you will be better off selecting a flat monthly service fee instead of per check charges. Note that some bank officers may give general financial advice.

SOLVED PROBLEM 7.1

You write at least 20 checks a month and are charged $.15 per check. Another checking account charges a flat monthly fee of $2.50.

(*a*) What is your minimum monthly service charge?

(*b*) Should you switch to that other account?

SOLUTION

(*a*) $3.00 (20 checks × $.15)

(*b*) You would be better off switching to that other account.

Some banks link the balances in your checking, savings, and money market accounts to your free checking privileges. Most banks give you free checking if you keep a certain minimum monthly amount in your accounts.

2. *Do you have the right checking account?* There are basically four types available:

Regular checking accounts. You can write as many checks as you want, make any number of deposits, keep any kind of balance, but you won't earn any interest. Usually, there is a monthly service charge. Some banks will allow deposit in other accounts, such as savings or certificates of deposit (CDs), to count toward your minimum.

Passbook savings account. It permits frequent deposit or withdrawal of funds. It has the fewest restrictions and is the simplest for savers to use. Low minimum-balance requirements make this a top choice for small savers.

NOW accounts. You have restricted checkwriting privileges, but earn fixed interest at the savings passbook rate. You have to maintain a specified minimum balance. Otherwise, you may lose interest.

Super NOW accounts. You can write any number of checks, but you must keep the bank's predetermined minimum balance in order to earn interest and avoid service charges. Interest fluctuates but is higher than the savings passbook rate and lower than the money market rate. Consider whether it pays to keep the minimum balance in NOW or Super NOW accounts to avoid service charges or get better rates elsewhere, such as CDs or money market mutual funds.

SOLVED PROBLEM 7.2

You have an average balance of $3,000. Comparison between NOW and Super NOW shows the following. Amounts above minimum requirements are deposited in a CD. Fill in the columns. With which account are you better off?

	NOW	SUPER NOW
Interest rate	5.5% rate	8% rate
Service charges	None	None
Minimum monthly balance	$1,000	$3,000
Interest earned on each account	(a)	(b)
Amount deposited in a CD	2,000	0
Interest earned from the CD (8.5% rate)	(c)	0
Total interest earned	(d)	(e)

SOLUTION

(a) $55   (5.5% × $1,000)   (b) $240   (8% × $3,000)   (c) $170   (8.5% × $2,000)   (d) $225
($55 + $170)   (e) $240

You are better off with the Super NOW account because you earned $15 more in interest.

Money market deposit accounts (MMDA).   You must keep the bank's predetermined minimum balance. There are also restrictions on the number of checks you can write. However, you will earn a higher interest rate than with any other kind of checking account. If you can afford to tie up $1,000 or more in a NOW account, consider putting your cash in an MMDA, where all of it will earn market rates, and transferring only what you need each month to your regular checking account. Note that the single most important advantage of money market accounts over money market mutual funds, other than its competitive interest rate, is the insurance protection of up to $100,000 per depositor. Savings and loan institutions failing and the problems with banks indicate that it is important not to exceed the insured amount of $100,000. Also a depositor can restructure accounts to obtain additional insurance such as having a joint account with a child.

Do comparison shopping. Choose an arrangement based on your checkwriting habits and ability to keep a certain minimum balance. You may want to decide on a combination that serves you best. To do so, first estimate how much you expect to leave in your account as a minimum. Then estimate the interest you would earn and the fees you would pay.

SOLVED PROBLEM 7.3

You expect to keep a minimum balance of $1,500. You are considering a regular checking account with NOW. The amount of the minimum requirement ($200) is deposited in a NOW account. Fill in the columns.

	REGULAR CHECKING WITH NOW
Service charges	$3.00/month
Amount per year	(a)
Minimum monthly balance	$200
Amount deposited in NOW	$1,300
Interest earned from NOW (5.5% rate)	(b)
Net interest earned (annual)	(c)

SOLUTION

(a) $36 ($3 × 12 months)   (b) $71.50 (5.5% × $1,300)   (c) $35.50 ($71.50 − $36.00)

TRY TO AVOID OVERDRAFTS

It is very costly to write a bad check. You will be charged $10 or more for each check bounced and possible penalties from the check's payee. Also, too many bounced checks can have your account closed and create a bad credit rating. Some states, such as New York, impose stringent penalties. *Note:* An individual should never send out a check hoping to make a later deposit to cover it before the check clears. This is a risky procedure. Only mail a check when the funds are already in the account.

The possible ways to avoid overdrafts include:

Keep scrupulous records and, at the end of each month, balance your checkbook.

Open an overdraft line of credit although the interest rate is high and there is often an advance fee.

Obtain immediate credit on deposits. Banks usually slap a "hold" on the checks drawn on a bank other than your own. That means you do not have use of your own deposit. Ask for immediate credit on all of your deposits. Here are some pointers for achieving this goal.

— Consider establishing your checking account at the bank on which your paycheck is drawn. The reason is that banks put holds only on checks from other banks.

— Apply for immediate credit privileges by getting some sort of written authorization of preapproval.

— Ask that any holds be placed on your savings account rather than on your checking account so that at least you will be able to write checks during the hold period.

Try to earn more interest on your savings. You can maximize your interest earnings by

— Only investing money you can afford to do without, no matter how attractive the interest rate. Early withdrawals can cost a lot in terms of penalties or lost interest.

— Keeping on top of interest fluctuations.

— Shopping around. When comparison shopping, ask if interest is compounded and how often.

Get a faster loan at a cheaper rate. Be friendly with your loan officer who understands your lending needs and has the authority to approve your request. Schedule an appointment and arrive prepared. Ask the following questions:

— How much do you want to borrow?

— Why do you want this loan?

— Over what period of time would you repay it?

— From what sources would you repay it?

Fill out the loan application form neatly and back it up with all the necessary evidence of your sources of income, credit history, and net worth. Spend less time asking for money and more time proving that you have the ability and the willingness to repay it. Have your accountant assist you in preparing the needed financial information on a loan application so it is professionally done. Do not be afraid to ask for a rate reduction or to negotiate for better terms. Many banks offer a better rate if you agree to their automatic loan deduction plan from your deposit account.

Consider opening up a personal line of credit. It is one little-advertised loan program you should seek out, since they can easily slice your borrowing costs by 6 percent or more. A personal line of credit can be secured by the equity you have built up in your home. These mortgage-secured lines of credit are increasingly popular for the following reasons:

— It is easier to get since it is based on your home's equity and your ability to pay.

— It is the only type of credit line available to most consumers in sizable dollar amounts for long time periods—sometimes up to 10 years.

— The interest charged is generally less than on unsecured lines of credit.

— Interest is tax-deductible when incurred on a home loan.

For more details about a home equity line, refer to Chapter 8 (Consumer Credit and Loans). Parents with college-bound children will find this an excellent alternative for financing tuition over a 4-year period.

Don't waste time in line. Try the following to reduce the time you spend in bank lobbies:

— Visit the bank during slack periods.

— Use automatic teller machines (ATMs) as often as possible and for as many transactions as possible.

Get better service overall. Get to know a banker, not a bank. Introduce yourself to the branch manager, loan officer, or anybody higher. These people have the clout to waive fees, bend rules, approve immediate credit on deposits, and approve loan requests.

ARE YOUR DEPOSITS SAFE?

Your checking and savings deposits are safe for an amount up to $100,000 if they are deposited in federally insured financial institutions (see below). Federal regulations set forth several ownership categories for personal accounts. Generally, you would be safe even if you had more than $100,000 in an insured institution.

FEDERAL AGENCY	INSURED INSTITUTIONS	AMOUNT OF INSURANCE
Federal Deposit Insurance Corp. (FDIC)	Commercial banks and mutual savings banks	$100,000 per depositor
Federal Savings and Loan Insurance Corporation (FSLIC)	Savings and loan associations	$100,000 per depositor
National Credit Union Administration (NCUA)	Federal and state-charted credit unions	$100,000 per depositor in share accounts

RECONCILING YOUR CHECKING ACCOUNT

Each month when the bank sends you a statement showing your bank balance, you should compare it with your checkbook balance. The two balances should match. In other words, the checkbook balance must be the same as the bank balance at the end of the period. Reconciling differences relate to (1) items shown on your checkbook but not on your bank statement and (2) items shown on your bank statement but not on your checkbook. Note a certified check that is still outstanding should not be deducted because the bank knows about it.

To reconcile the bank balance:

1. Deduct outstanding checks (checks not cleared).
2. Add deposits in transit (not yet received at the bank).
3. Add: Your account was charged in error with someone else's check.
4. Deduct: Your account was credited in error with someone else's deposit.

To reconcile your checkbook balance:

1. Deduct service charge.
2. Add collections made by the bank.
3. Deduct a check you received and deposited that "bounced" because of insufficient funds.
4. Deduct automatic charges (for example, monthly insurance and contribution deductions).
5. Add: The deficiency that resulted from entering a deposit in the checkbook that was lower than the actual amount you entered on the deposit slip (assume deposit slip is correct).
6. Deduct: The deficiency that resulted from entering a check that was less than the actual amount of the check (assume the check was correct).

Upon receiving the bank statement, review each entry and check off, on the proper stub, each returned check. Add or deduct necessary items as illustrated.

SOLVED PROBLEM 7.4

Your bank statement shows a balance of $348.50 on September 30, 19X1. Your checkbook balance on the same date is $277.00. Check no. 325 for $45.20 and check no. 333 for $29.30 are not enclosed with your statement. The bank has deducted a service charge of $3.00. Reconcile your statement.

SOLUTION

September 30, 19X1

Bank balance		$348.50	Checkbook balance	$277.00
Less: Outstanding checks:			Less: Service Charge	3.00
No. 325	$45.20			
No. 333	29.30	74.50		
Adjusted bank balance		$274.00	Adjusted checkbook balance	$274.00

SOLVED PROBLEM 7.5

Your records showed the following for the month of April:

(1) Cash balance per books—April 30, $15,000.

(2) Cash balance per bank statement—April 30, $12,850.

(3) On April 30, the checks outstanding were $642.

(4) The following two checks deposited by you were returned because of insufficient funds: $300 and $840.

(5) A deposit of $3,100 was made on April 30 but was not included on the bank statement.

(6) The bank collected a $2,000 note for you.

(7) The bank service charge was $25.

(8) The bank charged your account in error $527.

Prepare a bank reconciliation.

SOLUTION

Balance per books		$15,000
Add: Note receivable collected		2,000
		$17,000
Less: NSF check	$1,140	
Service charge	25	1,165
Adjusted book balance		$15,835
Balance per bank		$12,850
Add: Deposit in transit	$3,100	
Bank error	527	3,627
		$16,477
Less: Outstanding checks		642
Adjusted bank balance		$15,835

HOW TO DETERMINE THE SAVINGS ACCOUNT BALANCE BY INTEREST CALCULATIONS

Banks calculate interest on depositors' account balances in four different ways: FIFO (first in, first out), LIFO (last in, first out), minimum-balance, and DDDW (day-of-deposit–to–day-of-withdrawal). Each method has advantages and disadvantages to a depositor.

FIFO (FIRST-IN, FIRST-OUT) METHOD

Under the FIFO method, withdrawals are first deducted from the balance at the start of the interest period and then, if the balance is not sufficient, from later deposits. The method works to the disadvantage of savers, since interest is automatically lost on money on deposit early in the interest period if it is withdrawn.

LIFO (LAST-IN, FIRST-OUT) METHOD

Under this method, withdrawals are first deducted from the most recent deposits and then from the less recent ones, and so on. It does not penalize depositors as much as the FIFO method does, but it is still not a fair representation of actual funds on deposit during the period.

MINIMUM-BALANCE METHOD

The minimum (low)-balance method pays interest on the minimum balance in the account. This method, which discourages withdrawals, is the most unprofitable for the depositor.

DDDW (DAY-OF-DEPOSIT–TO–DAY-OF-WITHDRAWAL) METHOD

The DDDW method, also called the actual-balance method, is the fairest method to the saver. Under the method, each saver earns interest for the total number of days money was actually in the account. When withdrawals occur, interest is earned for the number of days the money remained before the day of withdrawal.

The following problem illustrates the interest calculations for each of the four methods discussed above.

SOLVED PROBLEM 7.6

The following activities have taken place during the 90-day period:

DAY	DEPOSIT (WITHDRAWAL)	BALANCE
1	$1,000	$1,000
30	1,000	2,000
60	(800)	1,200
90	Closing	1,200

With a 6 percent stated (nominal) interest rate, calculate interest under FIFO, LIFO, minimum balance, and DDDW.

SOLUTION

FIFO (first-in, first-out) method

(a) $\quad\$\ 200 \times .06 \times \frac{90}{360} = \$\ 3.00$

(b) $\quad\underline{1,000} \times .06 \times \frac{60}{360} = \underline{10.00}$

$\qquad\$1,200 \qquad\qquad\qquad \$13.00$

LIFO (last-in, first-out) method

(a) $\quad\$1,000 \times .06 \times \frac{90}{360} = \$15.00$

(b) $\quad\underline{200} \times .06 \times \frac{60}{360} = \underline{2.00}$

$\qquad\$1,200 \qquad\qquad\qquad \$17.00$

Minimum-balance method

$$\$1,000 \times .06 \times \tfrac{90}{360} = \$15.00$$

DDDW (day-of-deposit–to–day-of-withdrawal) method

(*a*) $$\$1,000 \times .06 \times \tfrac{30}{360} = \$\ 5.00$$

(*b*) $$\$2,000 \times .06 \times \tfrac{30}{360} = \ \ 10.00$$

(*c*) $$\$1,200 \times .06 \times \tfrac{30}{360} = \ \ \underline{\ \ 6.00}$$

$$\$21.00$$

INVESTING IN MONEY MARKET FUNDS

Money market funds are special forms of mutual funds. You can own a portfolio of high-yielding CDs, Treasury bills, and other similar securities of short-term nature, with a small investment. There is liquidity and flexibility in withdrawing funds through checkwriting privileges (the usual minimum withdrawal is $500). Money market funds are considered very conservative, because most of the securities purchased by the funds are safe. For more about money market funds, refer to Chapter 17 (Mutual Funds and Diversification).

SHOULD YOU PUT YOUR MONEY IN CERTIFICATES OF DEPOSIT?

Certificates of deposit (CDs) are fixed-time deposits that require savers to deposit money for minimum amounts of time, commonly ranging from 32 days to 8 years. Deposits can range from $1,000 to $100,000. These savings certificates are often referred to as a "parking place," since you can put your money there on a short-term basis until you find another investment that meets your long-term goals. There are no ceilings on rates. If money is withdrawn before maturity, there are usually interest penalties.

Banks compete for deposits by offering attractive yields. To compare CDs, look at the *effective annual yield,* which takes into account the effects of compounding. The figures in Table 7-1 indicate how much difference compounding can make on the rate of interest paid. For example, the annual return on a 6 percent CD with annual compounding is 6 percent, but the same CD with quarterly compounding could yield as much as 6.14 percent.

Table 7-1   Nominal and Effective Interest Rates with Different Compounding Periods

Nominal Rate	Effective Annualized Yield				
	Annually	Semiannually	Quarterly	Monthly	Daily
6%	6%	6.09%	6.14%	6.17%	6.18%
7	7	7.12	7.19	7.23	7.25
8	8	8.16	8.24	8.30	8.33
9	9	9.20	9.31	9.38	9.42
10	10	10.25	10.38	10.47	10.52
11	11	11.30	11.46	11.57	11.62
12	12	12.36	12.55	12.68	12.74

Banks calculate interest in various ways, so true yield varies widely on CDs with the same maturity and interest rate. Note that true yields are not always spelled out in bank advertising, but banks normally post the true yields inside bank offices, list them on window displays, or make them available over the phone.

BROKERED CDs

CDs can be purchased through banks, savings and loan institutions, credit unions, or even brokerage firms. Although you can usually find a better rate at a local bank or savings and loan institution, a CD purchased through a stockbroker offers greater liquidity without sacrificing federal deposit insurance. "Brokered CDs," as they are known in the industry, have several advantages.

Brokers typically do not charge a commission, rather they collect a finder's fee from the bank.

There is the full $100,000 deposit insurance.

Many brokers participate in the secondary market for these accounts, buying and selling them like stocks or bonds. This allows savers to cash out of their CD without paying an interest penalty—and to cash in on interest rate changes.

HOW TO BUY A TREASURY BILL

Treasury bills are short-term obligations of the U.S. government, which may be purchased for a minimum of $10,000, with maturities of 3 months, 6 months, or 1 year. Treasury bills are perhaps the safest investment, 100 percent guaranteed by the U.S. government. They are available through banks or other financial institutions for a small fee, or through Federal Reserve offices. Although Treasury bills cannot be cashed early, they are usually fairly easy to sell since there is an active secondary market.

The interest is exempt from state and local taxes. Treasury bills are sold at a discount to face value.

SOLVED PROBLEM 7.7

A 1-year, Treasury bill is sold for a stated interest rate of 8.5 percent.

(*a*)   What is the amount of discount?

(*b*)   What is the price you will pay?

(*c*)   What is the effective annual yield?

SOLUTION

(*a*) $850 (8.5% × $10,000)

(*b*) $9,150 ($10,000 − $850)

(*c*) $850 represents the yield. The effective annual yield is 9.29 percent ($850/$9,150).

For more on effective annual yield calculations, see Chapter 15 (Investing in Fixed-Income Securities).

BUYING U.S. SAVINGS BONDS

There are two types of U.S. savings bonds: Series EE and Series HH. A *Series EE bond* is purchased for half of its face value. It pays no periodic interest, since the interest accumulates between the purchase price and the bond's maturity value. For example, a Series EE bond can be purchased for $100 and redeemed at maturity for $200. Series EE bonds can be purchased in denominations from $25 to $5,000, with a maximum purchase limit of $15,000 annually. Early redemption is penalized with a lower interest rate than stated on the bond. When held for at least 5 years, Series EE bonds earn market-based interest or a guaranteed minimum, whichever is higher. Bonds held for less than 5 years earn a lower rate of return. The market-based rate, announced each May and November, is 85 percent of the market average on 5-year Treasury securities.

Series HH bonds are issued only in exchange for Series E and EE savings bonds. They are purchased at face value and pay interest semiannually until maturity 5 years later. Early redemption will be penalized at slightly less than face value.

SOLVED PROBLEM 7.8

A $10,000 Series HH pays 7 percent interest annually. How much is the semiannual interest?

SOLUTION

$$\$10,000 \times 7\% \times \tfrac{6}{12} = \$350$$

SOLVED PROBLEM 7.9

George Lee has decided to invest $5,000 in a Series EE savings bond for his retirement. If the interest averages 8 percent after 10 years, how much will he have after 10 years? (Assume semi-annual interest accrual.)

SOLUTION

The future value of $1 (Appendix Table 1 factor) for 20 periods at a semiannual rate of 4 percent is 2.191.

$$\$5,000 \times 2.191 = \$10,955$$

ADVANTAGES

Both Series EE and Series HH interest income is exempt from state and local taxes. Federal income taxes can be deferred on Series EE bonds until they are redeemed.

There are no service charges when you purchase or redeem savings bonds, as there are with many other investments.

Safety and complete security backed by the U.S. government.

DISADVANTAGES

Lack of liquidity

Relatively lower yield

United States savings bonds can be purchased at most banks and other financial institutions or through payroll deduction plans. They can be replaced if lost, stolen, or destroyed. Both series must be held at least 6 months before redeeming.

HOW ABOUT AN "ALL-IN-ONE" ACCOUNT OR ASSET MANAGEMENT ACCOUNT?

If you have $5,000 to $20,000 in cash or securities, many banks offer a package of services, including

Automated cash management

Certain investment services

Preferential personal treatment

On the cash management side, the bank covers checks you write by transferring the right amount from your money market account balance to your checking account, leaving the rest to earn interest.

On the investment side, the bank offers their facilities not only for trading securities at a discount but also for personal financial planning.

On top of this, the bank issues an exhaustive monthly statement that lists such items as stock and bond transactions as well as checking, CD, money market, and loan balances. Annual fees for these comprehensive services can be substantial, so ask yourself how many of these services you need. For example, if you are mainly interested in trading stocks and bonds, using a discount broker would be cheaper and more practical than the bank's asset management service.

Money market funds offer similar services including checking, savings, investments, and a credit card. Like the bank's asset management account, an asset management account of a fund centralizes bookkeeping, allows the writing of unlimited checks, and provides for the automatic crediting of stock dividends and bond interest. Disadvantages of the account are a high deposit required to open it (usually $5,000 to $20,000), annual fees ranging from $25 to $100, and failure to return checks by some funds.

HOW MANY WAYS ARE THERE TO ENDORSE CHECKS?

Before depositing a check or transferring it to another person, you as payee must endorse the check. Whenever you endorse a check you become liable for payment of it. There are several types of endorsements: blank, special, and restrictive.

Blank.   A blank endorsement is simply the payee's signature. It transfers title to anyone holding it at the time. *Warning:* Since it can be cashed by anyone, you should not use this endorsement until you are actually giving it to someone.

Special.   A special endorsement names an endorsee, who is the person you are giving the check to and the next person who must endorse it. No one else can negotiate the check.

Restrictive.   A restrictive endorsement specifies what can be done with the check and restricts further endorsement. An example is "for deposit only."

Figure 7-1 shows examples of each.

Blank	Restrictive	Special
John Doe	*For deposit only* *John Doe*	*Pay to the order of* *Mary Smith* *John Doe*

Fig. 7-1

Review Questions

(1)   When shopping for a bank, you should consider some elements which include _____, clarity of information, convenient hours and services, quick crediting of deposits, and good deals on loans.

(2)   If you are a frequent checkwriter, you will be better off by selecting a _____ instead of a per-check charge.

(3)   There are four types of checking accounts: _____, _____, _____, and _____.

(4)   MMDA stands for _____.

(5)   The most important advantage of money market accounts compared to _____ is the insurance protection of up to $100,000 per depositor.

(6)   Banks usually slap a "_____" on the checks drawn on a bank other than your own.

(7)   Interest is tax-deductible when incurred on a _____.

(8) Your checking and saving deposits are safe up to _____ if they are in federally insured financial institutions.

(9) To reconcile the bank balance the outstanding checks should be _____ from the bank balance.

(10) Banks calculate interest on depositors' accounts four different ways: _____, _____, _____, and _____.

(11) The DDDW method is also called _____.

(12) To compare CDs, look at the _____, which takes into account the effects of compounding.

(13) _____ are short-term obligations of the U.S. government, which may be purchased for a minimum of $10,000.

(14) Treasury bills are sold at a _____ to face value.

(15) There are two types of U.S. savings bonds: _____ and _____.

(16) In doing a bank reconciliation, _____ deposits in transit to the _____ balance.

(17) When preparing a bank reconciliation, a "bounced check" you received should be _____ from the _____ balance.

(18) If your account was charged in error by the bank with another person's check, you should _____ the amount to the _____ balance.

Answers: (1) comparison of rates and fees; (2) flat monthly service fee; (3) regular checking account, passbook savings account, NOW account, Super NOW account; (4) money market deposit account; (5) money market mutual funds; (6) hold; (7) home loan; (8) $100,000; (9) deducted; (10) FIFO, LIFO, minimum-balance, DDDW; (11) the actual-balance method; (12) effective annual yield; (13) Treasury bills; (14) discount; (15) Series EE, Series HH; (16) add, bank; (17) deducted, checkbook; (18) add, bank.

Additional Solved Problems

7.1 John Monat estimates that he will be writing, on the average, seven checks each month. An activity account would carry a service fee of $.90 per month. The bank has a service charge of $.08 per check and a deposit charge of $.10 per deposit. John will be making about two deposits per month. The bank also offers a minimum checking balance. With this account, the bank would not charge any service fees as long as he maintained a minimum balance of $300. John could withdraw $300 from his credit union account, which is currently paying 7 percent interest. Should John open the activity account or the minimum-balance account? Why?

SOLUTION

John Monat's monthly costs for an activity account would be $.90 + ($.08 × 7) + ($.10 × 2) = $1.66. His annual costs would be $1.66 × 12 = $19.92. With minimum-balance checking, he would lose $300 × .07 = $21 annually in interest. He would be better off staying with the activity account since it is cheaper.

7.2   Diane Gilbert writes about 10 checks and makes about two cash deposits each month. The local bank has offered her two service packages. The first package would carry a service charge of $1 per month. Each check written and each deposit made would carry a service charge of $.15. The second package has a service charge of $4 per month, and no service charges are assessed for either checks or deposits. Which of these checking packages is the better deal for Ms. Gilbert? Explain your answer.

SOLUTION

Ms. Gilbert's cost for the first package would be $(10 \times \$.15) + (2 \times \$.15) + \$1 = \$2.80$. Since this cost is less than the $4 cost for the second package, she would be better off with the first package.

7.3   The Kergers can open a special package account, which would include free checking, free traveler's checks, a safe deposit box, and an 8 percent rebate on interest charges on loans taken out. The cost of the package account is $6 per month. The Kergers can open an activity account that would cost, on the average, $3 per month. A safe deposit box can be rented for $15 per year. The Kergers borrow regularly from the bank and expect that they would pay about $200 in interest every year. The Kergers do not travel regularly, although they are considering taking an annual 1-week vacation. Which plan appears to be better for the Kergers? Justify your answer.

SOLUTION

The annual cost of the special package is $\$6 \times 12 = \$72$. The 8 percent rebate on $200 in annual interest charges is $\$200 \times .08 = \$16$. The safe deposit box rents for $15 per year. The effective cost of the package is $\$72 - \$16 - \$15 = \$41$. The activity account would cost them $\$3 \times 12 = \$36$ annually. Unless they buy a lot of traveler's checks, the Kergers should choose the activity account.

7.4   The Bradleys have noticed that a local bank is offering a free toaster if someone buys a $1,000 1-year certificate of deposit that has a 10 percent interest rate. The toaster normally sells for about $20 at a local discount department store. The Bradleys were thinking about buying a new toaster. They have their money in a money market fund that pays them about 12.4 percent annually in interest. What options do the Bradleys have? What should they do?

SOLUTION

The Bradleys have two options:

(1)   Buy the toaster.
(2)   Move $1,000 from the money market fund into the bank CD and get the toaster from the bank. In following option 2, they would lose $12.4\% - 10.0\% = 2.4\%$ in interest on $1,000 for 1 year. This amounts to a loss of $.024 \times \$1,000 = \$24$. Whether option 2 is more desirable depends on their tax situation. If they are in a low tax bracket, they should go with option 1. However, if they are in a high tax bracket then option 2 is better. For example, if they are in the 50 percent tax bracket, then they would get to keep only $12 of the extra $24 in income from the money fund. By moving the funds, they would lose only $12 in after-tax income but will be able to obtain a $20 toaster.

7.5   Mary Kay has $300 in traveler's checks left over from a vacation she took recently. She plans to take another vacation in 3 months. She can either keep the $300 in traveler's checks for her next vacation or cash them in and put the money in a savings account that pays 5.25 percent effective interest using the DDDW method. The bank charges her a service fee of 1 percent for issuing traveler's checks. What should she do? Why?

SOLUTION

On $300, she would earn $\$300 \times .0525/4 = \$3.94$ in interest in 3 months. She should go ahead and cash in the traveler's checks and deposit the money in the savings account. The interest received will be more than the $3 cost of buying new traveler's checks.

7.6 Until her recent graduation from college, Anne Bacher was writing about five to seven checks each month. She pays $1.50 monthly as a service fee and $.10 for each check written. After graduation she found herself writing about 25 checks each month. She feels that the activity account that she has had from her college days no longer adequately serves her needs. Her bank also offers a minimum checking balance plan. As long as Anne keeps at least $500 in her checking account, she would not have to pay any service charges. She can move $500 from a money market fund to her checking account. The money market fund has been paying about 10 percent after taxes annually. Should Ms. Bacher switch to the minimum checking balance plan?

SOLUTION

Her current monthly costs are $1.50 + ($.10 \times 25) = $1.50 + $2.50 = $4. The annual costs are $4 \times 12 = $48. If she transfers money from the fund, she will be losing $500 \times .1 = $50 in interest income annually. On the surface, it appears that she should stay with the activity account because with switching, she will be losing $50 in income to save $48 in costs. Note, however, that Anne is a recent college graduate. It is possible that in the near future, she may begin to write even more checks. In fact, even if she started to write only two more checks monthly, her annual checking account expenses would exceed $50: [$1.50 + ($.10 \times 27)] \times 12 = $4.20 \times 12 = $50.40. Ms. Bacher should go ahead and switch to the minimum checking balance plan.

7.7 Joan put $4,000 in a savings account that pays interest at the rate of 6 percent, compounded annually.

(a) How much will she have in 5 years?

(b) How much will she make in interest?

SOLUTION

(a)

$$\text{Future value} = \text{Amount deposited} \times \text{Future value of \$1} \quad \text{(Appendix Table 1)}$$
$$= \$4,000 \times 1.338$$
$$= \$5,352$$

(b) $1,352 ($5,352 − $4,000)

7.8 Kay decided to put $4,000 each year for the next 5 years in a savings account that pays 6 percent per year. How much would be accumulated at the end of 5 years?

SOLUTION

$$\text{Future value} = \text{Amount deposited each year}$$
$$\times \text{Future value of an annuity of \$1} \quad \text{(Appendix Table 2)}$$
$$= \$4,000 \times 5.637 = \$22,548$$

7.9 Calculate the future value of each series of deposits below.

	Amount Deposited per Year	Annual Interest Rate	Number of Years
A	$5,000	12%	4
B	2,000	10	10
C	500	7	5

SOLUTION

Deposit	Amount Deposited	× Future Value Annuity Factor	= Future Value
A	$5,000	4.779	$23,895
B	2,000	15.937	31,874
C	500	5.751	2,876

7.10 Lynne Stoke wants to buy a $1,000 certificate of deposit for 1 year. S&L A offers her 6.2 percent interest paid and compounded annually. S&L B offers her a 6.0 percent annual interest paid and compounded quarterly. What are the effective interest rates for these two CDs? Which one should Lynne select? Why?

SOLUTION

The effective interest rate for the CD from S&L A is 6.2 percent. The interest rate on the CD from S&L B can be calculated as follows:

QUARTER	PRINCIPAL	INTEREST	ENDING BALANCE
1	$1,000.00	$15.00	$1,015.00
2	1,015.00	15.23	1,030.23
3	1,030.23	15.45	1,045.68
4	1,045.68	15.69	1,061.37
		$61.37	

Interest was calculated by multiplying the principal by 1.5% (6%/4). Total interest received is $61.37. The effective interest rate on the CD is $61.37/$1,000 = .06137 = 6.137 percent. Thus, Lynne should select the CD from S&L A since it has the higher effective interest rate.

7.11 Your bank statement shows a balance of $238.79 on October 31, 19X1. Your checkbook balance as of the same date is $97.18. Check no. 25 for $84.89 and check no. 33 for $59.72 are not enclosed with your statement. The bank has deducted a service charge of $3.00. Reconcile your statement.

SOLUTION

October 31, 19X1

Bank balance		$238.79	Checkbook balance	$97.18
Less: Outstanding checks:			Less: Service charge	3.00
no. 25	$84.89			
no. 33	59.72	144.61		
Adjusted bank balance		$ 94.18	Adjusted checkbook balance	$94.18

7.12 Your bank statement shows a balance of $484.75 on January 31, 19X2. A deposit of $220 was not recorded on the bank statement. Your checkbook balance as of the same date is $365.75. Check no. 425 for $149 and check no. 433 for $195 are not enclosed with your statement. The bank has deducted a service charge of $5.00. Reconcile your statement.

SOLUTION

January 31, 19X2

Bank balance	$484.75	Checkbook balance	$365.75
Add: Deposit in transit	220.00		
Less: Outstanding checks:		Less: Service charge	5.00
no. 425	$149.00		
no. 433	195.00 344.00		
Adjusted bank balance	$360.75	Adjusted checkbook balance	$360.75

7.13 The checking account register for D. Klammer is shown below:

Number	Date	Description	Payment	Deposit	Balance
401	9/03	Osaka, food	$ 47.35		$ 212.53
402	9/05	GTE, phone	37.60		174.93
403	9/05	SCE, electricity	98.40		76.73
	9/09	Deposit		$ 80.00	156.73
404	9/17	LMN, food	17.95		138.78
405	9/24	Fashion Gal	60.00		78.78
406	10/01	Sears, clothing	210.25		(131.47)
407	10/01	ERA Realty, rent	350.00		(481.47)
	10/01	Deposit		769.22	287.75
408	10/03	LMN, food	32.37		255.38

The bank statement for D. Klammer's account is as follows:

D. KLAMMER
3981 Myra Ave.
Cypress, CA 90723

Beginning balance	$259.88
Plus: Deposits	849.22
Less: Checks	761.35
Less: Service charge	3.00
Ending balance	$344.75

Checks			Deposits	Date	Balance
47.35				9/05	212.53
37.60	98.20		80.00	9/09	156.73
17.95				9/20	138.78
			769.22	10/01	908.00
210.25	350.00	3.00 SC*		10/04	344.75

*SC = service charge

From the information provided, prepare an account reconciliation for D. Klammer.

SOLUTION

The two checks outstanding are no. 408 for $32.37 and no. 405 for $60. Both deposits have cleared. We use the following format to reconcile the account:

October 31

Bank balance	$344.75	Checkbook balance	$255.38
Less: Outstanding checks:		Less: Service charge	3.00
no. 425 $60.00			
no. 433 32.37	92.37		
Adjusted bank balance	$252.38	Adjusted checkbook balance	$252.38

7.14 Prepare a bank reconciliation as of November 30 using the following information:

(1) Balance per depositor's records, $11,550

(2) Balance per bank statement, $16,840

(3) Outstanding checks, $2,442

(4) Erroneous recording of check no. 1558 for telephone expense, $171; actual amount of check, $117

(5) Bank service charge, $6

(6) Deposit in transit, $2,760

(7) Note collected by bank for you, $6,400

(8) Check returned because of insufficient funds, $840

SOLUTION

Balance per depositor's records		$11,550
Add: Note collected	$6,400	
Error in check no. 1558	54	6,454
Deduct: Bank service charge	$ 6	
NSF check	840	846
Adjusted book balance		$17,158
Balance per bank statement		$16,840
Add: Deposit in transit		2,760
		$19,600
Deduct: Outstanding checks		2,442
Adjusted bank balance		$17,158

7.15 Determine the interest earned for the quarter using the

(a) Minimum-balance method

(b) FIFO method

(c) LIFO method

(d) Actual-balance method

The interest rate on the account is 8 percent. (Assume a 360-day year.)

Quarterly Activity

Day	Transaction	Account Balance
1	Opening balance	$40,000
30	Withdrawal	5,000
60	Deposit	10,000
90	Ending balance	45,000

SOLUTION

(a) Minimum balance method:

$$\$40{,}000 \times .08 \times \tfrac{90}{360} = \$800$$

(b) FIFO method:

$$\$35{,}000 \times .08 \times \tfrac{90}{360} = \$700$$
$$\$10{,}000 \times .08 \times \tfrac{30}{360} = \underline{67}$$
$$\$767$$

(c) LIFO method:

$$\$35{,}000 \times .08 \times \tfrac{90}{360} = \$700$$
$$\$10{,}000 \times .08 \times \tfrac{90}{360} = \underline{200}$$
$$\$900$$

(d) Actual-balance method:

$$\$40{,}000 \times .08 \times \tfrac{30}{360} = \$266.67$$
$$\$35{,}000 \times .08 \times \tfrac{30}{360} = 233.33$$
$$\$45{,}000 \times .08 \times \tfrac{30}{360} = \underline{300.00}$$
$$\$800.00$$

7.16 John Shubeck opened a savings account at his bank that paid 8 percent a year, compounded annually. Activity in his account for the quarter was as follows:

Beginning balance at day 1	$1,000
Deposit, 60 days after day 1	500
Withdrawal, 75 days after day 1	600
Ending balance for the quarter	900

Determine the interest earned for the quarter using the

(a) Minimum-balance method
(b) FIFO method
(c) LIFO method
(d) Day-of-deposit–to–day-to-withdrawal (DDDW) method

(Assume a 360-day year.)

SOLUTION

(a) Minimum-balance method:

$$\$900 \times .08 \times \tfrac{90}{360} = \$18$$

(b) FIFO method:

$$\$400 \times .08 \times \tfrac{90}{360} = \$8.00$$
$$\$500 \times .08 \times \tfrac{30}{360} = \underline{3.33}$$
$$\$11.33$$

(c) LIFO method:

$$\$900 \times .08 \times \tfrac{90}{360} = \$18$$

(d) Day-of-deposit–to–day-of-withdrawal (DDDW) method:

$$\$1,000 \times .08 \times \tfrac{60}{360} = \$13.33$$

$$\$1,500 \times .08 \times \tfrac{15}{360} = 5.00$$

$$\underline{\$900 \times .08 \times \tfrac{15}{360} = 3.00}$$

$$\$21.33$$

7.17 Listed below is the account activity for one quarter for Gladys Washington's savings account. Her account pays a 6 percent annual interest rate with quarterly compounding. (Assume a 360-day year.)

Date	Deposits (Withdrawals)	Balance
4/1		$ 500
4/2	$ 2,000	2,500
4/28	(1,000)	1,500
5/14	660	2,160
5/28	500	2,660
6/14	(1,700)	960
6/30		960

What amount of interest would she earn using each of the following methods?

(a) FIFO

(b) LIFO

(c) Minimum (low) balance

(d) Day-of-deposit–to–day-of-withdrawal (DDDW)

SOLUTION

Interest based on April 1–June 30 (90 days):

(a) FIFO

$$\$500 \times .06 \times \tfrac{90}{360} = \$7.50$$

$$\underline{\$460 \times .06 \times \tfrac{32}{360} = 2.45}$$

$$\$9.95$$

(b) LIFO

$$\$500 \times .06 \times \tfrac{90}{360} = \$7.50$$

$$\underline{\$460 \times .06 \times \tfrac{89}{360} = 6.82}$$

$$\$14.32$$

(c) Minimum balance

$$\$500 \times .06 \times \tfrac{90}{360} = \$7.50$$

(d) DDDW

$$\$500 \times .06 \times \tfrac{90}{360} = \$7.50$$

$$\$2,000 \times .06 \times \tfrac{89}{360} = 29.67$$

$$-\$1,000 \times .06 \times \tfrac{63}{360} = (10.50)$$

$$\$660 \times .06 \times \tfrac{46}{360} = 5.06$$

$$\$500 \times .06 \times \tfrac{36}{360} = 3.00$$

$$-\$1,700 \times .06 \times \tfrac{18}{360} = \underline{(5.10)}$$

$$\$29.63$$

7.18 Compute the quarterly interest earned under the four different methods with a 7 percent stated interest rate. (Assume a 360-day year.)

Activity in the Account

Day	Deposits (Withdrawals)	Balance
1	$1,500	$1,500
30	1,500	3,000
45	(500)	2,500
60	1,000	3,500
90	Closing	3,500

(*a*) FIFO

(*b*) LIFO

(*c*) Minimum (low) balance

(*d*) Day-of-deposit–to–day-of-withdrawal (DDDW)

SOLUTION

(*a*) FIFO

$$\$1,000 \times .07 \times \tfrac{90}{360} = \$17.50$$

$$\$1,500 \times .07 \times \tfrac{60}{360} = 17.50$$

$$\$1,000 \times .07 \times \tfrac{30}{360} = \underline{5.83}$$

$$\$40.83$$

(*b*) LIFO

$$\$1,500 \times .07 \times \tfrac{90}{360} = \$26.25$$

$$\$1,000 \times .07 \times \tfrac{60}{360} = 11.67$$

$$\$1,000 \times .07 \times \tfrac{30}{360} = \underline{5.83}$$

$$\$43.75$$

(*c*) Minimum balance

$$\$1,500 \times .07 \times \tfrac{90}{360} = \$26.25$$

(*d*) DDDW

$$\$1,500 \times .07 \times \tfrac{30}{360} = \$8.75$$

$$\$3,000 \times .07 \times \tfrac{15}{360} = 8.75$$

$$\$2,500 \times .07 \times \tfrac{15}{360} = 7.29$$

$$\$3,500 \times .07 \times \tfrac{30}{360} = \underline{20.42}$$

$$\$45.21$$

7.19 Barbara and Stanley opened a checking account on September 1.

(*a*) Use the following account transaction data to determine the balance on which Barbara and Stanley will be eligible to receive interest for the month of September 19X1 under each of the four techniques. (Assume that there are twelve 30-day months in the year.)

(b) Assuming the effective rate of interest is 6 percent and using the balance data given, calculate the amount of interest earned under each of the four techniques for the month ended September 30, 19X1.

Account Transaction for Month of September 19X1

Day	Transaction	Amount	Balance
1	—	—	$1,000
3	Deposit	$2,000	3,000
14	Deposit	1,000	4,000
17	Withdrawal	2,500	1,500
24	Withdrawal	1,000	500
25	Deposit	4,000	4,500
30	—	—	$4,500

SOLUTION

(a) Under the minimum-balance method you just look at the account transactions to see the lowest balance, which is $500.

Under FIFO, the balance is calculated as

Day 1	Balance	$1,000	
Day 3	Deposit	2,000	
	Balance	3,000	
Day 17	Withdrawal	2,500	
	Balance	500	
Day 14	Deposit	1,000	
	Balance	1,500	
Day 24	Withdrawal	1,000	
	Balance	500	from day 14 deposit
Day 25	Deposit	4,000	from day 25 deposit
	Ending Balance	4,500	

Under LIFO the balance would be

Day 1	Balance	$1,000	
Day 3	Deposit	2,000	
Day 14	Deposit	1,000	
	Balance	4,000	
Day 17	Withdrawal	2,500	or $1,000 from day 14 and $1,500 from day 3
	Balance	1,500	
Day 24	Withdrawal	1,000	or $500 from day 3 and $500 from day 1
	Balance	500	
Day 25	Deposit	4,000	
	Ending balance	4,500	

Under the actual-balance method the ending balance is still $4,500, but the days on deposit look as follows:

Day 1	Balance	$1,000 for 3 days
Day 3	Deposit	2,000
	Balance	3,000 for 11 days

Day 14	Deposit	1,000
	Balance	4,000 for 3 days
Day 17	Withdrawal	2,500
	Balance	1,500 for 7 days
Day 24	Withdrawal	1,000
	Balance	500 for 1 day
Day 24	Deposit	4,000
	Ending balance	$4,500 for 5 days

(b) Minimum balance interest earned is

$$\$500 \times .06 \times \tfrac{6}{360} = \$.50$$

FIFO interest earned is

$$\$500 \times .06 \times \tfrac{16}{360} = \$1.33$$
$$\$4,000 \times .06 \times \tfrac{5}{360} = \underline{\$3.33}$$

Total interest $4.66

LIFO interest earned is

$$\$1,000 \times .06 \times \tfrac{17}{360} = \$2.83$$
$$\$500 \times .06 \times \tfrac{14}{360} = 1.17$$
$$\$500 \times .06 \times \tfrac{7}{360} = .58$$
$$\$4,500 \times .06 \times \tfrac{5}{360} = \underline{3.75}$$

Total interest $8.33

Interest earned using the actual-balance method is

$$\$1,000 \times .06 \times \tfrac{3}{360} = \$ .50$$
$$\$3,000 \times .06 \times \tfrac{11}{360} = 5.50$$
$$\$4,000 \times .06 \times \tfrac{3}{360} = 2.00$$
$$\$1,500 \times .06 \times \tfrac{7}{360} = 1.75$$
$$\$500 \times .06 \times \tfrac{1}{360} = .08$$
$$\$4,500 \times .06 \times \tfrac{5}{360} = \underline{3.75}$$

Total interest $13.58

Chapter 8

Consumer Credit and Loans

Virtually everybody uses credit everyday. We live in an era of what seems to be abundant credit, which in turn allows people to spend more than ever before. Credit becomes a vicious cycle for many people. If you do not exercise caution, you can run into serious financial trouble, including the possibility of bankruptcy. In this chapter you will learn how to answer the following questions:

What are the advantages and disadvantages of credit?

How much credit can you handle?

How do you calculate the cost of credit?

How do you select a credit card?

Are you managing debt properly?

Should you pay off a loan early?

Where can you get help for credit problems?

Can you invest with borrowed money?

What are the pluses and minuses of a home equity line?

What is bankruptcy?

HOW TO EVALUATE CREDIT CARDS

Credit cards are an expensive way of borrowing. Their average interest rate nationally hovers around 18 percent. But increased competition among issuers (along with the outcry of consumer groups) is pushing rates down. So it pays to comparison shop.

1. *Interest rates and annual fees.*   A simple way to compare the costs of credit cards involves two steps. First, multiply the balance you usually carry by the percentage difference between the two cards.

SOLVED PROBLEM 8.1

Your average annual balance is $500 and the rate difference between credit cards is 5 percent. What will you save?

SOLUTION

$$5\% \times \$500 = \$25$$

Second, add in the annual fees. Do not skip this step: A card with a lower finance charge may carry a higher annual fee. One way to save on annual fees is to reassess whether you really need as many cards as you have in your wallet, and get rid of the cards you do not use. You can reduce the number of credit cards that you have by using each credit card to the maximum allowable amount. Thus, you can reduce total annual charges of your credit cards.

Some credit cards give you additional benefits. American Express, for example, provides its cardholders with its highly advertised Purchase Protection Plan. Also the Marriott First Card gives you charge points toward the Honored Guest Program.

2. *Grace periods.*   Do not forget the phase-out of deductibility of consumer credit interest. A 25- to 30-day period in which you can pay your bill in full and not incur an interest charge would be the best way to free money under the tax law. However, there is a growing trend to shorten or eliminate grace periods.

3. *Transaction fees.* Some issuers impose a small fee each time the card is used for a charge purchase. Many issuers also charge a fee for each cash advance, which can add up if you make frequent use of cash advances

4. *Other fees and charges.* These include late-payment fees and charges for exceeding your credit limit.

Rule of thumb: For most people, the best deal is a card with a low interest rate, no annual fee, and a 25- to 30-day grace period. For comparison shopping, check with Bankcard Holders of America's publications, including *Women's Credit Right* and *How to Shop for a Bank Card and Solving Your Credit Card Billing Questions* [Bankcard Holders of America, 333 Pennsylvania Avenue S.E., Washington, D.C. 20003, (800) 638–6407 (outside D.C.) and (202) 543–5805].

No matter how much your annual income is, you should not overload yourself with too many credit cards. It can be hazardous to your credit records. They count as debts on your credit file even though they were not used at all or to the maximum limit.

WHERE TO GET CREDIT COUNSELING

We are in an era where banks and stores are pushing credit cards and charge accounts on virtually anyone. It is not surprising that a lot of people have trouble handling the debts that go with "plastic money."

SOLVED PROBLEM 8.2

What financial difficulties will occur if your debt is excessive?

SOLUTION

Financial troubles include:

Inability to pay even the minimum amount due each month on every account

The situation where installment debts leave almost nothing for discretionary spending

No cushion for savings for an emergency

High interest cost

The worksheet in Fig. 8-1 will give you a quick picture of your credit obligations. Be sure to list all your consumer debts, noting the maturity dates for nonrevolving charges.

After you have totaled your monthly debt obligations, figure out the percentage of your take-home pay that they represent. If the figure is higher than 15 to 20 percent, you are in danger of credit overload. Also, ask yourself "Could you pay off all your debts within 18 to 24 months?" If not, you are probably in "over your head."

Name of Creditor	Interest Rate	Monthly Payment	Last Payment	Balance
	Total			

Fig. 8-1 Quick glance at your credit picture.

PAINSTAKING STEPS TO TAKE

If, after completing the worksheet, you find you need to trim your indebtedness, try the following steps:

1. Analyze your expenses. What are you spending, and where? Look for areas where you can cut back, at least temporarily, to free up cash and pay off debts.

2. Lock up your credit cards or get rid of some.

3. Establish a self-imposed repayment schedule. Start with the debts that carry the highest financial charges.

4. Do not take on new debts until your present ones are under control.

Here are some tips:

1. Try to talk to creditors and arrange a favorable repayment schedule.

2. Look for ads for debt consolidation loans, which are hopefully at lower interest rates with smaller monthly payments and longer repayment terms.

3. Look hard for impartial counseling from someone or an organization that does not attempt to take advantage of your situation. You may want to contact Consumer Credit Counseling Service, The National Foundation for Consumer Credit, 8701 George Avenue, Suite 507, Silver Spring, MD 20910. This is a nonprofit counseling service that offers counseling on various areas such as budgeting, design of a debt repayment plan, and management of credit. You might look up in your telephone White Pages directory for their local listings and locations.

HOW TO DEAL WITH A CREDIT BUREAU

Sometimes you find yourself totally shocked when your credit application is denied and you find out that you have a bad record at the credit bureau, which you were not aware of and it is inaccurate. But it is too late!!

There are about 2,000 credit bureaus around the country, serving as a clearinghouse for information about consumers' debts and their debt-paying habits. You do not choose a credit bureau because it does not work for you, but for creditors such as banks, financial institutions, and merchants. The credit files include not only reports from creditors but public-record information about bankruptcies, lawsuits, tax liens, and other matters that could affect your creditworthiness.

Unfortunately, the files may contain inaccurate information in your record. If your credit application is turned down, federal law requires that you be told why automatically. But it is good to check and find out whether outdated or erroneous data were the reasons. Here is what you should do:

1. Call the bureau for an appointment to review your file or to request that the bureau mail you a copy of your credit file.

2. If you find incorrect information in your file, demand that the credit bureau investigate the report. You might want to send them some supporting data. If the bureau cannot verify the accuracy of the item in dispute, it must drop the information.

3. Ask for a revised copy and also have them send it to credit grantors who received the erroneous version.

4. Regardless, review your credit record periodically even though you will be charged. It is worth it. Check your file each year to ensure no errors have slipped in.

HOW MUCH DEBT CAN YOU HANDLE?

It is not easy to determine the maximum debt to have. There are three methods to establish debt limits: the disposable income, ratio of debts to equity, and continuous debt methods.

DISPOSABLE INCOME METHOD

Keep your monthly consumer debt payments down to around 15 percent of your disposable personal income. Calculate the debt safety ratio:

$$\frac{\text{Monthly consumer debt payments}}{\text{Monthly take-home pay}}$$

Disposable personal income is the amount of your take-home pay left after all deductions are withheld for taxes, insurance, union dues, and the like. The absolute maximum of consumer debt payments should be 20 percent.

SOLVED PROBLEM 8.3

If your take-home pay is $2,000 for the month, how much should go toward paying off items bought on credit?

SOLUTION

$$20\% \times \$2,000 = \$400$$

Note that the maximum limit includes payments due on credit cards, and personal, school, and car loans–but not mortgages, home-equity loans, or rent. Those obligations can account for as much as an additional 35 percent of your total monthly expenditures. The following steps can assist in determining your debt limit:

1. Calculate your monthly consumer debt payments.
2. Determine your monthly net income (after all taxes, social security and IRA contributions).
3. To calculate the most you can afford each month, multiply your monthly income by 20 percent, 15 percent, or 10 percent (your personal permissible debt ratio, if you will). *Rule of thumb:* If you are single, middle-aged, and net $40,000 a year, you can perhaps afford 20 percent in debt. Reduce debt to 10 percent if your income is not stable (for example, based on commissions rather than salary). If you and your working spouse take home $50,000, you can afford 20 percent. If you have children, knock it back to 15 percent. If you are retired on a fixed income, make it 10 percent.
4. To find whether your payments are within your means, subtract (1) from (3). This figure is your safety margin. If (1) is larger than (3), however, you should start taking the steps suggested previously.

SOLVED PROBLEM 8.4

You are single, middle-aged, and take home $40,000 a year (or $3,333 a month). You carry an average monthly consumer debt payment of $1,000. According to the rule of thumb, what is the most you can afford each month? Are you over the limit?

SOLUTION

$667 (20% × $3,333). You are over the limit by $333 ($1,000 − $667). You should seriously consider cutting down on existing debts and avoid additional borrowing.

RATIO OF DEBTS TO EQUITY METHOD

Calculate the so-called debt/equity ratio. The ratio is your debts (not including a first mortgage) to your equity or net worth (not including the value of a first home). If your debts equal or exceed equity (that is, if their debt/equity ratio is equal to or greater than 1), you are probably at your maximum debt limit.

SOLVED PROBLEM 8.5

If you have $58,000 in net worth and owe $29,000, what is your debt/equity ratio.

SOLUTION

$$\frac{\$29,000}{\$58,000} = .50$$

CONTINUOUS DEBT METHOD

If you cannot get completely out of debt every 3 years (except for mortgage and education loans), you are probably too heavily in debt.

ARE YOU MANAGING DEBT PROPERLY?

Here are some tips for managing debt properly:

Avoid borrowing from the future to meet current living expenses. Are you borrowing against future raises or bonuses to pay for daily spending? If you are living beyond your means, danger lurks ahead.

Avoid borrowing for depreciating assets. Rather, only borrow for appreciating assets.

What is the interest rate on each type of debt? Keep track of who is charging a higher rate and move to the lower cost source.

Do not collaterize a loan with savings because a net cost will arise. Further, in the event of an emergency, the savings may not be withdrawn. Always try to buy something with cash rather than on credit.

Avoid using a bank credit card because of the high finance charge (for example, 18 to 20 percent). It is unwise to charge and incur an 18 percent financing cost while putting money in the bank and earning only 6 percent. You should withdraw the savings and pay off the credit card balance. Otherwise, you are losing 12 percent on your money.

Avoid using borrowed funds to invest unless the interest rate is very low and there is a dependable investment return.

SOLVED PROBLEM 8.6

You have $100,000 in a money market account earning 8 percent. You owe $7,000 on your credit cards at 20 percent interest. In this case, your net worth is declining since the borrowing cost exceeds the return on the bank account by 12 percent. $7,000 should be taken out from the bank account to pay the credit cards. What is the reduction in wealth on an annual basis?

SOLUTION

Cost of credit card ($7,000 × 20%)	$1,400
Return on bank account (7,000 × 8%)	560
Decline in wealth	$ 840

Establish a line of credit before it is necessary. There is usually no charge for a preapproved line until borrowing takes place.

To reduce credit payments, the loan may be extended over a longer time period (for example, financing the purchase of a car over 4 years rather than 3 years).

SOLVED PROBLEM 8.7

What are the advantages and disadvantages of buying on credit?

SOLUTION

The advantages of buying on credit are:

Convenience. You do not have to pay by cash or give a check.

Safety. You do not need to carry lots of currency.

You can buy high-ticket items and pay it out.

Emergency use when an unexpected expenditure occurs and you are temporarily out of cash.

Inflationary protection because you can buy goods or services before large inflationary price increases take place.

Ease of returning merchandise bought since you have not paid cash for them yet.

No charge for credit. If you pay within the credit-billing period, you may not have to pay a finance charge.

The disadvantages of buying on credit are:

You can overextend by buying items you cannot afford.

High financing cost.

Insecurity. Credit may create insecurity and anxiety on the part of many people.

BORROWING ON OPEN ACCOUNT

Credit on open account, often known as charge accounts, is a form of credit extended to a consumer in advance of any transactions. Department store cards and bank credit cards such as Master-Card and Visa are examples of open account credit. Open account credit offered by retail merchants is called store charges. It is important to understand how they compute finance charges on your credit purchases. There are four basic methods: the previous balance method, the average daily balance method, the adjusted balance method, and the past due balance method.

PREVIOUS BALANCE METHOD

This is the most expensive for the customer because interest is computed on the outstanding balance at the beginning of the period.

AVERAGE DAILY BALANCE METHOD

Under this method, the interest is charged on the average daily balance of the account over the billing period. The average daily balance method is less expensive than the previous balance method and widely used by stores that offer revolving charge accounts.

ADJUSTED BALANCE METHOD

With this method, the interest is applied to the balance remaining at the end of the billing period ignoring purchases or returns made during the billing period. This will result in lower interest charges than the other methods discussed above.

PAST DUE BALANCE METHOD

This method is used to stimulate customers to fully repay their accounts. With this method, customers who pay their accounts in full within a specified time period, such as 30 days from the billing date, do not have to pay a finance charge.

SOLVED PROBLEM 8.8

Assume that the monthly interest rate is 1.5 percent, which represents an annual rate of 18 percent. The previous balance is $400 and a payment of $300 was made on the fifteenth day of the month. What are the finance charges under each of the four methods?

SOLUTION

Previous balance method:

$$\$400 \times 1.5\% = \$6.00$$

Average daily balance method: Average daily balance is

NUMBER OF DAYS	BALANCE	WEIGHTED BALANCE
15 days	$400	$6,000
15 days	100	1,500
Total 30 days		Total $7,500

Average daily balance ($7,500/30 days) = $250

$$\$250 \times 1.5\% = \$3.75$$

Adjusted balance method: The balance remaining at the end of the billing period is $100 ($400 − $300), so the interest charge is $100 × 1.5% = $1.50.

Past due balance method: If the payment is made prior to a specified date, the finance charge would be zero; otherwise it would be equal to one of the figures calculated using one of the three methods illustrated above.

Summary of Finance Charges in Solved Problem 8.8

Method	(1) Balance	(2) Monthly Interest Rate	(1) × (2) Finance Charge
Previous balance	$400	1.5%	$6.00
Average daily	250	1.5	3.75
Adjusted balance	100	1.5	1.50
Past due balance	—	1.5	0.00

HOW TO DETERMINE MONTHLY INSTALLMENT LOAN PAYMENTS

When simple interest is used with installment loans, which is the case for most lenders, interest is charged only on the outstanding balance of the loan. In practice, to determine the monthly payment amount, finance tables are widely available for use. For example, Appendix Table 6 provides the monthly payment required to retire a $1,000 installment loan for a selected interest rate and term. The monthly payment covers both principal and interest, since the table has the interest charges built into it.

SOLVED PROBLEM 8.9

You want to take out a $15,000, 12 percent, 48-month loan.

(*a*)　What is the monthly installment loan payment?

(*b*)　What is the total loan payment?

(*c*)　What is the total finance charge?

SOLUTION

Using Appendix Table 6, you need to follow these three steps:

Step 1: Divide the loan amount by $1,000.

$$\frac{\$15,000}{\$1,000} = 15$$

Step 2: Find the payment factor from Appendix Table 6 for the specific interest rate and loan maturity. The Appendix Table 6 payment factor for 12 percent and 48 months is $26.34.

Step 3: Multiply the factor obtained in Step 2 by the amount from Step 1.

$$\$26.34 \times 15 = \$395.10$$

(*a*) Monthly installment loan payment = $395.10.

(*b*) Total loan payments = $18,964.80 ($395.10 × 48 months).

(*c*) The difference between $18,964.80 and the principal ($15,000) represents the finance charge on the loan, that is, $3,964.80.

HOW DO YOU DETERMINE THE TRUE COST OF CREDIT?

You can determine the cost of credit in two ways: (1) in terms of total dollars, and (2) in terms of an annual percentage rate (APR).

TOTAL DOLLAR COST

In terms of total dollar cost, you can immediately see your out-of-pocket expense for the use of credit. Many banks offer different mortgage programs varying in interest rate quoted and up-front points.

SOLVED PROBLEM 8.10

You want to take out a $100,000 mortgage for a new house. Bank A has an interest rate of 8 percent and points of 2 percent. Bank B has an interest rate of 9 percent with no points. The mortgage is for 20 years. Which bank arrangement should you go for?

SOLUTION

First, the yearly payments can be computed as follows:

Bank A   10 × $83.65 (from Appendix Table 5) = $836.50 × 12 months = $10,038

Bank B   10 × $89.98 = $899.80 × 12 months = $10,798

The total interest and point charge for the mortgages from both banks are

Bank A:
  Interest charge
    Total payments ($10,038 × 20) $200,760
    Less: Principal   100,000 $100,760
  Points in first year ($100,000 × 2%)   2,000
    Total $102,760

Bank B:
  Interest charge
    Total payments ($10,798 × 20) $215,960
    Less: Principal   100,000 $115,960
  Points in first year   0
    Total $115,960

The mortgage from Bank A should be selected because its overall cost is lower by $13,200 ($115,960 − $102,760).

ANNUAL PERCENTAGE RATE (APR)

The lender is required by the Truth-in-Lending Act (Consumer Credit Protection Act) to disclose to a borrower the effective annual percentage rate (APR) as well as the finance charge in dollars. The borrower can then compare the costs of the loans for the best deal.

Banks often quote their interest rates in terms of dollars of interest per hundred dollars. Other lenders quote in terms of dollars per payment. This leads to confusion on the part of borrowers. Fortunately, APR can eliminate this confusion.

The APR is a true measure of the effective cost of credit. It is the ratio of the finance charge to the average amount of credit in use during the life of the loan and is expressed as a percentage rate per year. Presented below is a discussion of the way the effective APR is calculated for various types of loans.

Single-Payment Loans

The single payment loan is paid in full on a given date. There are two ways of calculating APR on single-payment loans: the simple interest method and the discount method.

1. *Simple interest method.*   Under the simple interest method, interest is calculated only on the amount borrowed (proceeds). The formula for the simple interest method is

$$\text{Interest} = p \times r \times t$$
$$= \text{Principal} \times \text{Rate} \times \text{Time}$$

$$\text{APR} = \frac{\text{Average annual finance charge}}{\text{Amount borrowed or proceeds}}$$

SOLVED PROBLEM 8.11

You took out a single-payment loan at $1,000 for 2 years at a simple interest rate of 15 percent.

(a) What will the interest charge be?

(b) What is the APR?

SOLUTION

(a) $300 ($1,000 × 15% × 2 years)

(b) APR = 15% ($150/$1,000)

Under the simple interest method, the stated simple interest rate and the APR are always the same for single-payment loans.

2. *Discount method.*   Under this method, interest is determined and then deducted from the amount of the loan. The difference is the actual amount the borrower receives. In other words, the borrower prepays the finance charges.

SOLVED PROBLEM 8.12

Using the same figures as in Solved Problem 8.11, the actual amount received is $700 ($1,000 − $300), not $1,000 to be paid back. What will the APR be?

SOLUTION

APR = 21.43% ($150/$700). 21.43 percent is the rate the lender must quote on the loan, not 15 percent.

The discount method always gives a higher APR than the simple interest method for single-payment loans at the same interest rates.

Installment Loans

Most consumer loans use the add-on method. There are several methods for calculating the APR on add-on loans. They are (1) the actuarial method, (2) the constant-ratio method, (3) the direct-ratio method, and (4) the *N*-ratio method.

The *actuarial method* is the most accurate in calculating the APR and the one lenders most use. It can be defined as interest computed on unpaid balances of principal at a fixed rate, with each payment applied first to interest and the remainder to principal. Since calculation by this method involves complicated formulas, annuity tables or computer programs are commonly used.

The *constant-ratio method* is used to approximate the APR on an installment loan by the use of a simple formula, but it overstates the rate substantially. The higher the quoted rate, the greater the inaccuracy of the method. The constant-ratio formula is

$$APR = \frac{2MC}{P(N + 1)}$$

where M = number of payment periods in 1 year
  N = number of scheduled payments
  C = finance charges in dollars (dollar cost of credit)
  P = original proceeds

The *direct-ratio method* uses a somewhat more complex formula but is still easier than the actuarial method. It slightly understates the APR as compared to the actuarial method. The direct-ratio formula is

$$APR = \frac{6MC}{3P(N + 1) + C(N + 1)}$$

The *N-ratio method* gives a much more accurate approximation to the APR than either the constant-ratio or the direct-ratio method for most loans. The results of the *N*-ratio method may be either slightly higher or lower than the true rate, depending on the maturity of the loan and the stated rate itself. The *N*-ratio formula is

$$APR = \frac{M(95N + 9)C}{12N(N + 1)(4P + C)}$$

SOLVED PROBLEM 8.13

Assume you borrow $1,000 to be repaid in 12 equal monthly installments of $93.00 each for a finance charge of $116.00. What is the APR under each of the four methods? (Assume an annuity table or computer program gives an APR of 20.76 percent.)

SOLUTION

Actuarial method: The APR under this method is 20.76 percent, obtained from an annuity table or computer program.

Constant-ratio method:

$$APR = \frac{2MC}{P(N + 1)}$$
$$= \frac{2 \times 12 \times 116}{1,000(12 + 1)} = \frac{2,784}{13,000} = 21.42\%$$

Direct-ratio method:

$$APR = \frac{6MC}{3P(N + 1) + C(N + 1)}$$
$$= \frac{6 \times 12 \times 116}{3 \times 1,000(12 + 1) + 116(12 + 1)} = \frac{8,352}{40,508} = 20.62\%$$

N-ratio method:

$$APR = \frac{M(95N + 9)C}{12N(N + 1)(4P + C)}$$

$$= \frac{12 \times (95 \times 12 + 9) \times 116}{12 \times 12 \times 13 \times [4(1,000) + 116]} = \frac{1,599,408}{7,705,152} = 20.76\%$$

These approximation formulas should not be used if there is any variation in the amounts of payments or in the time periods between payments—for example, balloon payments or extended first payment loans. Note that some lenders charge fees for a credit investigation, a loan application, or for life insurance. When these fees are required, the lender must include them in addition to the finance charge in dollars as part of the APR calculations.

SOLVED PROBLEM 8.14

Bank A offers a 7 percent car loan if you put 25 percent down. Therefore, if you buy a $4,000 auto you will finance $3,000 over a 3-year period with carrying charges amounting to $630 (7% × $3,000 × 3 years). You will make equal monthly payments of $100.83 for 36 months.

Bank B will lend $3,500 on the same car. You must pay $90 per month for 48 months. Which of the above quotes offers the best deal? (Use the constant-ratio formula.)

SOLUTION

The APR calculations (using the constant-ratio formula) follow:

Bank A:

$$APR = \frac{2 \times 12 \times 630}{3,000(36 + 1)} = \frac{15,120}{111,000} = 13.62\%$$

Bank B:

$$APR = \frac{2 \times 12 \times 820}{3,500(48 + 1)} = \frac{19,680}{171,500} = 11.48\%$$

In the case of Bank B, it was necessary to multiply $90 × 48 months to arrive at a total cost of $4,320. Therefore, the total credit cost is $820 ($4,320 − $3,500).

Based on the APR, you should choose Bank B over Bank A.

IS IT A GOOD IDEA TO OBTAIN A HOME EQUITY LOAN?

Under the Tax Reform Act of 1986, interest incurred on your first and second homes is deductible for tax purposes. However, limitations exist on the deductibility of other types of interest—especially, interest on consumer loans, which is being phased out completely. As a result, you should convert your consumer loan interest to interest on a home equity loan in order to continue the full tax-deductibility of your interest expenses. The home equity loan comes in two forms: a second trust deed (mortgage) and a line of credit.

Second trust deed. A second trust deed is similar to a first trust deed (mortgage), except that in the event of foreclosure, the holder of the first mortgage has priority in payment over the holder of the second mortgage.

Line of credit. Under the line of credit provision for an equity loan, you may write a check when you need funds. You are charged with interest only on the amount borrowed.

Before you join the rush to a home equity loan, you should consider the pluses and minuses of the home equity loan.

ADVANTAGES OF A HOME EQUITY LOAN

Low interest rates, because (*a*) the loan is secured by your house, and (*b*) it usually bears variable rates.

No loan processing fees. You do not have to go through a loan application and incur fees each time you borrow money.

Convenience. You may write a check only when you need money. You are charged interest only on the amount borrowed.

DISADVANTAGES OF A HOME EQUITY LOAN

High points. Points imposed on an equity loan are based on the amount of the credit line, not on the amount actually borrowed.

Many home equity loans have no caps on interest rates.

Long payback period. It is convenient to have to pay a small minimum amount each month, but stretching out the loan payback period usually means higher interest rates over the period.

High balloon payments. Some loans require a large balloon payment of the principal at the end of the loan period.

Risk of home loss. Unlike other loans, you risk losing your home. You may not be so lucky to sell your home fast enough and at a fair market price to be able to meet the balloon.

Frivolous spending habit. You may get into the habit of spending on unnecessary things. Use home equity loans very conservatively. You may easily end up borrowing up to the limit and struggling through each month with heavy repayment burden. Don't forget: Your home—and the equity it represents—is probably your biggest investment. Anything borrowed against it must be repaid upon its sale. You could lose your home if your equity line becomes greater than your ability to pay it back.

Recommendation: You should shop around and carefully compare the various equity loan alternatives in terms of each of the above pitfalls. You could obtain a traditional second trust deed.

SHOULD YOU PAY OFF YOUR LOAN EARLY?

Most lenders allow you to pay off a loan before its scheduled maturity without prepayment penalty. In fact, they will refund your interest charges. The question then is: How early should you pay off your loan? The key is that you should know your interest savings prior to a prepayment decision, because you might be better off investing the funds elsewhere rather than prepaying the loan. You might think you save an equal amount of interest each month.

Unfortunately, lenders compute interest differently. They use the rule of 78—sometimes called the "sum of the digits," which results in your paying more interest in the beginning of a loan when you have the use of more of the money, and less and less interest as the debt is reduced. Therefore, it is important to know how much interest you can save by repaying after a certain month and how much you still owe on the loan.

SOLVED PROBLEM 8.15

You borrow $3,180 ($3,000 principal and $180 interest) for 12 months, so your equal monthly payment is $265 ($3,180/12). You want to know how much interest you save by prepaying after six payments.

SOLUTION

You might guess $90 ($180 $\times \frac{6}{12}$), reasoning that interest is charged uniformly each month. Good guess, but wrong. Here is how the rule of 78 works:

First, add up all the digits for the number of payments scheduled to be made, in this case the sum of the digits 1 through 12 ($1 + 2 + 3 + \cdots + 12 = 78$). Generally, you can find the sum of the digits (SD) using the following formula:

$$SD = \frac{n(n + 1)}{2} = \frac{12(12 + 1)}{2} = \frac{(12)(13)}{2} = \frac{156}{2} = 78$$

where $n =$ the number of months. {The sum of the digits for a 4-year (48-month) loan is 1,176 $[(48)(48 + 1)/2 = (48)(49)/2 = 1,176].$}

Refer to Table 8-1 (Loan Amortization Schedule).

In the first month, before making any payments, you have the use of the entire amount borrowed. You thus pay 12/78ths (or 15.39 percent) of the total interest in the first payment. In the second month, you pay 11/78ths (14.10 percent); in the third, 10/78ths (12.82 percent); and so on down to the last payment, 1/78ths (1.28 percent). Thus, the first month's total payment of $265 contains $27.69 (15.39% × $180) in interest and $237.31 ($265 − $27.69) in principal. The twelfth and last payment of $265 contains $2.30 (1.28% × $180) in interest and $262.70 in principal.

Table 8-1   Loan Amortization Schedule
[Based on a loan of $3,180 ($3,000 principal and $180 interest)]

Payment Number	Fraction (Percent) Earned by Lender	Monthly Payment	Interest	Principal
1	$\frac{12}{78}$ (15.39%)	$ 265	$ 27.69*	$ 237.31†
2	$\frac{11}{78}$ (14.10%)	265	25.39	239.61
3	$\frac{10}{78}$ (12.82%)	265	23.08	241.92
4	$\frac{9}{78}$ (11.54%)	265	20.77	244.23
5	$\frac{8}{78}$ (10.26%)	265	18.46	246.54
6	$\frac{7}{78}$ (8.97%)	265	16.15	248.85
7	$\frac{6}{78}$ (7.69%)	265	13.85	251.15
8	$\frac{5}{78}$ (6.41%)	265	11.54	253.46
9	$\frac{4}{78}$ (5.13%)	265	9.23	255.77
10	$\frac{3}{78}$ (3.85%)	265	6.92	258.08
11	$\frac{2}{78}$ (2.56%)	265	4.62	260.38
12	$\frac{1}{78}$ (1.28%)	265	2.30	262.70
78	$\frac{78}{78}$ (100%)	$3,180	$180.00	$ 3,000.00

*$27.69 = $180.00 × $\frac{12}{78}$ (15.39%)
†$237.31 = $265 − $27.69

In order to find out how much interest is saved by prepaying after the sixth payment, you merely add up the digits for the remaining six payments. Thus, using the above formula, 6(6 + 1)/2 = 21. This means that 21/78ths of the interest, or $48.46 ($\frac{21}{78}$ × $180), will be saved.

To calculate the amount of principal still owed, subtract the total amount of interest already paid, $131.54($180 − $48.46), from the total amount of payments made, $1,590 (6 × $265), giving $1,458.46. Then subtract this from the original $3,000 principal, giving $1,541.54 still owed.

Does it pay to pay off after the sixth payment? It depends on how much return you can get from investing elsewhere. In this example, you needed $1,541.54 to pay off the loan to save $48.46 in interest.

Note: For loans of longer maturities, the same rules apply, though the actual sum of the digits will be different. Thus, for a 48-month loan, in the first month you would pay 48/1,176ths of the total interest, in the second month, 47/1,176ths, and so on.

BANKRUPTCY LAW

A legal process, bankruptcy, is available for individuals who are overextended financially and are unable to pay their debts. They can file for bankruptcy in order to seek to legally eliminate some or all of their debts.

Under Chapter 7 of the Bankruptcy Law, often called *straight bankruptcy,* the intent is to liquidate assets to pay the debts. Should this method be elected, the bankrupt can claim certain property as "exempt" and this property can be retained to preserve the basic necessities of life (such as a certain amount of equity in their home, economical car, and personal clothing and effects). Once a person has declared bankruptcy, he or she cannot be discharged from debts again for 6 years.

Under Chapter 13, often called *wage-earner plans,* the assets are not liquidated. Instead, interest and late charges are eliminated and arrangements are made to pay off some or all of the debts over several years.

Note that bankruptcy will not discharge all the debts. Debts that cannot be eliminated through bankruptcy proceedings include income taxes, child support, alimony, student loans, and debts incurred under false pretenses. Bankruptcy should not be taken lightly. Be sure to consult an attorney on various decisions surrounding the issue and on how to get the greatest benefit from the new financial start.

Review Questions

(1) When you shop for a credit card, you have to compare interest rate and annual fees, _____, transaction fees, and other fees and charges.

(2) After you have totaled your monthly debt obligations, figure out the percentage of your take-home pay that they represent. If it is higher than _____ percent, you are in danger of credit overload.

(3) There are about 2,000 _____ around the country, serving as a clearinghouse for information about consumers' debts and their debt-paying habits.

(4) There are three methods to establish debt limits: the disposable income, _____, and continuous debt methods.

(5) Under the _____ method you should keep monthly consumer debt payments down to around 15 percent of your disposable personal income.

(6) Always pay off the _____-interest loans first.

(7) Advantages of buying on credit include _____, emergency use, _____, ease of returning merchandise, and no charge for credit.

(8) Credits on open accounts are often known as _____.

(9) Examples of bank credit cards are _____ and _____.

(10) There are four basic methods to calculate finance charges: _____, _____, _____, and _____.

(11) In practice, to determine the monthly loan payment, _____ are widely used.

(12) You can determine the cost of credit in two ways: _____ and _____.

(13) The lender is required by the _____ to disclose to a borrower the effective annual percentage rate.

(14) The _____ loan is to be paid in full on a given date.

(15) The _____ is considered the most accurate method of calculating the APR.

(16) The home equity loan comes in two forms: _____ and _____.

(17) _____ is often called straight bankruptcy.

(18) Debts that cannot be eliminated through bankruptcy proceedings include _____, child support, alimony, student loans, and debts incurred under false pretenses.

(19) *Women's Credit Right* is published by _____.

Answers: (1) grace periods; (2) 20; (3) credit bureaus; (4) ratio of debts to equity; (5) disposable income; (6) high; (7) convenience, inflationary protection; (8) charge accounts; (9) MasterCard, Visa; (10) the previous balance method, the average daily balance method, the adjusted balance method, the past due balance method; (11) finance tables; (12) total dollars, annual percentage rate; (13) Truth-in-Lending Act; (14) single-payment; (15) actuarial method; (16) second trust deed, line of credit; (17) Chapter 7; (18) income taxes; (19) Bankcard Holders of America.

Additional Solved Problems

8.1   Rob has a monthly take-home pay of $2,500 and average total monthly consumer credit payments of $625.

   (a)   Calculate Rob's debt safety ratio.

   (b)   Can Rob increase his monthly credit expenditures? Should he reduce his monthly credit expenditures?

   SOLUTION

   (a)

$$\text{Debt safety ratio} = \frac{\text{Total monthly consumer credit payments}}{\text{Monthly take-home pay}}$$

$$= \frac{\$625}{\$2,500}$$

$$= .25 \text{ or } 25\%$$

   (b)   The guideline for consumer credit levels recommends that the maximum debt safety ratio should not exceed 20 percent. Since Bill's exceeds 20 percent, he should probably reduce his expenditures.

8.2   The McDonalds have a monthly take-home pay of $4,200. The monthly installment payments are as follows: furniture, $87, credit cards, $247, sedan, $234, and station wagon, $150.

   (a)   Calculate the McDonalds' debt safety ratio.

   (b)   The McDonalds' plan to buy a third car for their son costing $200. What will their new debt safety ratio be?

SOLUTION

(a) Their total current monthly debt payments are $718 ($87 + $247 + $234 + $150). The debt safety ratio is 17.1 percent ($718/$4,200).

(b) The new debt safety ratio will be 21.9 percent ($918/$4,200).

8.3 The Parkers have take-home pay of $2,800 per month. They are paying $350 per month on a car loan. Other monthly credit payments include $200 for charge accounts and $150 for another car loan. What is their credit use situation?

SOLUTION

The total credit payments for the Parkers are $350 + $200 + $150 = $700. The amount equals 25 percent ($700/$2,800) of their monthly take-home pay. Using the 20 percent rule here, it appears that they are overextended.

8.4 The Saigals have a monthly take-home income of $5,600. Their monthly credit payments equal $1,100 per month. They are planning to lease a fancy car that would require monthly payments of $399 per month. Would you suggest they buy the new car?

SOLUTION

Using the 20 percent rule, they should not exceed $1,120 ($5,600 × 20%). With the car purchase, their monthly payments would be $1,499 ($1,100 + $399) per month, which would overextend them. They could lease a cheaper car or try to reduce their other credit payments.

8.5 The Johnsons own $54,000 in assets and have $30,000 in liabilities.

(a) What is their debt/equity ratio?

(b) Should they take out more debts?

SOLUTION

(a) The Johnsons' equity (net worth) = assets − liabilities = $54,000 − $30,000 = $24,000. Hence, their debt/equity ratio = $30,000/$24,000 = 1.25.

(b) No, since their ratio is greater than 1 (that is, their debts exceed equity).

8.6 Robert Barker has a monthly take-home pay of $1,200; he makes a monthly payment of $250 on his outstanding consumer credit (excluding the mortgage on his home). How would you characterize Robert's debt burden? What if his take-home pay were $850 a month and his monthly credit payments $90?

SOLUTION

If Barker makes payments of $250 and his take-home pay is $1,200, his debt safety ratio is $250/$1,200 = .21 or 21 percent, which is slightly above the maximum allowable limit and Robert should be cautious about incurring any more debt before he pays off his current obligations.

If his take-home pay was $850 and his payments were $90 per month, his debt safety ratio would be $90/$850 = .11 or 11 percent, which is well within the recommended guidelines and is even considered low.

8.7 Calculate the APR for a $1,000, 14 percent, 18-month single-payment loan using

(a) The simple interest method

(b) The discount method

SOLUTION

The finance charge = $1,000 × 14% = $140.00.

(a)   APR = $140/$1,000 = 14%

(b)   APR = $140/($1,000 − $140) = $140/$860 = 16.28%

8.8   Bank A will lend Thomas Sparks $4,000 for 12 months through a single-payment loan at $13\frac{1}{2}$ percent *discount,* while Bank B offers the same loan at 15 percent simple interest. Which loan should Sparks choose?

SOLUTION

APR on the Bank A loan is calculated as

$$APR = \frac{\$4,000 \times 13.5\%}{\$4,000 - \$540} = \frac{\$540}{\$3,460} = 15.6\%$$

APR on the Bank B loan is

$$APR = \frac{\$4,000 \times 15\%}{\$4,000} = \frac{\$600}{\$4,000} = 15\%$$

Sparks should borrow the money from Bank B since the APR is lower.

8.9   A washing machine is listed for cash sale at $239. It may be bought for $39 down and nine monthly installments of $25. What is the annual percentage rate, using the constant-ratio formula?

SOLUTION

$$\text{Principal} = \$239 - \$39 = \$200$$

Interest charge:

$$\$25 \times 9 \text{ months} = \$225 \qquad \$225 - \$200 = \$25$$

Using the constant-ratio formula:

$$APR = \frac{2 \times 12 \times 25}{200(9 + 1)} = \frac{600}{2,000} = 30\%$$

8.10   Kris Kringel borrowed $1,000 to be repaid in 12 monthly installments of $91.67.

(a)   How much interest would be paid on this loan?

(b)   What is the APR using the constant-ratio method?

(c)   If simple interest were charged at an annual rate of 10 percent on the outstanding balance, what is the APR on this loan?

SOLUTION

(a)   Total payments = $91.67 × 12 months = $1,100

$$\text{Interest} = \$1,100 - \$1,000 = \$100$$

(b)   *Constant-ratio method:*

$$APR = \frac{2MC}{P(N + 1)}$$

$$= \frac{2 \times 12 \times 100}{1,000(12 + 1)} = \frac{2,400}{13,000} = 18.46\%$$

(c)
$$\text{Finance charge} = \$1,000 \times 10\% = \$100$$

$$\text{APR} = \frac{\$100}{\$1,000} = 10\%$$

8.11   Daniel Weil needs $3,000 for 3 years. Bank X offers a 36-month loan that is to be repaid with monthly payments of $108. Bank Y offers a 42-month loan with monthly payments of $94.

(a)   What is the total interest charge for each of the two loans?

(b)   What are the APRs for each loan? (Use the constant-ratio method.)

(c)   Which loan should Weil choose?

SOLUTION

(a)

	BANK X	BANK Y
Total payments	$3,888 ($108 × 36)	$3,948 ($94 × 42)
Loan amount	3,000	3,000
Interest	$ 888	$ 948

(b)   Using the constant-ratio method:

$$\text{APR} = \frac{2MC}{P(N+1)}$$

Bank X:

$$\text{APR} = \frac{2 \times 12 \times 888}{3,000(36+1)} = \frac{21,312}{111,000} = 19.2\%$$

Bank Y:

$$\text{APR} = \frac{2 \times 12 \times 948}{3,000(42+1)} = \frac{22,752}{129,000} = 17.64\%$$

(c)   Weil should borrow at Bank Y since it has the lower APR.

8.12   Jennifer Hardie plans to borrow $5,000 to be repaid in 36 monthly installments. A 13 percent interest is applied using the add-on method.

(a)   What is the total interest charge? (Assume that the interest charge is the only finance charge).

(b)   What is the monthly payment on this loan?

(c)   What is the approximate APR on this loan using the constant-ratio method, the direct-ratio method, and the *N*-ratio method?

SOLUTION

(a) $$\text{Finance charge} = \$5,000 \times 13\% \times 3 \text{ years} = \$1,950$$

(b)   The monthly loan payment is $193.06.

$$\frac{\$5,000 + \$1,950}{36 \text{ months}} = \frac{\$6,950}{36} = \$193.06$$

(c)   Note that $M = 12$, $C = \$1,950$, $P = \$5,000$, and $N = 36$.

Constant-ratio method:

$$APR = \frac{2MC}{P(N + 1)}$$

$$= \frac{2 \times 12 \times 1,950}{5,000(36 + 1)} = \frac{46,800}{185,000} = 25.30\%$$

Direct-ratio method:

$$APR = \frac{6MC}{3P(N + 1) + C(N + 1)}$$

$$= \frac{6 \times 12 \times 1,950}{3 \times 5,000(36 + 1) + 1,950(36 + 1)} = \frac{140,400}{623,250} = 22.53\%$$

N-ratio method:

$$APR = \frac{M(95N + 9)C}{12N(N + 1)(4P + C)}$$

$$= \frac{12 \times (95 \times 36 + 9) \times 1,950}{12 \times 36 \times 37[4(5,000) + 1,950]} = \frac{80,238,600}{350,848,800} = 22.87\%$$

8.13   Walter Helicks is 22 years old. He knows he will receive a $10,000 inheritance on his twenty-fifth birthday. He would like to borrow now to go to law school through a $10,000 discount method single-payment loan for 3 years. He can get such a loan at a 10 percent discount method interest rate.

(a)   How much will Walter actually receive now?

(b)   What is the total interest charge?

(c)   How much will he repay in 3 years?

(d)   What is the APR of the loan?

SOLUTION

(a) $7,000 ($10,000 − $3,000)

(b) $3,000 ($10,000 × 10% × 3 years)

(c) $10,000

(d)   APR = 14.29% ($1,000/$7,000)

8.14   Lori Goldman can obtain an 8 percent add-on interest rate installment loan to build a swimming pool in her backyard. She will need to borrow $7,500 and repay it over 4 years in monthly installments. The loan will also require a $100 filing fee and a $50 credit check fee payable at the time the contract is signed.

(a)   What is her finance charge in dollars?

(b)   What is the APR of the loan using the constant-ratio formula?

(c)   What is the APR of the loan using the *N*-ratio formula?

(d)   What is the monthly payment on the loan?

SOLUTION

(a)   Total finance charge = Interest charge + Filing fee + Credit check fee

$2,550 = ($7,500 × 8% × 4 years) + $100 + $50

(b) *Constant-ratio method:*

$$APR = \frac{2MC}{P(N + 1)}$$

$$= \frac{2 \times 12 \times 2,550}{7,500(48 + 1)} = \frac{61,200}{367,500} = 16.65\%$$

(c) *N-ratio method:*

$$APR = \frac{M(95N + 9)C}{12N(N + 1)(4P + C)}$$

$$= \frac{12 \times (95 \times 48 + 9) \times 2,550}{12 \times 48 \times 49[4(7,500) + 2,550]} = \frac{13,981,140}{91,869,120} = 15.22\%$$

(d) $208.33 ($10,000/48)

8.15 The Honigs have borrowed $5,000 at 12 percent simple interest for 1 year. Calculate the APR for this loan using each of the three following methods:

(a) Simple interest method

(b) Discount method

(c) Add-on methods: constant-ratio method and *N*-ratio method

SOLUTION

(a) Simple interest method:

$$12\% = \frac{\$600}{\$5,000}$$

(b) Discount method:

$$13.63\% = \frac{\$600}{\$5,000 - \$600}$$

(c) Add-on methods:

Constant-ratio method:

$$APR = \frac{2MC}{P(N + 1)}$$

$$= \frac{2 \times 12 \times 600}{5,000(12 + 1)} = \frac{14,400}{65,000} = 22.15\%$$

N-ratio method:

$$APR = \frac{M(95N + 9)C}{12N(N + 1)(4P + C)}$$

$$= \frac{12 \times (95 \times 12 + 9) \times 600}{12 \times 48 \times 49[4(7,500) + 600]} = \frac{8,272,800}{38,563,200} = 21.45\%$$

8.16 Calculate the payment necessary at the maturity date of the following single-payment notes using the simple interest method.

	PRINCIPAL	INTEREST RATE	TERM OF LOAN
(a)	$1,000	5%	3 years
(b)	5,000	7%	5 years
(c)	7,000	10%	10 years

SOLUTION

$$\text{Finance charge} = p \times r \times t$$

where p = principal amount of loan
   r = stated annual rate of interest
   t = term of loan stated in years

(a)

$$\$1,000 \times .05 \times 3 = \$150$$

Principal amount + Finance charge = Total payment due at the maturity date

$$\$1,000 + \$150 = \$1,150$$

(b)

$$\$5,000 \times .07 \times 5 = \$1,750$$

$$\$5,000 + \$1,750 = \$6,750$$

(c)

$$\$7,000 \times .10 \times 10 = \$7,000$$

$$\$7,000 + \$7,000 = \$14,000$$

8.17 Calculate the finance charge and the annual percentage rate on the following single-payment loans using the discount method.

	PRINCIPAL	INTEREST RATE	TERM OF LOAN
(a)	$ 7,500	8%	2 years
(b)	5,000	9%	1 year
(c)	12,000	10%	3 years

SOLUTION

(a)

$$p \times r \times t = \$7,500 \times .08 \times 2 = \$1,200$$

$$\text{APR} = \frac{\text{Average annual finance charges}}{\text{Average loan balance outstanding}}$$

$$\text{Average annual finance charges} = \frac{\$1,200}{2} = \$600$$

$$\text{Average loan balance outstanding} = \$7,500 - \$1,200 = \$6,300$$

$$\text{Annual interest} = \$600 \qquad (8\% \times \$7,500)$$

$$\text{APR} = \frac{\$600}{\$6,300} = 9.5\%$$

(b)

$$\$5,000 \times .09 \times 1 = \$450$$

$$\text{APR} = \frac{450}{\$5,000 - \$450} = \frac{\$450}{\$4,550} = 9.9\%$$

(c)

$$\$12,000 \times .10 \times 3 = \$3,600$$

$$\text{Annual interest} = \$1,200 \qquad (10\% \times \$12,000)$$

$$\text{APR} = \frac{\$1,200}{\$12,000 - \$3,600} = \frac{\$1,200}{\$8,400} = 14.3\%$$

8.18   Calculate the finance charge and the monthly payment on a $15,500 add-on installment loan with an interest rate of 7.5 percent and a term of 2 years.

SOLUTION

$$p \times r \times t = \$15,500 \times .075 \times 2 = \$2,325$$

$$\text{Monthly payments} = \frac{\$15,500 + \$2,325}{24} = \$742.71$$

8.19   Compare the total finance charges on the two loans described below:

Loan 1: A simple interest installment loan to be repaid in monthly payments at a 9 percent stated interest rate, $10,000 principal value, and a 1-year maturity term.

Loan 2: An add-on installment loan to be repaid in monthly payments at a 9 percent stated interest rate, $10,000 principal value, and a 1-year maturity term.

SOLUTION

Loan 1:   The monthly payment is $874.60.

$$\frac{\$10,000}{\$1,000} \times 87.46 = \$874.60$$

$$12 \text{ payments} \times \$874.60 = \$10,495.20$$

$$\$10,495.20 - \$10,000 = \$495.20 \qquad \text{interest}$$

Loan 2:

$$p \times r \times t = \$10,000 \times .09 \times 1 = \$900 \text{ interest}$$

The add-on method results in nearly double the interest paid over the term of the loan.

8.20   Calculate the APR for the following add-on loans with monthly installments, using the *N*-ratio method:

	PRINCIPAL	INTEREST RATE	TERM OF LOAN
(a)	$20,000	10%	2 years
(b)	15,000	9%	3 years
(c)	3,500	6%	5 years

SOLUTION

Using the *N*-ratio formula:

$$\text{APR} = \frac{M(95N + 9)C}{12N(N + 1)(4P + C)}$$

(a)

$$\text{APR} = \frac{12[95(24) + 9]\$4,000}{12(24)(24 + 1)[(4 \times \$20,000) + \$4,000]} = \frac{\$109,872,000}{\$604,800,000} = 18.2\%$$

(b)

$$\text{APR} = \frac{12[95(36) + 9]\$4,050}{12(36)(36 + 1)[(4 \times \$15,000) + \$4,050]} = \frac{\$166,649,400}{\$1,023,775,200} = 16.3\%$$

(c)

$$\text{APR} = \frac{12[95(60) + 9]\$1,050}{12(60)(60 + 1)[(4 \times \$3,500) + \$1,050]} = \frac{\$71,933,400}{\$660,996,000} = 10.9\%$$

8.21 Robin Fisher purchased a new car and after all charges and trade-in allowances he had an unpaid balance of $15,000. He arranged a loan at 12 percent for the $15,000 to be paid back in 5 years with monthly installment payments of $333.67.

(a) How much will he pay back?

(b) What is the total interest charge?

(c) What rate of interest is Robin actually paying? Use the constant-ratio formula.

SOLUTION

(a) $333.67 (monthly payments) × 60 months = $20,020

(b) $20,020 (total amount due) − $15,000 = $5,020, interest charge

(c)

$$\text{APR} = \frac{2 \times 12 \times 5,020}{15,000(60 + 1)} = \frac{120,480}{915,000} = 13.17\%$$

He is actually paying a rate of 13.17 percent.

8.22 David Davidson has an overdraft protection line. His October 1990 statement showed a latest (new) balance of $862. If the line had a minimum monthly payment requirement of 5 percent of the latest balance (round to the nearest $5 figure), what would be the minimum amount he would have to pay on his overdraft protection line?

SOLUTION

$862 × .05 = $43.10 or $45 when rounded to the nearest $5 figure.

8.23 Ron Jaffe has a balance of $380 on his retail charge card. If the store levies a finance charge of 21 percent per annum, how much monthly interest will be added to Ron's account?

SOLUTION

$$\$380\left(\frac{21\%}{12}\right) = \$380 \times 1.75\% = \$6.65$$

This calculation assumes that the balance was computed by either the previous balance method, the average daily balance method, or the adjusted balance method. If finance charges are calculated on the past due balance method and the $380 is not past due, then there would be no interest charge if Ron pays off the entire $380.

8.24 Cornell Givens wants to borrow $2,500 to buy a used car for his teenage son. His bank will lend him the money through a 24-month installment loan at 15 percent simple interest. Alternatively, he can borrow the money at Friendly Finance with a 24-month installment loan at 10 percent add-on.

(a) Find the monthly payments, total finance charges, and APR on these two loans (using the N-ratio method).

(b) Which loan would you recommend?

SOLUTION

(a) If Cornell borrows $2,500 for 24 months at 15 percent simple interest, the monthly payment (from Appendix Table 6) would be

$$\$48.49 \times \frac{\$2,500}{\$1,000} = \$121.23$$

Total finance charges would be

$$(\$121.23 \times 24 \text{ payments}) - \$2,500 = \$409.52$$

Since this a simple installment loan, the APR is the same as the stated rate or 15 percent.

If Cornell borrows the money from the finance company at a 10 percent add-on rate for 24 months the monthly payment would be calculated after the finance charges:

$$\text{Finance charges} = \$2,500 \times .10 \times 2 = \$500$$

$$\text{Monthly payment} = \frac{\$2,500 + \$500}{24} = \frac{\$3,000}{24} = \$125$$

Using the N-ratio method, the APR is

$$\text{APR} = \frac{M(95N + 9)C}{MN(N + 1)(4P + C)}$$

$$= \frac{12 \times (95 \times 24 + 9) \times \$500}{12 \times 24 \times (24 + 1)[(4 \times \$2,500) + \$500]} = \frac{\$13,734,000}{\$75,600,000} = 18.17\%$$

(b)   The first bank loan is the better one because it has a lower APR.

8.25   Assuming that interest is the only finance charge, how much interest would be paid on a $500 installment loan to be repaid in 6 monthly installments of $87.02? If simple interest were charged at an annual rate of 15 percent on the outstanding balance, how much would the APR be on this loan? Explain.

SOLUTION

If the installment loan contract calls for a monthly payment of $87.02 for 6 months, the total payback would be $87.02 × 6 = $522.12. Therefore, $522.12 − $500.00 gives a balance of $22.12 that is set aside for interest. Since the interest is charged only on the outstanding balance of the loan, the annual percentage rate (APR) of interest on the installment loan determined by the simple interest method equals the stated rate, 15 percent.

8.26   Calculate the monthly installment loan payment for the following simple interest loans:

(a)   12 months, 10%, $25,000

(b)   24 months, 15%, $10,000

(c)   48 months, 8%, $5,000

SOLUTION

Using Appendix Table 6, we obtain

(a)   ($25,000/$1,000) × 87.92 = $2,198

(b)   ($10,000/$1,000) × 48.49 = $484.90

(c)   ($5,000/$1,000) × 24.42 = $122.10

8.27   Find the monthly payments and total finance charges on each of the following simple interest installment loans:

(a)   Borrow $3,600 at 12 percent for 48 months.

(b)   Borrow $10,000 at $10\frac{1}{2}$ percent for 5 years.

(c)   Borrow $750 at 15 percent for 12 months.

SOLUTION

Monthly payments are found in Appendix Table 6.

(a)   26.34 × 3.6 = $94.82. The total finance charges would be a total payment of $94.82 × 48 = $4,551.36 less the amount borrowed of $3,600. $4,551.36 − $3,600.00 = $951.36 total finance charge.

(b) $21.50 × 10 = $215.00. The total finance charges would be a total payment of $215 × 60 months = $12,900 less the amount borrowed of $10,000. $12,900 − $10,000 = $2,900 total finance charge.

(c) $90.26 × .75 = $67.70. The total finance charges would be a total payment of $67.70 × 12 months = $812.40 less the amount borrowed of $750. $812.40 − $750.00 = $62.40 total finance charge.

8.28 Janet Lynn's revolving credit card statement reveals the following for the month of June:
Billing date: June 30
Previous balance (May 31): $600

Transactions	Charges	Amount
6/5	Purchase	$ 80
6/10	Payment	200
6/15	Purchase	100
6/30	Purchase	50
New balance		630

Interest Rate 1.5% per month or 18% APR.

Compute the monthly finance charge for her statement using the

(a) Previous balance method

(b) Average daily balance method

(c) Adjusted balance method

SOLUTION

(a) Previous balance method:

$$\$600 × .015 = \$9.00$$

(b) Average daily balance method: Average daily balance is

Period	Number of days	Balance		Weighted Balance
6/1–6/4	4	$600		$ 2,400
6/5–6/9	5	680	($600 + $80)	3,400
6/10–6/14	5	480	($680 − $200)	2,400
6/15–6/29	15	580	($480 + $100)	8,700
6/30	1	630	($580 + $50)	630
Total	30			$17,530

Average daily balance:
$$\frac{\$17,530}{30 \text{ days}} = \$584.33$$

$$\$584.33 × 1.5\% = \$8.76$$

(c) Adjusted balance method:

$$\$600 + \$230 − \$200 = \$630$$

$$\$630 × .015 = \$9.45$$

8.29 Francine's bank credit card statement is shown for the month of July.

Billing date: July 31

Previous balance (June 30): $315.25

Transactions	Charges	Amount
7/2	Sam's Supermarket	$ 75.89
7/5	Longs Drug	29.40
7/10	Claim Jumpers Deli	25.10
7/12	The Images	152.00
7/14	Super Cuts	45.00
7/20	Crown Bookstores	19.50
7/25	Buffum's	195.27
7/25	American Airlines	654.00
		$1,196.16
7/30	Payment	500.00

Interest rate 1.5 percent per month or 18 percent APR.

Compute the monthly finance charge for her statement using the

(*a*)   Previous balance method

(*b*)   Average daily balance method

(*c*)   Adjusted balance method

SOLUTION

(*a*)   Previous balance method:

$$\$315.25 + \$1,196.16 = \$1,511.41$$

$$\$1,511.41 \times .015 = \$22.67$$

(*b*)   Average daily balance method:

7/1	$315.25	7/16	$ 642.64
7/2	391.14	7/17	642.64
7/3	391.14	7/18	642.64
7/4	391.14	7/19	642.64
7/5	420.54	7/20	662.14
7/6	420.54	7/21	662.14
7/7	420.54	7/22	662.14
7/8	420.54	7/23	662.14
7/9	420.54	7/24	662.14
7/10	445.64	7/25	1,511.41
7/11	445.64	7/26	1,511.41
7/12	597.64	7/27	1,511.41
7/13	597.64	7/28	1,511.41
7/14	642.64	7/29	1,511.41
7/15	642.64	7/30	1,011.41

(*c*)   Adjusted balance method:

$$\$315.25 + \$1,196.16 - \$500 = \$1,011.41$$

$$\$1,011.41 \times .015 = \$15.17$$

8.30 Brian Barrison borrowed $4,000 at a 9 percent add-on rate to be repaid in 36 monthly payments. What is the amount the lender will receive using the rule of 78 if Brian repays the loan after 3 months? What is the "payoff" on the loan at that time?

SOLUTION

The total finance charge = $4,000 × 9% × 3 years = $1,080. Monthly payment = ($4,000 + $1,080)/ 36 months = $5,080/36 = $141.11. The interest factor for 3 months by the rule of 78 is

$$\frac{36 + 35 + 34}{(36)(37)/2} = \frac{105}{666} = .1577$$

Total finance charges earned by the lender in the 3-month period is

$$\$1,080 \times .1577 = \$170.32$$

To calculate the loan payoff

Principal	$5,080.00	
Less: Refund to borrower	909.79	($1,080 − $170.21)
	$4,170.21	
Less: Payments to date	510.63	($170.21 × 3 months)
Loan payoff	$3,659.58	

8.31 Paula Baez takes out a 3-month loan for $500. The monthly interest rate is 1.5 percent. Paula repays the loan with monthly payments of $171.69 each.

(*a*) Set up a loan amortization schedule.

(*b*) Paula wants to repay the loan after the first payment. How much of a refund will Paula receive? Interest will be refunded by the rule of 78.

SOLUTION

(*a*) The loan amortization schedule follows:

MONTH	BEGINNING BALANCE	MONTHLY PAYMENT	INTEREST	PRINCIPAL	ENDING BALANCE
0	$500.00	—	—	—	$500.00
1	500.00	$171.69	$ 7.50	$164.19	335.81
2	335.81	171.69	5.04	166.65	169.15
3	169.15	171.69	2.54	169.15	0.00
			$15.08		

Interest for month 1 is $500 × 1.5% = $7.50. Principal repayment in month 1 is $171.69 − $7.50 = $164.19.

(*b*) Interest charged for month 1 will be $3/(3 + 2 + 1) = \frac{3}{6}$. The refund will be $1 - \frac{3}{6} = \frac{3}{6} = \frac{1}{2}$, or $15.08 × $\frac{1}{2}$ = $7.54.

8.32 The Bakers take out a 5-month bank loan for $1,000. The APR is 24 percent. They will pay off the loan by making five equal monthly payments of $212.16.

(*a*) Set up a loan amortization schedule.

(*b*) What is the total amount of interest to be paid?

SOLUTION

(*a*)   The loan amortization schedule follows:

MONTH	BEGINNING BALANCE	MONTHLY PAYMENT	INTEREST	PRINCIPAL	ENDING BALANCE
0	$1,000.00	—	—	—	$1,000.00
1	1,000.00	$212.16	$20.00	$192.16	807.84
2	807.84	212.16	16.16	196.00	611.84
3	611.84	212.16	12.24	199.92	411.92
4	411.92	212.16	8.24	203.92	208.00
5	208.00	212.16	4.16	208.00	0.00
			$60.80		

Interest for month 1 is $1,000 × 2% = $20. Total interest paid on this loan is $60.80.

8.33   Carla Marchese takes out a $2,500, 15-month loan from a bank, which is to be repaid with monthly payments of $200. After making nine payments, she decides to pay off the loan. The bank uses the rule of 78 to refund finance charges. It also charges $25 as a prepayment penalty. Determine the loan payoff.

SOLUTION

The total finance charge = ($200 × 15) − $2,500 = $500. The interest factor for 9 months by the rule of 78 is

$$\frac{15 + 14 + 13 + \cdots + 9}{(15)(16)/2} = \frac{84}{120} = .7$$

Total finance charges earned by the lender in the 3-month period is $500 × .7 = $350.
To calculate the loan payoff

Principal	$2,500	
Less: Refund to borrower	150	($500 − $350)
	$2,350	
Less: Payments to date	1,800	($200 × 9 months)
Loan payoff	$ 550	

The loan payoff including a prepayment penalty will be $575 ($550 + $25).

8.34   Laura borrowed $7,500 to be repaid in 48 monthly installments; the loan was made at an add-on interest rate of 6 percent. If Laura repays the loan after 12 months, how much will the lender receive as the loan payoff?

SOLUTION

Total finance charges are

$$p \times r \times t = \$7,500 \times .06 \times 4 = \$1,800$$

Monthly payments are then

$$\frac{\$7,500 + \$1,800}{48} = \$193.75$$

$$\text{Sum of the digits} = \frac{N(N + 1)}{2} = \frac{(48)(49)}{2} = 1,176$$

The lender is entitled to $(48 + 47 + 46 + 45 + 44 + 43 + 42 + 41 + 40 + 39 + 38 + 37)/1,176 = .4337 \times$ total finance charges $= .4337 \times \$1,800 = \$780.66$.

Amount of loan including add-on finance charges	$9,300.00
Less: Interest refunded to borrower	1,019.34
Payments to date (12 × $193.75)	2,325.00
Loan payoff	$5,955.66

Chapter 9

How to Determine and Save on the Costs of Living

There are many ways to save on living costs. When you purchase an automobile, you must calculate its real cost and search for ways to cut operating costs. You might also want to decide whether to purchase or lease. You can also do something about the food budget. Clothing can be expensive but there are several things you can do about it. With the rocketing costs of health care, steps must be undertaken to control costs. Finally, marital status is an important ingredient in cost control.

WHAT CAN YOU DO TO REDUCE COSTS?

Sound financial planning and management requires you to develop weapons to protect against increasing costs. The ways to reduce living costs are

Shop for the best buy without forgetting quality.

Redeem manufacturer or store coupons.

Watch for "real" sales and specials.

Stock up when you can get good buys.

Buy through computerized on-line stores (electronic malls) such as CompuStore. These are accessed through telecommunications.

Look for good warranties, service, and return policies.

Buy low-maintenance items.

When making home repairs, obtain competitive bids from three contractors.

Buy generic brands rather than name brands.

Always pay your credit card balance on time because of the high finance charge.

Use direct dialing and make calls during "low rate" periods (for example, weekends).

Save on electric bills by turning off lights, heating, and air conditioning in unused rooms.

Change to less costly versions of higher cost goods and services (for example, use public transportation rather than an automobile).

Buy discounted gasoline, which is for the most part indistinguishable from advertised gasoline. Also use self-service rather than full-service.

Have a checking account at a bank that does not charge for checks and pays interest on the checking balance.

HOW CAN YOU SAVE MONEY ON AN AUTOMOBILE, BOAT, OR OTHER MAJOR ACQUISITION?

There are many ways to save on a major acquisition, such as an automobile or boat.

You may save money when buying a major asset by paying cash rather than buying on credit, which typically involves finance charges.

SOLVED PROBLEM 9.1

A store reduces the list price of a major appliance it carries by 8 percent if the total payment is made with cash. How much will the cost be to purchase an appliance having a retail price of $500 if you pay cash?

SOLUTION

$$\$500 \times .92 = \$460$$

Other merchants may permit a grace period to pay and still obtain a discount from the list price. In many instances, brand-name goods can be bought from a discount store for less than the retail price in a regular store.

SOLVED PROBLEM 9.2

You can buy a brand-name TV set that retails for $700 at the department store for $600 in a discount store. What is your percentage saving if you buy at the discount store?

SOLUTION

$$\text{Percentage saving} = \frac{\$100}{\$700} = 14.3\%$$

SOLVED PROBLEM 9.3

You can buy a major appliance at a discount store at 15 percent below the list price of $650 quoted by the manufacturer. How much can you save by buying the item at the discount store?

SOLUTION

$$\$650 \times 15\% = \$97.50$$

When a discount is offered for early payment on a major acquisition, it is usually financially advantageous to pay within the discount period to obtain the discount. For example, if the terms of purchase are 3/10, net/30, you get a 3 percent discount if you pay within 10 days. In any event, you have to pay for the item by the thirtieth day.

SOLVED PROBLEM 9.4

You buy an item costing $750 on terms of 2/10, net/30.

(a)   How much discount will you receive if you pay within 10 days?
(b)   What will you pay within the discount period?
(c)   How much will you have to pay if your payment is received in 15 days?

SOLUTION

(a) $750 × 2% = $15
(b) $750 − $15 = $735
(c) $750

Sometimes you have a choice of paying cash or buying on an installment plan. The installment plan typically costs more money, since you can pay the purchase out over a longer period.

SOLVED PROBLEM 9.5

You can buy a range for a cash price of $450 or buy it on an installment purchase plan paying $50 down and 12 monthly payments of $40. If you take out the installment plan, what is your extra cost?

SOLUTION

Installment plan [$50 + 12($40)]	$530
Cash payment	450
Extra cost	$ 80

SOLVED PROBLEM 9.6

You can buy furniture for $1,800 cash or on the installment plan by paying $900 down and $200 a month for 6 months. How much does the installment price exceed the cash price?

SOLUTION

Down payment	$ 900
Monthly payments (6 × $200)	1,200
Installment price	$2,100

The installment price ($2,100) exceeds the cash price ($1,800) by $300.

SOLVED PROBLEM 9.7

You bought a boat that was advertised at a cash price of $2,000 or on the installment plan for $800 down and $250 a month for 6 months. What is the installment charge?

SOLUTION

Down payment	$ 800
Monthly payment ($250 × 6)	1,500
Total payments	$2,300
Less: Cash price	2,000
Installment charge	$ 300

SOLVED PROBLEM 9.8

You can buy a TV set for $650 cash or on the installment plan by paying 20 percent additional. You elect to make an installment purchase and make a down payment of $180, with monthly payments of $50. How many months will it take to pay for the TV?

SOLUTION

Installment purchase ($650 × 1.20)	$780
Less: Down payment	180
Balance	$600

$$\frac{\text{Balance (\$600)}}{\text{Monthly payment (\$50)}} = 12 \text{ months}$$

SOLVED PROBLEM 9.9

You can buy a typewriter on the installment plan by either of two methods: (a) by making a $100 down payment and paying $5 a week for 100 weeks or (b) by making a $150 down payment and paying $20 a month for 24 months. Which plan is less costly?

SOLUTION

Weekly plan:	
Down payment	$100
Weekly payments ($5 × 100 weeks)	500
Total cost	$600

Monthly plan:	
Down payment	$150
Monthly payment ($20 × 24 months)	480
Total cost	$630

The weekly plan is $30 cheaper.

The guidelines in buying a major item are

Establish a maximum price you are willing to pay.

Find out about the quality of the major item (for example, refer to *Consumer Reports*).

Try to buy a major item the dealer has in stock for some time since he or she may want to readily sell it.

Compare prospective major items in terms of price and quality.

AUTOMOBILES

Determine the expected cost per mile driven for cars and boats (including gasoline).

Estimate the life of the car.

Be sure you can meet the monthly payments for credit purchases. *Rule of thumb:* The monthly payments for an auto should not be more than one-half of your monthly housing costs.

SOLVED PROBLEM 9.10

Your annual cost of housing is $5,000. What is the maximum you can afford to pay per month on an auto loan?

SOLUTION

$$\frac{\$5,000}{12} = \$417 \times 50\% = \$208.50$$

Estimate the trade-in value. For example, some autos have a better trade-in value than others. Cars that are standardized (same features) generally have a better resale value. Also, certain car options such as air conditioning boost the resale value of the vehicle.

Avoid buying options since the dealer markup on them is often two to three times the profit margin on the car or boat itself. Where practical, you may be able to have the options installed more cheaply at a discount auto supply store.

The areas to save money with an automobile are purchasing, financing, insuring, running, repairing, and selling.

The cost of automobile ownership depends upon the size of the car (affecting initial cost) and the number of years of use. For example, a subcompact may cost one-third less than a standard-size model. Savings in cost per mile can arise by purchasing a smaller, less expensive automobile and holding the car for a long time. It is much more expensive to buy a new car every year.

The annual operating costs of an automobile include gasoline, oil, tires, replacement parts, general maintenance, insurance, registration fees, and depreciation representing the difference between the original cost less the trade-in value divided by the number of years of use.

Expenses for an auto used for *business* purposes are tax deductible.

SOLVED PROBLEM 9.11

The total expenses of using your car for the year is $6,000 and 70 percent of the mileage is for business purposes.

(*a*)   What amount is tax-deductible?

(*b*)   If you are in the 28 percent tax bracket, what is the tax savings?

SOLUTION

(*a*) $6,000 \times 70\% = \$4,200$

(*b*) $4,200 \times 28\% = \$1,176$

Insurance coverage is about 20 percent of the overall auto expenditure for the year. Insurance rates are higher for young drivers in urban population centers.

Your insurance rates increase if you are under 25, have traffic violations, and accidents. Accidents may not cost you penalty points for insurance purposes if you were legally parked, reimbursed by the other driver, you were "hit" from the rear, the other driver was given a traffic summons but not you, there was a hit-and-run, etc.

The ways of reducing auto insurance costs are

Take an accredited driver education course (this may also reduce penalty points on a license in some states).

If the auto is more than 3 years old or worth less than $1,000, collision coverage may be dropped. You can never receive more than the car's cash value.

If you are over 65 years of age, numerous states will give you lower insurance rates.

Take out coverage for emergency towing. For a *minimal* premium, you are typically covered from $25 to $50 for towing charges.

Insurance discounts may be given if the auto possesses certain items, such as various types of bumpers, air bags, antitheft devices, antilock brakes, and child safety seat. A discount is also typically given for a "clean" driving record.

Do not file a collision claim when your loss is marginally above the deductible because insurance rates may go up.

If your child takes one of the cars to a college where accidents and thefts are less likely, a reduction in the premium may be given.

Chapter 11 discusses insurance in detail.

The ways to improve gas mileage and reduce costs are buy a small car since it involves less initial and later costs, uses less gasoline, and involves lower insurance premiums; drive economically (45 to 50 miles per hour); and use radial tires. It is usually cheaper to finance and insure the car separately, not from the car dealer.

Are you thinking of buying a used car? The best used car is one that is no more than 3 years old because then things start breaking down. The benefits of used cars versus new cars are lower purchase price and lower ownership and operating costs.

Depreciation is highest in the earlier years of owning the car and lowest in the later years. However, maintenance charges do increase over the life of the car. In the earlier years, financing costs are higher. Insurance costs decrease in later years since the value of the car diminishes.

It is usually cheaper to repair a car and use it than trading it in for a new one.
The ways to save on auto repairs are

Get a detailed estimate of the job.

Get a time/mileage warranty for services performed.

Try to use your repair station regularly since regular customers are typically treated better.

Tell the mechanic clearly what is wrong. This will save the mechanic's time in trying to find out what the problem is.

Smaller engines not only cost you less initially but also result in maintenance savings.

Have periodic checkups.

WHAT DOES THE NEW CAR REALLY COST?

When buying a new car, try to stay with a dealer in the neighborhood. Find out if the dealer is a member of the National Automobile Dealers Association. You can approximate the dealer's cost. A typical car costs the dealer 85 percent to 90 percent of the sticker price. Domestic compacts and subcompacts are closer to 90 percent. Optional equipment usually costs the dealer about 85 percent of the sticker price.

SOLVED PROBLEM 9.12

You bought an auto having a sticker price of $14,000 which includes $2,000 of optional equipment. The dealer cost is 90 percent of the basic price and 85 percent for the optional equipment.

(a) How much does the auto cost the dealer?

(b) What profit did the dealer make?

SOLUTION

(a)

90% × $12,000		$10,800
85% × $ 2,000		1,700
Total cost		$12,500

(b) $14,000 − $12,500 = $1,500

SOLVED PROBLEM 9.13

An auto dealer will give 15 percent off the sticker price of a $15,000 new car. In addition, the salesperson offers you an additional 5 percent off the sales price if you order the car today.

(a) What will the car cost if you place the order?

(b) What percent of the retail price did you save?

SOLUTION

(a)

Retail price	$15,000.00
Less: Discount (.15 × $15,000)	2,250.00
Net sales price	$12,750.00
Less: Additional discount	
($12,750 × .05)	637.50
Purchase price	$12,112.50

(b) $15,000 - $12,112.50 = $2,887.50$ discount

$$\frac{\text{Discount}}{\text{Retail price}} = \frac{\$2,887.50}{\$15,000} = 19.25\%$$

To determine the cost of your new car subtract the trade-in value of the old car from the price of the new car and then add other charges (for example, taxes). An extended warranty contract is an added cost.

Some guidelines as to the extra cost of options as a percentage of the purchase price of the car are larger engine (about 5 percent), automatic transmission (about 3 percent), air conditioner (about 10 percent), power steering and brakes (about 4 percent), vinyl roof (about 3 percent), and power windows (about 3 percent).

Table 9-1 illustrates how the price for a new car may be determined.

Table 9-1   Determining a Reasonable Price for a New Car

Wholesale price including options	$16,000
Destination charge	750
Local dealer preparation	100
Dealer's cost	$16,850
Plus: Dealer's profit (10% on cost)	1,185
Selling price	$18,035
Sales tax at 8%	1,443
Title cost	30
Buyer pays	$19,508

SOLVED PROBLEM 9.14

A new car has a sticker price of $19,500. The wholesale price is 90 percent of list price. Destination charges are $500. Dealer preparation charges are $80. The sales tax is 8 percent. The title to the car costs $50. The dealer's profit is 5 percent of total cost. How much should you be willing to pay for this auto?

SOLUTION

List price	$19,500
Wholesale price (90%)	$17,550
Destination charges	500
Dealer preparation	80
Dealer's cost	$18,130
Dealer's profit (5%)	907
Purchase price	$19,037
Sales tax (8%)	1,523
Title	50
You pay	$20,610

SOLVED PROBLEM 9.15

The basic price of an auto is $23,000. You want to add a larger engine, automatic transmission, and air conditioning. The options will cost about 18 percent of the basic price. What is the total cost of the car?

SOLUTION

The approximate cost of the car is

Basic price	$22,000
Options (18% × $22,000)	3,960
Total cost before tax	$25,960

SOLVED PROBLEM 9.16

You buy a new car including options for $16,000. There is a trade-in allowance on your old car of $2,000. The sales tax is 8 percent. What is the total cost of the car?

SOLUTION

List price of new car plus options	$16,000
Less: Allowance for old car	2,000
Net price	$14,000
Sales tax (8% × $14,000)	1,120
Total cost	$15,120

SOLVED PROBLEM 9.17

You want to buy a car costing $19,000. In addition, options are $1,800 and preparation costs are $200. The sales tax is 8 percent. You also will take out a $1,000 extended warranty. What is the total cost of the car?

SOLUTION

Initial cost of car	$19,000
Cost of options	1,800
Preparation cost	200
Warranty	1,000
Total	$22,000
Sales tax (8% × $22,000)	1,760
Total cost	$23,760

You may have to determine whether you should give a down payment on a car.

SOLVED PROBLEM 9.18

You put 20 percent down on a $14,000 compact car. The going interest rate on a certificate of deposit is 8 percent. The car will be used for 4 years. What is the interest lost on the down payment?

SOLUTION

Down payment: $14,000 × .20 = $2,800

Interest lost: $2,800 × .08 × 4 years = $896

The initial cost of an auto is a far more important factor in determining the economy of a car than miles per gallon. *Remember:* Take into account sales taxes and finance charges when comparing the price of two cars.

SOLVED PROBLEM 9.19

You are looking at the financial difference between a compact and a subcompact car. The sales tax is 8 percent. You will be financing the car at 14 percent simple interest for 1 year. The difference in price of the cars is $2,000. What is the total difference?

SOLUTION

This difference involves the following total cost:

Basic price difference	$2,000
Tax (8% × $2,000)	160
Interest (14% × $2,160)	302
Total	$2,462

SOLVED PROBLEM 9.20

Refer to Solved Problem 9.19. You can save 10 miles per gallon on the subcompact. If you drive 5,000 miles per year, it translates to using 500 gallons (5,000/10).

(a) If the price per gallon is $1.10, what is the yearly savings in gasoline cost?

(b) Is the savings in miles per gallon adequate relative to the cost of buying the car?

SOLUTION

(a)
$$500 \text{ gallons} \times \$1.10 = \$550$$

(b) No. The savings in miles per gallon is only $550 compared to the extra cost of purchasing the car of $2,462.

You may have to evaluate whether you can afford buying a car in the future.

SOLVED PROBLEM 9.21

You want to buy a $30,000 car in 6 years. The inflation rate is 6 percent. How much would a comparable car cost today?

SOLUTION

$30,000 × Present value of $1 (Appendix Table 3) for $n = 6$, $i = 6\%$ is

$$\$30,000 \times .70496 = \$21,149$$

If you cannot accept paying $21,149 for an auto today, you will most likely not find it realistic purchasing a car for $30,000 six years from now.

How much do you have to save each year in order to buy a car?

SOLVED PROBLEM 9.22

You want to have enough money to buy a $24,000 auto in 4 years. The annual return rate is 15 percent. What is the annual amount you have to save?

SOLUTION

The annual amount you must save is computed below.
Factor for future value of annuity of $1 (Appendix Table 2) for $n = 4$, $i = 15\%$ is 4.99338.

$$\frac{\$24,000}{4.99338} = \$4,806$$

How much has your car depreciated since you bought it? There are two commonly used methods to determine depreciation: straight-line (constant depreciation per year) and mileage. The cost of your car less the accumulated depreciation equals its book value.

SOLVED PROBLEM 9.23

On January 1, 19X5, you buy an automobile for $15,000 having a salvage value of $2,000 and a life of 10 years. The salvage value is your estimated value of the car in 10 years when you expect to sell it.

(a)   What is the depreciation per year?

(b)   What is the book value of the automobile on December 31, 19X6?

(c)   What is the book value of the automobile on December 31, 19X9?

SOLUTION

(a)   The depreciation equals

$$\frac{\text{Cost} - \text{Salvage value}}{\text{Years}} = \frac{\$15,000 - \$2,000}{10} = \$1,300$$

(b)   The book value on December 31, 19X6 equals

Cost	$15,000
Less: Accumulated depreciation	
($1,300 × 2 years)	2,600
Book value	$12,400

(c)   The book value on December 31, 19X9 equals

Cost	$15,000
Less: Accumulated depreciation	
($1,300 × 5 years)	6,500
Book value	$ 8,500

To obtain the cost per mile divide the depreciable value of the car (purchase price less trade-in value) by the total expected miles. Depreciation for a given year would then be equal to depreciation per mile times the miles driven.

SOLVED PROBLEM 9.24

An auto costing $18,000 with a trade-in value of $3,000 has a total estimated mileage of 100,000 miles. Miles driven in the first year are 800.

(a)   What is the depreciation for the first year?

(b)   What is the book value of the car at the end of the first year?

SOLUTION

(a)   The depreciation for the first year is computed below:

$$\frac{\text{Cost} - \text{Salvage value}}{\text{Estimated total miles}} = \frac{\$18,000 - \$3,000}{100,000} = \frac{\$15,000}{100,000} = \$.15 \text{ per mile}$$

Depreciation for the first year equals

$$8,000 \text{ miles} \times \$.15 = \$1,200$$

(b)   The book value of the car at the end of the first year is

Cost	$18,000
Less: Accumulated depreciation	1,200
Book value	$16,800

You should compute the auto's operating costs.

SOLVED PROBLEM 9.25

The expected monthly operating costs for your car are loan payment, $300; plates, $50; insurance, $1,200; fuel, $.15 per mile; repairs, $.25 per mile; and depreciation, $2,000. You expect to drive 12,000 miles this year. What is the annual expected operating cost?

SOLUTION

Loan payment	$ 300
Plates	50
Insurance	1,200
Fuel ($.15 × 12,000 miles)	1,800
Repairs ($.25 × 12,000 miles)	3,000
Depreciation	2,000
Total cost	$8,350

SOLVED PROBLEM 9.26

You drove 12,000 miles during the year. The miles per gallon are 30. The cost of gasoline is $1.10 per gallon. What is the cost of gas for the year?

SOLUTION

$$\frac{\text{Miles driven}}{\text{Miles per gallon}} = \frac{12,000}{30} = 400 \text{ gallons}$$

$$400 \text{ gallons} \times \$1.10 = \$440$$

SOLVED PROBLEM 9.27

You travel about 1,000 miles a month in your car. You get 20 miles per gallon of gasoline at a cost of $.95 per gallon. You consume 1 quart of oil per month at a cost of $1.30 per quart.

(a)   What is your monthly cost for gasoline and oil?

(b)   What is the average cost per mile for gas and oil?

SOLUTION

(a)

$$\frac{\text{Miles driven}}{\text{Miles per gallon}} = \frac{1,000}{20} = 50 \text{ gallons}$$

Gas (50 gallons × $.95)	$47.50
Oil	1.30
Total monthly cost	$48.80

(b)

$$\frac{\text{Monthly cost}}{\text{Miles}} = \frac{\$48.80}{1,000} = \$.049$$

SOLVED PROBLEM 9.28

You buy a car for $20,000 having a salvage value of $2,000 and a 10-year life. Straight-line depreciation is used. The cost of insurance in the first year if $600. You expect insurance to increase by 10 percent in the second year. Estimated repairs for the first 2 years are $700 and $800, respectively. Gasoline is expected to cost over the 2-year period $900 and $1,200, respectively.

(*a*) Determine the total cost of operating the car in the first 2 years.

(*b*) If you drive 10,000 miles the first year and 11,000 miles the second year, what is the total cost per mile for each of the years?

SOLUTION

(*a*)

AUTO COSTS	YEAR 1	YEAR 2
Depreciation [($20,000 − $2,000)/10]	$1,800	$1,800
Insurance	600	660
Repairs	700	800
Gasoline	900	1,200
Total cost	$4,000	$4,460

(*b*)
$$\text{Year 1} = \frac{\$4,000}{10,000} = \$.40 \text{ per mile}$$

$$\text{Year 2} = \frac{\$4,460}{11,000} = \$.41 \text{ per mile}$$

WHAT SHOULD YOU KNOW IF YOU RENT A CAR?

Typically, auto rental companies hold you responsible for damage to the rental car, sometimes up to its full value, unless you take out collision coverage that may cost $7 to $9 a day. However, the policy on your owned car may cover insurance on the rented car. In addition, some credit cards automatically provide supplemental collision-damage coverage on rental cars paid for with the card.

Note that the rental car company's insurance will cover your legal liability in the event there is injury or property damage while driving the car. The rental company's insurance also will pay if an accident was caused by its negligence (for example, an improperly functioning car). If the rental company's insurance is inadequate, the liability coverage on your car will protect you up to the policy's limits.

SHOULD YOU BUY OR LEASE A CAR?

You may want to decide whether you are better off leasing or buying a car. In this connection, you have to determine the costs of leasing versus buying.

SOLVED PROBLEM 9.29

You lease a car for a monthly payment of $250. Sales tax is 8 percent. What is the total cost for a 3-year lease?

SOLUTION

Monthly payment	$ 250
Sales tax (8% × $250)	20
Cost per month	$ 270
	× 36 months
Total cost	$9,720

SOLVED PROBLEM 9.30

You can lease a car for $200 per month. Sales tax is 6 percent. The lease will be for 36 months. You can buy the same car for $9,500. $7,000 of the purchase price can be financed at 16 percent for 36 months. Monthly payments would be $246. Although licensing costs of $50 per year is included in the lease, you would have to pay them if you bought the car. The salvage value of the car at the end of 36 months would be $5,000. Is it cheaper to lease or buy?

SOLUTION

Cost of leasing:

Monthly payment	$ 200
Sales tax (6% × $200)	12
Monthly cost	$ 212
	× 36 months
Total cost for 36 months	$ 7,632

Cost of buying:

Monthly payment	$ 246
Total payments ($246 × 36)	$ 8,856
Down payment	2,500
Sales tax (6% × $9,500)	570
License cost ($50 × 3)	150
Cost of buying	$12,076
Less: Salvage value	5,000
Total cost of buying	$ 7,076

It is $556 ($7,632 − $7,076) cheaper to buy than lease.

HOW TO FINANCE A MAJOR ACQUISITION

A major acquisition may be financed by the dealer or an independent lender. You should be familiar with the financial computations to determine what your cost will really be. For example, you should know how to compute the monthly loan payment. You will want to compare alternative financing arrangements to see which one is best.

SOLVED PROBLEM 9.31

You buy a car for $14,000 making a down payment of $3,000. You will finance the balance at an interest rate of 24 percent payable monthly over 3 years.

(*a*)   What is the monthly loan payment?

(*b*)   What is the total loan payment?

(*c*)   What is the total interest?

SOLUTION

(*a*)

Cost of auto	$14,000
Less: Down payment	3,000
To be financed	$11,000

$$\text{Monthly interest rate} = \frac{24\%}{12} = 2\%$$

Months: $3 \times 12 = 36$

Present value of annuity of $1 (Appendix Table 4) for $i = 2\%$, $n = 36$ is a factor of 25.48884. The monthly loan payment is

$$\frac{\$11,000}{25.48884} = \$431.56$$

(b)   Total loan payments ($431.56 × 36) $15,536.16
                 Principal   11,000.00
(c)   Total interest $ 4,536.16

Table 9-2 shows what the monthly finance charge will be on a $1,000 loan for 12 months, 24 months, and 36 months.

Table 9-2   Finance Charge for each $1,000 Loan

Interest	12 Months	24 Months	36 Months
9%	$ 49.42	$ 96.43	$144.79
10	54.99	107.48	161.62
11	60.58	118.59	178.59
12	66.19	129.76	195.72
14	77.45	152.31	230.39
16	88.77	175.11	265.65
18	100.16	198.18	301.49

Many auto manufacturers either have their own sales finance company or have an agreement with one.

SOLVED PROBLEM 9.32

The purchase price of a new car is $12,000. Sales tax is 8 percent. In addition, you incur title and license fees of $40 and credit life insurance of $80. The trade-in on your old car is $2,000. Your cash down payment is $3,000. You will finance over 24 months at an annual interest rate of 24 percent.

(a)   How much will you have to finance?

(b)   What will the monthly payment be?

SOLUTION

(a)   Purchase price $12,000
              Sales tax (8% × $12,000)   960
              Title and license fees   40
              Credit and life insurance   80

              Total cost $13,080
              Less: Trade-in on old car $2,000
                    Down payment   3,000   5,000

              Balance to finance $ 8,080

(b)   Present value of annuity of $1 (Appendix Table 4) factor for $n = 24$, $i = 2\%$ (24%/12) is 18.91393.

$$\text{Monthly payment} = \frac{\$8,000}{18.91393} = \$427.20$$

You may be able to get a better deal on a car loan from another source (for example, credit union, bank) than from the auto dealer. Consider the provisions in the loan agreement regarding prepayment of the loan. Will there be a complete forgiveness of future finance charges if you can repay the loan in advance? What is the interest penalty for late payments? What rights do you have in the event of repossession? Is there an acceleration clause where all payments are due immediately if one payment is not made on time?

You should determine the operating cost of a major appliance.

SOLVED PROBLEM 9.33

You buy a freezer that has an estimated monthly operating cost of $7.25. What is the annual cost?

SOLUTION

$$\$7.25 \times 12 = \$87$$

ARE WARRANTIES AND SERVICE CONTRACTS WORTH THE COST?

Does it pay to take out an extended warranty? In financial terms, it generally does not. Typically, the repairs would cost less than the cost of taking out the warranty. The warranty varies depending upon the policy of the dealer and manufacturer. An extended warranty may also be taken out through the use of a credit card (for example, American Express). However, many people will take out an extended warranty for peace of mind knowing that if a major repair is needed they will be covered. Thus, personal preferences have to be considered. But, of course, taking out a policy for a low-priced item may be inappropriate. For example, taking out a $100 extended warranty for a $500 T.V. set is ridiculous.

SOLVED PROBLEM 9.34

You buy a major appliance. The dealer offers an extended warranty for two additional years after the second year which is already under warranty from the manufacturer. The cost of the warranty is $800 covering limited major repairs. Should you take out the warranty?

SOLUTION

If you do not expect to incur the cost of major repairs or you expect the cost to be less than $800, you should decline the extended warranty.

WHAT CAN YOU DO TO LOWER FOOD COSTS?

The ways to save on food costs are prepare a well-planned shopping list and do not buy an item not on the list except if there is an advertised special you will eventually need; do not shop when you are hungry; use discount coupons; shop at discount, "no frills" supermarkets; check the prices on "no-frills" items that can save you as much as 30 percent (the quality of the unmarked brand may be almost as good as the national brand); substitute for rising cost items, similar ones where prices are remaining steady (for example, substitute cereal for meat); and the *bottom* shelves may have lower prices on the items because stock people may not want to bend to reprice them. However, *bottom*-shelf merchandise may not be as fresh as top-shelf merchandise.

The ways to save costs on eating out are

Take advantage of restaurant promotions, such as Entertainment 1991 where two people can eat for the price of one. Another example is the "In Good Taste" credit card where 25 percent is deducted from the price of the meal at selected restaurants.

Avoid buying liquor drinks because they are very high priced. You may be paying a markup on cost of 200 percent or more.

Avoid high-priced restaurants even if the portions are oversized. It will cost you not only in the pocket but also in the waistline. What is worse is paying a higher price for a small portion.

SOLVED PROBLEM 9.35

You are at the supermarket. Brand A sells for $.80 and contains 12 oz. Brand B sells for $.60 and contains 8 oz. Which is least costly?

SOLUTION

	BRAND A	**BRAND B**
Cost per ounce	$\dfrac{\$.80}{12} = \$.067$	$\dfrac{\$60}{8} = \$.075$

Brand A is cheaper.

SOLVED PROBLEM 9.36

Five pounds of sugar sells for $4.00 per package while a 1-pound package sells for $.95. Which is the more economical purchase?

SOLUTION

	5-LB PACKAGE	**1-LB PACKAGE**
Unit price	$\dfrac{\$4.00}{5} = \$.80$ per lb	$.95 per lb

You save $.15 per pound by purchasing the 5-pound package.

HOW CAN YOU REDUCE CLOTHING COSTS?

Clothing costs are a material expense that can be curtailed. The ways to cut clothing costs are follow clothing care labels, avoid items that will discolor clothing, have protection in bad weather (for example, umbrella), hang up clothes after you take them off, have an air freshener in the closet, and launder or dry clean soiled clothes immediately.

SOLVED PROBLEM 9.37

You went to the department store, which was holding its year-end clearance sale. Boys and girls clothing was reduced 25 percent and 30 percent, respectively. You bought boys and girls clothing worth $100 and $150, respectively.

(a) What was your total savings?

(b) What was your percent savings?

SOLUTION

(a)

Boys clothing ($100 × 25%)	$25	saving
Girls clothing ($150 × 30%)	45	saving
Total saving	$70	

(b) Percent saving

$$\frac{\text{Saving}}{\text{Total regular price}} = \frac{\$70}{\$250} = 28\% \quad \text{saving}$$

SOLVED PROBLEM 9.38

You are shopping for clothing. The store offers 15 percent off the list price plus an additional 3 percent discount off the net sales price for cash purchases.

(a) What will be the savings on a total cash purchase of $300?

(b) What is the percentage savings?

SOLUTION

(a)
$$\$300 \times 15\% = \$45 \quad \text{discount}$$

$$\text{Net sales price} = \$300 - \$45 = \$255$$

$$\text{Cash discount} = \$255 \times 3\% = \$7.65$$

$$\text{Total savings} = \$45 + \$7.65 = \$52.65$$

(b)
$$\frac{\$52.65}{\$300} = 17.6\%$$

HOW MARITAL STATUS AFFECTS YOUR PERSONAL FINANCE

If you are living with someone, inquire with a lawyer as to how you should establish your status in the particular state with regard to the lease, insurance policy, will, etc. Keep careful records of who is entitled to what in case of separation.

If your spouse decides to get a job, the second income is lessened after taking into account the extra withholding tax, social security tax, and income tax.

You can package your fringe benefits to get the best from one employer. For example, you may take the best health care package from the husband's employer and the best disability plan from the wife's employer.

You may need a second car for the working spouse. Also, auto insurance premiums will increase. Child-care costs will have to be incurred. However, you can get a child-care credit on your income tax.

The disadvantages of a divorce include

Legal fees.

It may cost you more to live alone than with your spouse if you must pay alimony and child support. The same money has to cover the costs of two households rather than one.

Rule of thumb: A husband without children and with a nonworking wife may have to pay between 20 to 25% of gross income as alimony. If there are children, alimony and child support may total as much as 40 percent of gross income.

SOLVED PROBLEM 9.39

A husband's gross income is $60,000. The wife takes care of three children. If there is a divorce, what is the expected total cost the husband would have to pay for alimony and child support?

SOLUTION

$$\$60,000 \times 40\% = \$24,000$$

Tax implications. Alimony payments are tax-deductible to the former spouse who pays them and taxable to the former spouse who receives them. Child support is typically paid to a child until he or she reaches the age of 21. Child support is not tax deductible.

Review Questions

(1) _____ is a publication that reveals the quality of major products.

(2) The monthly payment for a major purchase should not exceed _____ of your monthly housing costs.

(3) The profit markup on options is _____ than the profit markup on the car.

(4)   Expenses for an auto used for business purposes is _____ .

(5)   The cost of insuring a car is about _____ of the total auto expenditures for the year.

(6)   A dealer's markup on a car usually ranges from _____ percent.

(7)   The _____ credit card gives you 25 percent off the price of a meal.

(8)   An extended warranty on a new car may be taken out with the use of an _____ credit card.

(9)   Alimony is _____ to the wife.

Answers: (1) *Consumer Reports*;   (2) one-half;   (3) greater;   (4) tax deductible;   (5) 20%;   (6) 15% to 25%;   (7) "In Good Taste";   (8) American Express;   (9) taxable.

Additional Solved Problems

9.1   You buy a range having a monthly operating cost of $5.35. What is the annual operating cost?

SOLUTION

$$\$5.35 \times 12 = \$64.20$$

9.2   A store reduces its list price on an item by 10 percent if the total payment is made with cash. How much will the cost be to buy an item having a retail price of $800?

SOLUTION

$$\$800 \times .90 = \$720$$

9.3   You can buy a major appliance at a discount store at 10 percent below the price of $425 charged at a department store. What will you save by buying the item at the discount store?

SOLUTION

$$\$425 \times 10\% = \$42.50$$

9.4   Ten pounds of sugar sells for $12 per package while a 2-pound package sells for $3. Which is the more economical purchase?

SOLUTION

	10-LB PACKAGE	**2-LB PACKAGE**
Unit price	$\dfrac{\$12}{10} = \$1.20$ per lb	$\dfrac{\$3.00}{2} = \$1.50$ per lb

You save $.30 per pound by buying the 10-pound package.

9.5   You can buy a brand-name VCR that retails for $625 at a department store for $550 in a discount store. What is your percentage saving if you buy at the discount store?

SOLUTION

$$\frac{\$75}{\$550} = 13.6\%$$

9.6 You are shopping at the grocery store. Brand X sells for $2.00 for 16 ounces while Brand Y sells for $1.50 for 10 ounces. Which is less costly?

SOLUTION

	BRAND X	BRAND Y
Cost per ounce	$\dfrac{\$2.00}{16} = \$.167$	$\dfrac{\$1.50}{10} = \$.150$

Brand Y is cheaper.

9.7 You put 30 percent down on a $15,000 car that you expect to use for 6 years. The going interest rate you could earn on your money is 7 percent. What is the interest lost on the down payment?

SOLUTION

$$\text{Down payment} = \$15,000 \times .30 = \$4,500$$

$$\text{Interest lost} = \$4,500 \times 7\% \times 6 \text{ years} = \$1,890$$

9.8 You can buy a boat at a cash price of $2,500 or on the installment plan for $1,000 down plus $150 per month for 12 months. What is the installment charge?

SOLUTION

Down payment	$1,000
Monthly payments ($150 × 12)	1,800
Total payments	$2,800
Less: Cash price	2,500
Installment charge	$ 300

9.9 You can purchase a microwave oven on the installment plan in either of two ways: (*a*) by making an $80 down payment and paying $6 a week for 80 weeks or (*b*) by making a $120 down payment and paying $25 a month for 18 months. Which plan is less costly?

SOLUTION

Weekly plan:	
Down payment	$ 80
Weekly payments ($6 × 80 weeks)	480
Total cost	$560
Monthly plan:	
Down payment	$120
Monthly payments ($25 × 18 months)	450
Total cost	$570

The weekly plan is $10 cheaper.

9.10 You can buy an appliance for $1,600 cash or on the installment plan by paying $600 down and $100 a month for 12 months. How much does the installment price exceed the cash price?

SOLUTION

Down payment	$ 600
Monthly payments (12 × $100)	1,200
Installment price	$1,800

The installment price is $200 more than the cash price ($1,800 − $1,600).

9.11   You can buy a refrigerator for a cash price of $800 or buy it on an installment purchase plan paying $100 down and 24 monthly payments of $35. If you take out the installment plan, what is the extra cost?

SOLUTION

Installment plan [$100 + 24($35)]	$940
Cash payment	800
Extra cost	$140

9.12   You can purchase a TV set for $800 or on the installment plan by paying an additional 10 percent. You select the installment plan and make a down payment of $280, with monthly payments of $60. How many months will it take to pay for the TV?

SOLUTION

Installment purchase ($800 × 1.10)	$880
Less: Down payment	280
Balance	$600

$$\frac{\text{Balance}}{\text{Monthly payment}} = \frac{\$600}{\$60} = 10 \text{ months}$$

9.13   You buy an item costing $800 on terms of 3/15, net/45.

(*a*)   How much discount will you receive if you pay within 15 days?

(*b*)   What will your payment be if you pay within the discount period?

(*c*)   How much will you have to pay if your payment is received in 25 days?

SOLUTION

(*a*) $800 × 3% = $24

(*b*) $800 − $24 = $776

(*c*) $800

9.14   You lease a car for a monthly payment of $300. Sales tax is 8 percent. What is the total cost of a 2-year lease?

SOLUTION

Monthly payment	$ 300
Sales tax (8% × $300)	24
Cost per month	$ 324
	× 24 months
Total cost	$7,776

9.15   You purchase an auto having a sticker price of $15,000 which includes $3,000 of optional equipment. The dealer cost is 85 percent of the basic price and 83 percent of the optional equipment.

(*a*)   How much does the auto cost the dealer?

(*b*)   What profit did the dealer make?

SOLUTION

(a)

85% × $12,000		$10,200
83% × $3,000		2,490
Total		$12,690

(b) $15,000 − $12,690 = $2,310

9.16 An auto dealer will give 10 percent off the sticker price of $14,000 on a new car. Further, the salesperson offers an additional 5 percent off the sales price if you place the order today.

(a) What will it cost if you accept the offer?

(b) What percentage of the retail price did you save?

SOLUTION

(a)

Retail price	$14,000
Less: Discount ($14,000 × .10)	1,400
Net selling price	$12,600
Less: Additional discount ($12,600 × .05)	630
Purchase price	$11,970

(b) $14,000 − $11,970 = $2,030 discount

$$\frac{\text{Discount}}{\text{Retail price}} = \frac{\$2,030}{\$14,000} = 14.5\%$$

9.17 You purchase a major household item for $12,000. The sales tax is 8 percent. Dealer preparation and options cost $1,000. What is the total cost?

SOLUTION

Purchase price	$12,000
Preparation and options cost	1,000
	$13,000
Sales tax (8% × $13,000)	1,040
Total cost	$14,040

9.18 You buy a new car for $15,000. The extra options cost 15 percent of the basic price. You trade in your old car for $3,000. What is the total cost of the new car? (Ignore taxes.)

SOLUTION

Basic price	$15,000
Options (15% × $15,000)	2,250
Total cost	$17,250
Less: Trade-in allowance	3,000
Net cost	$14,250

9.19 You are examining the financial difference between a compact and a subcompact car. The sales tax is 8 percent. You will be financing the car at 12 percent simple interest for 1 year. The difference in the price of the cars is $3,000. What is the total cost difference?

SOLUTION

Basic price difference	$3,000
Tax (8% × $3,000)	240
Interest (12% × $3,240)	389
Total	$3,629

9.20 The total expenses of operating your car were $2,000 for the year, of which 60 percent was for business.

　(a)　What is the amount of your tax-deductible expense?

　(b)　What is the tax savings if you are in the 28 percent tax bracket?

SOLUTION

　(a)　$2,000 × .60 = $1,200

　(b)　$1,200 × .28 = $336

9.21 You save 6 miles per gallon by buying a smaller car. You drive 12,000 miles during the year. The price per gallon of gasoline is $1.04. What is your yearly savings on gasoline cost?

SOLUTION

$$\frac{12,000}{6} = 2,000 \text{ gallons} \times \$1.04 = \$2,080$$

9.22 You buy an auto for $14,000. It has a salvage value of $2,000 and a life of 5 years.

　(a)　What is the depreciation per year?

　(b)　What is the book value of the auto at the end of the third year?

SOLUTION

　(a)

$$\frac{\text{Cost} - \text{Salvage value}}{\text{Years}} = \frac{\$14,000 - \$2,000}{5} = \$2,400$$

　(b)

Cost	$14,000
Less: Accumulated depreciation ($2,400 × 3)	7,200
Book value	$ 6,800

9.23 An auto costing $15,000 with a trade-in value of $2,000 has a total estimated mileage of 80,000 miles. Miles driven in the first year are 10,000.

　(a)　What is the depreciation for the first year?

　(b)　What is the book value of the car at the end of the first year?

SOLUTION

　(a)

$$\frac{\text{Cost} - \text{Salvage value}}{\text{Estimated total miles}} = \frac{\$15,000 - \$2,000}{80,000} = \$.1625 \text{ per mile}$$

Depreciation for the first year equals

$$10,000 \text{ miles} \times \$.1625 = \$1,625$$

(b)

Cost	$15,000
Less: Accumulated depreciation	1,625
Book value	$13,375

9.24 The expected monthly operating costs for your car are auto loan payment, $400; plates, $40; insurance, $1,100; fuel, $.12 per mile; repairs, $.30 per mile; and depreciation, $2,500. You expect to drive 8,000 miles this year. What is the annual expected operating cost?

SOLUTION

Monthly loan payment	$ 400
Plates	40
Insurance	1,100
Fuel ($.12 × 8,000 miles)	960
Repairs ($.30 × 8,000 miles)	2,400
Depreciation	2,500
Total cost	$7,400

9.25 You travel about 1,500 miles a month in your car. You get 25 miles per gallon of gasoline at a cost of $1.15 per gallon. You consume 2 quarts of oil per month at a cost of $1.25 per quart.

(a)   What is your monthly cost for gas and oil?

(b)   What is the average cost per mile for gas and oil?

SOLUTION

(a)

$$\frac{\text{Miles driven}}{\text{Miles per gallon}} = \frac{1,500}{25} = 60 \text{ gallons}$$

Gas (60 gallons × $1.15)	$69.00
Oil (2 × $1.25)	2.50
Total monthly cost	$71.50

(b)

$$\frac{\text{Monthly cost}}{\text{Miles}} = \frac{\$71.50}{1,500} = \$.048 \text{ per mile}$$

9.26 During the year, you incurred the following costs for your four-year-old car: new tires, $250; tune-ups, $140; oil and lubrication changes, $40; and a new muffler, $85. You drove 10,000 miles during the year.

(a)   What is your annual cost for maintenance and repairs?

(b)   What is your monthly cost for maintenance and repairs?

(c)   What is the average cost per mile?

SOLUTION

(a)

Tires	$250
Tune-ups	140
Oil and lubrication	40
New muffler	85
Annual cost	$515

(b)

$$\frac{\$515}{12} = \$42.92 \text{ monthly cost}$$

(c) $$\frac{\$515}{10{,}000 \text{ miles}} = \$.052 \text{ average cost per mile}$$

9.27 You purchase a car for $22,000 having a salvage value of $2,000 and a life of 10 years. The cost of insurance in the first year is $500 and you expect the cost to increase by 15 percent in the second year. Estimated repairs are $800 and $900 for the 2-year period. The gasoline cost is estimated at $750 and $925 for the 2-year period.

(a) Compute the total cost of operating the car for the first 2 years.

(b) If you drive 8,500 miles in the first year and 9,000 miles in the second year, what is the transportation cost per mile for each of the years?

SOLUTION

(a)

AUTO COSTS	YEAR 1	YEAR 2
Depreciation [($22,000 − $2,000)/10]	$2,000	$2,000
Insurance	500	575
Repairs	800	900
Gasoline	750	925
Total cost	$4,050	$4,400

(b) First year:

$$\frac{\$4{,}050}{8{,}500} = \$.48 \text{ per mile}$$

Second year:

$$\frac{\$4{,}400}{9{,}000} = \$.49 \text{ per mile}$$

9.28 The list price of a car is $20,800. The wholesale price is 85 percent of the list price. The dealer's profit is 10 percent of the total cost. Dealers are usually negotiable when it comes to price. Destination charges are $600. Dealer preparation costs are $150. The sales tax is 7 percent. The title to the car costs $60. How much should you be willing to pay for this car?

SOLUTION

List price	$20,800
Wholesale price (85% × $20,800)	$17,680
Destination charges	600
Dealer preparation costs	150
Dealer's cost	$18,430
Dealer's profit (10% × $18,430)	1,843
Purchase price	$20,273
Sales tax (7% × $20,273)	1,419
Title	60
You should pay	$21,752

9.29 You can lease an auto for $225 per month. Sales tax is 7 percent. The lease will be for 36 months. You can purchase the same car for $10,000. $7,000 of the purchase price can be financed at 16 percent for 36 months. Monthly payments will be $246. The licensing costs are $40 per year. The wholesale value of the car at the end of 36 months would be $4,500. Are you better off leasing or buying?

SOLUTION

Cost of leasing:	
Monthly lease payment	$ 225
Sales tax (7% × $225)	16
Monthly cost	$ 241
Number of months	× 36
Total cost of leasing	$ 8,676

Cost of buying:	
Monthly payment	$ 246
Total payments ($246 × 36)	$ 8,856
Down payment	3,000
Sales tax (7% × $10,000)	700
License cost ($40 × 3)	120
Cost of buying	$12,676
Less: Wholesale value	4,500
Total cost of buying	$ 8,176

It is $500 ($8,676 − $8,176) cheaper to buy than lease.

9.30 You want to buy a $30,000 car in 6 years. The inflation rate is 6 percent. What would a comparable car cost today?

SOLUTION

$30,000 × Present value of $1 (Appendix Table 3) for $n = 6$, $i = 6\%$ is

$$\$30,000 \times .70496 = \$21,149$$

9.31 You want to have sufficient funds to purchase a $25,000 auto in 4 years. The annual return rate is 15 percent. What is the annual amount you have to save?

SOLUTION

Factor for future value of annuity of $1 (Appendix Table 2) for $n = 4$, $i = 15\%$ is 4.99338.

$$\frac{\$25,000}{4.99338} = \$5,007$$

9.32 You purchase a car for $20,000 making a down payment of $4,000. You finance the balance at an interest rate of 24 percent payable monthly over 3 years.

(*a*) What is the monthly loan payment?

(*b*) What are the total loan payments?

(*c*) What is the total interest?

SOLUTION

(*a*) Amount to be financed is $20,000 − $4,000 = $16,000. The monthly interest rate is 24%/12 = 2%. The number of months is 3 × 12 = 36.
Present value of annuity of $1 (Appendix Table 4) for $i = 24\%$, $n = 36$ is a factor of 25.48884.

$$\text{Monthly loan payment} = \frac{\$16,000}{25.48884} = \$627.73$$

(*b*)   Total loan payments = $627.73 × 36 = $22,598.28

(c)	Total loan payments	$22,598.28
	Less: Principal	16,000.00
	Total interest	$ 6,598.28

9.33 The purchase price of a new car is $14,000. Sales tax is 6 percent. You incur title and license fees of $50 and credit life insurance of $100. The dealer will give you a trade-in on your old car of $4,000. Your cash down payment is $2,000. You will finance over 36 months at an annual interest rate of 24 percent.

(a)   How much will you have to finance?

(b)   What will the monthly payment be?

SOLUTION

(a)	Purchase price		$14,000
	Sales tax (6% × $14,000)		840
	Title and license fees		50
	Credit life insurance		100
	Total cost		$14,990
	Less: Trade-in on old car	$4,000	
	Down payment	2,000	6,000
	Balance to finance		$ 8,990

(b)   The present value of annuity of $1 (Appendix Table 4) factor for $n = 36$, $i = 2\%$* is 25.48884.

$$\text{Monthly payment} = \frac{\$8,990}{25.48884} = \$352.70$$

*Monthly interest rate = 24%/12 = 2%.

Chapter 10

Housing

Homeownership is perhaps the most sizable investment you will ever make. Further, your home is a tax shelter. There are many questions surrounding homeownership. In this chapter, you will find the answers to the following important questions:

Should you buy or rent?

How do you price a home?

How much can you afford to pay for a house?

How do you shop for an adjustable rate mortgage?

Should you refinance your home?

Should you pay off your mortgage early?

How good is your homeowners' policy?

How can you get top dollar for your house?

How can you sell your home yourself?

SHOULD YOU BUY A HOME OR RENT?

For many people, the decision to buy a home is more emotional than economic. But if you are wondering about whether or not to go on renting, here are some questions to help you decide when renting is right:

Do you have enough money to put down to buy a home? The initial cost of homeownership can be substantional. For example, for a $100,000 house you should figure on having anywhere between $10,000 to $20,000 (10 to 20 percent) for the down payment, $3,000 to $6,000 (3 to 6 percent) for closing costs and a $2,000 cushion for contingencies. Thus, at the time of purchase you will need to pay cash of anywhere between $15,000 to $28,000.

Are you the roving kind? If you stand a good chance of being relocated in a few years it doesn't make sense to buy because of high borrowing, closing, commission, and moving costs.

Do you live in an area where renting makes sense? In regions where there is a housing glut and rent controls and values are flat or falling, renting ends up being a bargain.

Are you lazy or a born renter? Can you deal with maintenance and lawn mowing? Or would you rather leave it up to a landlord by renting? Are you enjoying the appeal of community living and access to amenities such as swimming pools and tennis courts?

The disadvantages of renting are primarily financial and economic. Owning a home is still the best tax shelter there is. The renter does not receive any federal tax-deductible benefit from rent payments. Also, the rent payment does not contribute to building your equity. You are at the mercy of the landlord.

Homeownership has the following advantages:

You are building equity due to the appreciation in the value of the home.

Interest and property taxes are deductible on your tax return.

Usually owning is less costly than renting.

You may enjoy extra living space and privacy.

Single-family homes are usually in better locations than apartments.

You will have a sense of stability and roots in the community.

You will enjoy pride of ownership.

Note that the disadvantages of homeownership tend to be the advantages of renting and vice versa. In comparing rental and purchase costs, the worksheet in Table 10-1 can be useful.

Table 10-1   Comparison of Rental and Purchase Costs

Rental Cost	
Annual rental cost ($850 × 12)	$10,200
Purchase Costs (assuming a 30% tax bracket)	
Add:	
Mortgage payment ($100,000 @ 10%, 30 years)	$10,608
Principal = $608 (approximate)	
Interest = $10,000 (approximate)	
Property taxes	1,300
Property insurance	250
Maintenance	400
Cost of lost interest on $20,000 @ 5% (after-tax rate of return)	1,000
Subtract:	
Principal reduction in loan balance	(608)
Tax savings due to mortgage interest deduction ($10,000 × .3)	(3,000)
Tax savings due to property tax deduction ($1,300 × .3)	(390)
Net annual after-tax purchase costs	$ 9,560
Annual benefit of buying	$ 640*

*Note that the annual benefit does not include appreciation in the value of your home.

WHAT PRICE TO PAY

After you find the house you like, you must decide what price to pay for it. In most cases, there is room between the price sellers ask and the price that they are willing to accept. Make sure that you are not paying more for a property than its market value. To determine the maximum price to pay for the property is not an easy task. Two methods are widely used.

1. Have your real estate agent run "comparative sales" on a computer. The computer should be able to give you the recent history of sales in the neighborhood. The price that a subject property can bring must be adjusted upward or downward to reflect the difference between the subject property and comparables. Since this particular approach is based on selling price, not asking price, it can give you a good idea about the market.

2. Use an expert. You might want to hire a professional real estate appraiser for a fee. Appraisal is not a science, but a complex and subjective procedure that requires good information about specific properties, their selling prices, and applicable terms of financing. The use of an expert may well be worth the cost if you worry about the possibility of paying too much.

DETERMINING THE MONTHLY MORTGAGE PAYMENT

The monthly mortgage payment consists partly of principal repayment on a loan and partly of interest charges. It is determined through a loan amortization formula. In practice, however, *comprehensive mortgage payment tables* are available to determine monthly payments. These tables contain monthly payments for virtually every combination of loan size, interest rate, and term. Table 5 of the Appendix provides selected combinations for $10,000 fixed-rate loans.

SOLVED PROBLEM 10.1

You want to find the monthly mortgage payment on a $95,000, 10 percent, 30-year mortgage (use Appendix Table 5).

SOLUTION

Using Appendix Table 5, you need the following three steps:

Step 1:   Divide the amount of the loan by $10,000 (that is, $95,000/$10,000 = 9.5).

Step 2:   Find the payment factor for a specific interest rate and loan maturity. The Appendix Table 5 payment factor for 10 percent and 30 years is 87.76.

Step 3:   Multiply the factor obtained in Step 2 by the amount from Step 1.

$$\$87.76 \times 9.5 = \$833.72$$

The resulting monthly mortgage payment would be $833.72.

HOW MUCH CAN YOU AFFORD TO SPEND FOR HOUSING?

An accurate way to determine what kind of house you can afford is to make two basic calculations: How much can you pay each month for the long-term expenses of owning a home (for example, mortgage payments, maintenance and operating expenses, insurance and property taxes)? And, how much cash do you have to spend for the initial costs of the purchase (for example, the down payment, points and closing costs)?

Many lenders use various rules of thumb to determine a borrower's ability to afford a house. They include:

1. *Thirty-five percent rule of thumb.*   A borrower can afford no more than 35 percent of monthly take-home pay.

SOLVED PROBLEM 10.2

Your gross annual income is $33,000 per year and take-home pay is $2,095 per month. At 35 percent, you could afford a monthly payment of $733.

(*a*) Assuming an interest rate of 13 percent and a 30-year term, determine how much you can qualify for.

(*b*) Assume that your budget has already provided for property taxes, insurance, and maintenance expenses and you have $20,000 available for a down payment (after point charges and closing costs). How much house can you afford?

SOLUTION

(*a*) With an interest rate of 13 percent and a 30-year term, you could borrow $66,260. (From Appendix Table 5, the monthly payment for a $10,000 loan is $110.62. Hence, $733/$110.62 = 6.626, 6.626 × $10,000 = $66,260.)

(*b*) You could buy a house that costs about $86,260 ($20,000 + the $66,260 mortgage).

2. *Multiple of gross income rule.*   The price should not exceed roughly $2\frac{1}{2}$ times your family's gross annual income.

SOLVED PROBLEM 10.3

Your annual gross income is $40,000. What is the maximum price you could afford?

SOLUTION

$100,000 (2.5 × $40,000)

3. *Percent of monthly gross income rule.*   Your monthly mortgage payment, property taxes, and insurance should not exceed 25 percent of your family's monthly gross income [or about 35 percent for a Federal Housing Administration (FHA) or Veterans Administration (VA) mortgage].

SOLVED PROBLEM 10.4

You and your spouse have gross income of $60,000 ($5,000 a month). Under the above rule, what is the amount that your monthly mortgage payment, property taxes, and insurance should not exceed?

SOLUTION

$$25\% \times \$5,000 = \$1,250$$

4. Your debt payments on loans of 10 months or longer, including your mortgage, should not exceed 36 percent of your gross income (or 50 percent for an FHA or VA loan).

SOLVED PROBLEM 10.5

You and your spouse have gross income of $60,000 ($5,000 a month). If you have a monthly debt load of $500 or less, how much could you spend for a home?

SOLUTION

You might look for a $120,000 house with total monthly housing payments of about $1,300, since total debt payments of $1,800 ($1,300 + $500) equals or is close to 36 percent of your $5,000 monthly gross income. That means you could most likely qualify for a 30-year fixed-rate loan (with 10 to 20 percent down) even if interest rates hit 12 percent.

DOES IT PAY TO REFINANCE YOUR HOUSE?

Whether refinancing is worthwhile depends on the costs of refinancing and the time required to recoup those costs through low mortgage payments. The costs of refinancing are the closing costs, which can vary widely. Closing costs include:

Title search

Insurance (such as hazard, title, and private mortgage insurance)

Lender's review fees

Buyer's loan points

Reappraisal fees

Credit report

Escrow fees

Lawyer fees

Document preparation fees, judgment reports, notary fees, and recording fees

To get a rough estimate of the closing costs, take the costs of refinancing (3 to 6 percent of the outstanding principal) and multiply it by the amount of the loan.

SOLVED PROBLEM 10.6

If the loan amount is $100,000 and the cost is 5 percent, what are the dollar closing costs?

SOLUTION

$$5\% \times \$100,000 = \$5,000$$

Rule of thumb: To refinance successfully, you should plan on staying in the house for at least 3 years and should be able to reduce the rate paid on the mortgage by at least two percentage points.

If you are a fixed-rate mortgage holder, you might look for another fixed-rate home loan at least two to three percentage points below the mortgage currently held.

If you have an adjustable loan, you might consider what the expected rate on the adjustable rate mortgage (ARM) will be several years hence. If the current rates on fixed mortgages are substantially below the expected rate on the ARM, it might pay to refinance.

Rule of thumb: Consider when refinancing the amount of time it will take to recoup the costs of refinancing.

SOLVED PROBLEM 10.7

Assume you are refinancing $75,000. A 14 percent mortgage involves closing fees of $3,750, and the new interest rate is 10 percent. How long does it take to recover your total financing cost of $3,750?

SOLUTION

At the new rate of 10 percent, the monthly payment on a 30-year fixed-rate loan would be $658. That is a savings of $231 from the monthly payment of $889 required on a 14 percent loan. Dividing the total refinancing cost of $3,750 by $231 gives a recovery period of about 16 months. Table 10-2 below illustrates the monthly and yearly savings from refinancing to a 10 percent 30-year fixed rate mortgage for $75,000.

Table 10-2   Savings from Refinancing

Present Mortgage Rate, %	Current Monthly Payment	Monthly Payment at 10%	Monthly Savings at 10%	Annual Savings at 10%
12.0	$771	$658	$113	$1,356
12.5	800	658	142	1,704
13.0	830	658	172	2,064
13.5	859	658	201	2,412
14.0	889	658	231	2,772
15.0	948	658	290	3,480

HOW TO SHOP FOR AN ADJUSTABLE RATE MORTGAGE?

An adjustable rate mortgage (ARM) is a mortgage where the interest rate is not fixed but changes over the life of the loan. ARMs are often called variable- or flexible-rate mortgages.

ARMs often feature attractive starting interest rates and monthly payments. But you face the risk that your payments will rise. Pluses of ARMs include:

You pay lower initial interest (often two or three percentage points below that of a fixed rate) and lower initial payments, which can result in considerable savings. This means that ARMs are easier to qualify for.

Payments come down if interest rates fall.

Loans are more readily available and their processing time is quicker than fixed-rate mortgages.

Many adjustables are assumable by a borrower, which can help when it comes time to sell.

Many ARMs allow you to prepay the loan without penalty.

Some of the pitfalls of ARMs include:

Monthly payments can go up if interest rates rise.

Negative amortization can occur meaning the monthly payments do not cover all of the interest cost. The interest cost that is not covered is added to the unpaid principal balance. This means after making many payments you could owe more than you did at the beginning of the loan balance.

The initial interest rates last only until the first adjustment, typically 6 months or 1 year. And the promotional or tease rate is often not distinguished from the true contract rate, which is based on the index to which the loan is tied.

Tip: It pays to get an ARM if you are buying a starter home or expect to move or be transferred in 2 to 3 years.

You should consider a fixed-rate loan over an ARM if you

Plan to be in the same home for a long time.

Do not expect your income to rise.

Plan to take on sizable debts, like auto or educational loans.

Prize the security of constant payments.

When you shop for an ARM (or for any other adjustable-rate loan), you should carry the following checklist of questions to ask lenders:

What is the initial loan rate and the annual percentage rate (APR)? What costs besides interest does the APR reflect? What are the points?

What is the monthly payment?

What index is the loan tied to? How has the index moved in the past? Will the rate always move with the index?

What is the lender's margin above the index? *Tip:* The margin is an important consideration when comparing ARM loans, because it never changes during the life of the loan. *Remember:* Index rate + margin = ARM interest rate.

SOLVED PROBLEM 10.8

You are comparing ARMs offered by two different lenders. Both ARMs are for 30 years and amount to $65,000. Both lenders use the 1-year Treasury index, which is 10 percent. Lender A uses a 2 percent margin and Lender B uses a 3 percent margin. How would the difference in margin affect your initial monthly payment?

SOLUTION

	LENDER A	LENDER B
ARM interest rate	12% (10% + 2%)	13% (10% + 3%)
Monthly payment*	$668.59 at 12%	$719.03 at 13%

*From Appendix Table 5.

How long will the initial rate be in effect? Will there be an automatic increase at the first adjustment period, even if the index has not changed? What effect will this have on monthly payments?

How often can the rate change?

Is there a limit on each rate change and how will the limit affect monthly payments?

What is the "cap," or ceiling on the rate change over the life of the loan?

Does the loan require private mortgage insurance (PMI) and how much does it cost per month?

Is negative amortization possible?

Is the loan assumable?

Is there a prepayment penalty?

SHOULD YOU PAY OFF YOUR MORTGAGE EARLY?

Suppose you have decided to refinance your home with a lower fixed-rate mortgage. You should consider the term of the loan. Although the standard 30-year mortgage is still very much alive, you might want to consider a loan with a shorter term such as a 15-year fixed-rate loan. The overall savings in interest paid to the lender over the life of the 15-year mortgage can be quite substantial, yet the monthly payment is not significantly higher. *Recommendation:* Even if you decide to stay with your current 30-year mortgage, you might be able to save a bundle by paying off more each month, treating the 30-year loan as if it were a 15-year loan.

SOLVED PROBLEM 10.9

You currently have a $100,000 30-year fixed-rate mortgage at 13 percent. Your monthly payment for principal and interest is $1,106.20. You have decided to refinance your home with a fixed-rate loan at 10 percent. You have two options available: a 30-year loan at 10 percent versus a 15-year loan at the same rate. Which one should you choose?

SOLUTION

Look at Table 10-3 to compare the monthly payment and total interest over the life of the loan. *Note:* In either case, the monthly payment is less than the 13 percent mortgage. Between 30 years and 15 years, however, the monthly payment increases about 22.45 percent while the savings in total interest payments over the life would be almost 57 percent.

From this example, you learn some valuable lessons:

1. It was a good decision to refinance your home, since, in either case, you save in your monthly payments [$1,106.20 versus $877.57 (30-year) or $1,074.61 (15-year)]. In this example, a 3 percent drop in the fixed rate made this possible.

2. You would be able to save $122,495 in total interest payments by election of a 15-year loan without increasing your monthly burden.

3. Among other things, you will be a 100 percent equity holder in your home within 15 years instead of 30 years.

Table 10-3   Comparison of 30-Year Versus 15-Year Fixed-Rate Mortgage

	30-Year	15-Year	$ Increase (Decrease)	% Increase (Decrease)
Principal	$100,000	$100,000	—	—
Interest rate	10%	10%	—	—
Monthly payment	$877.57	$1,074.61	$197.04	22.45
Total interest	$215,925	$93,430	$(122.495)	(56.73)

CONSIDER BIWEEKLY MORTGAGES

If you pay the equivalent of an extra installment each year, you will dramatically lower the ultimate interest costs. This plan is called a biweekly payment loan. These plans provide a dramatic buildup of equity, saving you thousands of dollars in interest.

These plans do not change your existing mortgages. You are not reapplying or refinancing anything, so there are no points, no need for costly appraisals, and no credit constraints. Instead of making one monthly payment, you make a half-payment every 14 days. This results in 26 half-payments yearly, or an extra monthly payment annually. This way you achieve the following:

The reduction you will achieve on the loan more than doubles, even over the short term. For example, on a $100,000 loan, after 3 years in the biweekly program you would have $7,023 in equity available, as opposed to $3,425.61 if you had stayed on your regular monthly plan.

The loan is also shortened if you keep your property for the full term of the loan. A typical 30-year loan is completely paid off in a little more than 20 years, with a savings of more than $65,000 in interest per every $100,000 borrowed.

Biweekly payment plans are offered by various firms that are hired to act as money managers to assist the owner. Once in the program, everything is automatic. Every 14 days an electronic wire transfer of half your monthly payment is sent from your local bank or savings account. Then, after the second monthly half-payment, the funds are combined and the entire payment is transferred to your lender.

When shopping for a biweekly, there are five things to look for:

A reasonable, one-time start-up fee.

Reasonable wire transfer fees.

The program holds your funds in a major bank, not in a trust account or other privately controlled account.

The program pays you interest on all funds held.

You have the ability to go off, and back on, the program or transfer at no additional charge.

HOW TO GET TOP DOLLAR FOR YOUR HOUSE

Getting top dollar for your house when you sell hinges upon a number of factors. They are

Ask the right price. Get several brokers to look at your house. Have them do comparisons ("comps") to other homes on their computer.

Sell by July. Statistics show that of all home sales, over 70 percent occur in just four months, April through July. Most buyers want to move before school starts for their children.

Put some cosmetics on your house.

Pick a top sales agent. See if you can find a Realtor of the Year type because he or she is a performing broker.

Don't be stingy on the standard commission. A full-price broker may give up some portion of the commission to clinch your sale.

Sign up for a shorter term listing (such as no more than 90 days).

Take advantage of a multiple listing. The multiple listing is a listing, usually an exclusive right to sell, taken by a member of an organization made up of real estate brokers, with the provisions that all members will have the opportunity to find a buyer; a form of cooperative listing.

Do not oversell. Sit back and let the broker do the talking.

Avoid any offer that is contingent on the buyer's selling his or her own house. Avoid any chance the deal may fall through.

WOULD YOU WANT TO SELL YOUR HOME YOURSELF?

Where houses are selling briskly "For Sale by Owner" deals are becoming popular. Although this may not necessarily be a good idea in order to do away with the broker's commission, here are some tips:

Advertise.   Don't rely 100 percent on a "For Sale" sign on the lawn. You should circulate flyers, run ads in the local newspapers and Pennysavers, and put notices on bulletin boards. Try to be creative in advertising. Highlight good points (such as an assumable mortgage and a low fixed interest rate).

Do not overprice.   Compare your house to others in the neighborhood that have recently been sold, and factor in any improvements. Figure part of your savings in brokerage commissions into the asking price.

Screen buyers.   Before accepting an offer, ask the buyer to fill out a financial statement. You do not want the deal to fall through because of the buyer's failure to qualify for a mortgage loan. Ask how much of a down payment can be made. A serious buyer would not resist.

Review Questions

(1) _____ is still the best tax shelter there is.

(2) Two methods are widely used to determine the price of property: _____ and _____ .

(3) One rule of thumb to determine a borrower's ability to afford a house is that the borrower should not extend himself beyond _____ percent of monthly take-home pay.

(4) Whether refinancing is worthwhile depends on the costs of refinancing and the _____ required to recoup those costs through low mortgage payments.

(5) An _____ is a mortgage where the interest rate is not fixed but changes over the life of the loan.

(6) _____ amortization occurs when the monthly payments do not cover all of the interest cost.

(7) _____ is an important consideration when comparing ARM loans.

(8) If you pay the equivalent of an extra installment each year, you will dramatically lower the ultimate _____ .

(9) The best figure to use in determining your home insurance need is the _____ , the amount it would cost to rebuild, excluding land.

(10) _____ is known as the basic coverage.

(11) _____ differs from other policies in that the coverage is on an actual cash value basis rather than on a replacement cost basis.

(12) Statistics show that over 70 percent of home sales occur in just 4 months, _____ .

(13) Under the gross income rule, the price of a home should not exceed about _____ times the family's gross annual income.

Answers: (1) Owning a home; (2) comparative sales on computer, use of expert; (3) 35; (4) time; (5) adjustable-rate mortgage; (6) Negative; (7) Margin; (8) interest costs; (9) replacement value; (10) Homeowners-1 (HO-1); (11) HO-8; (12) April through July; (13) $2\frac{1}{2}$.

Additional Solved Problems

10.1 Property values in your neighborhood are increasing at a rate of 5 percent per year. If your home is presently worth $120,000, what will it be worth in 5 years?

SOLUTION

The future value of $1 for 5 years at 5 percent (from Appendix Table 1) is 1.276.

$$\$120,000 \times 1.276 = \$153,120$$

10.2 Tom Silver recently bought a second home as an investment. The purchase price was $85,600, of which he paid $15,000 down. Assume the land value was $15,600.

(a) What was the loan-to-value ratio?

(b) How much depreciation is tax deductible each year?

SOLUTION

(a) $70,600/$85,600 = 82.5%

(b) $\dfrac{\$85,600 - \$15,600}{27.5 \text{ years}} = \$2,545.45$

10.3 Janet Tannenbaum is about to close on the purchase of a $78,000 home. Her mortgage loan is for $62,400. She will be required to pay three points at closing. What is the dollar amount of that fee?

SOLUTION

$$\$62,400 \times 3\% = \$1,872$$

10.4 Jack and Jill have arranged for a mortgage of $100,000 with loan fees of 2 points. At the time the loan is granted, how much will Jack and Jill owe in mortgage points?

SOLUTION

$$.02 \times \$100,000 = \$2,000$$

10.5 The Republic Bank requires that mortgage loan applicants make a down payment. The bank's loan-to-value ratio requirement is 70 percent. The Tripps have applied for a mortgage loan with the bank for a property which will cost $250,000.

(a) Calculate the required down payment.

(b) Calculate the maximum mortgage available on this property from the bank.

SOLUTION

(a) (.30) ($250,000) = $75,000

(b) (.70) ($250,000) = $175,000

10.6 The Smiths decide to buy a house in the suburbs. They realize that they should not pay more than $2\frac{1}{2}$ times their combined annual gross income, which is $50,000. Up to what amount should they pay for a house?

SOLUTION

$$\$50,000 \times 2\tfrac{1}{2} = \$125,000$$

10.7 The Franks have been house-hunting for several months. They found a dream house at $210,000. How much should their annual gross income be in order to afford the house? (Use the $2\frac{1}{2}$ times rule.)

SOLUTION

$210,000/2\frac{1}{2} = $84,000 is required.

10.8 Your gross annual income is $35,000 and take-home pay is $2,400 per month. Using the 35 percent rule, how much monthly payment can you afford?

SOLUTION

$$\$2,400 \times 35\% = \$840$$

10.9 The Kings found an attractive house in the country with an appraised value of $210,000. After searching for a mortgage loan, they found a bank that would arrange a conventional loan in the amount of 80 percent of the appraised value.

(*a*) How much will the bank lend the Kings?

(*b*) How much will they have to put down?

SOLUTION .

(*a*)   Loan amount = $210,000 × 80% = $168,000

(*b*) $210,000 − $168,000 = $42,000

10.10 The Blocks want to buy a house for $79,000. Their monthly housing costs (mortgage payment, taxes, utilities, and so on) will amount to $890. The Blocks' gross annual income is $39,000. If the lender uses the gross monthly income rule, do the Blocks qualify for a loan? If not, by how much would they have to reduce their monthly housing costs to qualify?

SOLUTION

Using the annual gross income rule, the Blocks can buy a house for up to $39,000 × 2.5 = $97,500. The Blocks' monthly income is $39,000/12 = $3,250. Based on the monthly gross income rule, they should pay no more than $3,250 × .25 = $812.50 monthly in housing expenses. Their expected housing costs of $890 are too high. They will need to reduce their housing costs to about $812 before they might qualify for a mortgage.

10.11 The Allens have annual gross income of $40,000.

(*a*) Using the annual gross income rule, what is the maximum purchase price that they could afford for a house?

(*b*) Based on the monthly gross income rule what is the maximum amount per month that they should plan on spending for housing costs?

SOLUTION

(*a*) Using the gross income rule, the Allens can purchase a house that costs up to $40,000 × $2\frac{1}{2}$ = $100,000.

(*b*) Using the monthly income figure, they should plan to spend no more that $40,000 × $\frac{1}{12}$ × .25 = $833.33 per month on housing.

10.12 Jeanne Sedelo is considering making an offer of $100,000 on a ranch house that she likes. Her housing costs other than mortgage payments (that is, taxes, utilities, insurance, and maintenance) would be $500 per month. A lender has indicated to her that with a 20 percent down payment and a 12 percent, 25-year, fixed-rate mortgage, she would just meet the monthly gross income requirement. What is Jeanne's annual gross income?

SOLUTION

From Appendix Table 5, note that a $40,000 fixed-rate mortgage at 12 percent for 25 years would carry monthly payments of $421.32.

On a $100,000 home, Jeanne's 20 percent down payment would be $100,000 × .20 = $20,000. Thus, her mortgage would be $100,000 − $20,000 = $80,000. This is twice $40,000, meaning that Jeanne's monthly mortgage payment would be $421.32 \times 2 = $842.64. Her other monthly housing costs are $500. Thus, her total housing costs would be $842.64 + $500 = $1,342.64.

Since she just meets the monthly gross income rule, her monthly gross income would be four times $1,342.64, since monthly gross income $\times$ .25 = $1,342.64. Thus, her annual gross income would be about $1,342.64 \times 4 \times 12 = $64,446.72.

10.13 Dave and Linda are thinking of buying houses costing $80,000. Dave would make a 20 percent down payment, and Linda, 30 percent. Both mortgages are for 25 years, with Dave paying 12 percent interest, and Linda, 10 percent. Dave's and Linda's monthly payments are $674 and $509, respectively. Taxes, utilities, maintenance, and insurance are $250 a month for both.

(a)   Dave's annual gross income is $34,000, and Linda's is $38,000. If the lender uses the annual gross income rule, do both qualify for a mortgage? Explain your answer.

(b)   Using the monthly gross income rule, do both qualify for a mortgage? Explain your answer.

SOLUTION

(a)   Using the annual gross income rule, Dave could buy a house for up to $34,000 \times 2.5 = $85,000, and Linda could buy one for up to $38,000 \times 2.5 = $95,000. Neither one would qualify on the annual gross income rule.

(b)   Dave's monthly gross income is $34,000/12 = $2,833. He can afford monthly payments of up to $2,833 \times .25 = $708.25. Dave cannot qualify for the mortgage using the monthly gross income rule since his actual housing costs ($674 + $250 = $924) exceed $708.25. Linda can afford actual monthly housing costs of up to ($38,000/12) \times .25 = $791.67. She qualifies for the mortgage since the actual housing costs would be $509 + $250 = $759.

10.14 The Merrills are considering buying a home for $100,000. Their annual gross income is $42,000. The mortgage payments at current interest rates would be about $1,000 per month. Taxes would be $110 per month and utilities would be $140 per month. Will the Merrills qualify for a loan at a bank that uses the monthly gross income rule? What advice do you have for the Merrills?

SOLUTION

The Merrills' monthly income is $42,000/12 = $3,500. Based on the monthly gross income rule, they should not be spending more than $3,500 \times .25 = $875 per month on housing. Since their anticipated housing expenses are $1,000 + $110 + $140 = $1,250 per month, the bank will not loan them the mortgage money.

The Merrills have two options for buying a house. They can either increase the down payment on the house they are currently considering, or they can look for a cheaper one. In either case, they will have to reduce shelter expenses to around $875 per month before a bank might be willing to lend them money.

10.15 How much would you have to put down on a house costing $80,000 if the home had an appraised value of $85,000 and the lender requires an 80 percent loan-to-value ratio?

SOLUTION

If the loan-to-value ratio is 80 percent, the down payment must be 20 percent. If the appraised value of the house is $85,000 and the lender is willing to lend 80 percent of the value or $68,000, the required down payment for an $80,000 selling price would be $12,000 ($80,000 − $68,000). Note that the appraised value of a house may be different than its selling price.

10.16 Find the monthly mortgage payments on the following mortgage loans:

(a) $60,000, 10 percent, 30 years

(b) $50,000, $13\frac{1}{2}$ percent, 20 years

(c) $85,000, $10\frac{1}{2}$ percent, 15 years

SOLUTION

From Appendix Table 5

(a) For a $60,000, 10 percent, 30-year loan

$$\frac{\$60,000}{\$10,000} = 6$$

$$\$87.76 \times 6 = \$526.56 \text{ payment}$$

(b) For a $50,000, $13\frac{1}{2}$ percent, 20-year loan

$$\frac{\$50,000}{\$10,000} = 5$$

$$\$120.74 \times 5 = \$603.70 \text{ payment}$$

(c) For a $85,000, $10\frac{1}{2}$ percent, 15-year loan

$$\frac{\$85,000}{\$10,000} = 8.5$$

$$\$110.54 \times 8.5 = \$939.59 \text{ payment}$$

10.17 How much would a home buyer have to pay if the lender wanted to charge $2\frac{1}{2}$ points on a $75,000 mortgage? What effect do points have on the mortgage's rate of interest?

SOLUTION

If a lender wanted to charge $2\frac{1}{2}$ points on a $75,000 loan the buyer would have to pay $1,875 ($75,000 × .025) in points. Lenders use points as a way of charging interest on their loans. They can vary the interest rate along with the number of points they charge to come up with comparable effective rates.

10.18 What would the monthly payment be on a $50,999 loan if the mortgage were set up as

(a) A 15-year, 10 percent, fixed-rate loan?

(b) A 30-year adjustable-rate mortgage in which the lender added a margin of $2\frac{1}{2}$ points to the index rate (which presently stands at 6 percent)? Find the monthly mortgage payments for the first year only.

SOLUTION

From Appendix Table 5, using a factor of $50,000/$10,000 = 5,

(a) A 15-year, 10 percent, fixed-rate loan

$$\$107.47 \times 5 = \$537.35 \text{ payment}$$

(b) A 30-year adjustable-rate loan at $2\frac{1}{2}$ points above the index rate of 6 percent. The first year monthly payment would be based on 30 years at $8\frac{1}{2}$ percent:

$$\$76.90 \times 5 = \$384.50 \text{ payment}$$

10.19 The Masons have a home with an appraised value of $180,000 and a mortgage balance of $90,000. An S&L is willing to lend money at a loan-to-value ratio of 75 percent.

(a) How much of a home equity credit line can the Masons obtain?

(b) How much, if any, of this line would qualify for tax-deductible interest if their house originally cost $100,000 and they have spent $20,000 on home improvements?

SOLUTION

(a) If the Masons have a home appraised at $180,000 and they have a mortgage balance of $90,000, they have equity in the home of $90,000 ($180,000 − $90,000). If an S&L will lend money on the home at a loan-to-value ratio of 75 percent, the S&L would be willing to lend up to $135,000 (.75 × $180,000). Subtracting the first mortgage of $90,000, the Masons could qualify for a home equity loan of $45,000.

(b) Since the Masons paid $100,000 for the home and spent $20,000 on improvements, the portion of the home equity loan on which interest would be deductible is the difference between the $120,000 original cost plus improvements and the $90,000 first mortgage or $30,000.

Under the 1986 tax revisions any interest charged on an amount above $30,000 would not be tax deductible unless the money was used to cover the cost of home improvements or it was needed for educational or medical purposes.

10.20 Assume an affordable monthly mortgage payment of $650, and a mortgage interest rate of 10 percent on a 30-year loan.

(a) What is the size of the affordable mortgage?

(b) If you can make a 20 percent down payment, what is the affordable purchase price?

SOLUTION

(a) From Appendix Table 5, you get 87.76 for a monthly payment per $10,000 of mortgage loan.

$$\frac{\$650}{\$87.76} = 7.41$$

$$7.41 \times 10,000 = \$74,100 \qquad \text{(affordable mortgage)}$$

(b) The affordable purchase price with a 20 percent down payment is $74,100/(1 − .2) = $92,625.

10.21 You bought a $120,000 house that is expected to appreciate at 10 percent annually over the next 5 years. What will be the capital gain on the house on selling it and paying a sales commission of 6 percent?

SOLUTION

From Appendix Table 1, the furture value of a $1 after 5 years at 10 percent is 1.611.

$$\$120,000 \times 1.611 = \$193,320$$

After paying a sales commission of 6 percent, the capital gain is $81,721, as calculated below.

$$\$193,320 \times (1 - .06) = \$181,721$$

$$\$181,721 - \$120,000 = \$81,721$$

10.22 A lender is offering a 9 percent fixed-rate mortgage, and requiring a down payment of 10 percent of the home's purchase price. The lender estimates that closing costs should be equal to 3 points in loan origination and $750. What would be the closing cost on a $150,000 home?

SOLUTION

Each point is equal to 1 percent of the amount borrowed. The amount borrowed is $135,000 ($150,000 − $15,000). Total closing costs are $750 + (3% × $135,000) = $750 + $4,050 = $4,800.

10.23 You are a potential buyer. You and your spouse together earn $80,000 annually. Interest rates are 12 percent on a 30-year loan. What price can you afford to pay for a house if you base your calculations

(a) On the 25 percent standard?

(b) On the 35 percent standard?

SOLUTION

(a) Using the 25 percent standard, monthly payments are $1,667 ($80,000/12 × .25). From Appendix Table 5, we note that for a 12 percent, 30-year, $10,000 loan monthly payments are $102.86.

$$\frac{\$1,667}{102.86} = 16.21$$

$$16.21 \times \$10,000 = \$162,100$$

You could afford a $162,100 house.

(b) Using the 35 percent standard, monthly payments are $2,333 ($80,000/12 × .35). From Appendix Table 5, we note that for a 12 percent, 30-year, $10,000 loan monthly payments are $102.86.

$$\frac{\$2,333}{102.86} = 22.69$$

$$22.69 \times \$10,000 = \$226,900$$

You could afford a $226,900 house.

10.24 Jason Leigh has been in the market for a new home. He has signed a purchase contract to pay $58,900 for a two-bedroom ranch-style home. Now he is looking for a mortgage loan. Three of his applications have been approved. Loan A calls for a 15 percent down payment and a 13 percent interest rate for 25 years. Loan B calls for a 20 percent down payment and a 12 percent interest rate for 30 years. Loan C is an adjustable-rate mortgage (ARM) with a 10 percent down payment at 11 percent interest for 20 years. The ARM has 1-year interest rate and payment caps. (Use Appendix Table 5.)

(a)   What is the monthly payment for Loan A?

(b)   What is the monthly payment for Loan B?

(c)   What is the monthly payment (during the first year) for Loan C?

(d)   Jason has decided to accept Loan B. How much interest will he have paid at the end of the first year?

(e)   How much equity will he have in the home at the end of the first year if the market value of the home goes up $2,700?

SOLUTION

(a)   The loan amount is $50,065, because

$$\$58,900 - (15\% \times \$58,900) = \$58,900 - \$8,835 = \$50,065$$

The monthly payment is

$$11.2784 \times 50.065 = \$564.65$$

(b)   The loan amount is $47,120, because

$$\$58,900 - (20\% \times \$58,900) = \$58,900 - \$11,780 = \$47,120$$

The monthly payment is

$$11.2784 \times 47.120 = \$484.68$$

(c)   The loan amount is $53,010, because

$$\$58,900 - (10\% \times \$58,900) = \$58,900 - \$5,890 = \$53,010$$

The monthly payment is

$$11.2784 \times 53.010 = \$547.16$$

(d) $5,645.21 (see accompanying chart)

(e) $2,870.95 = $170.95 (see accompanying chart) + $2,700

The First Year of Jason Leigh's Mortgage

Month	Monthly Payment	Principal	Interest	Balance
1	$ 484.68	$ 13.48	$ 471.20	$47,106.52
2	484.68	13.61	471.07	47,092.91
3	484.68	13.79	470.93	47,079.16
4	484.68	13.88	470.80	47,065.28
5	484.68	14.03	470.65	47,051.25
6	484.68	14.17	470.51	47,037.08
7	484.68	14.31	470.37	47,022.77
8	484.68	14.45	470.23	47,008.32
9	484.68	14.60	470.08	46,993.72
10	484.68	14.74	469.94	46,978.98
11	484.68	14.89	469.79	46,964.09
12	484.68	15.04	469.64	46,949.05
Totals	$5,816.16	$170.95	$5,645.21	

10.25 Calculate the monthly mortgage payment using the Table of Monthly Mortgage Payments (Appendix Table 5) for each of the following mortgages:

Case	Rate of Interest, %	Loan Maturity, Years	Mortgage Amount
A	8	15	$100,000
B	12	10	50,000
C	9.5	30	75,000
D	14	20	30,000
E	10	25	65,000

SOLUTION

Case	(1) Amount of Loan per $10,000	(2) Loan Payment Factor	(3) Monthly Payment (1) × (2)
A	10	95.57	$955.70
B	5	143.48	717.40
C	7.5	84.09	630.68
D	3	124.36	373.08
E	6.5	90.88	590.72

10.26 Calculate the amount of interest paid over the full term of the mortgage for each case described.

Case	Rate of Interest	Loan Maturity, Years	Mortgage Amount
A	8%	15	$75,000
B	8	20	75,000
C	8	30	75,000

SOLUTION

Case	Amount of Loan per $10,000	Loan Payment Factor	Monthly Payments	Interest over Term of Loan
A	7.5	95.57	$716.78	$ 54,020.40
B	7.5	83.65	627.38	75,570.00
C	7.5	73.38	550.35	123,126.00

(Monthly payments × Number of months in the term of the loan) − Loan amount

= Total interest paid over term of loan

For example, Case A   [$716.78 × (15 × 12)] − $75,000 = $54,020.40

Note how the length of term greatly increases the total interest paid on the mortgage.

10.27 Affordability guidelines stipulate

Monthly mortgage payments should not exceed 25 percent of the borrower's monthly gross income.

Total monthly installment obligations should not exceed 36 percent of the borrower's gross income.

Calculate the maximum mortgage advisable in each of the following cases:

Case	Gross Income	Other Installment Loan Obligations
A	$4,000	$ 500
B	1,200	100
C	3,000	250
D	5,000	1,000

SOLUTION

	Maximum Total Monthly Installment Loan Payments	Other Installment Loan Payments	Maximum Monthly Mortgage Payment
A (.36) ($4,000)	$1,440	$ 500	$940
B (.36) ($1,200)	432	100	332
C (.36) ($3,000)	1,080	250	830
D (.36) ($5,000)	1,800	1,000	800

10.28 Consider the following two situations:

1. You had $5,000 in mortgage interest payments during the year, and you were in the 28 percent tax bracket.

2. You had the same amount in rental payments during the year, and you are in the 45 percent tax bracket.

What is the after-tax real cost of mortgage interest payments and what is the after-tax real cost of rental payments?

SOLUTION

The real cost of mortgage interest payments after taxes is $5,000 × (1 − .28) = $3,600. However, since rental payments are not tax deductible, the real cost of rental payments after taxes is still $5,000.

10.29 The West family is comparing the costs of renting versus buying a home. Jean West has compiled all of the relevant costs of each option. Using the form provided compare the costs of each option and recommend whether the West family should rent or buy their home.

Cost of Renting	
Monthly payment	$ 1,000
Renter's insurance	750
Cost of Buying	
Purchase price of home	$100,000
Mortgage payments	1,290
Homeowner's insurance	625
Property taxes	3,750
Maintenance	2,500
Principal reduction in loan balance	1,730
Annual interest (year 1)	13,750
Marginal tax rate	28%
Expected appreciation in the value of the home	2.5%
Down payment and closing costs	20,000
After-tax rate of return	5%

SOLUTION

RENT OR BUY ANALYSIS

A. **Cost of Renting**

1.	Annual rental costs (12 × monthly rental rate of $1,000)	$12,000	
2.	Renter's insurance	750	
	Total cost of renting		$12,750

B. **Cost of Buying**

1.	Annual mortgage payments (12 × monthly mortgage payment of $1,290)	$15,480	
2.	Property taxes	3,750	
3.	Homeowner's insurance	625	
4.	Maintenance	0	
5.	After-tax cost of interest lost on down payment and closing costs ($20,000 × 5% after-tax rate of return)	1,000	
6.	Total cost		$20,855
7.	Principal reduction in loan balance	$ 1,730	
8.	Tax savings due to interest deductions (interest portion of mortgage payments $13,750 × tax rate of 28%)	3,850	
9.	Tax savings due to property tax deductions	1,050	
10.	Total deductions		6,630
11.	Annual after-tax cost of home ownership		$14,225
12.	Less: Estimated annual appreciation in value of home		2,500
	Total cost of buying		$11,725

10.30 The Biblers can rent a home for $310 per month or buy it for $37,000. Assume that whether they buy or rent, maintenance, insurance, and utilities costs will remain the same. Monthly real estate taxes are $50. The house can be bought with a $7,000 down payment. Monthly mortgage payments are $316; $300 is interest, and $16 is payment on the principal. The house is expected to go up in value at a rate of $80 per month on an after-tax basis. If the Biblers do not buy the house, they will put the $7,000 in a savings account paying 8 percent per year. Their tax rate is 30 percent. Is it cheaper for them to buy or rent? Show your calculations.

SOLUTION

Item	Rent	Buy
Shelter expenditures		
Rent	$310	
Loan repayment		$316
Taxes		50
Total expenditures	$310	$366
Shelter benefits		
Interest on down payment	$ 33*	
Tax savings, interest		$ 90†
Tax savings, taxes		15‡
Payment on principal		16
Increase in shelter value		80
Total benefits	$ 33	$201
Net cost	$ 277	$165

*$7,000 $\times$ .08 $\times$ (1 − .3)/12 = $33
†$300 $\times$ .3 = $90
‡$50 $\times$ .3 = $15

It is $112 ($277 − $165) cheaper to buy than to rent.

10.31 In Problem 10.30, assume that the Biblers' tax rate is 0 percent and that the house increases in value at a rate of $125 per month. Show your calculations to indicate whether it is cheaper for them to buy or rent.

SOLUTION

We need to redo only the benefits portion here.

Item	Rent	Buy
Shelter expenditures	$310	$366
Shelter benefits		
Interest on down payment	$ 47	
Payment on principal		$ 16
Increase in shelter value		125
Total benefits	$ 47	$141
Net cost	$263	$225

It is $38 ($263 − $225) cheaper to buy.

10.32 The Hirts are looking for a house. They have located a house that can be either rented or bought. The rent is $350 per month on a 12-month lease. Renters' insurance on the house would be $9 per month. Their utility bills are expected to average $80 per month. The house can be bought for $42,000. A bank is willing to provide an 80 percent loan at 12 percent interest. Monthly payments to repay the loan are $354, of which $336 is for interest, and the rest is payment on the principal. Real estate taxes on the house are $720 per yer. Homeowners' insurance is $300 per year. Maintenance expenses are $50 per month. The Hirts' tax rate is 25 percent. The house is expected to increase in value by $140 per month on an after-tax basis. If the Hirts do not buy the house, they will put the down payment in a savings account paying 8 percent before taxes. Calculate the net cost of renting and buying. Which is better financially?

SOLUTION

Item	Rent	Buy
Shelter expenditures		
Rent	$350	
Loan repayment		$354
Utilities	80	80
Insurance	9	25
Taxes		60
Maintenance		50
Total expenditures	$439	$569
Shelter benefits		
Interest on down payment*	$ 42[†]	
Tax savings, interest		$ 84[‡]
Tax savings, taxes		15[§]
Payment on principal		18[¶]
Increase in shelter value		140
Total benefits	$ 42	$257
Net cost	$ 397	$312

*$42,000 \times .2 = \$8,400$
[†]$\$8,400 \times .08 \times (1 - .25)/12 = \$42$
[‡]$\$336 \times .25 = \$84$
[§]$\$60 \times .25 = \$15$
[¶]$\$354 - \$336 = \$18$

It is $85 ($397 − $312) cheaper to buy than rent.

10.33 Lynne Chamberlain has an option to either rent a house for $350 per month or buy it for $40,000. Whether the house is bought or rented, utilities will remain the same. Maintenance would be about $40 per month and would be paid by the owner. Renters' insurance is $5 per month, while homeowners' insurance is $20 per month. Lynne can buy the house with a 20 percent down payment. The mortgage payment would be $410 per month, of which $400 would be for interest. Real estate taxes are about $60 per month. Lynne expects the house to increase about $100 per month in value. She can earn about 12 percent, tax-free, on her investments. Lynne is in the 25 percent tax bracket. Should she buy or rent this house?

SOLUTION

Item	Rent	Buy
Shelter expenditures		
Rent	$350	
Loan repayment		$410
Insurance	5	20
Taxes		60
Maintenance		40
Total monthly expenditures	$355	$530
Shelter benefits		
Interest on down payment	$ 60	
Tax savings, interest		$100
Tax savings, taxes		15
Payment on principal		10
Increase in shelter value		100
Total shelter benefits	$ 60	$225
Net cost	$295	$305

Down payment is 20 percent of $40,000, or $8,000. Interest received on this amount is $8,000 × (1 − .25) × .12/12 = $60 per month. Since Lynne is in the 25 percent tax bracket, she derives a $400 × .25 = $100 per month benefit from paying interest. Her equity in the house would increase by $410 − $400 = $10 per month. Lynne would be better off renting than buying the house by $10 ($305 − $295).

10.34 Tracy Key sold her old home for $83,000 and bought a new one for $97,000. Expenses related to the sale of her house were $6,000. Her purchase price for the old home was $61,000. How much profit did Tracy make on the sale of her house? What tax advice do you have for her?

SOLUTION

Selling price	$83,000
Less: Selling expenses	6,000
Net amount realized	$77,000
Cost basis	61,000
Gain on sales	$16,000

Tracy made a $16,000 profit on the sale of her house. She should adjust the holding cost basis for her new house rather than pay taxes on the gain.

Purchase price	$97,000
Less: Gain on sale	16,000
Adjusted basis	$81,000

Her adjusted cost basis for the new house would be $81,000.

10.35 The Chens bought a house for $40,000, spent $7,000 on home improvements, and then sold the house for $80,000. Sales commissions and other closing costs were $6,000. Three months later they bought a new house for $90,000. What is the adjusted cost basis for the new house?

SOLUTION

The adjusted cost basis for the house was $40,000 + $7,000 = $47,000.

Selling price	$80,000
Less: Selling expenses	6,000
Net amount realized	$74,000
Adjusted basis	47,000
Gain on sale	$27,000

The adjusted basis for the new house is calculated as follows:

Purchase price	$90,000
Less: Gain on sale	27,000
Adjusted basis, new home	$63,000

10.36 Bob Teweles, 42, purchased a home twelve years ago for $43,800. He lived in it for the past 10 years, then sold it last month for $67,900, paying a 6 percent real estate commission. Bob is in the 28 percent tax bracket.

(a) How much profit did he make on the sale after paying the real estate commission?

(b) Yesterday Bob closed on the purchase of a new home for $76,000. How much federal income tax will he pay on the profit from his previous home?

(c) If Bob moved instead into an apartment and did not buy housing again, how much federal income tax will he pay on the profit from his previous home?

(d) How would the answer to part c change if Bob were fifty-seven years old?

SOLUTION

(a) $20,026 = $67,900 − $43,800 − $4,074 (or $67,900 × 0.06)

(b) 0, since he purchased a new home of equal or greater value within 2 years.

(c) $5,607.28 = $20,026 × 0.28

(d) Bob's tax liability would be zero since there is a one-time $125,000 income tax exclusion on the profit from the sale of a home for persons age fifty-five and over.

10.37 The Wyches want to refinance their home. Refinancing is $100,000. Details on the current loan and refinancing are

Current loan:	
Amount	$100,000
Term	30 years
Interest rate	14%
Monthly payments	$1,185
Refinancing:	
Amount	$100,000
Term	30 years
Interest rate	10%
Refinancing costs:	
Closing costs	$1,200
Points	2

Determine:

(*a*)   New monthly payments

(*b*)   Monthly savings

(*c*)   Total refinancing costs

(*d*)   Payback (recovery) period

SOLUTION

(*a*)   From Appendix Table 5, $10 \times \$87.76 = \$878$

(*b*) $\$1,185 - \$878 = \$307$

(*c*) $\$1,200 + (2\% \times \$100,000) = \$3,200$

(*d*) $\$3,200/\$307 = 10.4$ months

Chapter 11

Life, Health, and Property and Liability Insurance

An integral part of any financial plan is insurance protection. Insurance provides a vital means of meeting your financial objectives. The type and amount of insurance depends on your age, assets, income, and needs. Insurance is basically "replacement": life insurance provides income lost at the death of the wage earner; disability insurance assures income when you are not able to work full time; health insurance covers medical bills; and property/casualty policies pay most of the costs of theft, fire, or accident. With the variety of insurance products on the market, you are faced with a number of decisions. This chapter answers the following questions:

Which policy is right for you?

How much insurance should you buy?

How do you evaluate insurance coverage?

WHICH LIFE INSURANCE POLICY IS RIGHT FOR YOU?

Life insurance is the most important tool of estate planning and one of the most valuable aids to financial planning. Taking out an insurance policy is one way to obtain tax-deferred interest income since taxes are not paid until the policy is cashed in.

There are two basic types of life insurance policies—term insurance and whole life insurance. All other kinds of policies are variations on one or more of the two basic types.

TERM INSURANCE

Term insurance is death protection for a specified period of time and provides no cash value or savings element. It pays a benefit only if the insured dies during the period covered by the policy. It provides for a level premium rate for the set period after which the policy ceases and becomes void, except when renewed or changed to some other form of policy. It is the cheapest form of life insurance because it provides the most coverage for the least money. It is appropriate for young people who need large amounts of insurance, those who desire only death protection, and those whose insurance need will decrease over time.

Term insurance has many variations. *Level* term insurance premiums stay the same over the life of the policy, but these premiums are higher than with the straight term in early years and lower in later years. With *decreasing* term, the amount of coverage decreases each year while the premium stays the same. A *convertible* term policy can be converted to a whole life policy without a medical examination.

ASPECTS OF TERM INSURANCE

Protection for a specified period of time.

Low initial premium.

May be renewable and/or convertible.

Premium rises with each new term.

You or your dependents get nothing back if you survive the term.

The term rates increase as the insured ages. Many people, in fact, discontinue needed coverage because of the increasing cost. When evaluating term policies, compare (1) initial premiums as well as those charged in later years and (2) renewal provisions.

WHOLE LIFE INSURANCE

Whole life insurance is also called *cash value, straight,* or *ordinary life* insurance and provides insurance protection by the payment of a fixed premium throughout the lifetime of the insured. However, in addition to death protection, whole life insurance has a savings element called "cash value." As the policies mature, they develop cash values representing the early surplus plus investment earnings.

ADVANTAGES OF WHOLE LIFE INSURANCE

Future uninsurability, old age, or other contingencies cannot terminate the policy.

When you are older and no longer need a large face amount of insurance protection you can cash in the policy and use the cash as a source of retirement income.

Interest earned on cash value is tax-deferred until you surrender the policy, or tax-free if you hold it for life.

DISADVANTAGES OF WHOLE LIFE INSURANCE

More death protection can be purchased with term insurance.

The interest rate on cash value generally is below prevailing market rates. Therefore, high yields can be obtained on other investment or savings plans.

Cash values grow slowly in early years because of large up-front commissions and start-up expenses.

ASPECTS OF WHOLE LIFE INSURANCE

Protection for life.

Fixed premium.

Growing cash value.

Higher initial premium than term.

You or your dependents always receive benefits.

Available in several different forms such as universal, variable, or single-premium life.

Should be purchased with the intention of keeping for life or for a long period of time.

Whole life policies are most appropriate for those who want lifetime coverage and desire a structured savings plan.

There are many variations of whole life insurance: universal life, variable life, and single-premium whole life.

Universal life.   Universal life is a combination of term insurance and a tax-deferred savings plan that pays a flexible interest, either indexed to a particular investment such as the 90-day Treasury bill, or formulated by the company. The guaranteed minimum rate typically is 4 or 5 percent. *Tip:* It is most appropriate for those who desire flexibility and wish to vary premiums to reflect changing life situations and needs.

Variable life.   Variable life offers lifetime protection with level premiums. The cash value is invested, at your choosing, in any combination of stocks, bonds, or money market funds. The investment risk is yours. There is no guaranteed minimum rate. The death benefit can grow if the cash value increases. *Tip:* It is best suited for those who are investment oriented, desire high yields on policy premiums, and are willing to accept investment risk.

Single-premium life is explained later.

HOW DO YOU EVALUATE WHOLE LIFE POLICIES?

When shopping for whole life insurance policies, here are some tips for evaluation, especially universal and variable life policies:

Load charges.

Investment return.

Death benefits and net annual premium amounts.

Guaranteed cash value growth.

Insurance costs. What is the charge for the term coverage?

Policy loan rates, in case you borrow money against the cash value.

Cost-index numbers. The smaller the number, the lower the policy's net cost.

Cash surrender values and charges, if any.

How projected annual dividends, if any, would offset premium payments.

Medical requirements, for increasing the policy's face amount.

WHAT TYPE OF LIFE INSURANCE SHOULD YOU BUY?

When you buy life insurance from your agent, the chances are you will be steered to some form of whole life policy, since commissions are higher for that type. Here are some basic tips:

1. If you want the most protection, buy term insurance. Term premiums can be very expensive in your later years, but by then you may have enough protection for your dependents through your pension, social security, and other sources of income. Hopefully, you should be able to drop or reduce your insurance. *Recommendation:* Keep your options open by buying a term policy that is convertible as well as renewable.

2. If you want a guaranteed right to continue the face amount until death and an assured level premium, and if you have a bad record of investment performance, you would be better off with a whole life policy. If you decide on a whole life policy, consider a relatively new insurance product, single-premium whole life (SPWL).

SOLVED PROBLEM 11.1

You are 25 years old and are considering two insurance policies:

Type of Insurance	Insurance Protection	Annual Premium	Cash Value at Age 65
Term to 65	$50,000	$150*	$ 0
Whole life	50,000	450	28,500

*Premium remains constant to age 65.

(a) If you keep each policy until age 65, what is the total premium for each?

(b) If you die at age 45, what would each policy pay your beneficiaries?

(c) What rate of return would you have to earn on the premium savings (whole life term minus term to 65) from the term policy to match the whole life policy?

SOLUTION

(a)

Type of Insurance	Annual Premium	Period of Policy	Total Payments
Term to 65	$150	40 years	$ 6,000
Whole life	450	40 years	18,000

(b) Both policies would pay $50,000 should you die at age 45.

(c) Annual premium savings: $450 − $150 = $300
     Investment period: 40 years
     Terminal value: $28,500

We set up the equation as follows:

$$\$300 \times \text{Appendix Table 2 (future of an annuity of \$1) factor} = \$28,500$$

$$\text{Appendix Table 2 factor} = \frac{\$28,500}{\$300} = 95$$

Based on Appendix Table 2, annual deposits of $300 for 40 years would have to earn 4 percent return for the fund to be worth $28,500.

WHAT IS SINGLE-PREMIUM WHOLE LIFE (SPWL) INSURANCE?

Single-premium whole life insurance is a policy with a low risk investment flavor. For a minimum amount of $5,000, paid once, you get a paid-up insurance policy. Your money is invested at a guaranteed rate of interest, for 1 year or longer. SPWL has the following features:

1. Its cash value earns interest immediately at competitive rates.

2. It allows you to borrow interest earned annually after the first year.

3. It allows you to take out a loan for up to 90 percent of principal at lower rates.

4. It allows you to receive permanent life insurance coverage.

5. Withdrawals and loans are not subject to tax.

6. It provides tax-deferred accumulation of cash values.

7. It provides tax-free death benefits to named beneficiaries.

Minuses of SPWL include:

1. There are usually surrender charges if you withdraw your money.

2. Interest rate generally is guaranteed for only 1 year and could drop.

If you consider SPWL, get answers to the following questions:

1. What is the "net interest" rate at which your cash value will grow? The net interest rate is the yield after subtracting costs of the insurance and administrative expenses.

2. What is the surrender charge?

3. Are there any loan-processing fees? What is the loan interest rate?

4. Is there a bailout plan, which enables you to cash in the policy without penalty if interest rates drop below the initial rate?

Select only a company with an A or A+ rating by A.M. Best Company (Best's Insurance Reports available from a broker, company, or library) that has been in business at least 5 to 10 years. Note that rate comparison can be very confusing and difficult because of the existence of many variations.

Try to deal with the most consistent and reputable agent instead of shopping around for better rates. You might want to use various services offered by SelectQuote Insurance Services [140 Second Street, San Francisco, CA 94105, (800)-343-1985]. It is an insurance brokerage agency that (1) provides rate comparisons, (2) searches the rates of 1,600 companies to find the 16 that have a reputation for low rates on the type of coverage you want and have maintained an A or A+ rating from A.M. Best, and (3) sells one of the policies via its toll-free number.

HOW TO REVIEW YOUR LIFE INSURANCE COVERAGE

Your life insurance coverage requires periodic reevaluation as needs change and new insurance products present new possibilities. When reviewing coverage, ask yourself the following questions:

Will the death benefit meet your dependents' lifestyle, support, debt, and education needs?

Have your dependents' needs exceeded or diminished the current death benefit of your coverage? You may have to increase your coverage if you have incurred additional debt or if there is a need to provide liquidity to your estate and the estate grows. Or you may want to decrease your coverage, if you fund your children's education expenses or if your spouse returns to work.

Are the policy beneficiaries appropriate given your family and personal situation. Divorce, death, or disability may change the beneficiaries and their needs.

If you have cash value insurance, what is the current cash value? Have you considered using policy loan provisions to borrow against the cash value? How would a loan reduce the death benefits? Will this reduction have adverse effects on your beneficiaries?

HOW MUCH LIFE INSURANCE IS ENOUGH?

Unfortunately, there is no fixed formula in assessing the amount of life insurance a family should have. There are basically two approaches to use in determining the amount of insurance you need. They are:

The multiple-of-income approach.   Under this method, you simply multiply your gross annual income by some selected number. Some experts suggest that life insurance should equal 5 to 10 times your annual gross income.

SOLVED PROBLEM 11.2

You have a gross annual income of $30,000. If the multiplier is 5, how much insurance coverage should you have?

SOLUTION

$150,000 ($30,000 × 5)

This rule of thumb, however, may not always be appropriate because no two families are exactly the same. The amount will vary with family needs, goals, net worth, future expenses and income, and lifestyle requirements.

The needs approach.   This approach determines the financial needs of your family and other dependents in the event of your death. The needs approach emphasizes meeting financial objectives and obligations while the human life value approach stresses replacement of your future earnings. The idea is to first add up the total financial needs and then to deduct accumulated assets. If you decide to use the needs approach, consider the following funds:

1. *Emergency and administrative fund.*   Funds for the costs of final illness, funeral and burial bills, probate costs, uninsured medical costs, debts, and estate taxes.

2. *Special fund.*   Fund needed for other specific needs, such as educational expenses and paying mortgages.

3. *Retirement fund.*   Additional money set aside to support your spouse and dependents.

4. *Family income fund.*   Fund to support surviving dependents until they are self-supporting.

Figure 11-1 illustrates the use of the needs approach to help estimate the amount of life insurance to buy.

Keep in mind that life insurance is not a static product. Family needs may change; family income might vary; family size may alter. Therefore, basic insurance needs can vary over time. It is wise to reassess your coverage periodically in keeping with the changes that occur in your life.

	Sample Entries	Your Entries
(A) Funding needs		
1. Emergency and administrative fund	$ 15,000	_____
2. Special fund	125,000	_____
3. Family income fund	80,000	_____
4. Retirement fund	60,000	_____
Total needs	$280,000	_____
(B) Available resources		
1. Savings	$ 30,000	_____
2. Investments	60,000	_____
3. Life insurance		
a. Group insurance	50,000	_____
b. Social security	500	_____
Total resources	(140,500)	( )
Life insurance gap	$139,500	_____

Fig. 11-1   How much life insurance?

COST COMPARISONS FOR LIFE INSURANCE

The price people pay for life insurance depends on their age, health, and lifestyles. Comparing life insurance prices is a difficult task since policies and plans vary from company to company. Two popular methods of cost comparisons are described below.

THE NET COST METHOD

This method is publicized by insurance agents for cash value life insurance. The net cost of a life insurance policy is the total of all premiums to be paid minus any accumulated cash value and accrued dividends. This is computed for a specified point in time during the life of the policy. If the net cost is negative, it means that the policy will pay for itself.

SOLVED PROBLEM 11.3

You are considering the purchase of a $100,000 cash value policy. Your annual premiums will be $1,664 and the policy will have a cash value at the end of 20 years of $25,008. Total dividends accumulated for the 20 years will be $9,300. What is the net cost of the policy after 20 years?

SOLUTION

$$\text{Net cost} = (\$1,664 \times 20) - \$25,008 - \$9,300 = -\$1,028$$

INTEREST-ADJUSTED COST INDEX

This is a measure of the cost of life insurance that takes into account the interst that would have been earned had the premiums been invested rather than used to buy insurance. This index should be made available by insurance agents. If the agent is not willing to supply the value for this index, you should not buy the policy. Generally, the lower the index, the lower the cost for a given dollar amount of insurance protection. Certainly, the policies with a positive index should be avoided.

SOLVED PROBLEM 11.4

Using an interest rate of 5 percent in Solved Problem 11.3, the total dividends amount to $12,719. Calculate the 20-year, interest-adjusted cost index.

SOLUTION

Step 1: Accumulate annual premium at 5 percent deposited at the beginning of each
year for 20 years

$1,664 × 34.719* (Appendix Table 3) $57,772.42

Step 2: Accumulate total dividends at 5 percent compounded annually to end of
twentieth year and subtract   − 12,719.00

$45,053.42

Step 3: Subtract cash value at end of twentieth year   − 35,008.00

$10,045.42

Step 4: Divide by 34.719, which is what $1 deposited at the beginning of each
year in a 5 percent compounded account will grow to in 20 years. The
result is the amount that would have to be saved to reach the sum
derived in Step 3 $ 289.33

Step 5: Divide by the number of thousands of policy's face amount, in this
case, 100, to compute the annual interest-adjusted cost per $1,000
of face amount $ 2.89

You may use this figure to compare similar cash value policies from other agents and companies.

*Note that the value 34.719 here is the Appendix Table 3 value for 21 years at 5 percent *less* 1 year (35.719 − 1). The
reason for using this value is that the deposit is made at the beginning of the year, not the end of the year.

HOW DO YOU EVALUATE YOUR DISABILITY OR LOSS-OF-INCOME INSURANCE?

This insurance provides regular cash income when an insured person is unable to work as a result
of a covered illness, injury, or disease. Most disability payments are tax-exempt as long as the individual policyholder pays the premium. In evaluating your disability coverage, consider the following:

*Whether it is sufficient to meet the financial objectives and needs of you and your dependents should
you become disabled.*

How disability is defined.   Are benefits available if you can no longer perform any job or only a job
for which you are qualified for your training, education, or experience? If the definition is too restrictive, the financial burden of your disability may increase. If the definition is too broad, the
cost of such insurance coverage may be substantial. Some policies exclude disabilities resulting
from pregnancy, foreign travel, aviation, etc.

The waiting (elimination) period.   How long must you wait before benefits begin? Can you afford
to wait that long?

Cost-of-living adjustments.   You should include a cost-of-living clause in your policy.

You should also

Make sure the policy cannot be canceled or raised arbitrarily.

Look for any discount. For example, a premium discount may be available if you are a nonsmoker.

Make sure the policy has a residual clause for partial disabilities. A *residual clause* allows for some
reduced level of benefits when income is reduced but not eliminated.

It is important to estimate how much disability insurance you need. Figure 11-2 can be used for
that purpose. *Rule of thumb:* An adequate disability plan should provide at least 60 percent of your current gross income. (This figure is based on the assumption that some of your disability benefits will be
tax-free.) If you own a business or practice, you may need higher coverage to provide cash flow to
cover business overhead.

SOLVED PROBLEM 11.5

You earn $40,000 annually. What should your disability coverage be?

SOLUTION

$24,000 (60% of $40,000)

Like other insurance, your disability coverage must be reviewed regularly to ensure that it reflects your current financial needs and conditions.

---

(1) Income replacement requirements
     (60% of your monthly gross income) $_____
(2) Existing disability benefits:
     a. Social security benefits $_____
     b. Other government benefits   _____
     c. Company plans   _____
     d. Group disability policy benefits   _____
     e. Early retirement benefits   _____
         Total $_____
(3) Additional monthly disability
     benefits needed [(1) − (2)] $_____

Fig. 11-2 How much disability insurance?

HOW TO REVIEW YOUR MEDICAL AND HEALTH INSURANCE COVERAGE

For most people, health insurance is provided by the employer as a major fringe benefit. Otherwise, individual policies can be purchased. Policies can include any or all of the following coverages:

Hospitalization. Covers hospital room and board, medications, tests, and services.

Surgical. Covers operations.

Medical. Covers visits to the doctor's office and diagnostic laboratory tests.

Major medical. Covers expenses that exceed the dollar limit of the basic coverage.

Comprehensive. Includes all of the above.

Dental. Covers most dental expenses.

Prescriptions. Pays for prescribed medication.

Here are some tips for buying medical and health insurance:

Shop carefully before you buy. Policies vary widely as to coverage, cost, and service.

Check for preexisting condition exclusions. Many policies exclude coverage for preexisting conditions.

Review your coverage to determine what additional insurance you need to provide adequate protection for hospital, surgical, and medical expenses. In evaluating coverage, make sure your deductible matches your ability to bear the cost of injury or illness.

Consider ceilings on benefits provided by your policy. What are they and on what basis will they be applied—per illness, per plan year, or per lifetime? Your out-of-pocket cost may vary significantly depending on how each applies to you.

Determine the type of deductible your policy has—per person, per illness, per calendar year, or per group of participants.

Coinsurance and *copayment*. A coinsurance clause requires you to pay a proportion of any loss suffered, usually 20 to 25 percent. A variation of coinsurance, a copayment clause, requires you to pay a specific dollar portion of specific covered expense items (for example, prescription drug coverage). The following formula will determine the loss that will be reimbursed when there is a deductible and a coinsurance clause:

$$\text{Reimbursement} = (1 - \text{Coinsurance percentage})(\text{Loss} - \text{Deductible})$$

SOLVED PROBLEM 11.6

You bought a health insurance policy with a $100 deductible per hospital stay and a 20 percent coinsurance requirement. If the hospital bill is $2,225, what will the reimbursement be?

SOLUTION

$$\text{Reimbursement} = (1 - .20)\,(\$2,225 - \$100)$$
$$= .80(\$2,125)$$
$$= \$1,700$$

Check for a *grace period*. The grace period in health insurance is commonly 31 days. This prevents the lapse of a policy if a payment is late.

HOW ABOUT PROPERTY, LIABILITY, AND CASUALTY INSURANCE?

Property, liability, and casualty insurance are important to your financial security. You can be successful in your job, investments, and the like, and yet be almost destroyed financially by an accident, disaster, or lawsuit for which you do not have adequate property, liability, and casualty insurance. It is wise to carry such insurance to protect family assets and future income from a catastrophic event. *Note:* Auto insurance and homeowners' insurance policies contain liability coverages that provide a base level of protection.

In today's litigious society, you might want to buy additional liability insurance in the form of an umbrella policy. It provides supplemental coverage that picks up where the liability protection in auto, homeowners', and other policies leave off. Compare terms, exclusions, and prices of policies.

HOW GOOD IS YOUR HOMEOWNERS' POLICY?

Not all homeowners' policies offer equal protection. When a loss occurs, it is painfully easy to find out too late that a small extra premium could have saved you a large sum of money. You also may be missing out on discounts that have come along in recent years. The time to find out is before something happens. Here are some tips:

Determine your insurance needs. The best figure to use is your home's replacement value; that is, the amount it would cost to rebuild, excluding land. Your minimum protection should be 80 percent of replacing your house. If you fail to meet the replacement cost requirement, the amount of reimbursement for any loss will be calculated using the formula

$$R = L \times \left(\frac{I}{\text{RV} \times 80\%}\right)$$

where R = reimbursement payable
    L = the amount of loss <u>less</u> deductible
    I = amount of insurance actually carried
  RV = replacement value

SOLVED PROBLEM 11.7

You have a home with a replacement value of $100,000 and suffer a $50,000 fire loss. You insured your home for $80,000.

(a) What is the amount of insurance reimbursement?

(b) Are you fully reimbursed?

SOLUTION

(a) $50,000 × [$80,000/($100,000 × 80%)] = $50,000

(b)   Yes. You are fully reimbursed for your entire fire loss of $50,000.

Know the basic policy from the broad policy. Look for the broadest coverage for the dollar. But for maximum peace of mind, choose the "all risk" form. Compare the cost of each form.

Find out if in case of loss of the contents of a room, you will be paid based on book value replacement cost. Do not be surprised when you file a claim only to learn that policies that promise "actual cash value" are actually referring to your original cost minus depreciation over years of use. The formula for determining the actual cash value (ACV) is

$$ACV = P - \left[CA \times \left(\frac{P}{n} \right) \right]$$

where P = purchase price of the item, CA = current age in years, and n = expected life in years.

SOLVED PROBLEM 11.8

Your 6-year old VCR was stolen. The new VCR costs $400 and has an expected life of 8 years. What is its actual cash value (ACV) at the time it was stolen?

SOLUTION

$$\$400 - \left[6 \times \left(\frac{\$400}{8} \right) \right] = \$100$$

Make sure your policy includes an inflation endorsement that is tied to a state or regional index, instead of a national index, to keep in line with current construction costs.

Make sure potential calamities are covered. Fire and storm damage will be included, but damage from ice and snow may not be.

Look into a floater policy for furs, jewelry, silver, personal computers—theft protection for such valuables may be limited.

Consider an umbrella liability policy. A lawsuit over an accident on your property or away from home could wipe you out. *Note:* Umbrella protection is written over an underlying homeowners' policy and an auto policy. It takes over when the liability limits on these policies are reached. For example, if your homeowners' policy covers liability up to $50,000, an umbrella policy can cover you from losses in excess of $50,000.

You can achieve substantial savings by accepting a higher deductible (for example, $250 or $500 instead of $100).

Realize discounts by installing dead-bolt locks, smoke detectors, and fire extinguishers. See what other discounts are available.

Keep pictures of your valuables and personal belongings.

Review your insurance at least once a year to make sure your coverage is keeping pace with inflation.

WHEN YOU HAVE TO FILE A CLAIM

Report any theft or vandalism to the police.

Immediately call your insurance agent.

Protect your property from further damage.

Save all receipts for reimbursement.

Make a list of damaged articles.

Review the settlement steps outlined in your policy. In case there is a significant difference between what the insurer offers and what you believe you are entitled to, submit the dispute to arbitration.

If you are unhappy with your experience with the insurance carrier (for example, delay in receiving payment, inadequate reimbursement), "shop around" for another insurance company.

TYPES OF HOMEOWNER POLICIES

Seven different types of homeowner policies have been designed to meet the needs of buyers. Each of them is briefly described below.

Homeowners-1 (HO-1).   Known as the basic coverage, HO-1 offers protection against 11 of the 18 major property-damage perils—for example, fire, windstorm, hail, vandalism, explosion, lightning, riot, and smoke. Losses from these perils may be limited in the amount of coverage. The policy provides protection from the three liability exposures—comprehensive personal liability, damage to other peoples' property, and medical payments.

Homeowners-2 (HO-2).   Known as the broad form, HO-2 offers broader coverage than HO-1, in that HO-2 covers the 18 major perils that cause property damages—for example, falling objects, collapse of buildings, freezing of plumbing. It also provides protection from the three liability exposures.

Homeowners-3 (HO-3).   Often known as the special form, HO-3 provides all-risk coverage on the dwelling itself. *All-risk coverage* on the dwelling means that if a loss is not excluded in HO-3, it is covered.

Renters (HO-4).   HO-4 is designed for people who are renting an apartment or a home. It insures renters' personal property on the same basis as HO-2.

Comprehensive (HO-5).   HO-5 is the most comprehensive coverage you can buy. Obviously, it is much more expensive than the other forms.

Condominium (HO-6).   This is very similar to HO-4 except that it is designed for condominium owners, not renters.

HO-8.   HO-8 is designed for owners of older buildings that have been remodeled and would have replacement costs high in comparison with replacement costs for similar homes. This particular form differs from other policies in that the coverage is on an actual cash value basis rather than on a replacement cost basis.

HOW ABOUT AUTO INSURANCE?

The objective of automobile insurance is to protect you against two basic risks:

Liability coverage for bodily injuries, property damages, and medical expenses to you and others when you are at fault. These coverages usually have certain limits. For example, $10/$20 limit would pay $10,000 for loss from bodily injury liability for any one person, or $20,000 for all persons involved in any one accident. Property damage liability is usually expressed as a single limit, such as $10,000 or $20,000, for any one accident.

Physical coverage for damage or loss of your car due to fire, theft, or collision.

Premiums for auto insurance vary from company to company, but all rates generally reflect your age, sex, marital status, driving record, location, frequency of use, and your car's age.
Here are some tips for buying auto insurance:

Shop around for the lowest cost coverage. Auto policies vary as to cost, coverage, and claim service. High deductibles can save you money in premiums. For example, doubling the collision deductible from $100 to $200 can lower the collision premium by 25 percent. Figure 11-3 can be helpful in comparing the cost.

Look for discounts resulting from owning two cars or installation of alarm systems. Study exclusions.

Company _____

	Limits	Deductible	Annual Premium
Liability	_____		_____
Medical payments	_____		_____
Uninsured motorists	_____		_____
Collision	_____		_____
Comprehensive	_____	_____	_____
Total cost			_____

Discounts

Name	Percentage Discount	Dollar Discount	
1. _____	_____	_____	
2. _____	_____	_____	
3. _____	_____	_____	
etc.	_____	_____	
Total dollar discounts			_____
Total cost after discounts			_____

Fig. 11-3   Auto insurance comparison worksheet.

SOLVED PROBLEM 11.9

You have a 3-year-old car on which you are carrying the following auto insurance coverages: liability, 50/100/25; uninsured motorist, 15/30; collison, $50 deductible; comprehensive, $50 deductible. Recently, somebody who has no insurance ran into your car. Your medical costs totaled $5,400 and you lost 8 weeks' wages at $450 per week. Damage to your car totaled $4,000.

(*a*)   Will your policy pay any part of the medical cost and lost wages?

(*b*)   Which section, if any, will cover the damage to your car?

SOLUTION

(*a*)   Your uninsured motorist section should cover both your medical expenses and lost wages. That reimbursement would be

Medical expenses	$5,400
Lost wages from accident:	
8 weeks @$450	3,600
Total reimbursement	$9,000

(*b*)   Damage to your car will be covered by your collision section. The reimbursement would be

Repairs to your car	$4,000
Less: Deductible	50
Total reimbursement	$3,950

HOW TO SELECT AGENTS AND COMPANIES

It is important to select the right insurance agents and companies. However, you should know enough about what you are buying so that an agent can recommend the right insurance policy. The reason is that if you are unable to explain precisely what your insurance needs are, agents are unable to recommend and tailor for you the right combination of coverages. Usually, you have the following options:

A direct-writing company, whose salespeople are employees or exclusive agents

An independent agent or broker, who usually deals in the policies of several companies

Here are some tips:

Go to your local library. Check out the companies the agents represent, as well as the direct-writing companies you are considering. Deal only with the best companies, which are rated A or A+ by Best's Insurance Reports.

Get recommendations from friends, including business and professional people who have significant insurance needs.

Engage in comparison shopping among agents being seriously considered. Ask for proposed solutions to your insurance problems. Compare them in terms of deductibles, exclusions, and prices.

WHERE TO GET INSURANCE ANSWERS

If you have an unsettled claim or complaints about your insurance agent or company, the best place to call is your state insurance department. You will obtain impartial information and recommendations on what to do. In the case of an unsettled claim, the state insurance department cannot order payment but they can ask the insurance company to take a second look.

Review Questions

(1) _____ provides income lost at the death of the wage earner.

(2) There are two basic types of life insurance policies: _____ and _____ .

(3) _____ is death protection for a specified period of time and provides no cash value or savings element.

(4) _____ is the cheapest form of life insurance because it provides the most coverage for the least money.

(5) _____ is also called cash value, straight, or ordinary life insurance.

(6) _____ is a combination of term insurance and a tax-deferred savings plan that pays flexible interest.

(7) _____ offers lifetime protection with level premiums.

(8) _____ whole life insurance is a policy with a low risk investment flavor.

(9) There are basically two approaches you can use to determine the amount of insurance you need: _____ and _____ .

(10) The price people pay for life insurance depends on their age, health, and _____.

(11) _____ allows for some reduced level of benefits when income is reduced but not eliminated.

(12) A rule of thumb says that an adequate disability plan should provide at least _____ percent of your current gross income.

(13) _____ requires you to pay a proportion of any loss suffered.

(14) _____ in a health insurance policy is commonly 31 days.

(15) The objective of automobile insurance is to protect you against two basic risks: _____ and _____.

(16) Under the multiple-of-income approach, life insurance should equal _____ times annual gross income.

(17) _____ is the most comprehensive homeowners' insurance that can be bought.

(18) An _____ insurance policy is designed for condominium owners.

(19) The basic homeowners' insurance is referred to as _____.

Answers: (1) Life insurance; (2) term insurance, whole life insurance; (3) Term insurance; (4) Term insurance; (5) Whole life insurance; (6) Universal life; (7) Variable life; (8) Single-premium; (9) the multiple-of-income approach, the needs approach; (10) lifestyles; (11) A residual clause; (12) 60; (13) A coinsurance clause; (14) The grace period; (15) liability, physical damage; (16) 5 to 10; (17) HO–5; (18) HO–6; (19) HO–1.

Additional Solved Problems

11.1 A life insurance agent presented two insurance policy options:

> Plan A $10,000, 20-year term insurance with an annual premium of $30
>
> Plan B $10,000, 20-year cash value whole life, plus estimated dividends of $4,000, with an annual premium of $500

Which plan is more attractive? (Assume an after-tax rate of return of 8 percent.)

SOLUTION

If you purchase Plan A and save the difference in annual premium of $470 ($500 − $30) a year in a savings plan paying an after-tax rate of return of 8 percent, it will accumulate to $21,508, calculated as follows:

$$\$470 \times 45.762 \text{ (Appendix Table 2)} = \$21,508$$

as compared with Plan B that provides a total of $14,500.

The death protection during the 20-year period is $10,000 (face value) plus the accumulation in the side savings plan. Thus, the term insurance (Plan A) is more attractive.

11.2 Given the following data:

	WHOLE LIFE INSURANCE	TERM LIFE
Term	20 years	20 years
Annual premium	$400	$65
Value	Cash value of $11,000	Face value of $10,000
	Dividends of $5,500	

Assume an after-tax return of 8 percent. Which plan is more attractive?

SOLUTION

The difference in annual premiums of $335 ($400 − $65) will accumulate at a compound rate of 8 percent to $335 × 45.762 = $15,330, which is less than $16,500 ($11,000 + $5,500). Therefore, the whole life insurance policy is more attractive.

11.3 An insurance agent has offered to sell John Lee a $100,000 whole life nonparticipating policy. The annual premiums would be $1,700. The policy would be paid up at age 65 and would have a cash value of $70,000. A $100,000 renewable term insurance policy would cost John only $300 the first year. But over the next 35 years to age 65, the premiums would average about $1,450 per year. John has two alternatives:

1. Buy the whole life policy.
2. Buy the term insurance and invest the difference in premiums at a rate of return of 12 percent per year.

Which option should John take?

SOLUTION

The difference in annual premiums between whole life and term is $1,700 − $1,450 = $250. The present value of $250 for 35 years at 12 percent is $250 × 8.33 (from Appendix Table 4) = $2,082.50. With whole life, John would build up a cash value of $70,000 after 35 years. The present value of $1 received 35 years from today is 1.9 cents if the rate of return is 12 percent. Therefore, the present value of this $70,000 is $70,000 × .019 (from Appendix Table 3) = $1,330. He should buy the term insurance because the present value associated with it is larger.

11.4 Dolores Parras earns $35,000 annually as a college teacher. Her monthly take-home pay is $2,000. She receives an additional $200 per month in dividends and interest income. Her monthly expenses are as follows: shelter, $600; transportation, $250; food, $250; loans, $200; insurance, $200; vacation, $100; miscellaneous, $200; total, $1,800; and savings, $400.

If she were disabled, she would be able to eliminate transportation expenses. Insurance expenses would decline by $50 per month. She would also do without a vacation. Her miscellaneous expense would increase by $40 per month.

How much disability insurance should she carry? Show your calculations.

SOLUTION

Monthly expenses	$1,800
Less: Transportation	(250)
Insurance	(50)
Vacation	(100)
Plus: Miscellaneous	40
Insurance needs	$1,440

11.5 Ken and Mary Morgan are both 35 years old, and both work as independent management consultants. Each has take-home income of about $20,000 annually. They have two children, aged 5 and 7 years. Their total investable assets of about $150,000 earn 12 percent annually. Their annual living expenses are about $35,000. If either spouse dies, living expenses would not decline because the surviving spouse would have to hire child and home care help. Answer the following questions, assuming that either Ken or Mary could die prematurely:

(a) Perform all life risk evaluations for the surviving spouse.

(b) How much life risk could the surviving spouse retain?

(c) How much life insurance, if any, should each of the Morgans buy? (Assume that the surviving spouse will not receive any social security benefits and that the rate of return is 12 percent.)

SOLUTION

(a) Immediate cash needs:

Funeral*	$ 7,000
Contingency†	3,333
Total cash needs	$ 10,333
Living expense needs‡	$291,550
Total dollar life risk	$301,883

*Assumed
†Two months' salary, $20,000 × $\frac{2}{12}$
‡$35,000 × 8.33; 8.33 is the present value at 12 percent for 30 years.

(b) The surviving spouse can retain $150,000, the amount of the investable assets.

(c) The amount of insurance coverage needed is $301,883 − $150,000 = $151,883.

11.6 You earn $50,000 annually and want 65 percent of your income during your disability. You receive from existing benefits the following:

1. Social security benefits $950
2. Group disability policy benefits   650
3. Early retirement benefits   300

What additional disability income insurance do you need?

SOLUTION

Worksheet

(1) Income replacement requirements		
(65% of your monthly gross income)		
($50,000/12 × .65)		$2,708
(2) Existing disability benefits:		
a. Social security benefits	$950	
b. Group disability policy benefits	650	
c. Early retirement benefits	300	
Total		1,900
(3) Additional monthly disability		
benefits needed [(1) − (2)]		$ 808

11.7 Cathy Warty has a gross annual income of $32,000. If the multiplier is 7.9, how much life insurance does she need? Use the multiple-of-earnings approach.

SOLUTION

$$\$32,000 \times 7.9 = \$252,800$$

11.8 Terri Shell is a 32-year-old mother of two children, ages 3 and 7. She earns \$42,000 per year as a radio producer. She has no life insurance currently but estimates that her family would qualify for \$1,200 per month in social security survivors' benefits based on her income over the past 10 years. She wants to provide income replacement until her youngest child is 21, \$10,000 for her burial, \$37,000 to replace her husband's income for 1 year of readjustment if she were to die, and \$3,000 to pay off most of her short-term debts. She assumes that her husband, David, could earn 3 percent after taxes and inflation on the proceeds of any death benefit.

(*a*)   Use the multiple-of-earnings approach to calculate the dollar loss from Terri's premature death.

(*b*)   What is the projected dollar loss from her death using the needs approach? (Assume about 75 percent of the take-home pay of the deceased will need to be replaced.)

(*c*)   Explain why there is such a big difference between the answers to (*a*) and (*b*).

(*d*)   What is the projected dollar loss from David's death if his estimated monthly social security survivors' benefits are \$1,000 per month? David would also want to replace Terri's salary for 1 year; all other information is the same as Terri's.

SOLUTION

(*a*)   \$756,000 = \$42,000 × 18 years

(*b*)   \$285,193.40 = [.75(\$42,000) − (\$1,200 × 12)]13.754 + \$10,000 + \$37,000 + \$3,000

(*c*)   The multiple-of-earnings approach overestimates the potential loss because it attempts to replace total annual income and fails to take into account the interest that would be earned on the lump-sum death benefit paid by life insurance.

(*d*)   \$271,625.50 = [.75(\$37,000) − (\$1,000 × 12)]13.754 + \$10,000 + \$42,000 + \$3,000

11.9 The following worksheet illustrates the use of the needs approach to help estimate the amount of life insurance to buy. Complete the form.

Worksheet

(*A*)   Funding needs

    1.   Emergency and administrative fund   \$ 10,000

    2.   Special fund   110,000

    3.   Family income fund   80,000

    4.   Retirement fund   <u>60,000</u>

       Total needs   _____

(*B*)   Available resources

    1.   Savings   \$ 20,000

    2.   Investments   55,000

    3.   Life Insurance

        a.   Group insurance   75,000

        b.   Social security   <u>500</u>

       Total resources   _____

(*A*)   Life insurance gap [(*A*) − (*B*)]   _____

SOLUTION

Worksheet

(A) Funding needs

1.	Emergency and administrative fund	$ 10,000	
2.	Special fund	110,000	
3.	Family income fund	80,000	
4.	Retirement fund	60,000	
	Total needs		$260,000

(B) Available resources

1.	Savings	$ 20,000	
2.	Investments	55,000	
3.	Life insurance		
	a. Group insurance	75,000	
	b. Social security	500	
	Total resources		150,500
	Life insurance gap [(A) − (B)]		$109,500

11.10 How much life insurance is right for this family?

Family Profile

Husband: John Tash, bank vice president, 40, salary $45,000
Wife: Jani Tash, designer, 35, salary $39,000
Children:
  Megan, 12
  Jonathan, 9

Annual combined income	$79,000
Equity in primary residence	50,000
Total installment loans	12,000
Mortgage balance on primary residence	70,000
Cash and investments	63,000
Anticipated final burial expenses	7,000
Survivors benefits of social security for children	500/month

John and Jani Tash are reviewing their insurance needs. Their life insurance goals are

> To provide their children with an income equal to their current income until age 21 should they both die
>
> To provide a means to pay off the liabilities should either spouse die
>
> To provide a college education fund that would provide $15,000 per child for 4 years

(a) Use the multiple-of-earnings approach to find the amount of insurance if they want to replace 65 percent of their lost earnings. Assume a multiplier of 8.6 for John and 8.7 for Jani.

(b) Use the needs approach to determine the amount of life insurance which meets the Tash's goals. Are the Tash's adequately insured?

(c) What type of life insurance policy do you recommend for the Tash's?

SOLUTION

(a) Multiple earnings approach

John   (8.6) ($40,000) = $344,000

Jani   (8.7) ($39,000) = $\underline{\text{339,300}}$

$\hspace{9cm}$ $683,300

(b) Planning life insurance needs
Name: John and Jani

       A. Family income needs

          1. Debt liquidation:

             a. House mortgage $\hspace{2cm}$ $70,000

             b. Other loans $\hspace{3cm}$ $\underline{\text{12,000}}$

             c. Total debt (*a* + *b*) $\hspace{3.5cm}$ $ 82,000

          2. Final expenses $\hspace{5cm}$ 7,000

          3. Annual income needs:

             a. Current monthly income $\hspace{1.5cm}$ $ 6,583

             b. Less: Social security

                  survivor's benefit $\hspace{2cm}$ (500)

             c. Net monthly income (*a* − *b*) $\hspace{1cm}$ $\underline{\text{\$ 6,083}}$

             d. Net yearly income (*c* × 12) $\hspace{1cm}$ $72,996

             e. Number of years until

                  children are grown $\hspace{2.5cm}$ $\underline{\text{12}}$

             f. Total funding needed (*d* × *e*) $\hspace{2cm}$ 875,952

          4. Spouse reeducation fund $\hspace{4cm}$ 0

          5. Children's opportunity fund $\hspace{3cm}$ 120,000

          6. Other needs $\hspace{5.5cm}$ $\underline{\text{0}}$

          Total income needs

             (1*c* + 2 + 3*f* + 4 + 5 + 6) $\hspace{2cm}$ $1,084,952

       B. Financial resources available

          1. Savings and investments $\hspace{2cm}$ $63,000

          2. Group life insurance $\hspace{2.5cm}$ 30,000

          3. Other life insurance $\hspace{2.5cm}$ 50,000

          4. Other resources $\hspace{3cm}$ $\underline{\text{50,000}}$

          Total resources avaiable

             (1 + 2 + 3 + 4) $\hspace{3.5cm}$ $\underline{\text{193,000}}$

       C. Additional life insurance needed

          (*A* − *B*) $\hspace{4.5cm}$ $ 891,952

          (*Note:* No additional insurance is needed

          if number is negative.)

(c) The two basic goals of providing a steady income stream until 21 years of age for the children and setting up an education fund can be met in a variety of ways. A term life insurance policy can provide the death protection and the cash for the education fund (only in the event of a death). Or a whole life or universal life policy can provide the death protection but also through its savings feature, provide the education fund (not contingent upon death).

    Since the Tash's have a large insurance need, it is most economical to purchase a term insurance policy. To provide for the education fund, they have two choices: (1) buy a whole life or universal life policy for the savings/investment feature, or (2) buy term insurance with a large enough death benefit to cover all needs in the event of a death while establishing an independent savings plan. The term policy could be a decreasing term which sets a level premium but a decreasing death benefit. This would coincide with the independent savings plan which would have an increasing balance simultaneously.

11.11 Stella and Steve have a young family with four sons under the age of 6. Stella is an aspiring actress. Her salary from the acting company is $5,000 per month after taxes (for 6 months) and her income from advertisements is $500 per month after taxes (for 12 months). This work is independent of the acting company. She is covered by the acting troupe's group health insurance policy. The policy provides disability coverage of 60 percent of the employee's monthly take-home pay. (Since Stella works only 6 months per year, the disability benefit is based on earning $2,500 per month.) In the instance of complete disability, Stella would also be eligible for $500 per month from social security.

Stella's husband, Steve, is self-employed and earns $3,000 per month after taxes. Steve has purchased a comprehensive major medical policy which provides disability income of 70 percent of the insured's monthly take-home pay. In the event of being disabled, Steve is also eligible for social security benefits of $800 per month.

Stella and Steve currently spend 75 percent of their combined take-home pay to meet their living expenses. Another 5 percent is spent on entertainment and travel. The remaining 20 percent is put into savings and investments.

(a) How much disability insurance do Stella and Steve, individually, require to ensure adequate protection in the event of becoming disabled?

(b) Are Stella and Steve currently adequately covered?

(c) What recommendations would you make to Stella and Steve regarding their disability coverage?

SOLUTION

(a)

A Worksheet to Determine Disability Benefit Needs

Name: Stella   Date:

1.	Estimated current monthly take-home pay		$3,000
2.	Estimated existing disability benefits:		
	a. Social security benefits	$ 500	
	b. Other government benefits	0	
	c. Company programs	0	
	d. Group disability policy benefits	1,500	
3.	Total existing disability benefits		2,000
4.	Estimated monthly disability benefits needed		$1,000

A Worksheet to Determine Disability Benefit Needs

Name: Steve   Date:

1.	Estimated current monthly take-home pay		$3,000
2.	Estimated existing disability benefits:		
	a. Social security benefits	$ 800	
	b. Other government benefits	0	
	c. Company programs	0	
	d. Group disability policy benefits	2,100	
3.	Total existing disability benefits		2,900
4.	Estimated monthly disability benefits needed		$ 100

(b) Present annual expenditures:

Income	$72,000
Less: Living expenses (.75)	54,000
Entertainment and travel (.05)	3,600
Savings and investment (.20)	14,400
	$ 0

Annual expenditures (Stella is disabled):

Income	$60,000
Less: Living expenses	54,000
Entertainment and travel	3,600
Savings and investment	14,400
	−$12,000

Steve could adequately compensate the shortfall of his disability with an increase in savings.

11.12 Mike and Kim own a small corner grocery which is insured for fire with a policy limit of $250,000 and a 75 percent coinsurance clause. The value of the building and its contents is estimated at $400,000. If the building is destroyed by fire, how much could Mike and Kim recover from the insurance company?

SOLUTION

The 75 percent coinsurance clause requires that the policy limits must equal or exceed 75 percent of the building [(.75) ($400,000) = $300,000]. Since the building is not insured adequately according to the coinsurance clause, the insurance company would be obligated to pay only ($250,000/$300,000) of the claim up to the policy limit.

$$\left(\frac{\$250,000}{\$300,000}\right) \times \$250,000 = \$208,333$$

11.13 Richard Allen is held liable in a car accident. He carries liability limits of 20/40/10. Losses are as follows: $18,000 for bodily injury to A, $32,000 for bodily injury to B, $1,000 for bodily injury to C, and $12,000 for damage to the other car. How much of the losses will Richard's policy cover?

SOLUTION

Richard's policy will pay $18,000 for loss to A, buy only $20,000 to B due to the $20,000 limit of loss applying to any one individual. The loss of $1,000 to C is covered. Total bodily injury recovery is thus $39,000, which does not exceed the $40,000 limit for all parties. The policy will also pay $10,000 (not $12,000) of property damage since there is a $10,000 limit for property damage.

11.14 The Newmans have a color television set that is 6 years old. Its original cost was $600, and its useful life is considered to be 10 years. Replacing that television now would cost $800.

(a) Calculate the actual cash value for the television.

(b) Would the Newmans be better off with a policy that provided replacement cost coverage? Explain your answer.

SOLUTION

(a) Annual depreciation for an asset with a 10-year life is 100%/10 = 10 percent. After 6 years, the TV retains 100% − (10% × 6) = 40% of its value, or $800 × .4 = $320.

(b) In case of an insured loss of the TV, a replacement cost policy would pay $800, while an actual cash value policy would pay $320. Depending on the cost, the replacement cost policy might be desirable.

11.15 The Crawfords own a reasonably large collection of signed prints by Calder and Chagall, first edition collector's plates, a limited edition bronze statue by Remington, first edition novels by Faulkner, and African artifacts. They have relied on their HO–3 policy to provide insurance for their collections. What advice do you have for them?

SOLUTION

The HO–3 policy provides limited coverage on collectible items. In case of loss, the Crawfords may receive perhaps $1,000 for their collection. This amount would not be sufficient to replace even a small portion of their collection. They should give serious consideration to buying a floater policy to cover the replacement cost of their collection.

11.16 The Klugs have a $120,000 home on which they carry $80,000 in insurance coverage. How much would the insurance company pay if the Klugs were to suffer losses of (a) $60,000, (b) $80,000, (c) $100,000? What advice do you have for the Klugs?

SOLUTION

Insurance coverage is $80,000/$120,000 = 67 percent of replacement cost; therefore, payment is based on the coinsurance clause. The coinsurance ratio is $80,000/(.8 × $120,000) = .83. The losses paid are as follows:

(a) $60,000: $60,000 × .83 = $49,800

(b) $80,000: $80,000 × .83 = $66,400

(c) $100,000: $100,000 × .83 = $83,000   limited to $80,000

The Klugs should increase their coverage to at least .8 × $120,000 = $96,000.

11.17 The Hoffmans have recently bought a new home in Phoenix. They have an $80,000 mortgage on the house and an insurance policy for the same amount. They have a brand new car and a 7-year-old car. Mr. Hoffman has an extensive collection of antique Hummels. Mrs. Hoffman likes to collect proof sets of coins and has a significant dollar investment in her collection. Mrs. Hoffman is a branch manager for a consumer goods company. Mr. Hoffman teaches accounting on a part-time basis at a local college and is also trying to establish his own accounting practice. Briefly explain the risks the Hoffmans face and the best method for handling these risks.

SOLUTION

The Hoffmans face property risks for their home, cars, and collectibles. The home already has $80,000 in homeowners' insurance. The amount is tied in to the mortgage balance. It is possible that they need more than $80,000 in coverage. They should check with their insurance agent to see if the amount of coverage should be increased. The new car, if damaged, may be expensive to repair. Therefore, they should carry collision and comprehensive insurance on it. The old car is probably not worth much, and they may carry just comprehensive insurance. The Hoffman collections appear to be expensive and should be insured against theft and damage through a scheduled policy.

With the home and the car, the Hoffmans should carry appropriate liability insurance. Since Mr. Hoffman practices accounting, a comprehensive liability insurance policy would provide protection against malpractice.

Mrs. Hoffman probably has group health insurance available at work. Mr. Hoffman should be added to her health plan. Both should have disability insurance for about 50 percent of their earnings. Each of them should have life insurance for about 6 to 8 times their annual earnings.

11.18 Jerry Jones carries $60,000 in insurance coverage on his home. The replacement value of the home is $90,000 with an 80 percent coinsurance requirement. Calculate the insurance payout for $24,000 in damage caused by a covered peril.

SOLUTION

Using the formula

$$R = L \times \left(\frac{I}{RV \times 80\%} \right)$$

where R = reimbursement payable, L = the amount of loss less deductible, I = amount of insurance actually carried, RV = replacement value,

$$\$24,000 \times \left(\frac{\$60,000}{\$90,000 \times 80\%} \right) = \$20,000$$

11.19 James Price carries $100,000 in insurance coverage on his Lake Elsinore lake-front condominium.

(*a*)   If it turns out that the replacement cost value of his condo is $150,000, how much would the insurance company pay on losses of

    (1) $50,000

    (2) $90,000

    (3) $110,000?

(*b*)   How much insurance should he carry?

SOLUTION

(*a*)   Using the formula

$$R = L \times \left(\frac{I}{RV \times 80\%} \right)$$

    (1) $41,667 = \$50,000 \times [\$100,000/(\$150,000 \times 80\%)]$

    (2) $75,000 = \$90,000 \times [\$100,000/(\$150,000 \times 80\%)]$

    (3) $91,667 = \$110,000 \times [\$100,000/(\$150,000 \times 80\%)]$

(*b*)   Mr. Price should carry at least $120,000 in insurance on his condo.

11.20 Each of two brothers, Jim and Johnny, owns a condo with a replacement value of $120,000 and each suffers a $50,000 fire loss. Jim has insured his condo for $96,000 and Johnny has insured his condo for $90,000. Calculate the amount Jim and Johnny will be reimbursed for the loss to their dwellings.

SOLUTION

For Jim: $$\$50,000 = \$50,000 \times \left(\frac{\$96,000}{\$120,000 \times 80\%} \right)$$

For Johnny: $$\$46,875 = \$50,000 \times \left(\frac{\$90,000}{\$120,000 \times 80\%} \right)$$

Thus, Jim will be fully covered, while Johnny will be reimbursed for only $46,875.

11.21 Your 8-year-old TV was stolen. The TV when new cost $800 and had an expected life of 10 years. What is the actual cash value of the TV?

SOLUTION

Use the formula

$$ACV = P - \left[CA \times \left(\frac{P}{n} \right) \right]$$

where P = purchase price of the item, CA = current age in years, and n = expected life in years.
The ACV of the TV at the time it was stolen was

$$\$160 = \$800 - \left[8 \times \left(\frac{\$800}{10} \right) \right]$$

Chapter 12

What You Should Know About Investments and Planning

This chapter distinguishes between financial assets and real assets, looks at short-term versus long-term investing, enumerates investment considerations and guidelines, presents marketable investments, discusses economic and market factors, evaluates inflation, and analyzes risk versus return.

FINANCIAL ASSETS AND REAL ASSETS

The two basic kinds of investments are financial assets and real assets. *Financial assets* comprise all intangible assets: they might represent equity ownership of a company, or provide evidence that someone owes you a debt, or show the right to buy or sell your ownership interest at a later date.

SOLVED PROBLEM 12.1

What are some financial assets?

SOLUTION

Financial assets include savings and money market accounts, money market certificates, Treasury bills, commercial paper, common stock, options and warrants, preferred stock, bonds, mutual funds, commodity futures, and financial futures.

Real assets are those investments you can put your hands on. They are what we call real property.

SOLVED PROBLEM 12.2

What do real assets include?

SOLUTION

Real assets include real estate, precious metals, collectibles and gems, and oil.

SHORT-TERM AND LONG-TERM INVESTMENTS

An investment may be short-term or long-term. Short-term investments are held for 1 year or less, whereas long-term investments mature after more than 1 year. An example of a short-term investment is a 1-year certificate of deposit; a typical long-term investment is a 10-year bond. (Some long-term investments have no maturity date.) Equity securities (common stock and preferred stock) are considered long-term investments. But you can purchase a long-term investment and treat it as a short-term investment by selling it within 1 year.

FIXED-DOLLAR AND VARIABLE-DOLLAR INVESTMENTS

Fixed-dollar investments have principal and/or income guaranteed in advance. Examples are bonds, preferred stock, U.S. government securities, and municipal bonds. Variable-dollar investments do *not* have principal and/or income guaranteed. Examples are common stock and real estate.

SOURCES OF INVESTMENT MONEY

There are several ways of financing your investment choices. They include

Discretionary income.   After-tax income is disposable income, money available to you for spending or saving. You must commit much of your disposable income to fixed or semifixed expenditures such as housing, food, and transportation. Discretionary income is what is left after these expenses.

Home equity.   You may have a substantial amount of money in your home. You can cash out some of it by taking either a home equity loan or an equity line.

Life insurance.   If you have a cash value (for example, whole life or variable life) life insurance policy, you can borrow up to a certain amount.

Profit sharing and pension.   If you own some form of annuity, you may borrow up to a certain amount at a low interest rate.

Gift.

OPM (other people's money).

SOME INVESTMENT CONSIDERATIONS

Your financial situation and future expectations are essential in formulating an investment strategy.

SOLVED PROBLEM 12.3

Before you decide to make a particular investment, what should you consider?

SOLUTION

You should consider the following as they apply to your particular situation: current and future income needs; need to provide for heirs; need to hedge against inflation; ability to withstand financial losses; security of principal and income; rate of return; liquidity and marketability; diversification; tax and estate status; long-term versus short-term potential; amount of investment; denomination of investment [for example, $5,000 minimum investment, as required by some real estate investment trusts (REITs)]; need for loan collateral; protection from creditor claims; callability provisions; and risk level (high risk/ higher reward versus low risk/greater security).

It may not pay to invest small amounts because of the high percentage cost.

SOLVED PROBLEM 12.4

The minimum brokerage fee on a transaction is $40. You buy 100 shares of stock at $5 per share. What is your percentage cost of the transaction and does it pay financially?

SOLUTION

$$\frac{\text{Cost}}{\text{Investment}} = \frac{\$40}{\$500} = 8\%$$

It costs 8 percent for this transaction so to break even you must earn an 8 percent return. This transaction is not financially sound.

The return on an investment consists of dividend income or interest income plus capital gain (or loss). When comparing investments, the annual return is important to consider.

Dollar return on stock = Dividend income +/− Change in price

Dollar return on bond = Interest income +/− Change in price

SOLVED PROBLEM 12.5

You own stock in a company that will pay a quarterly dividend of $1.25 per share. You own 100 shares.

(a) What is the annual dividend per share?

(b) What is the total dividend you will receive?

SOLUTION

(a) $1.25 × 4 = $5

(b) 100 × $5 = $500

SOLVED PROBLEM 12.6

You invest in a stock paying a 9 percent dividend per year.

(a) If you are in the 15 percent tax bracket, what is the after-tax yield?

(b) If you are in the 28 percent tax bracket, what is the after-tax yield?

SOLUTION

(a) 9% × .85 = 7.7%

(b) 9% × .72 = 6.5%

SOLVED PROBLEM 12.7

You buy 1,000 shares of a company's stock for $3 a share and incur a brokerage commission of $50. The stock pays no dividends. After 1 year, you sell it for $5 a share. The brokerage commission is 2 percent of the selling price. What is your capital gain or loss?

SOLUTION

Selling price [1,000 × $5 = $5,000 − (2% × $5,000)]	$4,900
Cost (1,000 × $3 = $3,000 + $50)	3,050
Capital gain	$1,850

SOLVED PROBLEM 12.8

You bought 100 shares of a stock 2 years ago for $40 per share. In the current year, you received a dividend of $1.50 per share. You sold the 100 shares this year at $45 per share.

(a) What is your capital gain or loss?

(b) What is your dividend this year?

(c) What is your total return?

(d) Assuming a 28 percent tax rate, what is the after-tax gain?

SOLUTION

(a) Capital gain: ($45 − $40 = $5 × 100) = $500

(b) $1.50 × 100 = $150

(c) $500 + $150 = $650

(d) $650 × .72 = $468

SOLVED PROBLEM 12.9

You bought a stock for $5,000 plus brokerage commission of $100. After holding it for 1 year and receiving a dividend of $300, you sold it for $5,500 less a brokerage commission of $120. What is your total return or loss on the stock investment?

SOLUTION

Dividend income		$300
Plus: Price appreciation		
Net proceeds ($5,500 − $120)	$5,380	
Net cost ($5,000 + $100)	(5,100)	280
Total return		$580

SOLVED PROBLEM 12.10

Assume the same facts as in Solved Problem 12.9 except you sold the stock for $4,600 less a brokerage commission of $90.

(*a*)   What is your total return or loss on the stock investment?

(*b*)   Explain what happened.

SOLUTION

(*a*)

Dividend income		$300
Less: Price decrease		
Net proceeds ($4,600 − $90)	$4,510	
Net cost ($5,000 + $100)	(5,100)	(590)
Total loss		$ 290

(*b*)   Even though you received a dividend of $300, there is a negative return of $290 because of the decline in the price of the stock by $590.

SOLVED PROBLEM 12.11

You purchased a $3,000 face value bond for $2,950 plus brokerage commission of $60. The interest rate is 8 percent. After holding the bond 1 year, you sold it for $3,200. The brokerage commission on the sale was $70. What is your total return or loss on the bond investment?

SOLUTION

Interest income ($3,000 × 8%)		$240
Plus: Price increase		
Net proceeds ($3,200 − $70)	$3,130	
Net cost ($2,950 + $60)	(3,010)	120
Total return		$360

SOLVED PROBLEM 12.12

You bought a $4,000 face value bond for $4,000 plus brokerage commission of $75. The bond pays interest of 10 percent. After holding the bond 1 year, you sold it for 102 percent of its face value. The brokerage commission on the sale was $90.

(*a*)   What is your total return or loss on the bond investment?

(*b*)   Explain what happened.

SOLUTION

(a)

Interest income ($4,000 × 10%)		$400
Less: Price decrease		
Net proceeds ($4,000 × 102% = $4,080 − $90)	$3,990	
Net cost ($4,000 + $75)	(4,075)	(85)
Total return		$315

(b) Even though you received interest income of $400, the total return was only $315 because of a net decline in price of the bond of $85. It is interesting that even though you sold the bond at a *gross* price increase of $80 ($4,080 − $4,000), you still lost $85 because of the total brokerage commissions of $165 ($90 + $75). Hence, there is a *net* price decline of $85 ($165 − $80).

THE KEY QUESTIONS TO ASK

You must always be open and inquisitive in personal financial planning. The answers you give for the following questions will significantly shape investment strategy:

What proportion of funds do you want safe and liquid?

Are you willing to invest for higher return but greater risk?

How long a maturity period are you willing to take on the investment?

What should be the mix of your investments for diversification purposes (for example, stocks, bonds, real estate)?

Do you need to invest in tax-free securities?

You should invest during good and bad times because we can never be sure of the exact market timing. Such a strategy will typically provide rewarding returns. For example, in the stock market crash of October 1987, there were many good buys of significantly undervalued securities.

Investment return is affected by risk, liquidity, and size.

AGGRESSIVE AND DEFENSIVE INVESTMENT STRATEGY

Aggressive investment policies attempt to maximize profits and take above-average risk. Defensive investment policies are designed to reduce risk but also provide less return. If you invest aggressively, you tend to buy and sell more frequently. In a defensive strategy, you "buy and hold." Aggressive investment may include buying securities on margin (credit) so as to increase profit potential. Defensive investment does not rely on leverage. Diversification is a defensive policy. Aggressive investing involves concentration by investing in a few securities at one time in anticipation of a high return.

ARE YOUR INVESTMENTS MARKETABLE AND LIQUID?

Marketability should be distinguished from liquidity. Marketability means you can find a ready market if you want to sell the investment. Liquidity means the investment is not only marketable and easily accessible but also has a highly stable price.

Liquidity may be important if you have limited investments or are saving for a specific personal or business item (for example, down payment on a house). However, liquid investments typically earn less of a return than illiquid ones. You desire to minimize delays and transaction costs to convert the investment into immediate cash.

SOLVED PROBLEM 12.13

What are examples of liquid investments?

SOLUTION

Liquid investments include savings accounts, money market funds, and certificates of deposit.

Table 12-1 depicts marketability and liquidity factors for an investment.

Table 12-1   Asset Marketability and Liquidity

	Marketability	Liquidity
Savings accounts	Not applicable	Good
Money market funds	Good	Good
Corporate bonds	Good	Average
Municipal bonds	Good	Average
Short-term U.S. government securities	Good	Good
Long-term U.S. government securities	Good	Average
Common stock	Good	Poor
Real estate	Average	Poor

WHAT DO YOU WANT WHEN YOU INVEST?

If you want a safe investment with predictable but low return, invest in U.S. government securities, bank accounts, or money market accounts of a mutual fund.

If you are retired, you may favor safe investments providing fixed yearly returns. Appreciation in the price of a security is not as important as stable, guaranteed income. Risky investments are undesirable due to uncertainty. For example, a retiree may be satisfied with a long-term government bond.

There is a risk/return trade-off in investing. Generally, the higher the return to be earned, the riskier is the investment. For example, a higher return is generally earned on investing in stocks than in Treasury bills because of the greater risk.

The more money you invest in one source, the higher the rate of return. For example, a bank will usually pay you a higher interest rate on a $100,000 investment compared to a $10,000 investment.

Be cautious in taking salespeople (for example, brokers, mutual fund representatives) advice because their prime motivation is to earn a commission.

WHAT YOU SHOULD DO IN DIFFERENT SCENARIOS

Your personal finance strategy will differ depending upon whether there is inflation or depression.

SOLVED PROBLEM 12.14

What should you do in high inflation?

SOLUTION

A rapid increase in inflation will cause interest rates to rise, and bond prices to fall. Therefore, you should avoid fixed-income securities. However, the prices of precious metals (for example, gold and silver) and real estate will increase.

SOLVED PROBLEM 12.15

What should you do in a depression?

SOLUTION

In a depression, purchase long-term Treasury bonds. Interest rates will drop close to zero, and you will have a security all others wish to buy that is safe.

After you have an emergency fund and necessities, you may want capital accumulation. You will want an investment that grows consistent with your risk tolerance. In order to have growth, the after-tax return on the investment portfolio has to exceed the inflation rate. If inflation is high, your investment may not outpace inflation.

SOLVED PROBLEM 12.16

What investments usually provide long-term growth?

SOLUTION

Investments that typically provide long-term growth include common stock, convertible securities, growth mutual funds, and real estate.

SOLVED PROBLEM 12.17

You invest in a fixed-income portfolio (for example, bonds earning 9 percent). You are in the 28 percent tax bracket.

(*a*)   What is your after-tax yield?

(*b*)   Assuming an inflation rate of 5 percent, have you kept up with inflation?

SOLUTION

(*a*) $9\% \times .72 = 6.48\%$

(*b*)   You have only exceeded the inflation rate by 1.48% (6.48% − 5.00%).

SOLVED PROBLEM 12.18

You invest in a stock paying an 8 percent dividend per year. If you are in the 15 percent tax bracket, what is the after-tax yield?

SOLUTION

$$8\% \times .85 = 6.8\%$$

You may borrow money to make investments. This is known as leverage. You can dramatically increase the yield on an investment otherwise made entirely from your own funds. This increase occurs when the return on the investment exceeds the cost of borrowing. You can maximize return by buying stocks on margin or by putting down as little as possible when buying real estate.

SOLVED PROBLEM 12.19

What are examples of income-oriented investments that provide continual cash flow?

SOLUTION

Income-oriented investments include stocks paying high dividends (for example, utilities), bonds, income funds, certificates of deposit, and Treasury notes.

THE IMPACT OF ECONOMIC AND MARKET FACTORS

General economic conditions may affect your investments. Generally, problems in the economy will have a negative impact on your investments. Equity securities, for example, typically are highly sensitive to the overall economy. For instance, during an economic downturn, companies may have difficulty repaying their debts (adversely affecting their bond ratings) and have difficulty selling their products (adversely affecting stock prices).

If interest rates change, differing types of securities will be affected in varying ways.

SOLVED PROBLEM 12.20

What investments are at risk with changing interest rates?

SOLUTION

Investments at risk with changing interest rates are notes, bonds, mortgages, GNMA ("Ginnie Maes," issued by the Government National Mortgage Association), and stocks.

SOLVED PROBLEM 12.21

What investments offset the risk of interest rate changes?

SOLUTION

Investments offsetting the risk of interest rate changes are real estate and gold.

Long-term interest rates on high-quality bonds are about 3 percent more than the expected long-term inflation rate.

SOLVED PROBLEM 12.22

As interest rates increase, what happens to stock prices and why?

SOLUTION

With rising interest rates, stock prices decrease for the following reasons: Dividends are less attractive so many people sell stocks and put funds in the bank; buying stock on margin becomes more costly and thus discourages investment; financing becomes more costly for businesses resulting in decreased profits and inhibited expansion.

A change in economic conditions may have a material effect upon investments.

SOLVED PROBLEM 12.23

What investments are susceptible to changing economic conditions?

SOLUTION

Investments affected by a changing economy are bonds, stocks, mortgages, and real estate.

SOLVED PROBLEM 12.24

What investments are not susceptible to changing economic conditions?

SOLUTION

Investments not vulnerable to a changing economy are U.S. government securities, gold, and certificates of deposit.

SOLVED PROBLEM 12.25

What investments are susceptible to market cycles?

SOLUTION

Investments at risk during market cycle changes are common stock, real estate, collectibles, and gold.

SOLVED PROBLEM 12.26

What investments offset market cycle risk?

SOLUTION

Investments which offset market cycle risk are bonds, certificates of deposit, GNMAs, mortgages, and notes.

DID YOU CONSIDER A MUTUAL FUND?

A *direct* investment is when you buy a claim on a specific property. When you select an *indirect* investment, you invest in a portfolio of securities or properties. One popular indirect investment is a share of a *mutual fund,* which is a portfolio of securities issued by any one of several mutual investment companies. Mutual funds are discussed in more detail in Chapter 17.

SOLVED PROBLEM 12.27

What are some investment guidelines to follow in investing in mutual funds?

SOLUTION

Some investment guidelines in mutual fund investing are

If you want to speculate, do it in a stock mutual fund, where the gains can be significant, not in a bond mutual fund.

You can reduce risk by investing in a mutual fund with high-quality bonds, rather than low-quality ones.

Buy into a mutual fund that shows consistent long-term performance (for example, over a 5-year or 10-year period). A mutual fund may show great performance in 1 year only because of luck or unusual circumstances, or because the risky stocks they bought shot up.

Do not invest in a tax shelter mutual fund unless it appears to be a good investment.

Do not invest too heavily in a mutual fund of precious metals because of volatility in price.

SOLVED PROBLEM 12.28

Can you name a stock mutual fund that has an excellent track record?

SOLUTION

The answer will vary depending upon the respondent but an excellent stock mutual fund is Fidelity Magellan.

THE COST OF INVESTING

You might want to take into account the expenses associated with various investment instruments. The expenses vary widely.

SOLVED PROBLEM 12.29

Which investments require high expenses?

SOLUTION

Investments involving high expenses include over-the-counter and inactive stocks, load mutual funds, unit trusts, limited partnerships, collectibles, and certificates of deposit if withdrawn before maturity.

SOLVED PROBLEM 12.30

Which investments involve low expenses?

SOLUTION

Investments requiring low expenses include actively traded stocks and bonds and no-load mutual funds.

Buy in volume to obtain discounts. For example, as you increase the number of shares bought, the brokerage commission per share drops. The more you invest in certain mutual funds (for example, Fidelity Special Situations), the lower will be the sales commission. The greater the dollar purchase of a Treasury bill, the less the commission. If you buy a $50,000 or more Treasury bill from Merrill, Lynch, Pierce, Fenner, and Smith, there is a minimal commission.

HOW DOES INFLATION AFFECT YOU?

You have to take inflation into account in making personal financial planning decisions. Inflation is an increase in price for goods and services over a short time period. It reduces the purchasing power of the dollar and increases the cost of living. For example, inflation can push up the price of housing so severely that many young adults cannot afford to buy a house.

The Consumer Price Index (CPI) has more than tripled since 1967 (base year with an index of 100). From 1975 to 1985, inflation in the United States increased at an average compounded annual rate of 6.9 percent. Inflation has a negative impact if you have fixed-rate savings accounts or fixed-income investments (for example, bonds), or are living on a fixed income.

It is important to analyze your "real earnings," taking into account inflation and taxes. A change in "real earnings" may even be negative. If you are not keeping up with inflation, your standard of living and net worth will suffer. In 1970, for example, the average wage earner made $119 a week. In 1985, the average weekly wage was $300. However, in terms of purchasing power, the 1985 wage bought only $110 worth of goods and services. This represents a decrease in "real" income of 8 percent.

SOLVED PROBLEM 12.31

You get a 6 percent increase in income over the year. The inflation rate is 4 percent.

(a)   What has your real income increased by?

(b)   If the tax rate is 28 percent, what is the real income in after-tax dollars?

SOLUTION

(a)

$$6\% - 4\% = 2\%$$

(b)

After-tax nominal income (6% × .72)	4.32%
Inflation rate	4.00%
Real income rate	.32%

SOLVED PROBLEM 12.32

You invest $1,000 earning a 6 percent rate of return. Inflation averages 4 percent for the year. What is your real dollar rate of return?

SOLUTION

$$\$1,000 \times 2\% = \$20$$

SOLVED PROBLEM 12.33

You receive a 7 percent increase in salary. Your tax rate is 28 percent and the inflation rate is 4 percent. What is your raise in "real dollars"?

SOLUTION

Your raise in "real dollars" after taking into account inflation and taxes is

Increase in salary	7%
Taxes (.28 × 7%)	2%
Increase in salary after tax	5%
Inflation rate	4%
Increase in salary after tax and inflation	1%

DETERMINING YOUR LEVEL OF RISK

Personal risk means you may not be able to accomplish financial goals. Conservatism in financial planning is recommended, so that there is an aversion to high risk. Risk includes the chance of losing money on an investment. The more an investment can vary in value during the maturity period, the greater the risk you take when you buy it. Questions to be answered regarding losses include:

What potential losses exist, and what is the probability of loss?

How much money will be needed in the event of a major loss?

How much loss can be withstood, and for how long?

Risk can be reduced by having a diversified portfolio of securities that are negatively correlated (the price of the securities move in opposite directions). Perfect negative correlation is −1. An example of negatively correlated securities would be Ford Motor Company and Amtrack. The portfolio may also consist of securities having no correlation (0) such as pharmaceuticals and airlines. Avoid securities that are positively correlated because their prices always move in the same direction. Therefore, greater risk exists. Perfect positive correlation is +1. Examples of positively correlated securities are automobile, steel, and tire stocks. Note that correlation may be between −1 and +1.

SOLVED PROBLEM 12.34

The correlation between two stocks you own is −.90. What does that mean?

SOLUTION

A value of −.90 indicates that the two stocks are very highly negatively correlated. You are well diversified.

Figure 12-1 shows the degree of default risk associated with different types of securities.

Be careful that obligations do not become so excessive that personal assets have to be liquidated at losses to the extent you may never recover from its financial effects.

Review Questions

(1) An equity ownership interest in a company is an example of a _____ asset.

(2) An investment in real estate is an example of a _____ asset.

(3) An investment to be held for more than 1 year is referred to as a _____ investment.

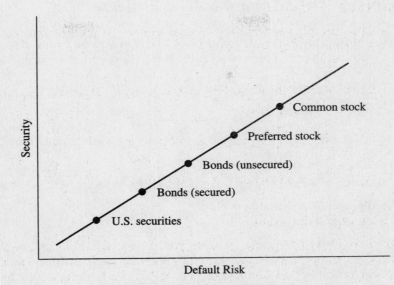

Fig. 12-1 Securities and default risk.

(4) Disposable income less fixed and semifixed expenditures equals _____ income.

(5) If interest rates rise, stock prices will _____ and bond prices will _____.

(6) During inflation, the price of real estate will _____ and the price of precious metals will _____.

(7) _____ means that an investment is both marketable and has a highly stable price.

(8) In a _____, it is best to purchase long-term Treasury bonds.

(9) You are effectively using _____ when the return on your investment exceeds the cost to borrow.

(10) You can diversify by investing in a _____ which holds a portfolio of many securities.

(11) The purchase of stock on margin is an example of an _____ investment strategy.

(12) "Buy and hold" is an example of a _____ investment strategy.

(13) The investment having the greatest default risk is _____.

(14) The prices of precious metals are _____.

(15) Investing in automotive and steel stocks is an example of _____ correlated securities.

(16) When securities have a correlation of −.4, they are _____ correlated.

(17) Diversification can be achieved by investing in securities with _____ or _____ correlations.

Answers: (1) financial; (2) real; (3) long-term; (4) discretionary; (5) fall, fall; (6) increase, increase; (7) Liquidity; (8) depression; (9) leverage; (10) mutual fund; (11) aggressive; (12) defensive; (13) common stock; (14) volatile; (15) positively; (16) negatively; (17) negative, no.

Additional Solved Problems

12.1 The minimum brokerage fee on a transaction is $35. You buy 50 shares of stock at a price per share of $9. What is the percentage cost of this transaction and is it worth doing?

SOLUTION

$$\frac{\text{Cost}}{\text{Investment}} = \frac{\$35}{\$450} = 7.8\%$$

This transaction already costs 7.8 percent so you must earn a minimum return of at least that. This transaction is not financially advisable.

12.2 You own 500 shares of a company that pays a quarterly dividend of $.80 per share.

(*a*)   What is the annual dividend per share?

(*b*)   What is the total dividend?

SOLUTION

(*a*) $.80 × 4 = $3.20

(*b*) $3.20 × 500 = $1,600

12.3 You invest in a bond earning 10 percent. You are in the 28 percent tax bracket and the inflation rate is 4 percent.

(*a*)   What is the after-tax yield?

(*b*)   What is the yield after taxes and inflation?

SOLUTION

(*a*)   10% × .72 = 7.2%

(*b*)   7.2% − 4.0% = 3.2%

12.4 You receive an 8 percent raise on your job. Your tax rate is 28 percent and the inflation rate is 5 percent. What is your raise in "real dollars" after considering taxes and inflation?

SOLUTION

Increase in salary	8.0%
Taxes (.28 × 8%)	2.2
Increase in salary after tax	5.8%
Inflation rate	5.0
Increase in salary after tax and inflation	.8%

12.5 You get a 7 percent increase in income over the year. The inflation rate is 5 percent.

(*a*)   What is the increase in your real income?

(*b*)   If the tax rate is 15 percent, what is the real income in after-tax dollars?

SOLUTION

(*a*)   7% − 5% = 2%

(*b*)

After-tax nominal income (7% × .85)	5.95%
Inflation rate	5.00%
Real income rate	.95%

12.6 You invest $5,000 earning an 8 percent rate of return. Inflation is 5 percent for the year.

    (*a*)   What is your real percentage rate of return?

    (*b*)   What is your dollar rate of return?

SOLUTION

    (*a*)   8% − 5% = 3%

    (*b*) $5,000 × 3% = $150

12.7 You bought 100 shares of a stock 3 years ago for $25 per share. In the current year, you received a dividend of $1.25 per share. You sold the 100 shares this year at $32 per share.

    (*a*)   What is your capital gain or loss?

    (*b*)   What is your dividend this year?

    (*c*)   What is the total return?

    (*d*)   Assuming a 30 percent tax rate, what is the after-tax gain?

SOLUTION

    (*a*)   Capital gain ($32 − $25) = $7 × 100 shares = $700

    (*b*) $1.25 × 100 = $125

    (*c*) $700 + $125 = $825

    (*d*) $825 × .70 = $578

12.8 You buy 500 shares of a company at $7 a share plus a brokerage commission of 2 percent. The stock pays no dividend. After holding it 4 years, you sell it at $5 per share. The brokerage commission is 2.5 percent. What is your capital gain or loss?

SOLUTION

Selling price [500 × $5 = $2,500
    − (2.5% × $2,500) = $2,500 − $62.50] $ 2,437.50
Cost [500 × $7 = $3,500 + (2%
    × $3,500) = $3,500 + $70]   3,570.00
Capital loss $(1,132.50)

12.9 You bought a stock for $3,000 plus brokerage commission of $80. After keeping it 1 year and receiving a dividend of $200, you sold it for $3,800 less a brokerage commission of $90. What is the total return or loss on the stock investment?

SOLUTION

Dividend income $200
Plus: Price appreciation
    Net proceeds ($3,800 − $90) $ 3,710
    Net cost ($3,000 + $80)   (3,080)   630
Total return $830

12.10 Assume the same facts as Solved Problem 12.9 except that you sold the stock for $2,700 less a brokerage commission of $85.

    (*a*)   What is your total return or loss?

    (*b*)   Explain what happened?

SOLUTION

(a)

Dividend income			$ 200
Less: Price decrease			
Net proceeds ($2,700 − $85)		$ 2,615	
Net cost ($3,000 + $80)		(3,080)	(465)
Total cost			$(265)

(b) Even though you received a dividend of $200, there is a negative return of $265 because of the drop in the price of the stock by $465.

12.11 You purchased a $6,000 face value bond for $6,185 plus brokerage commission of $100. The interest rate is 9 percent. After holding the bond 1 year, you sold it for $6,800. The brokerage commission on the sale was $125. What is your total return or loss on the bond investment?

SOLUTION

Interest income ($6,000 × 9%)		$540
Plus: Price increase		
Net proceeds ($6,800 − $125)	$ 6,675	
Net cost ($6,185 + $100)	(6,285)	390
Total return		$930

12.12 You bought an $8,000 face value bond for $8,100 plus brokerage commission of $125. The bond pays interest of 12 percent. After holding the bond 1 year, you sold it for 103 percent of its face value. The brokerage commission on the sale was $150.

(a) What is your total return or loss?

(b) Explain what happened.

SOLUTION

(a)

Interest income ($8,000 × 12%)		$960
Less: Price decrease		
Net proceeds ($8,000 × 103% = $8,240 − $15)	$ 8,090	
Net cost ($8,000 + $125)	(8,125)	(35)
Total return		$925

(b) Even though you received interest income of $960, the total return was only $925 because of the net decline in price of the bond by $35. It is interesting that even though you sold the bond at a *gross* price increase of $240 ($8,240 − $8,000) you still lost $35 because of the total brokerage commission of $275 ($150 + $125). Hence, there is a net decrease of $35 ($275 − $240).

Chapter 13

Investing in Common Stock

Common stock is an equity investment that represents ownership in a business (evidenced by a stock certificate which is transferable). For example, if you hold 3,000 shares of XYZ Company, which has 100,000 shares outstanding, your ownership interest is 3 percent. Share means a fractional ownership interest in a firm. You obtain an equity interest in the company by buying its stock. Before the stock may be sold to the public, it must be registered with the Securities and Exchange Commission. Details of a new issue and financial information are contained in a document referred to as the *prospectus*. Law requires that you receive a prospectus before you can purchase a security.

As a stockholder, you can vote for the directors of the corporation. There is no maturity date to an equity investment. Your return is in the form of dividend income and appreciation in the market price of stock.

Stocks are of two types: common and preferred. As a common stockholder, you bear part of the company's risk and share in its success. Preferred stock is similar to bonds, which are discussed in other chapters. You may buy common stock on the listed exchanges or the over-the-counter market. Table 13-1 presents characteristics of common stock.

Table 13-1 Characteristics of Common Stock

Voting rights	Yes, one vote per share
Risk	High
Appreciation in market price	Yes
Price fluctuation	Yes
Fixed annual return	No, income varies with corporate income
Inflation hedge	Yes
Preemptive right	Yes
Last in bankruptcy to collect	Yes, common stockholders are paid after all others

You should be familiar with the following common stock terms:

Par value.   The stated or face value of a stock. This figure exists primarily for legal reasons. Some stocks are issued with no par value.

Book value.   This equals the common stockholders' equity divided by the number of shares outstanding.

Market price.   The current price the stock can be bought or sold at. Market prices are listed in the newspapers (for example, *The Wall Street Journal*).

SOLVED PROBLEM 13.1

What are the advantages and disadvantages of owning common stock?

SOLUTION

Among the benefits of owning common stock are

Voting right

Share in dividends and increased market price

Better hedge against inflation than with fixed-income securities

Preemptive right to maintain your proportionate share of ownership in the company—that is, to buy new shares issued before they go on sale to the public

Assume you own 5 percent of the company and there is a new issuance of 50,000 shares. You have the right to purchase 2,500 shares.

Disadvantages to common stock ownership include

Possible decline in market price

Possible curtailment or elimination of dividends

Receipt of dividends only after preferred stockholders

Possible forfeiture of dividends omitted in a year

Greater price fluctuation than with fixed-income securities

SOLVED PROBLEM 13.2

You own 4 percent of a company that has a new issuance of 20,000 shares. How many shares can you buy by exercising a preemptive right?

SOLUTION

$$20,000 \times .04 = 800$$

Although equity ownership returns vary with business cycles, stocks have shown over the years to be rewarding investments and good hedges against inflation. However, you should invest in stocks only if you have extra disposable income after building up sufficient cash savings for unexpected emergencies, life insurance, and other necessities. If possible, try to invest about 15 percent of after-tax income. As a general rule, before you invest in stocks, your total assets should be two times your total liabilities.

WHAT TYPES OF STOCKS ARE THERE?

The stock you buy should be best for your particular circumstances and goals. The types of stock include

1. *Blue chips.*   These offer ownership in high-quality, financially strong companies (for example, General Electric). They have low risk and provide modest but dependable returns. They have good track records in earnings growth and dividend payments. "Blue chips" are less susceptible than other stocks to cyclical market swings. They typically sell at high price-earnings (P/E) ratios and have low risk of stock price variability. A "blue chip" is for those wanting a safe, long-term equity investment.

2. *Growth stocks.*   Companies evidencing faster growth rates than other firms (for example, high-technology businesses) and the economy in general. Growth stocks pay low or no dividends, since earnings are normally retained for future expansion. While growth stocks usually increase in price faster than others, they may fluctuate more. An example of a growth stock is MCI. A growth stock may be good if you are planning to retire many years from now.

3. *Income stocks.*   These are issued by companies having higher dividends and dividend payout ratios. These stocks are good if you desire high current income instead of capital appreciation, and want to have less risk. Income stocks are generally of companies in stable industries (for example, utilities). Income stocks give you the highest income with stability to satisfy your present living requirements. *Tip:* You may be interested in income stocks when greater uncertainty exists about economic conditions. Income stocks are attractive to retirees who depend on stability and periodic cash flow.

4. *Cyclical stocks.*   When a stock's price fluctuates based on economic changes, it is called a cyclical stock. These companies' earnings drop in recession and increase in expansion. The stocks are thus somewhat speculative. Examples are airlines, chemicals, and construction companies. A cyclical stock may be for a young individual who is willing to take risks and who is financially secure.

5. *Defensive stocks.* Stocks of companies that are basically not affected by a downturn in the business cycle. They are consistent and safe securities. However, a lower return is earned. Examples are utilities and consumer product companies. A defensive stock may be for an older person who prefers to avoid downward risk in the economy.

6. *Speculative stocks.* When companies without established track records issue stock, there is uncertainty in earnings but an opportunity for large profits. You may buy a speculative stock if you want a very high return and are willing to take high risk. Speculative stocks are for professional investors rather than the average person. Speculative stocks have high price-earnings ratios and price fluctuations. Examples are biotechnology companies and mining stocks.

Beware of "penny" stocks, which typically sell for less than $1 a share. Penny stocks are issued by companies with a short or erratic history of earnings, and are thus quite risky.

A part of your funds should be invested in equity securities for diversification. But do not put all your eggs in one basket; if all your funds are in stock, you may suffer a huge loss in a stock crash.

However, over the long run, stocks have outperformed most other investments including bonds, certificates of deposit, and gold.

WHAT TYPES OF ORDERS MAY YOU PLACE WITH YOUR BROKER?

The broker's commission is based on the dollar amount of the transaction and the number of shares traded. The greater the number of shares and the greater the dollar amount, the lower is the commission percentage.

The types of orders you may place for stock transactions are as follows:

Market order.   You buy or sell stock at the current market price.

Open order.   Your order is kept open for a specified time period.

Day order.   Your order is good only for the day.

Good till canceled (GTC).   There is no expiration date to the order. It is open until the transaction takes place or is withdrawn.

Limit order.   You agree to buy the stock at no more than a given price or sell at no less than a stated price. Your broker continues the order until a specified date or until you withdraw it. The brokerage commission is usually higher on a limit order than on a market order.

SOLVED PROBLEM 13.3

When is a limit order advisable?

SOLUTION

A limit order may be good to use when market prices are uncertain or fluctuate rapidly.

EXAMPLE 13.1   You place a limit order to buy at $9 or less a stock now selling at $10. If the stock increases, it is not bought. However, if it decreases to $9, it is immediately purchased.

Stop-loss order.   You agree to buy or sell a stock when it increases to or declines below a given price. *Recommendation:* Set a stop-loss order at 15 to 20 percent below your cost or the recent high. Stop-loss orders are not available for over-the-counter stocks.

SOLVED PROBLEM 13.4

When is a stop-loss order advisable?

SOLUTION

Use this order to protect yourself from further stock price declines by selling the shares at a predetermined price.

EXAMPLE 13.2   You own 100 shares of ABC Company at a current market price of $40 per share. You originally bought it at $25 a share. You may place a stop-loss order to sell the stock if it drops to $35, to lock in a gain of $10 ($35 − $25).

Time order.   You ask your broker to sell a stock at a particular price in a given time period (for example, month, week, day) unless you cancel the order.

EXAMPLE 13.3   You wish to sell 50 shares of XYZ Company at $40 per share. You believe the stock will rise to $40 in 2 weeks. You can place a time order to sell the shares at $40, specifying a limit of 2 weeks.

Scale order.   You give an order to purchase or sell a stock in specified amounts at specified price variations.

A settlement for a stock transaction takes place on the fifth full business day after a trade has occurred. For example, if you buy shares you must pay for them by the fifth business day (settlement date) after the date of purchase (trade date).

SOLVED PROBLEM 13.5

You buy stock on January 6, a Monday.

(*a*)   What is the trade date?

(*b*)   What is the settlement date?

SOLUTION

(*a*)   January 6 (Monday)

(*b*)   January 13 (Monday)

An odd-lot transaction is one involving less than 100 shares of a stock. A round-lot transaction involves units of 100 shares.

SOLVED PROBLEM 13.6

Does an odd-lot transaction cost more per share?

SOLUTION

Yes. If you buy fewer than 100 shares you usually have to pay more per share for the stock, typically one-eighth of a point higher; this goes to the specialist handling the transaction. Further, the brokerage commission per share will come out higher, because of the restricted volume.

The stock ticker (tape) is the record of each transaction taking place on the floor of the stock exchange.

YOUR DEALINGS WITH YOUR BROKER

Brokerage fees are paid when you buy or sell stock. The brokerage fee generally ranges from 1.5 percent to 3 percent of the transaction value. When you sell, you will also have to pay state transfer taxes and a nominal federal registration fee. *Tip:* You can save money, usually from 30 percent to 70 percent, by using a discount broker if you do not need full brokerage services. You can also negotiate commissions with your broker. A full-service broker's services include preparation of research reports and recommendations. Historically, brokerage stock recommendations have not outperformed investing at random. Also, you may get a lot of "selling talk."

SOLVED PROBLEM 13.7

When should you use a full-service broker instead of a discount broker?

SOLUTION

Your decision whether to use a full-service broker or a discount broker depends particularly on the investment help and advice you need. If you make your own stock choices, you should select a discount broker.

Tip: If you are a heavy trader, try to get information from your full-service broker(s) and place orders with a discount broker. This way you can get brokerage house recommendations and at the same time pay low commissions.

HOW DO STOCK SPLITS AND DIVIDENDS AFFECT YOU?

A company may issue additional shares through a stock split and/or stock dividend. A stock split is the issuance of a substantial amount of additional shares, thus reducing the par value of the stock on a proportionate basis. For example, a two-for-one split means for every one share you previously had, you now have two shares but the par value per share is halved so the total par value is the same. A stock dividend is a pro rata distribution of added shares of a company's stock to stockholders. For example, a 10 percent stock dividend means that for every 1 share you own you receive .10 share. Thus, for instance, if you owned 100 shares, you will have after the stock dividend 110 shares.

STOCK SPLITS

A stock split occurs when a company believes its stock price is too high and wants to lower the per share price to generate trading appeal.

SOLVED PROBLEM 13.8

Should you get excited about a stock split?

SOLUTION

No. All that has happened is that you have received more shares: the total cost and value remain the same. Thus, the cost per share has decreased proportionately. While a stock split may positively affect the stock price temporarily, because of psychological factors and because it's now cheaper for others to buy because of the lower price, it does *not* change the underlying value of the stock.

After a stock split, your ownership percentage of the company is still the same. The market price of the stock theoretically should decrease on a relative basis for the split.

SOLVED PROBLEM 13.9

You own 1,000 shares of Company XYZ at a cost of $10,000. What will be the effect of a two-for-one stock split?

SOLUTION

You will receive two new shares for each old share. The cost per share will be halved. Theoretically, the market price per share should also be halved. After Company XYZ's stock split you will have 2,000 shares at a cost per share of $5—still $10,000 in total.

DIVIDENDS

The two common types of dividends are cash and stock. On average, U.S. companies pay out about 50 percent of their earnings in dividends. You should track a company's dividend history (for example, 5 years) to predict what future dividends are likely to be. Is the company's dividend policy consistent with your needs?

Cash dividends are fully taxable to you and are typically paid quarterly. If a stock dividend differs in form from the security entitling you to the dividend (for example, you own common stock but receive a preferred stock dividend), you have to pay taxes on the dividends received. If it is the same (for example, you own common stock and receive common stock dividends), there is no tax on the dividends. Since the stock dividend becomes part of your asset base, tax is paid only when the stock is sold. You may wish to consider stocks paying stock dividends if you are in a high tax bracket. Refer to *Standard and Poor's Stock Guide* for dividend records and ratings of companies.

Important dates for dividends are

Declaration date.   The date a dividend is declared by the board of directors at which time it represents a legal liability of the company.

Date of record.   If you are a registered shareholder on the date of record, you will receive the dividend. The date of record comes after the date of declaration and before the payment date. *Caution:* Do not sell your stock before the date of record, because you will lose the dividend.

Payment date.   The date the dividend will be mailed to you—typically several weeks subsequent to the date of record.

EXAMPLE 13.4   A resolution approved at the January 15 (date of declaration) meeting of the board of directors might be declared payable February 15 (date of payment) to all stockholders of record February 1 (date of record).

Ex-dividend date.   This is 4 business days prior to the date of record. It determines who is eligible to receive the declared dividend. The ex-dividend date is the day on and after which the right to receive the current dividend is not automatically transferred from the seller to the buyer, and the stock begins to be traded ex-dividend. The dividend will be paid to the stockholder of record before the ex-dividend date.

A *cash dividend* is usually stated on a dividend per share basis (for example, $.75 per share). It may also be expressed as a percentage of par value. Par value is an arbitrary amount assigned to a stock certificate as per the corporation's charter.

SOLVED PROBLEM 13.10

You own 10,000 shares of a company that pays a cash dividend of $.50 per share. How much will you receive?

SOLUTION

$$10,000 \times \$.50 = \$5,000$$

SOLVED PROBLEM 13.11

You own 20,000 shares of a company's stock, which has a par value of $10 per share. A 12 percent dividend is declared based on total par value. How much will you receive?

SOLUTION

$$20,000 \times \$10 \times .12 = \$24,000$$

A *stock dividend* is payable in shares of stock. It is an issue of new shares expressed as a percentage of shares already held.

SOLVED PROBLEM 13.12

If you own 500 shares before a 5 percent stock dividend, how many additional shares will you receive?

SOLUTION

$$500 \text{ shares} \times 5\% = 25 \text{ shares}$$

You really receive nothing of value with a stock dividend. You receive more shares, but the total cost of your investment remains the same. The cost per share drops; so does the market value. Stock dividends basically have a psychological rather than a financial value.

SOLVED PROBLEM 13.13

You own 1,000 shares of ABC Company costing $20 per share, or $20,000. A 10 percent stock dividend is declared.

(*a*)   How many shares will you receive because of the stock dividend?

(*b*)   What is the new cost per share?

(*c*)   What is the gain or loss if you then sell 200 shares for $5,000?

SOLUTION

(*a*)   1,000 shares × 10% = 100 shares

(*b*) $20,000/1,100 = $18.18

(*c*)

Selling price	$5,000
Less: Cost (200 × $18.18)	3,636
Gain	$1,364

Although rare, a property dividend may be paid. The stockholder receives corporate assets such as inventory of the company's products or stock of another company owned by the firm. Also rare is a liability (scrip) dividend where the company issues a note which will be paid at a later date along with interest as the dividend.

SHOULD YOU TAKE ADVANTAGE OF DIVIDEND REINVESTMENT AND CASH OPTION PLANS?

An advantage of a dividend reinvestment plan is that the company reinvests your dividends to buy more shares without your having to incur a brokerage commission. Further, you may buy the additional shares at a discount price (for example, 5 percent) from market price. You may identify those companies offering a dividend reinvestment plan by referring to *Moody's Annual Dividend Record*.

SOLVED PROBLEM 13.14

What are the disadvantages of a dividend reinvestment plan?

SOLUTION

A drawback to dividend reinvestment is the delay in selling reinvested holdings, since the company typically holds the reinvested shares. Further, a company may not permit you to sell part of the reinvested shares; if you sell, you may have to sell all your holdings to close the dividend reinvestment account. There may be a delay in buying stock through the purchase plan. Finally, reinvested dividends are taxable as ordinary income when paid, even though the distributions are not received in cash. Some plans also allow you to invest additional cash (above the dividend payment).

In a cash option plan, you can also invest additional monies without brokerage or administrative charges.

An automatic reinvestment plan is a form of "dollar cost" averaging: It allows you to buy stock during price declines as well as price increases, thus "averaging out" the purchase prices.

WHAT IS YOUR RETURN ON COMMON STOCK?

You can determine the return on a stock investment by computing the total dollar return, percentage return, dividend yield, and earnings per share.

DOLLAR RETURN

Your dollar return from a stock investment represents dividend income and change in market price.

SOLVED PROBLEM 13.15

You buy a stock for $30 and subsequently sell it for $36. The annual cash dividend is $2.

(a) What is your return per share?

(b) What is your total return if you own 100 shares?

SOLUTION

(a)

Dividend income	$2
Gain ($36 − $30)	6
Total return per share	$8

(b) Total return = 100 shares × $8 = $800

PERCENTAGE RETURN (HOLDING-PERIOD RETURN)

The percentage return or holding-period return earned on your investment equals

$$\frac{\text{(Selling price} - \text{Investment)} + \text{Dividend}}{\text{Investment}}$$

SOLVED PROBLEM 13.16

You invested $80 in a stock which you sold 3 months later for $90. A $2.50 dividend was received.

(a) What is the quarterly return?

(b) What is the equivalent annual return?

SOLUTION

(a)

$$\frac{\text{(Selling price} - \text{Investment)} + \text{Dividend}}{\text{Investment}} = \frac{(\$90 - \$80) + \$2.50}{\$80} = \frac{\$12.50}{\$80} = 15.6\%$$

(b) 15.6% × 4 = 62.4%

SOLVED PROBLEM 13.17

You buy a stock for $60 and sell it for $100 after 4 years. Each year you receive a dividend of $3. What is the annual percentage return from your investment over the 4-year period?

SOLUTION

$$\frac{\dfrac{\text{Selling price} - \text{Investment}}{\text{Years}} + \text{Dividend}}{\text{Average investment}} = \frac{\dfrac{\text{Selling price} - \text{Investment}}{\text{Years}} + \text{Dividend}}{\dfrac{\text{Selling price} + \text{Investment}}{2}}$$

$$= \frac{[(\$100 - \$60)/4] + \$3}{(\$100 - \$60)/2} = \frac{\$13}{\$80} = 16.3\%$$

To get a relative idea of how you did, you can compare the return on your stock to the performance of a stock market index (for example, Standard & Poor 500).

DIVIDEND YIELD ON STOCK

The yield is the percentage return on your common stock investment at its initial cost or present market value. Note that the dividend yield is on a relative (percentage) rather than on an absolute (dollar) basis.

Yield based on original investment equals

$$\frac{\text{Dividends per share}}{\text{Investment}}$$

SOLVED PROBLEM 13.18

You paid $80 for a stock currently worth $90. The dividend per share is $4. What is your yield on the initial investment?

SOLUTION

$$\frac{\$4}{\$80} = .05$$

Dividend yield based on current market price equals

$$\frac{\text{Dividends per share}}{\text{Market price per share}}$$

SOLVED PROBLEM 13.19

Assuming the same facts as in Solved Problem 13.18, what is the dividend yield based on current market price?

SOLUTION

$$\frac{\$4}{\$90} = .044$$

SOLVED PROBLEM 13.20

You own X Company's common stock which has a current market price of $80 and pays dividends of $2 quarterly. You also own Y Company's common stock which has a current market price of $50 and has a stock dividend of 15 percent. What is the dividend yield for each of the stocks?

SOLUTION

X Company's common stock:

$$\frac{\text{Dividends per share}}{\text{Market price per share}} = \frac{\$2}{\$80} = 2.5\% \text{ per quarter}$$

$$2.5\% \times 4 = 10\% \text{ per year}$$

Y Company's common stock: The dividend yield is not relevant since a stock dividend is not cash.

SOLVED PROBLEM 13.21

What does a company's dividend yield indicate?

SOLUTION

You can use the dividend yield as an indication of the reasonableness of the stock's price, particularly when dividends are stable (for example, utilities). Yield on stock is also helpful if you're an income-oriented investor who wishes to compare equity dividend returns with those of fixed-income securities.

Dividend yields are highest when stock prices are low, since dividend payments are less volatile than stock prices. A higher dividend yield is desirable. *Special note:* The dividend yield on stock is usually less than the yield on a bond.

The ratio of market price to dividends per share (inverse of dividend yield) indicates what investors are willing to pay for $1 worth of dividends. If the market price-dividend ratio of the Dow Jones Industrial Average goes below 18 (5½ percent yield), the market is considered undervalued, and an opportunity to buy exists. On the other hand, a market price-dividend ratio of about 30 (approximately a 3 percent yield) indicates an overvalued market—time to sell. Historically, the average yield of the stock market has been about 5 percent. An extreme variation indicates you should proceed with caution.

DIVIDEND PAYOUT RATIO

The dividend payout ratio equals

$$\frac{\text{Dividends per share}}{\text{Earnings per share}}$$

SOLVED PROBLEM 13.22

Should you favor a high dividend payout stock?

SOLUTION

A higher payout ratio indicates the possibility of higher dividends, pointing to higher stock prices. If you're an individual desiring high dividends because you rely on fixed income (for example, if you are retired), you may favor a company with a high dividend payout ratio.

Over the last 100 years, the average payout ratio for "blue chips" has been about 67 percent.

EARNINGS PER SHARE

Dividends and market price of stock depend upon future earnings per share.
You can calculate estimated earnings at the end of the year as follows:

$$\text{Estimated sales at end of year} \times \text{After-tax profit margin}$$

Estimated earnings per share at end of year are computed this way:

$$\frac{\text{Estimated earnings at end of year}}{\text{Estimated outstanding shares at end of year}}$$

SOLVED PROBLEM 13.23

The sales last year were $2,000,000. You expect sales to grow at a 10 percent rate. The after-tax profit margin is 66 percent. The outstanding shares at year-end are expected to be 1,000,000.

(*a*) What are the estimated earnings for the year?

(*b*) What are the estimated earnings per share for the year?

SOLUTION

(*a*)

$$\text{Estimated sales at end of year} = \$2,000,000 \times 1.10 = \$2,200,000$$

$$\text{Estimated earnings} = \$2,200,000 \times 66\% = \$1,452,000$$

(*b*)

$$\frac{\$1,452,000}{1,000,000} = \$1.45 \text{ per share}$$

PRACTICAL APPROACHES TO VALUING STOCK

In valuing a stock investment, there are several techniques you may employ, including book value and price-earnings (P/E) ratio.

BOOK VALUE PER SHARE

Book value (net asset value, liquidation value) per share is the amount of corporate assets for each share of common stock. You may benefit by uncovering stock that is selling below book value or whose assets are significantly undervalued. A stock may represent a good value when its market price is below or close to book value because the security is undervalued. Companies with lower ratios of market price to book value have historically earned better returns than those with higher ratios.

SOLVED PROBLEM 13.24

What conclusions can you reach regarding the difference between book value per share and market price per share of a particular stock?

SOLUTION

Book value is based on historical cost, while market price is based on current prices. Thus, a stock may be undervalued relative to what the company is worth on the books. Because of inflation alone, market price should usually be higher than book value, since book value ignores inflationary increases. However, it should be noted that market price may be less than book value if the company is not doing well financially and/or has dim prospects.

Book value per share equals

$$\frac{\text{Total stockholders' equity}}{\text{Number of shares outstanding}}$$

where

$$\text{Total stockholders' equity} = \text{Total assets} - \text{Total liabilities}$$

SOLVED PROBLEM 13.25

You are thinking of investing in a company that has a market price per share of $40. Total stockholders' equity is $5,000,000 and 100,000 shares are outstanding.

(*a*) What is the book value per share?

(*b*) Is this a buying opportunity?

SOLUTION

(a) $5,000,000/100,000 shares = $50

(b) This may be a buying opportunity, since market price ($40) is well below book value ($50) and an upward movement in prices may occur.

PRICE-EARNINGS RATIO

The price-earnings ratio (multiple) equals

$$\frac{\text{Market price per share}}{\text{Earnings per share}}$$

SOLVED PROBLEM 13.26

The market price of a stock is $50 and the earnings per share is $5, what is the price-earnings multiple?

SOLUTION

$$\$50/\$5 = 10 \text{ times}$$

The price-earnings ratio measures what investors are willing to pay for $1 worth of earnings and shows stock price as a multiple of the earnings figure. The ratio indicates the faith of the investing public in the company and is a good measure of expectations (for example, earnings) and thus value. The higher the price-earnings ratio, the greater the expectation of investors for future growth in the value of the stock. Price-earnings ratios of companies are published in newspapers in the stock quote section.

You can use the price-earnings ratio to value a stock. Estimated market price can be determined by

$$\text{Estimated earnings per share} \times \text{Estimated price-earnings ratio}$$

SOLVED PROBLEM 13.27

You expect the sales for ABC Company to be $2,000,000, based on financial projections you read in a brokerage report and/or management's discussion in the annual report. The company's tax rate is 34 percent. The price-earnings ratio is 10.

(a) What is the after-tax profit?

(b) If expected shares outstanding are 1,000,000, what will the estimated earnings per share be?

(c) What is the expected market price?

SOLUTION

(a)

$$\$2,000,000 \times 66\% = \$1,320,000$$

(b)

$$\frac{\$1,320,000}{1,000,000} = \$1.32$$

(c)

$$\$1.32 \times 10 = \$13.20$$

SOLVED PROBLEM 13.28

What factors affect a company's price-earnings ratio?

SOLUTION

The price-earnings ratio is affected by the following factors, among others:

Growth rate in earnings

Cash flow from operations

Expected dividends

Riskiness of company

Instability in stock price and/or earnings

Degree of competition

Economic and political uncertainties

Company's management ability

Price-earnings ratios vary among industries and from company to company within an industry. The price-earnings ratio for a stock will also change with economic, industry, and company conditions. If a company's price-earnings ratio is much higher or lower than the average price-earnings ratio of other companies in the industry, you would want to know why! Historically, most large, stable, well-established companies sell at price-earnings ratios between 10 and 20.

Stocks in a given industry usually have about the same price-earnings ratios, and the ratios go up and down together.

SOLVED PROBLEM 13.29

Do growth stocks have higher P/E ratios than mature companies?

SOLUTION

Yes. Companies in growth industries (for example, computers) usually have higher price-earnings ratios than companies in established industries (for example, utilities).

SOLVED PROBLEM 13.30

Do cyclical stocks have higher P/E ratios than stable stocks?

SOLUTION

Yes. Cyclical stocks usually have lower price-earnings ratios than companies that are stable.

SOLVED PROBLEM 13.31

What are the implications of a high P/E stock?

SOLUTION

A high price-earnings ratio is typically justified when corporate earnings are anticipated to grow. A high multiple generally means the stock market expects the company's future earnings to be higher than its current earnings. You must consider a company's current price-earnings ratio in terms of present and future economic and stock market conditions.

A company with a high price-earnings ratio may be an excellent company but *not* necessarily a good buy. The high price-earnings ratio may reflect exaggerated investor expectations. *Warning:* If you are a long-term investor, a high price-earnings ratio company should perhaps be avoided. If you pay a price that is many times higher than the earnings figure, the stock may have difficulty holding on to that high price. The stock would have to do even better than the current high expectations for you to earn a profit.

Examine P/E multiples for competing companies in a particular industry. This is a good starting point for researching what is happening in the industry. The P/E ratio also reflects investor confidence in the overall stock market.

Also calculate a multiple for the stock market as a whole, or for a stock index. For example, a multiple for the Standard & Poor's 500 can be arrived at as follows:

$$\frac{\text{Average market price per share}}{\text{Average earnings per share}}$$

Average market price per share equals

$$\frac{\text{Total market price for all issues}}{\text{Number of issues}}$$

Average earnings per share equals

$$\frac{\text{Total earnings per share for all issues}}{\text{Number of issues}}$$

SOLVED PROBLEM 13.32

The total market price and earnings per share for all companies in an index are $1,200 and $200, respectively. There are 100 companies included in that index. What is the overall multiple for the companies in the index?

SOLUTION

$$\text{Average market price per share} = \frac{\$1,200}{100} = \$12$$

$$\text{Average earnings per share} = \frac{\$200}{100} = \$2$$

$$\frac{\text{Average market price per share}}{\text{Average earnings per share}} = \frac{\$12}{\$2} = 6$$

SOLVED PROBLEM 13.33

What is the significance of a low P/E ratio?

SOLUTION

A low multiple indicates investors look unfavorably on the stock, industry, or overall stock market. With a low price-earnings multiple stock, a short-term profit opportunity is unlikely. However, low multiples offer profit opportunities in the long term. *Suggestion:* A good time to buy stocks may be when multiples are less than traditional levels. *Tip:* Spot a stock selling at a low P/E ratio that has good earnings growth potential. You have less downside risk and good upside potential.

SOLVED PROBLEM 13.34

A company's stock had a P/E ratio ranging from 10 to 20. This information was obtained from reading financial advisory service reports (for example, Standard & Poor's), brokerage reports, or the company's annual report. The P/E ratio is now 11 (current P/E ratios of companies are listed in the stock pages of a newspaper), and the prospects for the industry and company are bright. Is this a buying opportunity?

SOLUTION

Yes. This may be a buying opportunity.

SOLVED PROBLEM 13.35

You are thinking of buying a stock whose price has ranged from $30 to $50 in the previous 52 weeks. The price is currently $49. What are the implications of this?

SOLUTION

There is greater risk when buying a stock near its high for the year. The upside may be limited. You are generally better-off buying a stock at its low point or at a middle price.

The price-earnings ratio may be distorted when a company has volatile earnings. In this case, it is difficult to normalize earnings to compute a meaningful P/E ratio. Instead of using the earnings per share for the last year, you may use average earnings for several years (total earnings/total years) or an average of past and estimated earnings.

SOLVED PROBLEM 13.36

X Company's earnings are quite unstable. The company's profits were as follows: 19X3, $600,000; 19X4, $2,000,000; 19X5, $1,000,000; 19X6, $1,500,000; and 19X7, $800,000. What is the average earnings over the 5-year period?

SOLUTION

$$\frac{\$600,000 + \$2,000,000 + \$1,000,000 + \$1,500,000 + \$800,000}{5} = \frac{\$5,900,000}{5} = \$1,180,000$$

Be cautious not to rely too heavily on the price-earnings ratio, because stock market conditions, economic factors, etc., may outweigh the significance of the P/E ratio. The price-earnings ratios for small or speculative companies and for firms with instability in earnings or no earnings records do not provide dependable data on which to base valuation estimates.

If your valuation of a stock differs from the current market price, you may buy it if it is undervalued or sell short if it is overvalued.

SOLVED PROBLEM 13.37

Company XYZ's stock price is $40 on the market and your valuation indicates it is worth $50. Should you buy the stock?

SOLUTION

Yes. You should purchase the undervalued stock.

SOLVED PROBLEM 13.38

A company has the following financial information: total assets, $40,000; total liabilities, $10,000; total preferred stock, $5,000; dividends on preferred stock, $4,000; net income, $16,000; outstanding common shares, 2,000; market price per share, $50; and dividends on common stock, $1.20 per share.

Compute the following:

(a) Dividend yield on common stock

(b) Book value per share

(c) Earnings per share

(d) Price/earnings ratio

SOLUTION

(a)

$$\frac{\text{Dividends per share}}{\text{Market price per share}} = \frac{\$1.20}{\$50.00} = 2.4\%$$

(b)   Common stockholders' equity equals:

$$\text{Assets} - (\text{Liabilities} + \text{Preferred stock}) \; \$40{,}000 - (\$10{,}000 + \$5{,}000) = \$25{,}000$$

$$\frac{\text{Common stockholders' equity}}{\text{Outstanding shares}} = \frac{\$25{,}000}{2{,}000} = \$12.50$$

(c)

$$\frac{\text{Net income} - \text{Preferred dividends}}{\text{Outstanding shares}} = \frac{\$16{,}000 - \$4{,}000}{2} = \$6$$

(d)

$$\frac{\text{Market price per share}}{\text{Earnings per share}} = \frac{\$50}{\$6} = 8.33$$

HOW TO READ STOCK QUOTATIONS

Newspapers (for example, *The New York Times, The Wall Street Journal*) publish price quotations of stocks for the preceding day. As an illustration, information regarding IT Co. on October 6, 19X7, appearing in the October 7, 19X7, issue of a financial newspaper's financial page follows:

| 52-Week | | | | | | | | | | |
High	Low	Stock	Dividend	Yield %	P/E Ratio	Sales 100s	High	Low	Last	Net Change
$66\frac{3}{8}$	$48\frac{3}{4}$	IT Co.	1.00	1.6	14	10761	$64\frac{3}{8}$	$62\frac{1}{4}$	$62\frac{3}{8}$	$-\frac{5}{8}$

The highest and lowest price the stock sold for over the last 52 weeks are indicated in the first two columns. The expected cash dividend in 19X7 is $1.00 per share, based on the latest quarterly declaration. The dividend yield is 1.6 percent computed by dividing the dividends per share ($1.00) by the closing stock price (62\frac{3}{8}$). The price-earnings ratio is the current market price divided by the prior year's earnings per share. The volume transacted is reflected in the Sales column, which is reported in lots of 100 shares. The shares traded on October 6 were 1,076,100 shares. The highest, lowest, and closing price for the day are listed in the High, Low, and Last columns. The net change in price of the stock from October 5 to October 6 was a drop of $\frac{5}{8}$ of a point. Additional details are sometimes provided in the "Explanatory notes" section after the newspaper's stock quotations.

SOLVED PROBLEM 13.39

(a)   If you bought 100 shares of IT Co. at the high price of the day, what would the cost have been? (Ignore commissions.)

(b)   If you bought 100 shares of IT Co. at the low price of the day, what would the cost have been? (Ignore commissions.)

(c)   What was IT Company's closing price on the previous day?

(d)   Is IT Company's current stock price closer to the high or low for the year?

SOLUTION

(a) $100 \times 64\frac{3}{8} = \$6{,}437.50$

(b) $100 \times 62\frac{1}{4} = \$6{,}225$

(c) $62\frac{3}{8} + \frac{5}{8} = 63$

(d)   It is closer to the high for the year since $62\frac{3}{8}$ is nearer to $66\frac{3}{8}$ than to $48\frac{3}{4}$.

HOW DO YOU USE BETA TO SELECT A STOCK?

Beta refers to the percentage change in the market price of a stock relative to the percentage change in a stock market index (for example, Standard & Poor's 500). Therefore, beta is a measure of the security's volatility relative to an average security. A high beta means a risky security. For example, a beta of 1.8 means that the firm's stock price can rise or fall 80 percent faster than the market.

SOLVED PROBLEM 13.40

What do the beta values mean in the following cases?
(a)   < 0   (d)   1
(b)   0   (e)   > 1
(c)   < 1

SOLUTION

BETA VALUE	MEANING
(a) < 0	The security's market price moves in the *opposite* direction from the market. Very few stocks have a negative beta.
(b) 0	The security's return is independent of the market (for example, risk-free U.S. Treasury security).
(c) < 1	The security's price moves in the same direction as the market, but the security's price fluctuates less than the market index. This is a conservative investment.
(d) 1	The security's market price moves in the same direction as the market index. The stock has the same risk as the market.
(e) > 1	The security's price moves in the same direction as the market, but the security's price fluctuates more than the market index. This is a risky security.

Many brokerage houses and investment services, including Merrill Lynch, Value Line, and Standard & Poor's, publish information on beta for various securities. For example, the beta values for Bordens and Consolidated Edison approximate .95 and .70, respectively.

After determining a security's beta value, you can estimate the required return as follows:

$$\text{Stock risk premium} = \text{Beta value} \times \text{Market risk premium}$$

SOLVED PROBLEM 13.41

A stock has a beta of +1.2 and the market risk premium is 7 percent. What is the stock risk premium?

SOLUTION

$$1.2 \times 7\% = 8.4\%$$

SOLVED PROBLEM 13.42

Stock X has a beta of .80, and the overall market rate of return increases by 15 percent. Predict how the return on the stock will be affected based on the market movement?

SOLUTION

$$15\% \times .80 = 12\% \text{ increase}$$

HOW CAN YOU USE DOLLAR-COST AVERAGING TO YOUR ADVANTAGE?

You may take advantage of dollar-cost averaging for a stock you consider to be a sound long-term investment. This entails buying a constant dollar amount of a given stock or stocks at regularly spaced intervals—in other words, time diversification. By investing a fixed amount each time, you buy more shares when the price is down and fewer shares when the price is up. This usually results in a lower average cost per share since you buy more shares of stock with the same dollars. Such an approach is advantageous when a stock price moves within a narrow range. If stock prices decline, you lose less money than you ordinarily would. If stock prices rise, you profit, but less than you usually would. However, dollar-cost averaging does involve greater transaction costs. *Note:* Dollar-cost averaging will not work when the stock price continually drops. In general, dollar-cost averaging is a conservative way to invest, because it screens out "whims" which could result in buying high and selling low.

SOLVED PROBLEM 13.43

What are the advantages of dollar-cost averaging?

SOLUTION

The advantages of dollar-cost averaging are

A conservative stock may be bought with relatively little risk, yielding benefits from long-term price appreciation.

Buying too many shares at high prices is avoided.

A bear market provides an opportunity to buy additional shares at particularly low prices.

SOLVED PROBLEM 13.44

You invest $100 a month in XYZ Company and have the following transactions. Assume no brokerage commission.

DATE	INVESTED	PRICE PER SHARE	SHARES BOUGHT
1/15	$100	$20	5
2/15	100	15	$6\frac{2}{3}$
3/15	100	12	$8\frac{1}{3}$
4/15	100	16	$6\frac{1}{4}$
5/15	100	25	4
		$88	$30\frac{1}{4}$

(a) What is the average price per share?
(b) What is the cost per share?
(c) What conclusion can be reached on May 15?

SOLUTION

(a) You have bought fewer shares at the higher price and more shares at the lower price. The average price per share is

$$\frac{\$88}{5} = \$17.60$$

(b) With your $500 investment you have acquired $30\frac{1}{4}$ shares, resulting in a cost per share of $16.53.

(c) On May 15, the market price of $25 exceeds your average cost of $16.53, reflecting an attractive gain.

HOW DOES A CONSTANT-RATIO PLAN WORK?

Under a constant-ratio plan, you maintain a portfolio that has a constant ratio of stocks to bonds. The plan usually provides for an arbitrary switching period (for example, quarterly). Typically, no buying or selling will occur except in a minimum amount (for example, $2,500).

SOLVED PROBLEM 13.45

Your desired ratio between stocks and bonds is 70 percent. At the present time, your portfolio consists of the following:

Average Stock Price	Average Shares	Value of Stock	Value of Bonds	Total Value	Ratio
$10	14,000	$140,000	$60,000	$200,000	70%

The stocks fell by an average of $2 in price.

(a) What is the value of the stocks and bonds after the drop in price?

(b) In order to maintain a constant ratio of 70 percent between stocks and bonds, how much in stocks have to be bought and how much in bonds have to be sold?

(c) What are the adjusted values of stocks and bonds?

SOLUTION

Average Stock Price	Average Shares	Value of Stock	Value of Bonds	Total Value	Ratio
(a) $8	14,000	$112,000	$ 60,000	$172,000	65.1%
(b)		+ 8,400	− 8,400		
(c)		$120,400	$ 51,600	$172,000	70%

WHAT ABOUT STOCK VALUATION?

There are several ways to derive a fundamental (theoretical) value for a stock investment. These include time value computations, primarily determining present value; capitalizing earnings; and dividend-based values.

TIME VALUE OF MONEY

The time value of money is important to consider when evaluating stocks. Compound interest computations are necessary to appraise the future value of an investment. Discounting computations are used to analyze the present value of a future cash flow from a stock.

Future Value (Compounding)

A dollar in your hand today is worth more than a dollar you will receive in the future because you can invest and earn interest on it. Compound interest occurs when interest earns interest. Future value indicates the worth of the investment in a later year (see Appendix Table 1).

Future Value of an Annuity

An annuity is a series of equal receipts for a specified time period; an example is constant dividends. The future value of an annuity involves compounding, since the payments accrue interest (see Appendix Table 2).

Present Value (Discounting)

Present value computation is the opposite of determining compounded future value (see Appendix Table 3).

Present Value of an Annuity

Constant dividends on stocks or interest on bonds constitute annuities. To compare the financial attractiveness of financial instruments, you have to determine the present value of annuities for each one (see Appendix Table 4).

COMMON STOCK VALUATION

Various financial services track industries and companies. They offer expectations as to future earnings, dividends, and market prices of stock. Examples are Standard and Poor's, Moody's, Value Line, and Dow-Jones Irwin. For example, reference may be made to Standard and Poor's *Stock Reports* and *The Outlook*. These provide a thorough analysis of companies and provide clues as to future expectations. Standard and Poor's *Industry Surveys* provide information on specific industries.

The objective of valuing common stock is to ascertain whether the current market price is realistic in view of expected future earnings, dividends, and price. The valuation process is directed at determining whether the stock is properly valued, undervalued, or overvalued.

You can determine a stock's value by computing the present value of a security's anticipated future cash flows, using your required rate of return (the return rate you want to earn on your money) as the discount rate. The value of the common stock is the present value of your expected future cash inflows (from dividends and selling price). Value equals

$$\text{Value of common stock} = \text{Present value of future dividends}$$
$$+ \text{Present value of selling price}$$

You use present value tables to find the appropriate factor that corresponds to the rate of return (i) and number of years involved in holding the security (y).

SOLVED PROBLEM 13.46

You are considering whether to buy a stock at the beginning of the year. The dividend at year's end is expected to be $2.00, and the year-end market price is anticipated to be $50. You intend to hold the stock for 1 year. The desired rate of return on your investment is 15 percent.

(*a*)   What is the value of the stock?

(*b*)   What if the market price of the stock is below the value you derive for it in part (*a*)?

SOLUTION

(*a*)   The value of the stock at the end of the year (using Appendix Table 3, present value of $1) equals

$$\$2.00 \times .86957 + \$50 \times .86957 = \$45.22$$

(*b*)   If the stock has a market price below $45.22, you should buy it since it is underpriced in the market.

SOLVED PROBLEM 13.47

You want to estimate the worth of a stock. You anticipate holding it for 10 years and receiving $10 in annual dividends per share. The expected selling price at the end of 10 years is $40 per share. The required rate of return is 10 percent.

(*a*)   What is the value per share?

(*b*)   If the market price of the stock was $95, would you buy it?

SOLUTION

(*a*)   The estimated value per share can be determined through the use of present value tables. The value per share is

Present value of annuity of $1 (Appendix Table 4) ($10 × 6.14457)	$61.45
Plus: Present value of $1 (Appendix Table 3) ($40 × .38554)	15.42
Total present value of dividends and selling price	$76.87

(b) If the stock's market price was $95 per share, you would not buy it, since that price is more than the $76.87 computed value based on your required rate of return.

SOLVED PROBLEM 13.48

You buy a stock with expected dividends growing at 10 percent, as follows:

YEAR	DIVIDEND
1	$1.20
2	$1.32
3	$1.45

At the end of year 3 you expect to sell the stock for $20. Your minimum rate of return is 12 percent.

(a) What is the value of the stock today?

(b) If the stock had a market price of $14, would you buy it?

SOLUTION

(a) The value of the stock today is computed using Appendix Table 3, "Present Value of $1," as follows:

YEAR		PRESENT VALUE (YEAR 0)
1	$1.20 × .89286	$ 1.07
2	$1.32 × .79719	1.05
3	$1.45 × .71178	1.03
3	$20 × .71178	14.24
	Total value	$17.39

(b) · If the stock was selling today at $14, you would buy it, since it is undervalued.

Perpetuities are annuities that continue forever. An example is a stock that yields a constant-dollar dividend indefinitely. The value of the stock equals

$$\frac{\text{Dividends per share}}{\text{Discount rate}}$$

Tip: Common stock valuation based on dividends is most appropriate for mature companies or those in the expansion stage.

SOLVED PROBLEM 13.49

You are thinking of buying a stock that pays the same dividend forever ($3.00). If you require a 10 percent return, what is the value of the stock?

SOLUTION

$$\frac{\$3.00}{.10} = \$30$$

Gordon's model, a traditional financial model named for the individual who derived it, can be used to determine the value of common stock assuming a constant growth rate in dividends. The model is

$$\text{Price} = \frac{\text{Dividends per share (current year)}}{\text{Required return rate} - \text{Growth rate in dividends}}$$

The model mostly applies to valuing the common stocks of larger, diversified companies.

SOLVED PROBLEM 13.50

You are considering buying a stock that paid a $5 dividend per share at the end of last year and is expected to pay a cash dividend each year at a growth rate of 10 percent. The required rate of return is 14 percent. What is the value of the stock?

SOLUTION

$$\text{Price} = \frac{\$5.50}{.14 - .10} = \frac{\$5.50}{.04} = \$137.50$$

IMPORTANCE OF STOCK VOLUME FIGURES

You may learn something by looking at the volume traded in stock. For example, declining volume traded and a strong increase in the price of the stock indicates that buyers are more wary. Increased volume along with a drop in the stock price indicates that institutions may be selling the stock. The situation is most positive when volume and price move together, when price rises on substantial volume. Most daily newspapers have a financial page listing the 15 most active stocks of the day.

It is generally best to trade in active stocks, because of readier marketability and less possible manipulation in price.

SOLVED PROBLEM 13.51

What is the difference between a "bull market" and a "bear market"?

SOLUTION

In a "bull market" there are rising stock prices and increasing volume while in a "bear market" there are decreasing prices and a pessimistic outlook.

SHOULD YOU BUY STOCK ON MARGIN (CREDIT)?

If you purchase stock on margin, you are buying securities on credit. Interest will be charged by your broker on the unpaid balance. The brokerage firm typically charges the borrowing investor 2 percent more than it is charged by the bank. A brokerage firm can lend you up to 50 percent of total value of stocks, up to 70 percent for corporate bonds, and up to 90 percent for U.S. Government securities. You have to put up more cash for equity securities than for bonds because of the greater risk involved. If the value of your portfolio declines enough to jeopardize the brokerage loan on your margin account, you will receive a "margin call" to put up additional money or securities, or sell some stock. A margin account requires a minimum of $2,000 in cash (or equity in securities) on deposit.

Buying on margin gives you the opportunity to improve your return through *leverage* (buying on credit). You make a partial payment for a stock that has appreciated in value. However, your loss can also be magnified, if the value of the security portfolio declines.

To open a margin account, you have to deposit a specified amount of cash or its equivalent in marginable securities. Securities bought on margin will be held by your broker in "street name"—that is, in the name of the brokerage firm.

SOLVED PROBLEM 13.52

You buy 50 shares of ABC Company at $40 per share, or $2,000. You pay 60 percent of the price, or $1,200 from your own funds, and borrow the remaining $800. The interest rate is 12 percent.

(a) What is the annual interest charge?

(b) If the stock price increases to $45, what is your rate of return before interest and brokerage fees?

(c)   If the total brokerage fees are $75, what is your rate of return after interest and brokerage fees?

SOLUTION

(a) $800 × .12 = $96

(b)   If the stock increases to $45 a year later, you can sell it for $2,250 ($45 × 50 shares). Your profit before interest and brokerage fees is $250 ($2,250 − $2,000), on an investment of only $1,200. The return rate is 20.8 percent ($250/$1,200).

(c)

$$\text{Net return} = \$250 - \$96 - \$75 = \$79$$

$$\text{Rate of return} = \$79/\$1,200 = 6.6\%$$

SOLVED PROBLEM 13.53

You bought 100 shares of XT Company at $20 per share on margin 1 year ago. The brokerage fee was $50. You paid 60 percent of the cost and borrowed the remainder at 12 percent. You just sold the stock for $35 per share less a brokerage fee of $100.

Fill in the two columns comparing the gain or loss and the return on initial investment without margin and with margin.

SOLUTION

	WITHOUT MARGIN		WITH MARGIN	
Cash paid	$2,050		$1,230	(a)
Borrowing on margin	0		820	(b)
Initial cost	$2,050		$2,050	
Interest charge	0		98	(c)
Total cost	$2,050		$2,148	
Net sales proceeds	$3,400	(d)	$3,400	
Gain or loss	$1,350		$1,252	
Return on initial cash investment	65.9%	(e)	101.8%	(f)

(a) $2,000 + $50 = $2,050 × 60% = $1,230

(b) $2,050 × 40% = $820

(c) $820 × 12% = $98

(d) $3,500 − $100 = $3,400

(e)   Gain/Initial cash investment = $1,350/$2,050 = 65.9%

(f)   Gain/Initial cash investment = $1,252/$1,230 = 101.8%

IS AN INITIAL PUBLIC OFFERING FOR YOU?

An initial public offering occurs when a company issues stock for the first time. Some new issues are offered by established, financially strong companies to obtain money or to go public. However, most new issues are offered by small, unknown, newly formed companies. Typically, they do not have track records. *Beware:* These companies represent speculative investments. But new issues are potentially profitable, because these securities may have high returns in the *initial* period after the stock "goes public." On average, new issue performance is positive because the stocks are generally underpriced.

Your broker may call you about a "special offering." *Beware:* The brokerage firm may be trying to unload stock that professional money managers for mutual funds and institutional investors do not want. The retail broker receives a large sales incentive to push these shares. While no brokerage fee is charged to the buyer of such stock (the seller pays the fees), it is usually a stock that professionals do not want!

SHOULD YOU VENTURE INTO THE OVER-THE-COUNTER MARKET?

The over-the-counter market consists of unlisted securities (those not listed on the recognized stock exchanges). The over-the-counter market involves broker/dealers who buy and sell securities through a communications network referred to as the National Association of Security Dealers Automated Quotation (NASDAQ) System, instead of a trading floor. Unlisted securities are generally those of small companies.

Dealers keep over-the-counter shares in inventory.

Note: You have to incur the cost of the dealer's "spread" (difference between the price you buy shares at and the price remitted to the seller), which can be quite significant.

Watch out for "penny stocks" on the over-the-counter market, because they usually have high risk and low quality. Some firms whose market prices for stock are in pennies per share may be headed for bankruptcy, while others may be new to the market and barely surviving.

SOLVED PROBLEM 13.54

Stock XYZ has "bid and asked" prices of $8 and 8\frac{1}{2}$.

(a)   What does this quotation mean?

(b)   What is the dealer's spread?

(c)   In addition to the dealer's spread, is there also a brokerage commission?

SOLUTION

(a)   This means that if you buy the stock you pay 8\frac{1}{2}$, but if you sell the stock you receive only $8.

(b)   The dealer's spread is $$\frac{1}{2}$.

(c)   Yes. You must also pay brokerage commissions on the purchase and sale.

SOLVED PROBLEM 13.55

Refer to Solved Problem 13.54. Assume you buy 1,000 shares of XYZ Company and then sell it immediately. The total brokerage fees on buy and sell equal $150. How much do you have to absorb due to the spread and brokerage fees?

SOLUTION

Spread (1,000 shares $\times \frac{1}{2}$)	$500
Brokerage fees	150
Total	$650

Note: Some newspapers do not list "bid and asked" prices anymore. The last price listed is the *final* sale of the day as of 4 P.M.

SHOULD YOU SELL SHORT A STOCK?

Short selling is used to profit from a decline in stock price. To make a short sale, your broker borrows stock from someone and then sells it for you to someone else. When the stock price falls, you buy shares to replace the borrowed ones. If you buy the shares back at a lower price than the broker sold them for, you earn a profit. You "sell short against the box" when you sell short shares you actually own (not borrowed shares).

SOLVED PROBLEM 13.56

When do you experience a loss in short selling?

SOLUTION

You incur a loss with short selling when the repurchase price is higher than the original selling price. Significant losses are possible, since the stock price may increase indefinitely. No matter how high it goes, you will have to buy securities to "cover," or replace, the borrowed ones.

To sell short, you must have a margin account with cash or securities valued at a minimum of 50 percent of the market value of the stock you want to sell short. While selling short normally requires no interest charge, you will have to retain the proceeds from the sale in your brokerage account. Of course, brokerage commissions will still have to be paid on the sale and repurchase.

SOLVED PROBLEM 13.57

What are some possible reasons to sell short?

SOLUTION

You may want to sell short when a decline in stock price is anticipated or you wish to postpone making a gain and paying taxes on it from one year to the next.

SOLVED PROBLEM 13.58

What are some guidelines in short selling a stock?

SOLUTION

When selling short a stock, consider the following: Do not go against an upward trend in stock prices; if stock prices go up 10 to 15 percent, cover the short sale; and do not short several stocks at once.

SOLVED PROBLEM 13.59

What are the possible times to sell short?

SOLUTION

You may sell short when officers of the company have sold a good part of their shares; prices for the stock are volatile; professionals forecast lower corporate earnings; the stock has "zoomed" up in a relatively short period of time; it is a "glamour" stock losing popularity; and it is a stock that has started to decline more than the market average.

SOLVED PROBLEM 13.60

Which stocks should you avoid selling short?

SOLUTION

Avoid selling short the following securities: issues with limited shares outstanding; securities with a large short interest; and stocks of companies that are candidates for takeovers.

A disadvantage of selling short a stock is that you have to pay the dividends declared by the company to the person or firm from whom you borrowed the shares. Your brokerage firm will deduct the dividend from your account and place it in the account of the individual who lent you the shares. *Tip:* Sell short a stock paying low or no dividends.

Recommendation: Place a limit order rather than a market order when you sell short. There is a danger in shorting a stock "at the market" since it can only be shorted on an "up tick" (that is, when the current price is higher than the previous one). However, over-the-counter stocks can be sold short at anytime. If the stock falls drastically, it may be some time before an "up tick" occurs.

EXAMPLE 13.5   If a stock was initially at $40 when you placed your order, and drastically falls by the time it is sold short, the price may be $35. It would have been better to protect yourself against such a situation by putting in a limit order to sell, say, for $38 or better.

SOLVED PROBLEM 13.61

You sell short 100 shares of stock with a market price of $30. The broker borrows the shares for you and sells them to someone else for $3,000. Subsequently, you buy the stock back at $25 a share, and return the shares to the broker. How much profit will you earn?

SOLUTION

You will earn a profit per share of $5, or a total of $500 before brokerage charges.

SOLVED PROBLEM 13.62

Refer to Solved Problem 13.61. Assume instead you bought the stock back at $32 per share. What is your loss?

SOLUTION

$$\$32 - \$30 = \$2 \times 100 \text{ shares} = \$200$$

THE PROPER TIMING FOR BUYING AND SELLING STOCKS

Do not buy your entire portfolio at the top of a bull market when stocks appear very attractive with much good news. You may have to wait a long time for gains, because it may take years for the market to retain a prior peak.

Recommendation: Buy stock when prices are at very depressed levels and stock market and economic conditions appear gloomy. Stocks will then be selling for below-average price-earnings ratios. If you buy for the long term, chances are that corporate earnings and multiples will increase.

Of course, great uncertainty may exist as to whether the market is at a peak or a bottom. No one can really predict accurately whether stocks will increase or decrease in price.

SOLVED PROBLEM 13.63

What should you do to avoid purchasing all your stock at market highs?

SOLUTION

To avoid buying your portfolio at a market peak, acquire a few securities at a time, staggering your stock acquisitions over months and years.

Do not be fully invested in stocks for the amount of money you have reserved for investment, keep some funds liquid for market declines, so you can take advantage of buying opportunities. Keep investing each year until your portfolio is diversified.

Buy a stock that no longer reacts negatively to bad economic news, since the news has already been discounted in its price. It probably will not decrease further.

If the price of a security is currently so high that it would *not* be a good buy, it may be time to sell. Selling should be done at one of the various phases of a bull market at the end of which a significant drop in prices may occur. In the last phase of a bull market, stock prices move above their intrinsic value and start to discount future possible events.

In timing the buying and selling of stocks, you should consider three sets of indicators: economic, monetary, and psychological.

ECONOMIC INDICATORS

Economic indicators apply to the business outlook.

SOLVED PROBLEM 13.64

How do economic factors influence stock price?

SOLUTION

A growing economy will lead to improved profitability and dividends; thus it is bullish for stocks. A decline in real gross national product will result in lower profits and dividends, causing a decline in stock prices. Buy stock when the economy has entered a recession—that is, when real gross national product declines for two consecutive quarters. Sell when the economy is growing at an unsustainable rate (for example, 10 percent annual rate for two quarters).

A low inflation rate is better for equity securities. During the "bull market" period of 1984 to 1986, the yearly percent increases in the Consumer Price Index were 4.0 percent, 3.8 percent, and 1.1 percent. Economic indicators can be used to confirm market direction. For example, if the economy is contracting at an unsustainable rate, stock prices will shortly do better, to reflect the better business environment that will emerge. Once the stock market does not react to bad news anymore, the market has already discounted the bad news and stock prices should start to move upward.

MONETARY INDICATORS

Monetary indicators apply to Federal Reserve actions and the demand for credit.

SOLVED PROBLEM 13.65

What should be considered in looking at monetary indicators?

SOLUTION

Monetary indicators involve long-term interest rates, which are important since bond yields compete with stock yields. Monetary and credit indicators are often the first signs of market direction. If monetary indicators move favorably, this is an indication that a decline in stock prices may be over.

A stock market top may be ready for a contraction if the Federal Reserve tightens credit, making consumer buying and corporate expansion more costly and difficult.

SOLVED PROBLEM 13.66

What are some good monetary indicators?

SOLUTION

Good monetary indicators include

Dow Jones 20-bond index
Dow Jones utility average
New York Stock Exchange utility average

Bonds and utilities are yield instruments and therefore money-sensitive. They are impacted by changing interest rates.

If the above monetary indicators are active and pointing higher, it is a sign the stock market will start to take off. In other words, an upward movement in these indicators takes place in advance of a stock market increase.

PSYCHOLOGICAL INDICATORS

Psychological indicators are important. If much emotion surrounds the market, than irrationality exists, and stocks are close to a reversal in trend. Psychological indicators apply to investor's attitudes regarding stocks.

SOLVED PROBLEM 13.67

What are some psychological indicators?

SOLUTION

Psychological indicators include whether stocks are in strong (financial institutions) or weak (average people's) hands; how much potential buying power is available; whether selling pressure has stopped; and whether the market is behaving emotionally.

SHOULD YOU DIVERSIFY YOUR PORTFOLIO?

To lower risk, diversify your stockholdings rather than investing in just one or two stocks and becoming highly vulnerable to stock price movements. Diversification reduces the volatility of your overall stockholdings. However, overall return will usually also be lessened.

SOLVED PROBLEM 13.68

How does diversification work?

SOLUTION

Diversification may mean a stock portfolio includes growth stocks, income-oriented stocks, stable stocks, and speculative stocks. It is also possible to gain some diversification by buying a stock of a company that is itself widely diversified in its manufacturing and holding activities. Diversification is a defensive technique and reduces the risk of loss.

You should also diversify your investments *over time* so as to offset the ups and downs of the market.

WHAT KIND OF STOCK STRATEGY CAN YOU EMPLOY?

After you have looked at the financial data of competing companies in an attractive industry and determined that a particular company is the best value, then buy it.

Standard and Poor's Stock Guide has a stock rating system emphasizing earnings, dividend stability, and growth. An "A+" rating indicates the highest growth and stability of earnings and dividends. A "C" rating signifies the lowest stability and growth of earnings and dividends. *Standard and Poor's Stock Reports* provide a brief interpretation of companies traded on the exchanges and in the over-the-counter markets.

SOLVED PROBLEM 13.69

What questions should you ask yourself in deciding whether to invest in a particular company?

SOLUTION

You should ask the following questions:

How is the company's cash flow?

What is the capital spending of the company for expansion purposes?

Is corporate debt excessive?

What is the variability and growth in stock price, dividends per share, and earnings per share?

Do earnings rise or fall in cycles?

Is the company excessively regulated by the government?

Invest in quality companies (financially strong leaders in their fields that have had consistent high, profitable growth) and in the long term you should profit.

Buy an undervalued stock, which may be indicated by

A P/E ratio no more than twice the prevailing interest rate (for example, a P/E ratio of 20 compared to an interest rate of 10 percent).

A market price of 20 percent or more under book value.

Value may be found in stocks that are at new 52-week lows. Value may also be found in industry groups that have had a washout and are now fully neglected. The future may be good if the industry satisfies a long-term need, providing a necessary function or service. *Tip:* Make sure all the bad news on the industry is out.

One strategy for investing is to buy stocks with relatively low P/E ratios and high dividend yields. Some investors use the "7 and 7" strategy, according to which a stock is bought if the P/E ratio is less than 7 and the dividend yield is greater than 7.

In general, do not stay with an unprofitable stock too long if the future prospects are also poor. Take your small loss now before things get worse.

When the worst that can possibly happen to the stock market does actually happen, stock prices are bound to move upward.

If a stock market index is very depressed (for example, Dow Jones Industrial Average), and you notice that advancing issues begin to exceed declining issues for the first time, an upward trend may be occurring.

About 2 weeks prior to the end of a calendar quarter (for example, June 30), buy high-grade stocks that have had a big move in the past 30 days. These stocks are being bought by institutional investors to enhance their reports. The upturn in those stocks should continue for a while.

One approach to investing in the market is practicing "contrary opinion." You determine what popular opinion is and do the opposite. When an idea is in the minds of a vast number of investors, it is likely that the idea is based on emotions rather than on rational thought. One way of telling this is when many odd-lot transactions occur, which indicates what "small" investors are doing. Usually, small investors do the wrong thing. For example, small investors typically buy when they should be selling. When you hear only good things about the stock market or individual industries, watch out for a possible trend reversal. For example, when a great number of investment advisory services are bullish, this may be a bearish sign.

WHAT KIND OF INVESTMENT PORTFOLIO SHOULD YOU HAVE?

A stock portfolio is one that is a list of investments that have been bought because each one satisfies your objectives. *Recommendation:* Have a conservative investment portfolio of high-grade stocks to assure security and stability. A conservative portfolio will generally result in steady income flows with relatively minor fluctuations in price.

SOLVED PROBLEM 13.70

What should you know about your investment portfolio?

SOLUTION

You should know the following about investments:

Invest for the long term. Frequent trading involves a lot of transaction costs. Further, it is difficult to predict the performance of a stock in the short run. Do not be concerned with temporary price changes.

Buy low and sell high. When the market looks worst, a buying opportunity exists because prices are low. When the market looks great, opportunities are minimal and risks are greatest indicating the time to sell.

Have a cash reserve to "pick up" bargains.

Avoid buying on margin since you may become nervous in a market decline at which time you may sell at close to the market bottom.

Avoid short selling a stock because it may be difficult to continue a short position as the stock rises in value.

Buy quality stocks since there is less likelihood of your losing money.

Do not expect to make a "killing" from speculation since earning money usually doesn't come easy. It is better to obtain a reasonable return.

Do not sell a stock just because you earned a profit on it when it reached your arbitrary selling price. The stock may go higher than you anticipate.

Do not sell during a panic because stock prices and conditions will probably improve.

Be wary when the market is moving in one direction contrary to news. For example, if the economy is good but the market is declining, you should be concerned.

In a bull market, most stocks eventually go up. Thus, do not sell a stock that has not moved yet because of impatience. You may sell it just before it rises.

Typically, buy or sell in a trendless period (prices and volume are steady) since you will obtain better values. You usually do not get the best price in a frenzy period.

Most stock movements go considerably beyond where they are anticipated to go. For example, if the consensus in a bull market is that the Dow Jones Industrial Average will go to 2,500, it may even reach 2,800.

Do not purchase a previous leader in a bull market because of profit taking. Wait until investors are disillusioned with the stock. Wait till bad news does not result in declining prices. Buy the stocks when they start to go up on bad or good news.

If stock prices hold up when volume decreases, it is a bullish sign and may be a time to buy.

The market usually goes lower in the fall and late spring, and moves higher around year's end and in the summer.

If you buy a stock in a young industry (for example, biotechnology), invest only in the companies already earning money since they already show success.

The bottom of a market may be indicated and a buying opportunity may exist when stocks show a resistance to further declines. It is a good sign for investing when the number of unchanged issues on the New York Stock Exchange are 500 or more daily.

Interesting note: Value Line Investment Advisory Service recommends you should have a portfolio of at least 15 stocks, drawing from at least eight industries.

SOLVED PROBLEM 13.71

How do you determine how your investment portfolio is doing?

SOLUTION

You can measure the performance of your investment portfolio, preferably on a quarterly basis, by using the following formula:

$$\text{Return} = \frac{\text{Ending price} - \text{Beginning price} + \text{Dividends}}{\text{Beginning price}}$$

The return on your portfolio can be compared to the return on the Standard and Poor's 500.

SOLVED PROBLEM 13.72

On July 1, 19X6, your portfolio was worth $60,000 and on September 30, 1986, it had a value of $68,000. You received dividends for the quarter of $3,000.

(*a*)   What was your rate of return for the quarter?

(*b*)   What if the quarterly return for the S&P 500 was 12 percent?

(*c*)   What was your equivalent annual return?

SOLUTION

(*a*)

$$\frac{\$68,000 - \$60,000 + \$3,000}{\$60,000} = \frac{\$11,000}{\$60,000} = 18.3\%$$

(*b*)   If the quarterly rate of return for the S&P 500 was 12%, your performance was superior to the average.

(*c*) $18.3\% \times 4 = 73.2\%$

SOLVED PROBLEM 13.73

At the end of a month, you want to determine the market value of your portfolio. Your records indicate the following:

STOCK	SHARES	PRICE PAID PER SHARE	MARKET PRICE PER SHARE
ABC Co.	1,000	$6	$7
XYZ Co.	500	2	3
LTM Co.	2,000	5	4

What is your portfolio worth?

SOLUTION

STOCK	MARKET VALUE
ABC Co. (1,000 × $7)	$ 7,000
XYZ Co.　(500 × $3)	1,500
LTM Co. (2,000 × $4)	8,000
Total	$16,500

THE TAX IMPLICATIONS OF YOUR STOCK INVESTMENTS

Some important tax rules are

Dividends received are fully taxable.

A capital gain occurs when the selling price exceeds the cost of stock you have held for more than 1 year. A capital loss occurs when the selling price is less than the cost of the stock you have held for more than 1 year.

Net capital gains (capital gains less capital losses) are taxed at your tax rate.

SOLVED PROBLEM 13.74

If your net long-term capital gain in 19X9 is $15,000 and the tax rate is 28 percent, what will your tax be?

SOLUTION

$$\$15,000 \times .28 = \$4,200$$

Capital losses are allowed to the extent of capital gains plus up to $3,000 ($1,500 for married individuals filing separately) of ordinary income. The excess capital loss (over $3,000) may be carried forward.

Capital losses offset ordinary income. An ordinary gain or loss occurs on stock held for less than 1 year. The tax rate for ordinary and capital gains or losses is the same under current law.

You must report your gains from the sale of stock on the trade date (date you sell the stock) instead of the settlement date (5 business days later, when the broker must make payment to you). The settlement date may be in a later year.

SOLVED PROBLEM 13.75

You sold shares of XYZ Company in 19X0 netting $8,000. The initial cost (including brokerage fees) was $6,700. You are in the 28 percent tax bracket. How much tax will you have to pay on the gain?

SOLUTION

Gain ($8,000 − $6,700)	$1,300
Tax rate	× .28
Tax	$ 364

A technique for postponing the tax on the gain from a disposition of stock while simultaneously protecting that gain is to sell short. If you own appreciated stock, you may sell short near the end of the year and then deliver the stock to the dealer and realize the gain after the new year.

Review Questions

(1) The return from stock consists of _____ and _____.

(2) _____ equals common stockholders' equity divided by outstanding shares.

(3) _____ are stocks of high-quality, financially strong companies.

(4) _____ stocks are stocks of companies providing higher dividend payout ratios.

(5) Stocks that fluctuate based on economic changes are referred to as _____ stocks.

(6) A stock that is not adversely impacted by a downturn in business is termed a _____ stock.

(7) A _____ is the execution of a buy or sell of a stock at the present market price.

(8) A _____ order has no expiration date.

(9) A _____ order is when you agree to purchase stock at no more than a specified price.

(10) In a _____ order, you agree to buy or sell a stock when it increases to or declines below a given price.

(11) The settlement date for a stock transaction is on the _____ business day after a trade is made.

(12) An _____ transaction involves units of 100 shares while a _____ transaction involves less than 100 shares.

(13) When you buy less than 100 shares, you typically have to pay _____ of a point higher.

(14) A good source of reference for the dividend records of companies is _____.

(15) You are entitled to receive a dividend if you are a registered shareholder on the _____.

(16) The ratio of dividends per share divided by earnings per share is referred to as the _____ ratio.

(17) Book value per share equals _____ divided by _____.

(18) The price-earnings ratio equals _____ divided by _____.

(19) _____ is the percentage change in the market price of a stock compared to the percentage change in a stock market index.

(20) The _____ market involves brokers/dealers who buy and sell securities through a communications network.

(21) If the "bid and asked" prices are \$10 and \$$10\frac{1}{2}$, you will have to pay \$_____ to buy the over-the-counter stock.

(22) _____ selling is when you expect the price of a stock to drop.

(23) An _____ order is good for a specified time period.

(24) A _____ order is one to buy a stock in specified amounts at specified price variations.

(25) If you owned 100 shares of a company's stock and the company decided to exchange it for 400 shares, this is referred to as a _____.

(26) The _____ date is 4 business days before the date of record.

(27) A company's security is riskier than the market average if its beta is greater than _____.

(28) An annuity that continues forever is referred to as a _____.

(29) _____ is the term used when you buy stock on credit.

(30) You are allowed a maximum capital loss on the tax return of \$_____.

Answers: (1) appreciation in market price, dividends; (2) Book value; (3) Blue chips; (4) Income; (5) cyclical; (6) defensive; (7) market order; (8) good till canceled; (9) limit; (10) stop-loss; (11) fifth; (12) odd-lot, round-lot; (13) $\frac{1}{8}$; (14) Standard and Poor's *Stock Guide* or Moody's *Annual Dividend Record*; (15) date of record; (16) dividend payment; (17) stockholders' equity, outstanding shares; (18) market price per share, earnings per share; (19) Beta; (20) over-the-counter; (21) \$$10\frac{1}{2}$; (22) Short; (23) open; (24) scale; (25) stock split; (26) ex-dividend; (27) 1; (28) perpetuity; (29) Margin; (30) \$3,000.

Additional Solved Problems

13.1 You sold shares of AB Company in 19X0 netting \$7,000. The initial cost (including brokerage fees) was \$6,100. If you are in the 28 percent tax bracket, what is the tax you will have to pay?

SOLUTION

Gain (\$7,000 − \$6,100)	\$ 900
Tax rate	× .28
Tax	\$ 252

13.2 You own 100 shares of ABC Company at a cost of \$1,500. There is a three-for-one stock split. After the stock split, how many shares will you have and what will be the cost per share and total cost?

SOLUTION

$$300 \text{ shares} \times \$5 = \$1,500$$

13.3 You own 5,000 shares of stock. The company pays a dividend per share of $.25. How much will you receive?

SOLUTION

$$5,000 \times \$.25 = \$1,250$$

13.4 You own 200 shares of stock having a par value of $20 per share. A 10 percent cash dividend is declared. How much will you receive?

SOLUTION

$$200 \times \$20 \times .10 = \$400$$

13.5 You own 500 shares of XYZ Company costing $10 per share. A 10 percent stock dividend is declared.

(*a*)   After receiving the stock dividend, what will be the new cost per share?

(*b*)   If you later sell 100 shares at $1,200, what will be your gain or loss?

SOLUTION

(*a*)

Shares to be received (500 × 10%) = 50

$$\text{New cost per share} = \frac{\$5,000}{550 \text{ shares}} = \$9.09$$

(*b*)

Selling price	$1,200
Less: Cost (100 × $9.09)	909
Gain	$ 291

13.6 You buy a stock for $50 and later sell it for $54. The annual cash dividend is $3. What is the return per share on the investment?

SOLUTION

Dividend income	$3
Gain ($54 − $50)	4
Total	$7

13.7 You own A Company's common stock which has a current market price of $60 and pays a quarterly dividend of $1.50. You also own B Company's common stock which has a current market price of $67 and gives a stock dividend of 5 percent. What is the dividend yield for each of the stocks?

SOLUTION

A Company's common stock:

$$\frac{\text{Dividend per share}}{\text{Market price per share}} = \frac{\$1.50}{\$60.00} = 2.5\% \text{ per quarter}$$

$$2.5\% \times 4 = 10\% \text{ per year}$$

B Company's common stock: The dividend yield is not relevant since a stock dividend is not cash.

13.8 Stock Y has a beta of 1.2 and the overall market rate of return decreases by 6 percent. Predict how the return on the stock will be affected based on the overall market movement.

SOLUTION

$$6\% \times 1.2 = 7.2\% \text{ decrease}$$

13.9 You invested $100 in a stock which you sold 6 months later for $120. A $2 dividend was received.

    (*a*) What is the semiannual return?

    (*b*) What is the equivalent annual return?

SOLUTION

$$\frac{(\text{Selling price} - \text{Investment}) + \text{Dividend}}{\text{Investment}}$$

(*a*)
$$\frac{(\$120 - \$100) + \$2}{\$100} = \frac{\$22}{\$100} = 22\%$$

(*b*)
$$22\% \times 2 = 44\%$$

13.10 You buy a stock for $70 and sell it for $130 after 5 years. Each year you receive a dividend of $4. What is your return over the 5-year period?

SOLUTION

$$\frac{(\text{Selling price} - \text{Investment})/\text{Years} + \text{Dividend}}{\text{Average investment}} = \frac{(\$130 - \$70)/5 + \$4}{(\$130 + \$70)/2} = \frac{\$24}{\$100} = 24\%$$

13.11 You sell short 500 shares of stock with a market price of $25 per share. Later, you buy back the stock at $20 per share. How much profit did you earn, if any?

SOLUTION

$$500 \times \$5 = \$2{,}500$$

13.12 You paid $90 for a stock presently worth $110. The dividend per share is $5.

    (*a*) What is the dividend yield on your initial investment?

    (*b*) What is the dividend yield on current market price?

SOLUTION

    (*a*) Dividends per share/Investment = $5/$90 = 5.6%

    (*b*) Dividends per share/Market price = $5/$110 = 4.5%

13.13 The present market price of a stock is $20 and the earnings per share is $2. Therefore, the P/E ratio is 10. An 8 percent annual growth rate in earnings is anticipated over the next 7 years. The P/E ratio is assumed to be the same in 7 years. What is the expected market price of the stock?

SOLUTION

$$\text{Current EPS} \times \text{Future Value of \$1 (Appendix Table 1) for } n = 8, i = 8\%$$

$$\$2 \times 1.71382 = \$3.43$$

$$\text{Expected market price} = \text{Expected EPS} \times \text{P/E ratio}$$

$$\$3.43 \times 10 = \$34.30$$

13.14 You are deciding whether to purchase a security at the beginning of the year. The dividend at year's end is anticipated to be $3.00, and the year-end market price is expected to be $60. The desired rate of return is 12 percent. What will the value of the stock be at the end of the year?

SOLUTION

Present value of $1 (Appendix Table 3) factor for $n = 1$, $i = 12\%$ is .89286.

$$(\$3.00 \times .89286) + (\$60 \times .89286) = \$2.68 + \$53.57 = \$56.25$$

13.15 You expect to hold a stock for 15 years and receive $30 in annual dividends per share. The anticipated selling price at the end of 15 years is $250 per share. Your required rate of return is 8 percent. What is the value per share of this stock today?

SOLUTION

Present value of annuity (Appendix Table 4) ($30 × 8.55948)	$256.78
Present value of $1 (Appendix Table 3) ($250 × .31524)	78.81
Total	$335.59

13.16 You purchase a stock with dividends anticipated to increase by 8 percent per year for the next 3 years. The dividends per share for the first year is $1.15. At the end of the third year you expect to sell the stock for $25. Your required rate of return is 10 percent.

(*a*) What is the value of the stock today?

(*b*) If you could buy the stock at $18, would you buy it?

SOLUTION

(*a*)

YEAR	DIVIDEND	PRESENT VALUE
1	$1.15 × .90909 (Appendix Table 3)	$ 1.05
2	$1.24* × .82645 (Appendix Table 3)	1.02
3	$1.34† × .75132 (Appendix Table 3)	1.01
3	$25.00 × .75132 (Appendix Table 3)	18.78
Total		$21.86

*$1.15 × 1.08 = $1.24
†$1.24 × 1.08 = $1.34

(*b*) Yes. Since the purchase price of $18 is below the value of the stock of $21.86, it should be bought.

13.17 L Company's EPS is currently $2 and it is selling at a P/E multiple of 15. It has a dividend yield of 10 percent. You anticipate that the market price will increase to $38 a share 1 year from now. What is the expected rate of return?

SOLUTION

$$\text{Current market price} = \text{EPS} \times \text{P/E multiple} = \$2 \times 15 = \$30$$

$$\text{Dividend yield} = \$30 \times .10 = \$3$$

$$\text{Rate of return} = \frac{\text{Dividends per share} + \text{Change in price}}{\text{Initial investment}}$$

$$= \frac{\$3 + (\$38 - \$30)}{\$30} = \frac{\$11}{\$30} = 36.7\%$$

13.18 At the end of a month, you wish to compute the market value of your portfolio. Your records indicate the following:

STOCK	SHARES	PRICE PAID PER SHARE	MARKET PRICE PER SHARE
TUV Co.	500	$9	$12
LCE Co.	750	7	5
XYZ Co.	1,000	7	8

What is the value of your portfolio?

SOLUTION

	STOCK		MARKET VALUE
TUV Co.	(500 × $12)		$ 6,000
LCE Co.	(750 × $5)		3,750
XYZ Co.	(1,000 × $8)		8,000
Total			$17,750

13.19 You invest $1,000 a month in ABC Company stock and have the following transactions. (Ignore brokerage commissions.)

DATE	INVESTMENT	PRICE PER SHARE	SHARES BOUGHT
3/12	$1,000	$10	100
5/3	1,000	12	83.33
7/7	1,000	7	142.86

(a) What is the average price per share?

(b) What is the average cost per share?

SOLUTION

(a) Total price per share/Number of purchases = $29/3 = $9.67

(b) Investment/Total shares bought = $3,000/326.19 = $9.20

13.20 XYZ Company has an EPS of $5 with an anticipated growth rate of 20 percent. The normal P/E multiple is 6. What is the value of the stock?

SOLUTION

$$\text{Estimated EPS} = \$5(1.20) = \$6$$

$$\text{Price of stock} = \$6 \times 6 = \$36$$

13.21 A company's future annual earnings are anticipated to be $5 per share. The risk rate of return (capitalization rate) is 12 percent. What is the value of the common stock?

SOLUTION

$$\frac{\$5}{.12} = \$41.67$$

13.22 You buy 70 shares of P Company at $30 per share. You pay 80 percent of the price, and borrow the remainder on margin. Assuming an interest rate of 15 percent, what will be your rate of return (*after* interest) if you sell the stock for $50 per share 1 year later?

SOLUTION

$$\text{Cost of stock} = 70 \times \$30 = \$2,100$$

$$\text{Down payment} = 80\% \times \$2,100 = \$1,680$$

$$\text{Margin} = 20\% \times \$2,100 = \$420$$

$$\text{Interest cost} = 15\% \times \$420 = \$63$$

$$\text{Selling price} = 70 \times \$50 = \$3,500$$

$$\text{Rate of return} = \frac{(\text{Selling price} - \text{Cost}) - \text{Interest}}{\text{Investment}}$$

$$= \frac{(\$3,500 - \$2,100) - \$63}{\$1,680} = \frac{\$1,337}{\$1,680} = 80\%$$

13.23 A company has the following financial characteristics: total assets, $20,000; total liabilities, $5,000; preferred stock, $2,000; dividends on preferred stock, $500; net income, $3,000; outstanding common shares, 1,000; market price per share, $30; and dividends on common stock, $1.50 per share. Compute the following:

(*a*)   Dividend yield on common stock

(*b*)   Book value per share

(*c*)   Earnings per share

(*d*)   P/E ratio

SOLUTION

(*a*)
$$\text{Dividend yield} = \frac{\text{Dividends per share}}{\text{Market price per share}} = \frac{\$1.50}{\$30.00} = 5\%$$

(*b*)
$$\text{Common stockholders' equity} = \text{Assets} - (\text{Liabilities} + \text{Preferred stock})$$
$$= \$20,000 - (\$5,000 + \$2,000) = \$13,000$$

$$\text{Book value per share} = \frac{\text{Common stockholders' equity}}{\text{Outstanding common shares}} = \frac{\$13,000}{1,000} = \$13$$

(*c*)
$$\text{Earnings per share} = \frac{\text{Net income} - \text{Preferred dividends}}{\text{Outstanding common shares}}$$

$$= \frac{\$3,000 - \$500}{1,000} = \frac{\$2,500}{1,000} = \$2.50$$

(*d*)
$$\text{P/E ratio} = \frac{\text{Market price}}{\text{EPS}} = \frac{\$30}{\$2.50} = 12$$

13.24 You have a constant ratio plan between stocks and bonds of 80 percent. At the current time, your portfolio consists of the following:

Average Stock Price	Average Shares	Value of Stock	Value of Bonds	Total Value	Ratio
$5	16,000	$80,000	$20,000	$100,000	80%

The stocks fell by an average of $1 in price.

(*a*)   What is the value of the stocks and bonds after the drop in price?

(*b*)   In order to maintain a constant ratio of 80 percent between stocks and bonds, how much in stock has to be bought and how much in bonds has to be sold?

(*c*)   What are the adjusted values of stocks and bonds?

SOLUTION

	Average Stock Price	Average Shares	Value of Stock	Value of Bonds	Total Value	Ratio
(*a*)	$4	16,000	$64,000	$20,000	$84,000	76.2%
(*b*)			+ 3,200	− 3,200		
(*c*)			$67,200	$16,800	$84,000	80%

13.25 You bought 100 shares of AB Co. at $40 per share on margin 1 year ago. The brokerage fee was $150. You paid 70 percent of the cost and borrowed the remainder at 14 percent interest. You just sold the stocks at $48 per share less a brokerage fee of $200. Fill in the columns below.

	WITHOUT MARGIN	WITH MARGIN
Cash paid	$4,150	(a)
Borrowing on credit	—	(b)
Initial cost	$4,150	$4,150
Interest charge	—	(c)
Total cost	$4,150	$4,324
Net sales proceeds	(d)	(d)
Gain or loss	$ 450	$ 276
Return on initial cash investment	(e)	(f)

SOLUTION

(a) $4,000 + $150 = $4,150 × 70% = $2,905

(b) $4,150 × 30% = $1,245

(c) $1,245 × 14% = $174

(d) $4,800 − $200 = $4,600

(e)   Gain/Initial cash investment = $450/$4,150 = 10.8%

(f)   Gain/Initial cash investment = $276/$2,905 = 9.5%

Chapter 14

Investing in Options: Rights, Warrants, Calls, and Puts

Options give you the right to buy a security at a particular price for a specified time period. Options have their own inherent value and are traded in secondary markets. You may buy an option so that you can take advantage of an expected increase in the price of the underlying stock. Option prices are directly tied to the prices of the common stock they apply to. The types of options include rights, warrants, calls, and puts. Investing in options is quite risky and requires specialized knowledge.

STOCK RIGHTS

In a stock rights offering, current stockholders have the first right to buy new shares to maintain their present ownership interest. This is referred to as a *preemptive right*.

SOLVED PROBLEM 14.1

You own 3 percent of ABC Company. The firm issues 5,000 additional shares and there is a stock rights offering. How many shares may you buy under the offering?

SOLUTION

$$3\% \times 5{,}000 = 150$$

A stock right enables you to buy new stock at a subscription price (sometimes termed an exercise price) for a short time, typically no more than several weeks. This subscription price, or exercise price, is lower than the current market price of the stock.

SOLVED PROBLEM 14.2

A company has 2 million shares outstanding and wants to issue another 100,000 shares. Each existing stockholder will receive one right per share owned. How many rights does a stockholder need to buy one new share?

SOLUTION

$$\frac{2{,}000{,}000}{100{,}000} = 20$$

One advantage of the stock rights option is the lower exercise price. Another is that stockholders do not have to pay a brokerage commission when they purchase the additional stock.

Stockholders who do not wish to purchase additional stock can sell their rights in the secondary market. (Of course, if a right is not exercised prior to the expiration date, it no longer has value.)

STOCK WARRANTS

A warrant is an option to buy a certain number of shares at a specified price for a given time period at a subscription price that is *higher* than the present market price. A warrant may or may not come in a one-to-one ratio with stock already owned. Unlike an option, a warrant is usually good for several years; some, in fact, have no maturity date.

Warrants are often given as sweeteners for a bond issue. This allows the company to float the debt or issue the bond at a lower interest rate. Generally, warrants are detachable from the bond, once it has been issued. Detachable warrants have their own market price. So even though warrants are exercised, the debt with which they are first issued still exists. Also stock warrants may be issued with preferred stock. Most warrants are traded on the American Stock Exchange, and some are traded on the New York Stock Exchange.

Warrants are not frequently issued and are not available for all securities. They pay no dividends and carry no voting privileges. The warrant enables you to take part *indirectly* in price appreciation of common stock and to obtain a capital gain. One warrant usually equals one share, but in some instances more than one warrant is required to get one share.

Warrants can be bought from a broker. The price of a warrant is usually listed along with that of the common stock of the company. Brokerage fees for warrants are the same as those for stocks and depend on the market price of the security.

SOLVED PROBLEM 14.3

What can you do with the warrant if the market price of the common stock rises?

SOLUTION

When the price per common share goes up, you may either sell the warrant (since the warrant also increases in value) or exercise it and get the stock.

SOLVED PROBLEM 14.4

Are warrants speculative?

SOLUTION

Yes. Trading in warrants is speculative; there is potential for high return, but high risk exists because of the possibility of variability in return.

Warrants are speculative since their value depends on the price of the common stock for which they can be exchanged. If stock prices fluctuate widely, the value of warrants will sharply vacillate.

As we said earlier, when warrants are issued, the exercise price is greater than the market price.

SOLVED PROBLEM 14.5

A warrant of ABC Company stock permits you to buy one share at $25.

(a)   If the stock goes beyond $25 prior to the expiration date, what happens to the value of the warrant?

(b)   If the stock goes below $25, what happens to the value of the warrant?

SOLUTION

(a)   Increases

(b)   Decreases

The exercise price for a warrant is typically constant over its life. However, the price of some warrants may rise as the expiration date approaches. Exercise price is adjusted for stock splits and large stock dividends.

The return on a warrant for a holding period of no more than 1 year equals

$$\frac{\text{Selling price} - \text{Acquisition price}}{\text{Acquisition price}}$$

SOLVED PROBLEM 14.6

You sell a warrant for $21 after holding it 1 year. That same warrant cost you only $12. What is your rate of return?

SOLUTION

$$\frac{\$21 - \$12}{\$12} = \frac{\$9}{\$12} = 75\%$$

The return on a warrant for a holding period in excess of 1 year equals

$$\frac{\text{(Selling price} - \text{Acquisition price)/Years}}{\text{Average investment}}$$

SOLVED PROBLEM 14.7

Refer to Solved Problem 14.6; assume there is a holding period of 4 years on the warrant you sold for $21. What is your rate of return?

SOLUTION

$$\frac{(\$21 - \$12)/4}{(\$21 + \$12)/2} = \frac{\$2.25}{\$16.50} = 13.6\%$$

The value of a warrant is greatest when the market price of the related stock is equal to or greater than the exercise price of the warrant. The value of a warrant thus equals

(Market price of common stock − Exercise price of warrant)

$$\times \text{ Number of common stock shares bought for one warrant}$$

The market price of stock will usually change daily. However, the exercise price of the warrant is fixed over the life of the warrant.

SOLVED PROBLEM 14.8

A warrant has an exercise price of $25. Two warrants equal one share. The market price of the stock is $30. What is the value of the warrant?

SOLUTION

$$(\$30 - \$25) \times .5 = \$2.50$$

Typically, the market value of a warrant is greater than its intrinsic value (premium) due to the speculative nature of the warrant. Premium equals the market price of the warrant less its intrinsic value.

SOLVED PROBLEM 14.9

If the warrant in Solved Problem 14.8 has a market price of $3.50, what will the premium be?

SOLUTION

$$\$3.50 - \$2.50 = \$1.00$$

SOLVED PROBLEM 14.10

Assume that $100,000 in bonds are issued. Thus, there are 100 bonds ($100,000/$1,000). Each bond has eight warrants attached. Each warrant allows the investor to buy one share of stock at $12 until 1 year from the date of the bond.

(a)   What is the value of the warrant if the stock is selling below $12?

(b)   If the stock increases in value to $25 a share, what will one warrant be worth?

(c)   What will the eight warrants be worth?

SOLUTION

(a) $0

(b) $25 − $12 = $13

(c) $13 × 8 = $104

You may also use the leveraging effect to increase your dollar return.

EXAMPLE 14.1   You have $7,000 to invest. If you buy common stock when the market price is $35 a share, you can buy 200 shares. If the price increases to $41 a share you will have a capital gain of $1,200. But if you invest the $7,000 in warrants priced at only $7 a share, you can buy 1,000 of them. (One warrant equals one share.) If the price of the warrant increases by $6, your profit will be $6,000. In this case, you earn a return of only 17.1 percent on the common stock investment but on the warrants you obtain a return of 85.7 percent. On the other hand, assume the market price of the stock declines by $6 a share. If you invest in the common stock you will lose $1,200 for a remaining equity of $5,800. But if you invest in the warrant you will lose everything (assuming no warrant premium exists).

If an investor is to obtain maximum price potential from a warrant, the market price of the common stock must equal or exceed the warrant's exercise price. Also, lower-priced issues provide greater leverage opportunity. Further, a warrant with a low unit price generates more price volatility and less downside risk (since there is less to lose), and thus is preferable to a warrant with a high unit price.

SOLVED PROBLEM 14.11

What are the advantages and disadvantages of warrants?

SOLUTION

The advantages of warrants are the price of the warrant follows the price of the related common stock, the low unit cost provides leverage opportunity, and there is less downside risk due to lower unit price. The disadvantages of warrants are the loss of the entire investment if price appreciation does not occur, no dividend income is received, and careful study is required.

SOLVED PROBLEM 14.12

$100,000 in bonds are issued. Each bond has five warrants attached. Each warrant allows the investor to buy one share of stock at $14 until 2 years from the date of the bond. The stock increases in price to $20.

(a)   What is each warrant worth?

(b)   How much are the five warrants worth?

SOLUTION

(a) $20 − $14 = $6

(b)   5 × $6 = $30

SOLVED PROBLEM 14.13

An individual invests $15,000. The common stock has a market price of $150 per share. The price of the stock increases to $155 per share. You decided to invest in warrants priced at $60 a share. One warrant equals one share. The price of the warrant increases by $10.

(a)   How many warrants are you able to buy?

(b)   What is your profit on the warrants?

(c)   What is your rate of return on the warrants?

(d)   If you purchased the stock rather than the warrants, how many shares would you have bought?

(e)   What would the capital gain on the stock have been?

(f)   What rate of return would you have earned on the stock?

SOLUTION

(a) $15,000/$60 = 250 warrants

(b)   250 × $10 = $2,500

(c) $2,500/$15,000 = 16.7%

(d) $15,000/$150 = 100 shares

(e)   100 × $5 = $500

(f) $500/$15,000 = 3.3%

CALLS AND PUTS

Calls and puts are another kind of stock option. You can buy or sell them in round lots, typically 100 shares.

When you buy a *call,* you are buying the right to purchase stock at a *fixed* price. You do this when you anticipate the price of that stock will go up. In buying a call you have the chance to make a significant gain from a small investment if the stock price increases, but you also risk the loss of your entire investment if the stock does not increase in price. Calls are in bearer negotiable form with a life of 1 month to 9 months.

If you purchase a *put,* you have the right to sell stock at a *fixed* price. You might buy a put when you anticipate a decline in the stock price. By purchasing a put you have the opportunity to make a significant gain from a small investment when the price of the stock declines, but you risk your entire investment if the stock price does not drop. Like calls, puts are in bearer negotiable form with a life ranging from 1 month to 9 months.

Calls and puts are usually written for widely held and actively traded stock on organized exchanges. Options can be traded for speculative or conservative purposes. Commissions and transaction costs are incurred when buying and selling a call or put.

SOLVED PROBLEM 14.14

What are the disadvantages of calls?

SOLUTION

Calls do not provide voting privileges, ownership interest, or dividend income. However, option contracts are adjusted for stock splits and stock dividends.

The life of calls and puts is shorter than that of warrants but longer than that of rights. They are similar to warrants in that they are an alternative investment to common stock, have leverage opportunity, and are a speculative investment.

SOLVED PROBLEM 14.15

Who issues calls and puts?

SOLUTION

Calls and puts are not issued by the company with the common stock but instead by option makers or option writers. The maker of the option receives the price paid for the call or put minus commission costs. The option trades on the open market. Calls and puts are written and can be acquired through brokers and dealers. The writer is required to purchase or deliver the stock when requested.

SOLVED PROBLEM 14.16

Do you have to actually exercise a call or put to make money?

SOLUTION

No. When you hold a call or put, you do not necessarily have to exercise it to earn a return. You can trade the call or put in the secondary market for whatever its value is. For example, the value of a call increases as the underlying common stock goes up in price. The call can be sold in the market before its expiration date.

Calls and puts are traded on listed option exchanges, which are secondary markets like the Chicago Board Options Exchange, American Stock Exchange, Philadelphia Stock Exchange, and Pacific Stock Exchange. They are also traded in the over-the-counter market. Option exchanges deal only in the purchase and sale of call and put options. *Listed options* are options traded on organized exchanges. *Conventional options* are those options traded in the over-the-counter market.

SOLVED PROBLEM 14.17

What does the Options Clearing Corporation do?

SOLUTION

The Options Clearing Corporation issues calls listed on the options exchanges. Orders are placed with this corporation, which then issues the calls or closes the position. No certificates are issued for options, so the investor must have a brokerage account. When a holder exercises a call, he goes through the Clearing Corporation, which picks at random a writer from member accounts. A call writer would be required to sell 100 shares of the common stock at the exercise price.

The price per share for 100 shares, which the purchaser may buy at (call), is referred to as the striking price (exercise price). For a put, it is the price at which the stock may be sold. The purchase or sale of the stock is to the writer of the option. The striking price is set for the life of the option on the options exchange. When stock price changes, new exercise prices are introduced for trading purposes reflecting the new value.

The option expires on the last day it can be exercised. Conventional options can expire on any business day while listed options have a standardized expiration date.

The cost of an option is termed the *premium*. It is the price the purchaser of the call or put has to pay the writer.

SOLVED PROBLEM 14.18

What does the premium for a call depend upon?

SOLUTION

The premium depends on the exchange the option is listed, prevailing interest rates, dividend trend of the related security, trading volume, market price of the stock it applies to, amount of time remaining before the expiration date, variability in price of the related security, and width of the spread in price of the stock relative to the option's exercise price (a wider spread means a higher price).

SOLVED PROBLEM 14.19

When are calls "in-the-money" and "out-of-the-money"?

SOLUTION

When the market price is greater than the strike price, the call is "in-the-money." When the market price is less than the strike price, the call is "out-of-the-money." Call options in-the-money have an intrinsic value equal to the difference between the market price and the strike price.

$$\text{Value of call} = (\text{Market price of stock} - \text{Exercise price of call}) \times 100$$

The market price of stock is at the current date. Of course, the market price will typically *change* on a stock each day. The exercise (strike) price of the call is *fixed* for its life. For example, the exercise (strike) price for a 3-month call is the same for the entire period.

SOLVED PROBLEM 14.20

The market price per share of a stock is $45, with a strike price of $40. Remember that one call is for 100 shares of stock. What is the value of the call?

SOLUTION

$$\$45 - \$40 = \$5 \times 100 \text{ shares} = \$500$$

Out-of-the-money call options have no intrinsic value.

SOLVED PROBLEM 14.21

If the total premium (option price) of an option is $7 and the intrinsic value is $3, there is an additional premium of $4 arising from other considerations. What are these other considerations?

SOLUTION

In effect, the total premium consists of the intrinsic value plus speculative premium (time value) based on factors such as risk, variability, forecasted future prices, expiration date, leverage, and dividend.

$$\text{Total premium} = \text{Intrinsic value} + \text{Speculative premium}$$

The definition of in-the-money and out-of-the-money is different for puts because puts allow the owner to sell stock at the strike price. When strike price exceeds market price of stock, we have an in-the-money put option. Its value equals

$$\text{Value of put} = (\text{Exercise price of put} - \text{Market price of stock}) \times 100$$

The exercise (strike) price of a put is *fixed* over the life of the put. The market price of the stock of course will *change* typically each day.

SOLVED PROBLEM 14.22

The market price of a stock is $53 and the strike price of the put is $60. What is the value of the put?

SOLUTION

$$(\$60 - \$53) = \$7 \times 100 \text{ shares} = \$700$$

When market price of stock exceeds strike price, there is an out-of-the-money put. Since a stock owner can sell it for a greater amount in the market than he or she could get by exercising the put, there is no intrinsic value of the out-of-money put.

	A Call at a $50 Strike Price	A Put at a $50 Strike Price
In-the-money	Over $50	Under $50
At-the-money	$50	$50
Out-of-the-money	Under $50	Over $50

The theoretical value for calls and puts indicates the price at which the options should be traded. Typically, however, calls and puts are traded at prices higher than true value when they have a long remaining time period. This difference represents the *investment premium*.

$$\text{Investment premium} = \frac{\text{Option premium} - \text{Option value}}{\text{Option value}}$$

SOLVED PROBLEM 14.23

A put has a theoretical value of $1,500 and a price of $1,750. What is the investment premium in percentage terms?

SOLUTION

$$\frac{\$250}{\$1,500} = 16.67\%$$

CALLS

The *call purchaser* takes the risk of losing the entire investment price for the option if a price increase does not take place.

SOLVED PROBLEM 14.24

A 2-month call option allows you to buy 500 shares of ABC Company at $20 per share. Within that time period, you exercise the option when the market price is $38.

(*a*)   What is your gain before commissions?

(*b*)   What would happen if the market price per share dropped below $20?

SOLUTION

(*a*)   Your gain is $9,000 ($38 − $20 = $18 × 500 shares).

(*b*)   If the market price had declined from $20 you would not have exercised the call option, and you would have lost your entire investment.

SOLVED PROBLEM 14.25

What are the advantages of buying a call?

SOLUTION

By purchasing a call you can own common stock for a fraction of the cost of purchasing regular shares. Calls cost significantly less than common stock. Leverage exists because a little change in common stock price can result in a major change in the call option's price. A part of the percentage gain in the price of the call is the speculative premium attributable to the remaining life on the call. Calls can be considered a means of controlling 100 shares of stock without a large dollar investment.

Significant percentage gains on call options are possible from the low investment compared to the price of the related common stock.

SOLVED PROBLEM 14.26

A stock has a current market price of $35. A call can be purchased for $300 allowing the acquisition of 100 shares at $35 each. If the price of the stock increases, the call will also be worth more. Assume that the stock is at $55 at the call's expiration date.

(a) What is your profit?

(b) What is your rate of return?

SOLUTION

(a) The profit is $20 ($55 − $35) on each of the 100 shares of stock in the call, or a total of $2,000 on an investment of $300.

(b) A return of 667 percent ($2,000/$300) is earned.

In effect, when you exercise the call for 100 shares at $35 each, you can immediately sell them at $55 per share. Note that you could have earned the same amount by investing directly in the common stock, but the investment would have been $3,500 so the rate of return would have been significantly lower.

SOLVED PROBLEM 14.27

You can buy XY Company stock at $30 a share, or $3,000 for 100 shares. You can acquire a $33 three-month call for $400. Thus, you could invest $2,600 cash and have the opportunity to buy 100 shares at $33 per share. Assume, however, that you decide to invest your $2,600 in a 3-month CD earning 14 percent interest. The CD will return $91 (14% × $2,600 × $\frac{3}{12}$).

(a) If the XY Company stock goes to $16, what is the option worth?

(b) If the stock goes to $43, would there be a gain or loss?

SOLUTION

(a) The option will be worthless but the significant loss on the stock of $14 a share did not occur. Instead, the loss is limited to $309 ($400 − $91). However, note that by not buying a stock you may have foregone a dividend.

(b) If the stock went up to $43, the call would be exercised at $33 resulting in a significant gain with little investment.

PUTS

The *put holder* may sell 100 shares at the strike price for a given period to a put writer. A put is purchased when there is an expectation of a price decline. The maximum loss is the premium cost (investment), which will be lost if the price of the stock does not drop.

SOLVED PROBLEM 14.28

A stock has a market price of $35. You acquire a put to sell 100 shares of stock at $35 per share. The cost of the put is $300. At the exercise date of the put, the price of the stock goes to $15 a share. What is your net gain or loss?

SOLUTION

You realize a profit of $20 per share, or $2,000 ($35 − $15 = $20 × 100 shares). As the holder of the put, you simply buy on the market 100 shares at $15 each and then sell them to the writer of the put for $35 each. The net gain after taking into account the cost of the put is $1,700 ($2,000 − $300).

SOLVED PROBLEM 14.29

Ark's stock price was $55 on March 2. You buy a $56 June put for $4. The speculative premium is therefore $3. On June 7, the stock price falls to $47 and the price of the June $56 put rises to $8.

(*a*)   What is the intrinsic value?

(*b*)   What is the speculative premium?

(*c*)   What is the gain or loss?

SOLUTION

(*a*) $56 − $47 = $9

(*b*) $9 − $8 = $1

(*c*)   Gain = $4 ($8 − $4)

Review Questions

(1)   An option allowing stockholders to buy new common stock at a subscription price, typically below market price, for a given period is referred to as a _____ .

(2)   Your right as an existing stockholder to maintain your fractional interest in the business when new common stock is issued is known as the _____ right.

(3)   The option to buy a given number of shares for a specified period at a subscription price that is higher than the current market price of the stock is referred to as a _____ .

(4)   The price of 100 shares which is fixed for the life of the stock is referred to as the _____ .

(5)   The life of a warrant is _____ than the life of a stock right.

(6)   Options can be traded in the _____ market.

(7)   Options are traded in terms of _____ lots of (typically) _____ shares.

(8)   A _____ is the option to sell common shares at a set price by a specified date.

(9)   Option contracts are adjusted for _____ and _____ .

(10)   The _____ acts as the issuer of calls listed on the options exchange.

(11)   The _____ price is the price per share to buy 100 shares under a call.

(12)   The _____ is the price paid for an option.

(13)   When market price is below the strike price, the call is said to be _____ .

(14)   If you do not exercise a call option, you will lose your _____ .

Answers: (1) stock right; (2) preemptive; (3) stock warrant; (4) striking price; (5) longer; (6) secondary; (7) round, 100; (8) put; (9) stock dividends, stock splits; (10) Options Clearing Corporation; (11) striking; (12) option premium; (13) out-of-the-money; (14) entire investment.

Additional Solved Problems

14.1 You pay $16,000 for warrants having a unit price of $8. One warrant equals one share. The warrant increases to $12.

(*a*)   How many warrants did you acquire?

(*b*)   What rate of return did you earn?

SOLUTION

(*a*)
$$\frac{\$16,000}{\$8} = 2,000 \text{ warrants}$$

(*b*)
$$\frac{\$4 \times 2,000}{\$16,000} = \frac{\$8,000}{\$16,000} = 50\%$$

14.2 If you do not exercise the warrant in Solved Problem 14.1, what value is assigned to it?

SOLUTION

0

14.3 You sell at $30 a warrant that cost $14. The holding period is 3 years. What is the rate of return?

SOLUTION

$$\frac{(\$30 - \$14)/3}{(\$30 + \$14)/2} = \frac{\$5.33}{\$22.00} = 24.2\%$$

14.4 One warrant equals one share. The exercise price is $12. The market price of the stock is $16. The warrants are traded at $5. Determine the percentage premium.

SOLUTION

$$(\$16 - \$12) \times 1 = \$4$$

$$\text{Premium} = \$5 - \$4 = \$1$$

$$\text{Percentage premium} = \frac{\$1}{\$4} = 25\%$$

14.5 $100,000 in bonds are issued. Each bond has seven warrants attached. Each warrant permits the investor to purchase one share of stock at $15 until 2 years from the date of the bond. The stock increases in price to $27.

(*a*)   What is each warrant worth?

(*b*)   How much are the seven warrants worth?

SOLUTION

(*a*) $27 − $15 = $12

(*b*)   7 × $12 = $84

14.6 Assume there are $200,000 bonds issued. Thus, there are 200 bonds ($200,000/$1,000). Each bond has five warrants attached. Each warrant permits the investor to buy one share of stock at $14 until 2 years from the date of the bond.

    (*a*)   What is the value of the warrant if the stock is selling below $14?

    (*b*)   If the stock increases in value to $20 a share, what will the warrant be worth?

    (*c*)   What will the five warrants be worth?

SOLUTION

    (*a*) $0

    (*b*) $20 − $14 = $6

    (*c*)   5 × $6 = $30

14.7 An individual invests $10,000. The common stock has a market price of $100 per share. The price of the stock increases to $106 per share. He decides to invest in warrants priced at $40 a share. One warrant equals one share. The price of the warrant increases by $8.

    (*a*)   How many warrants is he able to buy?

    (*b*)   What is his profit on the warrants?

    (*c*)   What is his rate of return on the warrants?

    (*d*)   If he bought the stock instead of the warrants, how many shares would he have bought?

    (*e*)   What would the capital gain on the stock have been?

    (*f*)   What rate of return would he have earned on the stock?

SOLUTION

    (*a*) $10,000/$40 = 250 warrants

    (*b*) $8 × 250 = $2,000

    (*c*) $2,000/$10,000 = 20%

    (*d*) $10,000/$100 = 100 shares

    (*e*) $6 × 100 = $600

    (*f*) $600/$10,000 = 6%

14.8 A stock has a present market price of $17.50. A call can be bought for $150 permitting the acquisition of 100 shares at $17.50 each. If the stock price goes to $27.50 at the call's expiration date, what is the rate of return?

SOLUTION

    The profit is $10 on each of the 100 shares of stock in the call, or a total of $1,000 on an investment of $150. The return rate is 667 percent ($1,000/$150).

14.9 A stock has a market price of $50. You buy a put to sell 100 shares of stock at $50 per share. The cost of the put is $250. At the exercise date of the put, the price of the stock goes to $30. What is your profit or loss?

SOLUTION

Gain on sale (100 shares × $20)	$2,000
Cost of put	250
Profit	$1,750

14.10 Assume the same facts as in Solved Problem 14.9 except that the stock increases in price to $58. What is the profit or loss?

SOLUTION

    Loss of the entire investment of $250.

Chapter 15

Investing in Fixed-Income Securities

Fixed-income securities generally stress current fixed income and offer little or no opportunity for appreciation in value. They are usually liquid and bear less market risk than other types of investments. Fixed-income investments perform well during stable economic conditions and lower inflation. As interest rates drop, the price of fixed-income investments increases. Examples of fixed-income securities include

Corporate bonds

Government bonds

Municipal bonds

Preferred stocks

Short-term debt securities

In this chapter, you will learn about

Basics of corporate and government bonds and the types of bonds issued

How to calculate the yield on bonds and how to read bond quotations

How to select the right bond for you

Basics about preferred stocks and other short-term fixed-income securities

WHAT IS A BOND?

A bond is a certificate or security showing that you loaned funds to a company or to a government in return for fixed future interest and repayment of principal. Bonds have the following advantages:

There is fixed interest income each year.

Bonds are safer than equity securities such as common stock. This is because bondholders come before common stockholders in the distribution of earnings and in the event of corporate bankruptcy.

Bonds suffer from the following disadvantages:

They do not participate in incremental profitability.

There is no voting right.

TERMS AND FEATURES OF BONDS

There are certain terms and features of bonds you should be familiar with, including:

1. *Par value.* The par value of a bond is the face value, usually $1,000.
2. *Coupon rate.* The coupon rate is the nominal interest rate that determines the actual interest to be received on a bond. It is an annual interest per par value.

SOLVED PROBLEM 15.1

You own a $1,000 bond having a coupon rate of 6 percent. What is the annual interest payment?

SOLUTION

$$\$1,000 \times 6\% = \$60$$

294

3. *Maturity date.* The maturity date is the final date on which repayment of the bond principal is due.

4. *Indenture.* The bond indenture is the lengthy, legal agreement detailing the issuer's obligations pertaining to a bond issue. It contains the terms of the bond issue as well as any restrictive provisions placed on the firm, known as *restrictive covenants.* The indenture is administered by an independent trustee. A restrictive covenant may include maintenance of (*a*) required levels of working capital, (*b*) a particular current ratio, and (*c*) a specified debt ratio.

5. *Trustee.* The trustee is the third party with whom the indenture is made. The trustee's job is to see that the terms of the indenture are actually carried out.

6. *Yield.* The yield is different than the coupon interest rate. It is the effective interest rate you are earning on the bond investment. If a bond is bought below its face value (that is, purchased at a discount), the yield is higher than the coupon rate. If a bond is acquired above face value (that is, bought at a premium), the yield is below the coupon rate.

7. *Call provision.* A call provision entitles the corporation to repurchase, or "call" the bond from their holders at stated prices over specified periods.

8. *Sinking fund.* In a sinking fund bond, money is put aside by the company periodically for the repayment of debt, thus reducing the total amount of debt outstanding. This particular provision may be included in the bond indenture to protect investors.

WHAT ARE THE TYPES OF BONDS?

There are many types of bonds according to different criteria including:

1. *Mortgage bonds.* Mortgage bonds are secured by physical property. In case of default, the bondholders may foreclose on the secured property and sell it to satisfy their claims.

2. *Debentures.* Debentures are unsecured bonds. They are protected by the general credit of the issuing corporation. Credit ratings are very important for this type of bond. Federal, state, and municipal government issues are debentures. Subordinated debentures are junior issues ranking after other unsecured debt as a result of explicit provisions in the indenture. Finance companies have made extensive use of these types of bonds.

3. *Convertible bonds.* These bonds are subordinated debentures which may be converted, at your option, into a specified amount of other securities (usually common stock) at a fixed price. They are hybrid securities having characteristics of both bonds and common stock in that they provide fixed interest income and potential appreciation through participation in future price increases of the underlying common stock.

4. *Income bonds.* In income bonds, interest is paid only if earned. They are often called reorganization bonds.

5. *Tax-exempt bonds.* Tax-exempt bonds are usually municipal bonds where interest income is not subject to federal tax, although the Tax Reform Act (TRA) of 1986 imposed restrictions on the issuance of tax-exempt municipal bonds. Municipal bonds may carry a lower interest than taxable bonds of similar quality and safety. However, after-tax yield from these bonds is usually more than a bond with a higher rate of taxable interest. *Note:* Municipal bonds are subject to two principal risks—interest rate and default.

6. *U.S. government securities.* They include bills, notes, bonds, and mortgages such as "Ginnie Maes." Treasury bills represent short-term government financing and mature in 12 months or less. United States government notes have a maturity of 1 to 10 years whereas U.S. bonds have a maturity of 10 to 25 years and can be purchased in denominations as low as $1,000. All these types of U.S. government securities are subject to federal income taxes, but not subject to state and local income taxes. "Ginnie Maes" represent pools of 25- to 30-year Federal Housing Administration (FHA) or Veterans Administration (VA) mortgages guaranteed by the Government National Mortgage Association.

7. *Zero-coupon bonds.* With zero-coupon bonds, the interest instead of being paid out directly is added to the principal semiannually and both the principal and accumulated interest are paid at maturity. This compounding factor results in your receiving higher returns on your original investment at maturity. Zero-coupon bonds are not fixed-income securities in the historical sense, because they provide no periodic income. The interest on the bond is paid at maturity. However, accrued interest, though not received, is taxable yearly as ordinary income. Zero-coupon bonds have two basic advantages over regular coupon-bearing bonds: (*a*) A relatively small investment is required to buy these bonds; and (*b*) you are assured of a specific yield throughout the term of the investment.

8. *Junk bonds.*   Junk bonds are bonds with a speculative credit rating of BB or lower by Moody's and Standard & Poor's rating systems. They are issued by companies without track records of sales and earnings and therefore are risky for conservative investors. Since junk bonds are known for their high yields, many risk-oriented investors specialize in trading them.

9. *Serial bonds.*   Serial bonds are bonds that mature in installments over time rather than at one maturity date.

HOW TO SELECT A BOND

When selecting a bond, you should take into consideration basically five factors:

1. Investment quality
       Rating of bonds
2. Length of maturity
       Short term (0–5 years)
       Medium (6–15 years)
       Long term (over 15 years)
3. Features of bonds
       Call or conversion features
4. Tax status
5. Yield to maturity

BOND RATINGS

The investment quality of a bond is measured by its bond rating which reflects the probability that a bond issue will go into default. The rating should influence your perception of risk and therefore have an impact on the interest rate you are willing to accept, the price you are willing to pay, and the maturity period you are willing to agree to.

Bond investors tend to place more emphasis on independent analysis of quality than do common stock investors. Bond analysis and ratings are done, among others, by Standard & Poor's and Moody's. Below is a listing of the designations used by these well-known independent agencies. Descriptions on ratings are summarized. For original versions of descriptions, see Moody's *Bond Record* and Standard & Poor's *Bond Guide*.

Description of Bond Ratings

Moody's	Standard & Poor's	Quality Indication
Aaa	AAA	Highest quality
Aa	AA	High quality
A	A	Upper medium grade
Baa	BBB	Medium grade
Ba	BB	Contains speculative elements
B	B	Outright speculative
Caa	CCC & CC	Default definitely possible
Ca	C	Default, only partial recovery likely
C	D	Default, little recovery likely

Note: Ratings may also have + or − sign to show relative standings in class.

You should pay careful attention to ratings since they can affect not only potential market behavior but relative yields as well. Specifically, the higher the rating, the lower the yield of a bond, other things being equal. It should be noted that the ratings do change over time and the rating agencies have "credit watch lists" of various types. See if you can select only those bonds rated Baa or above by Moody's or BBB or above by Standard & Poor's, even though doing so means giving up about $\frac{3}{4}$ of a percentage point in yield.

MATURITY

In addition to the ratings, you can control the risk element through the maturities you select. The maturity indicates how much you stand to lose if interest rates rise. The longer a bond's maturity, the more volatile its price. There is a trade-off: Shorter maturities usually mean lower yields. If you are a conservative investor, select bonds with maturities no further out than 10 years. The bond price is more susceptible to changing interest rates, the longer the maturity of the bond.

FEATURES

Check to see whether a bond has a call provision, which allows the issuing company to redeem its bonds after a certain date if it chooses to, rather than at maturity. You are generally paid a small premium over par if an issue is called but not as much as you would have received if you had been able to hold the bond until maturity. Bonds are usually called only if their interest rates are higher than the going market rate. Try to avoid bonds of companies that have a call provision and may be involved in "event risk" (mergers and acquisitions, leveraged buyouts, etc.).

Also check to see if a bond has a convertible feature. Convertible bonds can be converted into common stock at a later date. They provide fixed income in the form of interest. You also can benefit from the appreciation value of common stock. *Note:* If you have only a small amount to invest or would like to have someone else make the selection, you can buy shares in one of the bond mutual funds. (See Chapter 17 for more about bond funds.)

TAX STATUS

If you are in a high tax bracket, you may want to consider tax-exempt bonds. Most municipal bonds are rated A or above, making them a good grade risk. They can also be bought in mutual funds.

YIELD TO MATURITY

Yield has a lot to do with the rating of a bond. The calculation of yield is taken up later.
A bond may be bought at a discount (below face value) when

1. There is a long maturity period.
2. It is a risky company.
3. The interest rate on the bond is less than the "current market interest rate."

A bond may be bought at a premium when the aforementioned circumstances are opposite.

HOW DO YOU READ A BOND QUOTATION?

To see how bond quotations are presented in the newspaper, let us look at the data for an IBM bond.

Bonds	Cur Yld	Vol	High	Low	Close	Net Chg
IBM $9\frac{3}{8}$ 04	11.	169	$84\frac{5}{8}$	84	84	$-1\frac{1}{8}$

The numbers immediately following the company name gives the bond coupon rate and maturity date. This particular bond carries a 9.375 percent interest rate and matures in 2004. The next column, labeled "cur yld," provides the current yield calculated by dividing the annual interest income

($9\frac{3}{8}$ percent) by the current market price of the bond (a closing price of 84). Thus, the current yield for the IBM bond is 11 percent. This figure represents the effective, or real, rate of return on the current market price represented by the bond's interest earnings. The "vol" column indicates the number of bonds traded on the given day (that is, 169 bonds).

The market price of a bond is usually expressed as a percent of its par (face) value, which is customarily $1,000. Corporate bonds are quoted to the nearest one-eighth of a percent, and a quote of $84\frac{5}{8}$ in the above indicates a price of $846.25 or $84\frac{5}{8}$ percent of $1,000.

United States government bonds are highly marketable and deal in keenly competitive markets so they are quoted in thirty-seconds or sixty-fourths rather than eighths.

Moreover, decimals are used, rather than fractions, in quoting prices. For example, a quotation of 106.17 for a Treasury bond indicates a plus of $1,065.31 [$1,060 + ($\frac{17}{32}$ × $10)]. When a plus sign follows the quotation, the Treasury bond is being quoted in a sixty-fourth. We must double the number following the decimal point and add one to determine the fraction of $10 represented in the quote. For example, a quote of 95.16+ indicates a price of $955.16 [$950 + ($\frac{33}{64}$ × $10)].

HOW DO YOU CALCULATE YIELD (EFFECTIVE RATE OF RETURN) ON A BOND?

Bonds are evaluated on many different types of returns including current yield, yield to maturity, yield to call, and realized yield.

1. *Current yield.* The current yield is the annual interest payment divided by the current price of the bond, which was discussed in the previous section ("Bond Quotation"). This is reported in *The Wall Street Journal,* among others.

   The current yield is

$$\frac{\text{Annual interest payment}}{\text{Current price}}$$

SOLVED PROBLEM 15.2

A 12 percent coupon rate $1,000 par value bond is selling for $960. What is the current yield?

SOLUTION

$$\frac{\$120}{\$960} = 12.5\%$$

The problem with this measure of return is that it does not take into account the maturity date of the bond. A bond with 1 year to run and another with 15 years to run would have the same current yield quote if interest payments were $120 and the price were $960. Clearly, the 1-year bond would be preferable under this circumstance because you would not only get $120 in interest, but also a gain of $40 ($1,000 − $960) with a 1-year time period, and this amount could be reinvested.

2. *Yield to maturity (YTM).* The yield to maturity takes into account the maturity date of the bond. It is the real return you would receive from interest income plus capital gain assuming the bond is held to maturity. The exact way of calculating this measure is a little complicated and not presented here. But the approximate method is

$$\text{Yield} = \frac{I + (\$1,000 - V)/n}{(\$1,000 + V)/2}$$

where V = the market value of the bond

I = dollars of interest paid per year

n = number of years to maturity

SOLVED PROBLEM 15.3

You are offered a 10-year, 8 percent coupon, $1,000 par value bond at a price of $877.60.

(a) What is the rate of return (yield) you could earn if you bought the bond and held it to maturity?

(b) Is the yield greater or lower than the coupon rate?

SOLUTION

(a)

$$\text{Yield} = \frac{\$80 + (\$1,000 - \$877.60)/10}{(\$1,000 + \$877.60)/2} = \frac{\$80 + \$12.24}{\$938.80} = \frac{\$92.24}{\$938.80} = 9.8\%$$

(b) Since the bond was bought at a discount, the yield (9.8 percent) came out greater than the coupon rate of 8 percent.

3. *Yield to call.* Not all bonds are held to maturity. If the bond may be called prior to maturity, the yield to maturity formula will have the call price in place of the par value of $1,000.

SOLVED PROBLEM 15.4

A 20-year bond was initially issued at a 13.5 percent coupon rate, and after 2 years, rates have dropped. The bond is currently selling for $1,180, the yield to maturity on the bond is 11.15 percent, and the bond can be called 5 years after issue at $1,090. Thus if you buy the bond 2 years after issue, your bond may be called back after 3 more years at $1,090. Compute the yield to call.

SOLUTION

$$\frac{\$135 + (\$1,090 - \$1,180)/3}{(\$1,090 + \$1,180)/2} = \frac{\$135 + (-\$90/3)}{\$1,135} = \frac{\$105}{\$1,135} = 9.25\%$$

Note: The yield to call figure of 9.25 percent is 190 basis points less than the yield to maturity of 11.15 percent. Clearly, you need to be aware of the differential because a lower return is earned.

4. *Realized yield.* You may trade in and out of a bond long before it matures. You obviously need a measure of return to evaluate the investment appeal of any bonds you intend to buy and sell. Realized yield is used for this purpose. This measure is simply a variation of yield to maturity, as only two variables are changed in the yield to maturity formula to provide this measure. Future price is used in place of par value ($1,000), and the length of the holding period is substituted for the number of years to maturity.

SOLVED PROBLEM 15.5

In Solved Problem 15.3, assume that you anticipate holding the bond for only 3 years and that you have estimated interest rates will change in the future so that the price of the bond will move to about $925 from its present level of $877.70. Thus, you will buy the bond today at a market price of $877.70 and sell the issue 3 years later at a price of $925. Compute the realized yield.

SOLUTION

$$\text{Realized yield} = \frac{\$80 + (\$925 - \$877.70)/3}{(\$925 + \$877.70)/2} = \frac{\$80 + \$15.77}{\$901.35} + \frac{\$95.77}{\$901.35} = 10.63\%$$

Note: You can use a bond table to find the value for various yield measures. A source is *Thorndike Encyclopedia of Banking and Financial Tables* by Warren, Gorham & Lamont, Boston.

5. *Equivalent before-tax yield.* Yield on a municipal bond needs to be looked at on an equivalent before-tax yield basis, because the interest received is not subject to federal income taxes. The formula used to equate interest on municipals to other investments is

$$\text{Tax equivalent yield} = \frac{\text{Tax-exempt yield}}{1 - \text{Tax rate}}$$

SOLVED PROBLEM 15.6

If you have a marginal tax rate of 28 percent and are evaluating a municipal bond paying 10 percent interest, what is the equivalent before-tax yield on a taxable investment?

SOLUTION

$$\frac{10\%}{1 - .28} = 13.9\%$$

Thus, you could choose between a taxable investment paying 13.9 percent and a tax-exempt bond paying 10 percent and be indifferent between the two.

WHAT IS PREFERRED STOCK?

Preferred stock carries a fixed dividend that is paid quarterly. The dividend is stated in dollar terms per share, or as a percentage of par (stated) value of the stock. Preferred stock is considered a hybrid security because it possesses features of both common stock and a corporate bond. It is like common stock in that

It represents equity ownership and is issued without stated maturity dates.

It pays dividends.

Preferred stock is also like a corporate bond in that

It provides for prior claims on earnings and assets.

Its dividend is fixed for the life of the issue.

It can carry call and convertible features and sinking fund provisions.

Since preferred stocks are traded on the basis of the yield offered to investors, they are viewed as fixed-income securities and, as a result, are in competition with bonds in the marketplace. Corporate bonds, however, occupy a position senior to preferred stocks.

Advantages of owning preferred stocks include

Their high current income, which is highly predictable

Safety

Lower unit cost ($10 to $25 per share)

Disadvantages are

Their susceptibility to inflation and high interest rates.

They lack substantial capital gains potential.

Most preferred stock is cumulative. Cumulative preferred stock requires any dividends in arrears that have not been paid in prior years to be paid before common stockholders can receive their dividends.

PREFERRED STOCK RATINGS

Like bond ratings, Standard & Poor's and Moody's have long rated the investment quality of preferred stocks. S&P uses basically the same rating system as they do with bonds, except that triple A ratings are not given to preferred stocks. Moody's uses a slightly different system, which is given below.

These ratings are intended to provide an indication of the quality of the issue and are based largely on an assessment of the firm's ability to pay preferred dividends in a prompt and timely fashion. *Note:* Preferred stock ratings should not be compared with bond ratings as they are not equivalent.

Moody's Preferred Stock Rating System

Rating Symbol	Definition
aaa	Top quality
aa	High grade
a	Upper medium grade
baa	Lower medium grade
ba	Speculative type
b	Little assurance of future dividends
caa	Likely to be already in arrears

HOW TO CALCULATE EXPECTED RETURN FROM PREFERRED STOCK

The expected return from preferred stock is calculated in the same way as the expected return on bonds. Since preferred stock usually has no maturity date when the company must redeem it, you cannot calculate a yield to maturity. You can calculate a current yield as follows:

$$\text{Current yield} = \frac{D}{P}$$

where D = annual dividend and P = the market price of the preferred stock.

SOLVED PROBLEM 15.7

What is the current yield on a preferred stock paying $4.00 a year in dividends and having a market price of $25?

SOLUTION

16% ($4/$25)

PREFERRED STOCK QUOTATION

If preferred stocks are listed on the organized exchanges, they are reported in the same section as common stocks in newspapers. The symbol "pf" appears after the name of the corporation, designating the issue as preferred. Preferred stocks are read the same way as common stock quotations. The issues are listed in Moody's Bond Record.

OTHER FIXED-INCOME SECURITIES—SHORT-TERM "PARKING LOTS"

Besides bonds and preferred stock, there are other significant forms of debt instruments from which you may choose, and they are primarily short term in nature. You may treat them as "parking lots" until you decide what the next investment should be.

CERTIFICATES OF DEPOSIT (CDs)

These safe instruments are issued by commercial banks and thrift institutions and have traditionally been in amounts of $10,000 or $100,000 (jumbo CDs). You can invest in a CD for much less (for example, $2,000, $5,000). CDs have a fixed maturity period varying from several months to many years. *Warning:* There is a penalty for cashing in the certificate prior to the maturity date.

COMMERCIAL PAPER

Commercial paper is issued by large corporations to the public. Unfortunately, it usually comes in minimum denominations of $25,000. It represents an unsecured promissory note and usually carries a higher yield than small CDs. The maturity is usually 30, 60, and 90 days. The degree of risk depends on the company's credit rating.

TREASURY BILLS

Treasury bills have a maximum maturity of 1 year and common maturities of 91 and 182 days. They trade in minimum units of $10,000. They do not pay interest in the traditional sense; they are sold at a discount, and redeemed when the maturity date comes around, at face value. Treasury bills are extremely liquid in that there is an active secondary or resale market for these securities. They have an extremely low risk because they are backed by the U.S. government.

Yields on discount securities such as Treasury bills are calculated using the formula:

$$\frac{P_1 - P_0}{P_0} \times \frac{52}{n}$$

where P_1 = redemption price, P_0 = purchase price, and n = maturity in weeks.

SOLVED PROBLEM 15.8

Assume that P_1 = $10,000, P_0 = $9,800, and n = 13 weeks. What is the Treasury bill yield?

SOLUTION

$$\frac{\$10,000 - \$9,800}{\$9,800} \times \frac{52}{13} = \frac{\$10,400}{\$127,400} = .0816 = 8.16\%$$

MONEY MARKET FUNDS

Money market funds are special forms of mutual funds. You can own a portfolio of high-yielding CDs, Treasury bills, and other similar securities of short-term nature, with a small investment. There is a great deal of liquidity and flexibility in withdrawing funds through check-writing privileges (the usual minimum withdrawal is $500). Money market funds are considered very conservative, because most of the securities purchased by the funds are quite safe. For more about money market funds, refer to Chapter 17 (Mutual Funds and Diversification).

Review Questions

(1) Fixed-income securities perform well during stable economic conditions and _____ inflation.

(2) A _____ is a certificate or security showing you loaned funds to a company or to a government in return for fixed future interest and repayment of principal.

(3) The _____ of a bond is the face value.

(4) The _____ is the nominal interest rate that determines the actual interest to be received on a bond.

(5) The bond _____ is the lengthy, legal agreement detailing the issuer's obligations pertaining to a bond issue.

(6) _____ is the effective interest rate you are earning on the bond investment.

(7) A _____ entitles the corporation to repurchase bonds from their holders at stated prices over specified periods.

(8) _____ are bonds with a speculative credit rating of BB or lower by Moody's and Standard & Poor's ratings.

(9) When selecting a bond, you should take into consideration five factors: Investment quality, _____, features of bond, tax status, and yield to maturity.

(10) _____ is considered a hybrid security because it possesses features of both common stock and a corporate bond.

(11) _____ is unsecured debt issued by large financially sound corporations to the public.

(12) _____ have a maximum maturity of 1 year and common maturities of 91 and 182 days.

(13) A bond is a certificate or security showing you loaned funds to a company or to a government in return for _____ and _____.

(14) _____ bonds pay interest only if earned.

(15) As interest rates increase, the price of bonds _____.

(16) A _____ bond matures in periodic installments.

(17) _____ bonds are issued at a discount and pay interest only at the maturity date.

(18) The highest rating for a preferred stock by Moody's is _____ and the lowest rating is _____.

Answers: (1) lower; (2) bond; (3) par value; (4) coupon rate; (5) indenture; (6) Yield rate; (7) call provision; (8) Junk bonds; (9) maturity of bonds; (10) Preferred stock; (11) Commercial paper; (12) Treasury bills; (13) fixed interest, repayment of principal; (14) Income; (15) decreases; (16) serial; (17) Zero-coupon; (18) aaa, caa.

Additional Solved Problems

15.1 A 10 percent coupon rate $1,000 par value bond is selling for $950. What is the current yield?

SOLUTION

$$\frac{\text{Annual interest payment}}{\text{Current price}} = \frac{(.1)(\$1,000)}{\$950} = 10.53\%$$

15.2 Ten years ago the Mirage Products Corporation issued a series of $1,000 bonds at a 9 percent coupon rate of interest with a 30-year maturity. The current market price of the bonds is $950.

(*a*) What is the current yield of the bonds?

(*b*) What is the yield to maturity (YTM) of the bonds if purchased at the market price today?

SOLUTION

(*a*)

$$\text{Current yield} = \frac{\text{Annual interest payment}}{\text{Current price}}$$

$$= \frac{\$90}{\$950} = 9.47\%$$

(*b*)

$$\text{YTM} = \frac{I + (\$1,000 - V)/n}{(\$1,000 + V)/2}$$

$$= \frac{\$90 + [(\$1,000 - \$950)/20]}{(\$1,000 + \$950)/2} = 9.49\%$$

15.3 Calculate the current yield and the yield to maturity (YTM) on the following $1,000 par value bonds.

BOND	COUPON RATE	TERM TO MATURITY	MARKET PRICE
1	5%	20 years	$1,050
2	12	15	1,200
3	8	5	950
4	10	12	1,000

SOLUTION

$$\text{Current yield} = \frac{\text{Annual interest payment}}{\text{Current price}}$$

$$\text{YTM} = \frac{I + (\$1,000 - V)/n}{(\$1,000 + V)/2}$$

For Bond 1:
Current yield

$$\frac{(.05)(\$1,000)}{\$1,050} = 4.8\%$$

YTM

$$\frac{\$50 + [(\$1,000 - \$1,050)/20]}{(\$1,000 + \$1,050)/2} = 4.6\%$$

For Bond 2:
Current yield

$$\frac{(.12)(\$1,000)}{\$1,200} = 10\%$$

YTM

$$\frac{\$120 + [(\$1,000 - \$1,200)/15]}{(\$1,000 + \$1,200)/2} = 9.7\%$$

For Bond 3:
Current yield

$$\frac{(.08)(\$1,000)}{\$950} = 8.4\%$$

$$\frac{.12(\$1,000 + V)}{2} = \$130 + \frac{\$1,000 - V}{30}$$

$$\$60 + .06V = \$130 + \$33.33 - .0333V$$

$$.09333V = \$103.33$$

$$V = \$1,107.15$$

John Tash should be willing to pay \$1,107.15 for the bond.

15.10 Given the following bond quotation for an ABC Corporation bond:

Bonds	Cur Yld	Vol	High	Low	Close	Net Chg
ABC 9 10	9.7	75	$93\frac{1}{8}$	$92\frac{1}{2}$	$92\frac{1}{2}$	$+1\frac{1}{4}$

(*a*)   What do these numbers mean?

(*b*)   Calculate the bond's yield to maturity using the short-cut formula. Assume this year is 1990.

SOLUTION

(*a*)   This particular bond carries a 9 percent coupon interest rate and matures in 2010. The next column, labeled "cur yld," provides the current yield calculated by dividing the annual interest income (9 percent) by the current market price of the bond (a closing price of $92\frac{1}{2}$). Thus, the current yield for the ABC bond is 9.7 percent. This figure represents the effective, or real, rate of return on the current market price represented by the bond's interest earnings. The "vol" column indicates the number of bonds traded on the given day (that is, 75 bonds).

The market price of a bond is usually expressed as a percent of its par (face) value, which is customarily \$1,000. Corporate bonds are quoted to the nearest one-eighth of a percent, and a quote of $93\frac{1}{8}$ in the above, for example, indicates a price of \$931.25 or $93\frac{1}{8}$ percent of \$1,000.

(*b*)   Using the closing price, which is $92\frac{1}{2}$ percent of \$1,000, or \$925, the yield to maturity (YTM) is calculated as

$$\text{YTM} = \frac{I + (\$1,000 - V)/n}{(\$1,000 + V)/2}$$

$$= \frac{\$90 + (\$1,000 - \$925)/10}{(\$1,000 + \$925)/2} = \frac{\$90 + \$7.50}{\$962.50}$$

$$= \frac{\$97.50}{\$962.50} = 10.13\%$$

15.11 Bruce Gross wants to invest \$45,000 in bonds. He can buy a corporate bond with a yield of 8 percent or a municipal bond with a yield of 6 percent. Gross is in the 33 percent tax bracket. Based on yield, which bond should he select?

SOLUTION

$$\text{Tax equivalent yield} = \frac{\text{Tax-exempt yield}}{1 - \text{Tax rate}}$$

$$= \frac{6\%}{1 - .33}$$

$$= 8.96\%$$

He should choose the municipal bond, since it gives the higher after-tax yield than the corporate bond (8.96% versus 8%).

15.12 Walter Heller wants to invest $15,000 in bonds. He can buy a corporate bond with a yield of 9 percent or a municipal bond with a yield of 7 percent. Heller is in the 28 percent tax bracket. Based on yield, which bond is more attractive?

SOLUTION

$$\text{Tax equivalent yield} = \frac{\text{Tax-exempt yield}}{1 - \text{Tax rate}}$$

$$= \frac{7\%}{1 - .28}$$

$$= 9.72\%$$

He should choose the municipal bond, since it gives the higher after-tax yield than the corporate bond (9.72% versus 9%).

15.13 Steve Merriman is in the 30 percent tax bracket. His brother Robert is in the 15 percent tax bracket. Each brother is contemplating investing in bonds. They have narrowed their choices to the following two issues: a municipal bond with a coupon rate of 8 percent and a corporate bond with a coupon rate of 10 percent. Both bonds have face values of $1,000.

(*a*)   Which bond should Steve buy?

(*b*)   Which bond should Robert buy?

(*c*)   If choices of Steve and Robert are different, why?

SOLUTION

(*a*)   Steve should purchase the municipal bond. The tax equivalent yield of the municipal bond is 8%/(1 − .3) = 11.43%, which is higher than the yield of the corporate bond (10 percent).

(*b*)   Robert should buy the corporate bond, since his tax equivalent yield of the municipal bond is 8%/(1 − .15) = 9.41%, which is lower than the yield of the corporate bond.

(*c*)   The choices are different since the brothers are in different tax brackets. The tax advantage of the municipal bond is greater for Steve since he is in a higher tax bracket.

15.14 You can invest in a municipal bond yielding 7 percent or a corporate bond yielding 10 percent. Which one is the better of the two if your marginal federal income tax rate is

(*a*)   15 percent

(*b*)   28 percent

(*c*)   33 percent

SOLUTION

(*a*)

$$\text{Tax equivalent yield} = \frac{\text{Tax-exempt yield}}{1 - \text{Tax rate}}$$

$$= \frac{7\%}{1 - .15}$$

$$= 8.24\%$$

The corporate bond is more attractive.

(*b*)

$$\frac{7\%}{1 - .28} = 9.72\%$$

The corporate bond is still attractive.

(*c*)

$$\frac{7\%}{1 - .33} = 10.45\%$$

The municipal bond is more attractive if you are in the 33 percent tax bracket.

15.15 You have a preferred stock paying $5.00 a year in dividends and having a market price of $25. What is the expected rate of return (yield)?

SOLUTION

The yield of the preferred stock is

$$\frac{\text{Annual dividend}}{\text{Market price}} = \frac{\$5}{\$25} = 20\%$$

15.16 Laura Wix recently paid $9,800 for a U.S. Treasury bill with a maturity value after 120 days of $10,000. What is the yield (discount yield) on the Treasury bill? (Assume a 360-day year.)

SOLUTION

$$\frac{P_1 - P_0}{P_0} \times \frac{360}{n}$$

where P_1 = redemption price, P_0 = purchase price, and n = maturity in days.

$$\frac{\$10,000 - \$9,800}{\$9,800} \times \frac{360}{120} = \frac{\$200}{\$9,800} \times 3 = .0204 \times 3$$

$$= .0612 = 6.12\%$$

Chapter 16

Investing in Tangibles: Real Estate and Other Real Assets

Investing in tangibles such as real estate, precious metals, and collectibles is considered an inflation hedge. Real estate investing still provides some tax shelters to many investors. In this chapter, you will learn about

Advantages and pitfalls of real estate investing

Determination of after-tax cash flow

How to value an income-producing property

Other forms of real estate investing such as Real Estate Investment Trusts (REITs), limited partnerships, and mortgage-backed securities

How to use leverage and increase return

Basics about precious metals

INVESTING IN REAL ESTATE IS AN I.D.E.A.L. SITUATION

It has often been said that real estate is the I.D.E.A.L. investment. Each of the five letters in IDEAL stands for an advantage to real estate as an investment.

"I" stands for *interest deduction*. ("I" could mean inflation hedge or income tax benefits.) The mortgage interest paid on the first and second residential homes are tax deductible. On the average, real estate is a good hedge against inflation because property values and the income from properties rise to keep pace with inflation.

"D" stands for *depreciation*. The building on your land depreciates in book value each year and you can deduct this depreciation from your gross income. This is only true for investment property and not residential.

"E" is for *equity buildup*. This buildup of a capital asset is like money in the bank. As you amortize a mortgage, the value of your equity investment will steadily rise. In the case of income-producing property, this amortization could mean that your tenants help you build your estate.

"A" is for *appreciation*. Your property value goes up every year, hopefully. Be careful because this is not guaranteed.

"L" is for *leverage*. When you buy a house you make a down payment, say, 10 percent and you borrow the balance, say, 90 percent. You get the benefit of all 100 percent even though you put up only 10 percent of your own money. You can maximize return with other people's money (OPM). The use of mortgage and OPM means that you can use small amounts of cash to gain control of large investments and earn large returns on the cash invested.

Besides I.D.E.A.L., you could add the following advantages of investing in real estate:

Tax-free refinancing. Mortgage proceeds even from refinancing are not taxable income to you. Therefore, refinancing is a way to recover your cash investment and, in some cases, you profit tax-free.

Pride of ownership. You may find greater personal satisfaction in owning property than stock certificates.

Investment and consumption. Certain types of real estate, such as land and vacation homes, can serve both as investments and as sources of pleasure.

WHAT ARE THE DISADVANTAGES WITH REAL ESTATE?

Real estate investing is not free from problems. Watch out for the following:

High transaction costs, such as brokerage commissions and closing expenses. These costs eat up short-term profits. *Warning:* If you might need your money out in a hurry, do not invest in real estate.

Negative cash flow with little down (too much leverage). In jargon, we call it an alligator.

Balloon payment due. The balloon payment is the unpaid balance of a mortgage loan that is paid off in a lump sum at the end of the loan term. This is typically a large amount. You may be unable to make the final payment, and thus lose your property.

Limited marketability. Lack of a central market or exchange to make real estate investments more liquid.

Management headache, such as unreliable tenants, or otherwise high professional management fees.

HOW TO ENHANCE THE VALUE OF REAL ESTATE

You may enhance the value of real estate in the following ways:

Buying below market

Making cosmetic improvements

Beneficial zoning changes

Making financing available

Rent increases in multifamily units

Subdividing property

However, watch out for get-rich schemes lacking economic reality. A *beginning* investor in real estate should keep the following in mind:

Buy a property you can easily manage.

Buy a property at a price you can afford.

Select a good location, particularly an "emerging" attractive area.

Buy a residential property containing from one to four units. A single unit, such as a single family house, is generally preferable.

If you are going to buy a property needing work, make sure it has "curable" problems that could be solved at a cost below the increment in value.

Try to buy a property that will generate revenue to cover your annual cash outlay.

Buy a property that is in good condition.

Rule of thumb: Since real estate is typically not a liquid investment, you should maintain at least 3 months' income or 3 months' living expenses in liquid funds as a precaution in the event that an emergency develops.

WHAT TYPES OF REAL ESTATE INVESTMENTS ARE THERE?

Kinds of real estate to invest in include

Undeveloped land

Residential rental property (for example, single family houses for rental, and multiunit apartments)

Commercial property (for example, office buildings, shopping centers, and industrial property)

Real Estate Investment Trusts (REITs)

FACTORS TO BE CONSIDERED REGARDING A REAL ESTATE INVESTMENT

Location

Method of financing the purchase of the property

Before-tax cash flow

After-tax cash flow

Vacancy rate for rental property

Gain or loss for tax purposes

Management problems

HOW DO YOU DETERMINE CASH FLOW FROM REAL ESTATE?

A necessary task in analyzing an income-producing property is determining the before-tax cash flow. When you know the cash flow, you can figure the return on your investment, calculate the tax shelter, and evaluate the investment. You don't need to be a real estate expert to determine a property's cash flow, common sense and some uncomplicated research will provide you with a base figure.

EXAMPLE 16.1 John Smith recently calculated the cash flow of a property offered to him for investment. We will go through his analysis, step by step, as an example of the process and format which you can follow. Mr. Smith is considering a duplex apartment. The property is located in an attractive suburb. The cost of the building is $219,000 and a $175,000, 30-year mortgage at 12 percent fixed rate is anticipated. The projected figures are based on the first full year of operation.

Step 1: *Figuring gross income*

The building has 2 three-bedroom apartments. To judge how much the apartments could rent for, Mr. Smith compared his building to ones in the area which were similar in quality of location and construction. He studied advertisements and questioned real estate brokers in the area. After weighing this information, he decided the three-bedroom apartments could rent for $950. Thus, the total maximum yearly rental income was $22,800.

$$2 \times \$950 = \$1,900 \qquad \$1,900 \times 12 = \$22,800$$

Additional income of $800 from laundry fees would make the possible total gross income $23,600.

Step 2: *Vacancy and credit losses*

To estimate the reduction in gross income caused by vacancies and bad debts, Mr. Smith looked at the result of the survey conducted by the local realtors and apartment associations. He estimated that the vacancy and bad debt rate would be 2 percent of possible gross income or $472 (2 percent of $23,600). Refer to Table 16-1 (Annual Property Operating Data).

Table 16-1   Annual Property Operating Data (12 Months, Projected)

Gross scheduled income		$22,800
+Other income		800
Total Gross Income		$23,600
−Vacancy/credit losses (2%)		472
Gross operating income (GOI)		$23,128
Operating expenses (with percent of GOI)		
Property insurance	1.93%	$ 446
Real estate taxes	13.22%	3,058
Repairs and maintenance	1.45%	335
Sewer and water	2.90%	671
Total operating expenses (19.50%)		4,510
Net operating income (80.50%)		$18,618
−Debt service (principal and interest)		21,601
Before-tax cash flow		$ (2,983)

Step 3: Operating expenses

For estimates of operating expenses, Mr. Smith carefully examined the record of previous costs by category. He came up with the cost figures as shown in Table 16-1, which are basically the previous costs plus adjustments for inflation.

Step 4: Net operating income

The projected operating expenses totaled $4,510 or 19.50% of gross operating income ($23,128). This left a net operating income (NOI) of $18,618 ($23,128 − $4,510). Now we proceed to calculating before-tax cash flow:

Step 5: Debt service (principal and interest payments)

Payments at 12 percent on a $175,000, 30-year fixed-rate mortgage would be $1,800.08 per month or $21,601 annually (principal amount is $635).

Step 6: Before-tax cash flow

The estimated before-tax cash flow was $(2,983) on an investment of $44,000 ($219,000 − $175,000). In order to compute after-tax cash flow, we have to add principal payments and deduct annual depreciation as follows:

Before-tax cash flow	$(2,983)
Add: Principal	635
Less: Depreciation	(5,575)*
Taxable income (loss)	$(7,923)
Your income tax rate	× .35
Value of taxable loss	$ 2,773

Assumption: The depreciable base of the building is 70 percent of $219,000 = $153,300. Annual depreciation is therefore $5,575 ($153,300/27.5 years by straight line).

Then your after-tax cash flow is

Before-tax cash flow	$(2,983)
Add: Value of taxable loss	2,773
After-tax cash flow	$ (210)

Note: Due to the deductibility of interest payments and annual depreciation for income tax purposes, after-tax cash flow is reduced by a substantial amount (in this example, after-tax cash flow was only −$210 as compared to before-tax cash flow of −$2,983). *Don't forget:* We did not even take into account the potential appreciation of the property. The return on your investment in this building should be calculated on the basis of both annual after-tax cash flows and the selling price of the property at the end of the holding period.

HOW DO YOU VALUE AN INCOME-PRODUCING PROPERTY?

There are several methods to arrive at the estimated value of an income-producing property. They are the gross income multiplier, net income multiplier, capitalization rate, and discounted cash flow.

Gross income multiplier (GIM).   Gross income multiplier is calculated as

$$\frac{\text{Purchase price}}{\text{Gross rental income}}$$

SOLVED PROBLEM 16.1

In Mr. Smith's example, what is the gross income multiplier?

SOLUTION

$$\frac{\$219,000}{\$23,600} = 9.28$$

A duplex in a similar neighborhood may be valued at "8 times annual gross." Thus, if its annual gross rental income amounts to $23,600, the value would be taken as $188,800 (8 × $23,600).

This approach should be used with caution. Different properties have different operating expenses which must be taken into account in determining the value of a property.

Net income multiplier.   Net income multiplier is calculated as

$$\frac{\text{Purchase price}}{\text{Net operating income (NOI)}}$$

SOLVED PROBLEM 16.2

In Mr. Smith's example, what is the net income multiplier?

SOLUTION

$$\frac{\$219,000}{\$18,618} = 11.76$$

Note that NOI is the gross income less allowances for vacancies and operating expenses, except depreciation and debt payments.

Capitalization rate.   Capitalization rate, or cap rate, is almost the same as the net income multiplier, only it is used more often. Also known as *income yield*, it is the reciprocal of the net income multiplier, that is,

$$\frac{\text{Net operating income (NOI)}}{\text{Purchase price}}$$

The higher the cap rate, the lower the perceived risk to the investor and the lower the asking price paid. Whether a piece of property is overpriced or not depends on the rate of a similar type of property derived from the marketplace. The method has two limitations: (1) it is based on only the first year's NOI, and (2) it ignores return through appreciation in property value.

SOLVED PROBLEM 16.3

Let us go back to Mr. Smith's example.

(*a*)   What is the duplex's capitalization rate?

(*b*)   Is the duplex overpriced if the market cap rate is 10 percent?

SOLUTION

(*a*) $18,618/$219,000 = 8.5%.

(*b*)   If the market rate is 10 percent, the fair market value of a similar duplex is $18,618/ 10% = $186,180. Mr. Smith may be overpaying for this property.

Discounted cash flow.   This method uses the present value technique under which the asking price or value of a real estate investment is the present worth of the future after-tax cash flows from the investment, discounted at the rate of return required by the investor.

SOLVED PROBLEM 16.4

You require a rate of return of 10 percent on a piece of property advertised for sale at $150,000. You estimate that rents can be increased each year for 5 years. You expect that after all expenses you would have an after-tax cash flow of $5,000, $5,200, $5,400, $5,600, and $5,800 for each year. You also expect that this property can sell for $200,000 at the end of the fifth year. How much would you be willing to pay for this property?

SOLUTION

We can set up the present value table as follows:

Year	After-Tax Cash Flow	Present Value of $1 at 10%	Total Present Value
1	$ 5,000	.909	$ 4,545
2	5,200	.826	4,295
3	5,400	.751	4,055
4	5,600	.683	3,825
5	5,800	.621	3,602
Sell property	200,000	.621	124,200
Present value of property			$144,522

You would be willing to pay $144,522 for this property.

WHAT ARE REAL ESTATE INVESTMENT TRUSTS (REITs)?

In some situations, a direct investment in real estate is impractical, and yet you may be aware of the advantages of a real estate investment and want some of its qualities in an investment portfolio. There are three indirect ways of investing in real estate. These are through pooled real estate investment arrangements, such as real estate investment trusts, limited partnerships, and mortgage-backed investments.

Real estate investment trusts (REITs) are corporations that operate much like *closed-end mutual funds*, investing shareholders' money in diversified real estate or mortgage portfolios instead of stocks or bonds. Their shares trade on the major stock exchanges or over-the-counter.

By law, REITs must distribute 95 percent of their net earnings to shareholders, and in turn they are exempt from corporate taxes on income or gains.

HOW ABOUT REIT YIELDS?

Since REIT earnings are not taxed before they are distributed, you get a larger percentage of the profits than with stocks. REIT yields are high.

WHAT ARE THE TYPES OF REITs?

There are three types of REITs: Equity REITs invest primarily in income-producing properties, mortgage REITs lend funds to developers or builders, and hybrid REITs do both. Equity REITs are considered the safest; however, their total returns are the lowest of the three.

WHAT YOU SHOULD KNOW ABOUT REITs?

Where to buy	Stockbrokers
Pluses	• Dividend income with competitive yields
	• Potential appreciation in price
	• A liquid investment in an illiquid area
	• Means of portfolio diversification and participation in a variety of real estate with minimal cash outlay
Minuses	• Possible glut in real estate or weakening demand
	• Market risk: possible decline in share price
Safety	Low
Liquidity	Very high: shares traded on major exchanges or over-the-counter and therefore sold at any time
Taxes	Income subject to tax upon sale

HOW SHOULD YOU SELECT AN REIT?

Before buying any REIT, be sure to read the latest annual report, *The Value Line Investment Survey, Audit Investment's Newsletter,* or *Realty Stock Review.* Check the following points:

Track record.   How long in business as well as solid dividend record.

Debt level.   Make sure that the unsecured debt level is low.

Cash flow.   Make sure that operating cash flow covers the dividend.

Adequate diversification.   Beware of REITs investing in only one type of property.

Property location.   Beware of geographically depressed areas.

Type of property.   Nursing homes, some apartment buildings, shopping centers presently favored; "seasoned" properties preferred.

Aggressive management.   Avoid REITs that do not upgrade properties.

Earnings.   Monitor earnings regularly; be prepared to sell when the market or property location weakens.

WHAT ARE LIMITED PARTNERSHIPS (SYNDICATES)?

A limited partnership (syndicate) is another form of investing in real estate that enables investors to buy into real estate projects too large for a single investor. For example, a group of investors form a partnership, each putting up a specified amount of money to purchase a large project such as an apartment complex or a shopping mall.

Syndicates have both general and limited partners. The *general manager* usually originates and manages the project for a fee, while the *limited partners* invest funds and are liable only for the amount of their investment. The advantages of limited partnerships are

Enable you to invest in a large-size project with professional management

Offers possible price appreciation

Helps you obtain a tax-sheltered cash flow

The disadvantages, or risks, of syndicates are the following:

Suffers from illiquidity since there is no active secondary market, unlike REITs.

High management fees and expenses.

Difficult for average investors to understand the fine print of syndicates in terms of the complex risks and rewards associated with them.

Adverse tax rulings can destroy the widely publicized tax benefits of syndicates.

WHAT ARE MORTGAGE-BACKED INVESTMENTS?

A third way to get into the real estate market is through mortgage-backed (pass-through) securities. A mortgage-backed security is a share in an organized pool of residential mortgages, the principal and interest payments on which are passed through to shareholders, usually monthly. There are several kinds of mortgage-backed securities. They include:

1. *Ginnie Maes,* which is the pet name given for Government National Mortgage Association (GNMA) securities

2. *Freddie Macs,* which is the nickname for Federal Home Loan Mortgage Corporation (FHLMC) securities

3. *Fannie Mae,* which is the name given for Federal National Mortgage Association (FNMA) securities

4. *Collaterized mortgage obligations* (CMOs), which are mortgage-backed securities that separate mortgage pools into short-, medium-, and long-term portions

Mortgage-backed securities enjoy liquidity and a high degree of safety since they are either government-sponsored or otherwise insured. Most of them are sold, however, in minimum amounts of $25,000, which is out of reach for most small investors.

SHOULD YOU USE LEVERAGE WHEN INVESTING IN REAL ESTATE?

Leverage means the use of other people's money (OPM) in an effort to increase the reward for investing. To a lot of people, it means risk. The fact of the matter is using leverage in real estate investing is an exciting way to earn big yields on small dollars, and you should not fear taking a chance. When you are building real estate wealth, leverage will help you grow quickly without involving too much risk (as long as you watch out for some pitfalls, which will be discussed later). High-leveraged investing in real estate is especially powerful when inflation is in full swing. High-leverage investors have numbers going for them because property values rise faster than the interest charges on their borrowed money.

To see the full power of high-leverage investing, take a look at the following example:

EXAMPLE 16.2   You pay a seller $100,000 cash for a piece of property. During the next 12 months, the property appreciates 5 percent and grows in resale value to $105,000. The $5,000 gain equals a 5 percent yield on your investment. But suppose you had put down only 10 percent ($10,000) in the property and mortgaged the balance. Now, your return on investment leaps to an astonishing 50 percent ($5,000/$10,000). Another way of looking at the result is: Since you only put down $10,000 on $100,000 worth of property, you actually control an asset 10 times the value of your actual cash outlay. This means 5% × 10 times = 50%. (In this example, for simplicity, we've omitted mortgage interest costs as well as the return on the $10,000 you would have invested somewhere else, plus any rental income you would have earned from the property.)

Let us expand the scenario to further see the impact of leverage.

EXAMPLE 16.3   Instead of putting 100 percent down ($100,000), you put down 10 percent ($10,000) and bought nine more pieces of property, each costing $100,000, and each bought with 10 percent down ($10,000). Again assume that they appreciate at the rate of 5 percent. Therefore, your wealth increases: $5,000 apiece × 10 pieces = $50,000. All that in 1 year. *Tip:* Tying up your wealth in one property ($100,000) costs you $45,000 ($50,000 − $5,000). Conversely, by spreading your funds over more properties and leveraging the balance, you would multiply your earnings 10 times.

Remember: The lower the amount of cash invested, the higher your return (from value appreciation and/or rental income). On the other hand, the larger your cash investment, the lower your return.

Also, remember, a higher appreciation will greatly increase earnings on your leveraged investment.

PITFALLS OF HIGH-LEVERAGED REAL ESTATE INVESTING

High-leveraged real estate investing sounds real good as long as you watch out for some of the pitfalls. They are

Property values can go down as well as up. Some types of real estate and some parts of the country are experiencing value declines. An example is Texas.

— Select the property carefully.
— Anticipate a rising market due to a lower mortgage rate or a high inflation rate before you jump in a high-leverage world.

Look out for negative cash flow. Income from highly leveraged property may be insufficient to cover operating expenses and debt payments. Do not overpay for property and underestimate costs. *Warning:* Buying for little or nothing down is easy. The difficult part is making the payments. You should try to avoid negative cash flow. (*Note:* Losses are tax deductible, however.)

Watch out for deferred maintenance. Deferred maintenance can create lots of problems down the road. You can avoid hidden costs and potential future expenditure by bargaining for a fair (or less than market) price and reasonable terms. In any case, overrepair is poison to the high-leverage investor.

HOW ABOUT INVESTING IN PRECIOUS METALS?

Investments in tangible assets such as gold, silver, and other precious metals have gained popularity in the last decade. They offer

A hedge against inflation

An opportunity to diversify holdings

Psychic pleasure

It should be noted, however, that this type of defensive investment does not produce current income. Further, it is not an investment easily converted into cash. Appreciation may take years and resale may not be easy.

Gold and silver are two highly volatile forms of tangible assets in which price movements often run counter to events in the economy and the world. Bad news is good news (and vice versa) for precious metal investors. Gold and silver may be generally bought in bullion or bulk form, as coins, in the commodities futures market, indirectly through securities of firms specializing in gold or silver mining, or through mutual funds investing in gold or silver.

Precious gems and other collectibles, such as art, antiques, stamps, Chinese ceramics, and rare books, have attracted the attention of investors. Profits are often very high. But don't invest in these tangibles unless you have product and market knowledge.

Tangibles are inflation hedges. In the decade of the 1970s oil, gold, U.S. coins, silver, and stamps had the highest compound returns, above 20 percent. For 1980 to 1985, which is a period of rapid disinflation, financial assets such as bonds, stocks, and Treasury bills had higher returns than every category of tangible assets. In fact, gold and silver suffered huge losses (more than 11 percent) in the early 1980s.

Review Questions

(1) _____ stands for an advantage to real estate as an investment.

(2) The use of _____ means that you can use small amounts of cash to gain control of large investments and earn large returns on the cash invested.

(3) The _____ is the unpaid balance of a mortgage loan that is paid off in a lump sum at the end of the loan term.

(4) A necessary task in analyzing an income-producing property is determining the _____ .

(5) There are three indirect ways of investing in real estate: pooled real estate investment arrangements, limited partnerships, and _____ .

(6) A _____ is a form of organization that enables investors to buy real estate projects too large for a single investor.

(7) A _____ is a share in an organized pool of residential mortgages, the principal and interest payments on which are passed through to shareholders.

(8) _____ means the use of other people's money in an effort to increase the reward for investing.

(9)   The lower the amount of cash invested, the _____ your return.

(10)   _____ and _____ are two highly volatile forms of tangible assets in which price movements often run counter to events in the economy and the world.

(11)   REITs must distribute _____ percent of their net earnings to shareholders.

Answers: (1) IDEAL; (2) OPM; (3) balloon payment; (4) before-tax cash flow; (5) mortgage-backed investments; (6) limited partnership; (7) mortgage-backed security; (8) Leverage; (9) higher; (10) Gold, silver; (11) 95.

Additional Solved Problems

16.1 The advertised price on a duplex apartment is $240,000 and the gross rental income totals $30,000. What is the gross income multiplier (GIM)?

SOLUTION

$$GIM = \frac{\text{Asking price of property}}{\text{Gross rental income}}$$

$$= \frac{\$240,000}{\$30,000} = 8$$

16.2 Jon Stevenson is considering the purchase of a small apartment which has a current annual gross rental income of $41,500 as an investment. The gross rental multiplier (GIM) for similar properties in the same general area of the city is about 7. What is a likely value of the apartment?

SOLUTION

$$\text{Asking price} = \text{Gross rental income} \times \text{GIM}$$

$$\$290,500 = \$41,500 \times 7$$

16.3 In Problem 16.1, the net operating income (NOI) is $20,500. What is the net income multiplier?

SOLUTION

$$\text{Net income multiplier} = \frac{\text{Purchase price}}{\text{Net operating income (NOI)}}$$

$$= \frac{\$240,000}{\$20,500} = 11.71$$

16.4 The net operating income (NOI) is $36,000 on an office building with a total investment of $270,000. What is the capitalization rate?

SOLUTION

$$\text{Capitalization rate} = \frac{\text{Net operating income (NOI)}}{\text{Purchase price}}$$

$$= \frac{\$36,000}{\$270,000} = 13.33\%$$

16.5 John Tonneli is considering the purchase of a four-plex, which has a net operating income (NOI) of $33,500. If he requires a capitalization rate of 8 percent, what would be his asking price?

SOLUTION

$$\text{Asking price} = \frac{\text{NOI}}{\text{Capitalization rate}}$$

$$= \frac{\$33,500}{.08} = \$418,750$$

16.6 Glenn and Anne are comparing two residential income properties as investments. Given the financial data on two properties:

	TRIPLEX A	TRIPLEX B
Gross rental income	$ 30,000	$ 24,000
Net operating income (NOI)	15,000	15,000
Asking price	200,000	180,000

(a) Calculate the GIM for both properties.

(b) Which one should they buy, given that the GIM for comparable properties in their area is 7?

(c) Calculate the net income multiplier for both properties. Which one should they buy?

(d) What method should they use to make a selection?

SOLUTION

(a) The gross income multiplier (GIM) is calculated as

$$\frac{\text{Purchase price}}{\text{Gross rental income}}$$

Triplex A: $200,000/$30,000 = 6.67
Triplex B: $180,000/$24,000 = 7.5

(b) They should buy Triplex A.

(c) The net income multiplier is calculated as

$$\frac{\text{Purchase price}}{\text{Net operating income (NOI)}}$$

Triplex A: $200,000/$15,000 = 13.33
Triplex B: $180,000/$15,000 = 12
Based on the net income multiplier, they should buy Triplex B.

(d) They should use the net income multiplier since NOI accounts for expenses and allowances for vacancies.

16.7 Dana Carter is considering buying a duplex as an investment. The gross rentals are $30,000 a year. The gross income, less allowances for vacancies and expenses (except depreciation and mortgage payments), is $20,000 a year. The asking price is $180,000.

(a) What is the gross income multiplier?

(b) What is the capitalization rate?

(c) Assume that the typical cap rate for similar properties in the area is 10.3. Should Dana buy this property?

SOLUTION

(a) The GIM = $180,000/$30,000 = 6.0.

(b)

$$\text{Capitalization rate} = \frac{\text{Net operating income (NOI)}}{\text{Purchase price}}$$

$$= \frac{\$20,000}{\$180,000} = 11.11\%$$

(c) Yes, she should since 11.11 percent is greater than the market cap rate in the neighborhood.

16.8 You are considering the purchase of a duplex which is expected to generate the following after-tax cash flow in each of the next 5 years:

YEARS	AFTER-TAX CASH FLOW
1	$3,000
2	3,300
3	3,600
4	3,900
5	4,200

The expected selling price of the property will be $150,000 in 5 years. You desire an after-tax return of 10 percent.

(a) What is the present worth of this property?

(b) The seller is asking for $140,000. Should you buy this property?

SOLUTION

(a) We can set up the present value table (from Appendix Table 3) as follows:

Year	After-Tax Cash Flow	Present Value of $1 at 10%	Total Present Value
1	$ 3,000	.909	$ 2,727
2	3,300	.826	2,726
3	3,600	.751	2,704
4	3,900	.683	2,664
5	4,200	.621	2,608
Sell property	150,000	.621	93,150
Present value of property			$106,579

(b) No, since at the asking price of $140,000, the property is overpriced.
You might want to make an offer of around $106,579.

16.9 Christy expects to realize $4,000 a year from an investment in a small office condo and to sell it at the end of 5 years for $100,000 after selling costs and taxes. Her required rate of return is 12 percent. How much would she be willing to pay for this office condo?

SOLUTION

We will use the discounted cash flow method. The present value table (Appendix Table 3) looks as follows:

Year	After-Tax Cash Flow	Present Value of $1 at 12%	Total Present Value
1	$ 4,000	.893	$ 3,572
2	4,000	.797	3,188
3	4,000	.712	2,848
4	4,000	.636	2,544
5	4,000	.567	2,268
Sell property	100,000	.567	56,700
Present value of property			$71,120

Alternatively, using the table for present value of an annuity of $1 for 5 years (from Appendix Table 4) yields the same answer:

$$\$4,000 \times 3.605 = \$14,420$$

$$\$100,000 \times .567 = \underline{56,700}$$
$$\$71,120$$

$71,120 is the maximum price Christy would be willing to pay for the condo.

16.10 You are thinking of buying an income-producing property costing $200,000. It is expected to generate net income before interest and taxes of $30,000. You are in the 28 percent marginal tax bracket. You are offered the two options: (A) To put down the entire $100,000 or (B) to put down 10 percent. (Assume an interest charge of $22,226 based on a 12.5 percent, 30-year loan on $180,000.)

(a) Calculate the return on investment for both options.

(b) Comment on the effect of leverage (use of other people's money).

SOLUTION

(a)

OPTION	(A)	(B)
Your investment (1)	$200,000	$ 20,000 (10% × $200,000)
Amount of leverage	0	180,000
Total investment	$200,000	$200,000
Net income before interest and taxes	$ 30,000	$ 30,000
Less: Interest	0	22,226
Net income before taxes	$ 30,000	$ 7,774
Income tax (28%)	8,400	2,177
Net income after taxes (2)	$ 21,600	$ 5,597
Return on investment [(2)/(1)]	10.8%	28.0%

(b) The positive use of leverage tends to magnify your return on investment (28.0% versus 10.8%).

16.11 Gary Brennan recently bought a piece of property as an investment. The purchase price was $95,000, of which he paid $15,000 down.

   (a)   What was the loan-to-value ratio?

   (b)   What is the depreciation amount each year he can deduct from his income taxes? (Use the 27.5-year, straight-line method and assume a building value of 70 percent.)

SOLUTION

   (a)   The loan amount = $95,000 − $15,000 = $80,000.

$$\text{Loan-to-value ratio} = \frac{\$80,000}{\$95,000} = 84.2\%$$

   (b)   The value of the building which is depreciable is 70% × $95,000 = $66,500. The annual depreciation is $66,500/27.5 years = $2,418.

16.12 You bought a duplex for $100,000 which is expected to generate gross rental income of $10,000 annually. You are allowed to depreciate the building value (80 percent of the cost of the duplex) for 27.5 years. You are in the 28 percent marginal tax bracket.

   (a)   Calculate after-tax return on investment with and without depreciation. (Disregard operating and debt service expenses.)

   (b)   How much income taxes are saved due to depreciation?

SOLUTION

   (a)   The depreciable building value is $80,000/27.5 years = $2,909.

	WITHOUT DEPRECIATION	WITH DEPRECIATION
Gross rental income (1)	$10,000	$10,000
Less annual depreciation expense	—	2,909
Taxable income	$10,000	$ 7,091
Income taxes (28%) (2)	2,800	1,985
Return after taxes [(1) − (2)]	$ 7,200	$ 8,015
After-tax return (divided by $100,000)	7.2%	8.0%

   (b)   Due to the depreciation permitted, you save $815 in income taxes ($8,015 − $7,200) or 28% × $2,909.

16.13 Dave Steward has the choice of receiving $14,500 today as a down payment from someone who wants to purchase his rental property or a personal note for $24,000 payable in 6 years. If he could expect to earn 8 percent on such funds, which is the better choice?

SOLUTION

     The future value of $1 for 6 years at 8 percent (from Appendix Table 1) is 1.587. Hence the future value of $14,500 is $14,500 × 1.587 = $23,012. Thus, Dave would be better off taking the note for $24,000.

     Alternatively, using the concept of present value, the present value of $1 for 6 years at 8 percent (from Appendix Table 3) is .630. Hence the present worth of $24,000 is $24,000 × .630 = $15,120. Thus, the present worth of $24,000 received in 6 years is greater than $14,500 received now, and is the better choice.

16.14 Cindy Garvey purchased a small, four-unit apartment building 7 years ago for $138,500. Over the years she has added central air conditioning at a cost of $7,800, spent $1,830 on painting the interior and $1,300 on painting the exterior, replaced the carpeting in each apartment once at a cost of $485 each time, spent $2,340 on miscellaneous repairs, and built a four-bay carport at a cost of $1,600. Recently she sold the property for $179,200.

(a) How much did Cindy spend on capital improvements for the property?

(b) How much did she spend on repairs to the property?

(c) What was her price appreciation on this investment?

SOLUTION

(a) $9,400 = $7,800 + $1,600

(b) $7,410 = $1,830 + $1,300 + ($485 × 4) + $2,340

(c) $31,300 = $179,200 − $138,500 − $9,400

16.15 Mike Moore has the opportunity to purchase an office building for $400,000 with an expected life of 20 years. Looking over the financial details, he sees that annual net rental income is $50,000. If Mike wants a return of at least 15 percent, how much should he pay for the building?

SOLUTION

The present value of an annuity of $1 for 20 years at 15 percent (from Appendix Table 4) is 6.259. Hence the solution is $50,000 × 6.259 = $312,950. Thus, the price is too high for Mike to earn a 15 percent return.

16.16 John Van Decamp is considering the purchase of a 40-unit apartment building for which the asking price is $1.6 million. Rentals average $525 monthly for a gross income of $252,000. The building has an assumable first mortgage of $1 million for 25 years at 14 percent. John is asked to make a $600,000 down payment. The relevant financial data are given below.

Gross rental income			$252,000
−Vacancy/credit losses (5%)			12,000
Gross operating income (GOI)			$240,000
Operating expenses (with percent of GOI)			
Management expense	7.00%	$16,800	
Real estate taxes, repairs and			
maintenance, utilities	5.00%	12,000	
Total operating expenses (12%)			28,800
Net operating income (88%)			$211,200
−Debt service (principal and interest)*			145,498
Before-tax cash flow			$ 65,702

*From the mortgage amortization table (Appendix Table 5) for a 25-year, 14 percent loan.

(a) Calculate the gross income multiplier.

(b) Calculate the cap rate.

SOLUTION

(a) GIM = $1,600,000/$252,000 = 6.35

(b) Cap rate = $211,200/$1,600,000 = 13.2%

16.17 In Problem 16.16, assume further that:

1. Depreciation is 6.1 percent of the building value of $1,400,000, which is the asking price less the land value ($1,600,000 − $200,000), which may be deducted for income taxes.

2. John is in the 50 percent tax bracket.

3. The principal payment amounts to $5,498 [$145,498 − 14%($1,000,000)]. Calculate the after-tax cash flow for this property.

SOLUTION

In order to compute after-tax cash flow, we have to add principal payment and deduct annual depreciation as follows:

Before-tax cash flow	$ 65,702	
Add: Principal	5,498	
Less: Depreciation	85,400	(6.1% × $1,400,000)
Taxable income (loss)	$(14,200)	
Income tax rate	× .50	
Value of taxable loss	$ 7,100	

Then John's after-tax cash flow is

Before-tax cash flow	$65,702
Add: Value of taxable loss	7,100
After-tax cash flow	$72,802

Note that part of the mortgage payment represents loan repayment and produces "equity buildup" (the value of the property less indebtedness). This equity, which in this problem amounts to $5,498, is realized when the property is sold, and therefore is not included in the after-tax cash flow.

16.18 You are considering the purchase of a residential property for rental, with a 3-year holding period. Rental income for the first year is $10,000, and is expected to increase by 10 percent for each of the subsequent years. The property was financed by an $80,000 loan, at 10 percent for 30 years. Use the following worksheet format to calculate the after-tax cash flow for each of the 3 years:

Cash Flow Analysis Worksheet

	YEAR 1	YEAR 2	YEAR 3
Gross scheduled income	$10,000		
Less: Vacancy (5%)			
Gross operating income			
Less: Operating expenses	1,840	$1,940	$2,040
Net operating income			
Less: Annual debt service	8,485	8,485	8,485
Before-tax cash flow			
Add: Principal	153	437	719
Less: Depreciation	2,900	2,900	2,900
Taxable income (loss)			
Tax rate	33%	33%	33%
Value of taxable loss			
Add: Before-tax cash flow			
After-tax cash flow			

SOLUTION

Cash Flow Analysis Worksheet

	YEAR 1	YEAR 2	YEAR 3
Gross scheduled income	$10,000	$11,000	$12,100
Less: Vacancy (5%)	500	550	605
Gross operating income	$ 9,500	$ 10,450	$ 11,495
Less: Operating expenses	(1,840)	(1,940)	(2,040)
Net operating income	$ 7,660	$ 8,510	$ 9,455
Less: Annual debt service	(8,485)	(8,485)	(8,485)
Before-tax cash flow	$ (825)	$ 25	$ 970
Add: Principal	153	437	719
Less: Depreciation	(2,900)	(2,900)	(2,900)
Taxable income (loss)	$ (3,572)	$ (2,438)	$ (1,211)
Tax rate	33%	33%	33%
Value of taxable loss	1,179	805	400
Add: Before-tax cash flow	(825)	25	970
After-tax cash flow	$ 354	$ 830	$ 1,370

Chapter 17

Mutual Funds and Diversification

If you are an investor who is interested in receiving the benefit of professional portfolio management but do not have sufficient funds and/or time to purchase a diversified mix of securities, you will find the purchase of mutual fund shares attractive. In this chapter, you will learn the following:

Special features and advantages of investing in mutual funds

How to evaluate the performance of a mutual fund

Fees associated with mutual funds

Types of funds and how they fit into your investment goals

Special types of funds such as money market funds, bond funds, and unit investment-trusts

How to read mutual fund quotations

How to calculate your real return on mutual fund investments

What beta means in terms of risk of a fund

Where to buy mutual fund shares

What factors to consider in selecting a mutual fund

WHAT ARE THE SPECIAL FEATURES OF MUTUAL FUND INVESTING?

A mutual fund is an investment company, run by professional managers, that pools the money of many people to purchase a diverse portfolio of investments. Participation is characterized by ownership of shares of the fund which represents the fund's investments. Ownership of shares gains the investor a pro rata interest in each of the fund's investments.

SOLVED PROBLEM 17.1

ABC Mutual Fund owns the following:

STOCK	NUMBER OF SHARES
IBM	100
Xerox	200
GM	50

If you made a 2 percent investment in ABC Fund, how many shares is that equivalent to of the stock?

SOLUTION

Two shares of IBM, four shares of Xerox, and one share of GM.

Major advantages of investing in mutual funds are

1. *Diversification.*   Each share of a fund gives you an interest in a cross section of stocks, bonds, or other investments. You can own shares in a mutual fund with a diversified portfolio—many different investments. The variety and large number of holdings also help lessen risk. *Note:* By spreading money among many investments, there is a better chance of picking some that will do well.

2. *Small minimum investment.*   You can achieve diversification with a small amount of money ($250 or less) through the large number of securities in the portfolio. A handful of funds have no minimums.

3. *Automatic reinvestment.* Most funds allow you to automatically reinvest dividends and any capital gains which may arise from the fund's buying and selling activities. Funds typically do not charge a sales fee on automatic reinvestments.

4. *Automatic withdrawals.* Most funds will allow you to withdraw money on a regular basis.

5. *Liquidity.* You are allowed to redeem the shares owned.

6. *Switching.* You may want to make changes in your investments.

Your long-term goals may remain the same, but the investment climate does not. To facilitate switching among funds, such companies as Fidelity and Vanguard have introduced "families" of funds. You may move among them with relative freedom, usually at no fee.

WHAT IS NET ASSET VALUE (NAV)?

The price of a mutual fund share is measured by net asset value (NAV), which equals

$$\frac{\text{Fund's total assets} - \text{Liabilities}}{\text{Number of shares outstanding in the fund}}$$

SOLVED PROBLEM 17.2

In Solved Problem 17.1, assume that on a particular day, the market values below existed. Then the NAV of the fund is calculated as follows (assume the fund has no liabilities):

(a)	IBM ($100 per share × 100 shares)	$10,000
(b)	Xerox ($50 per share × 200 shares)	10,000
(c)	IBM ($75 per share × 50 shares)	3,750
(d)	Value of the fund's portfolio	$23,750
(e)	Number of shares outstanding in the fund	1,000
(f)	Net asset value (NAV) per share [(d)/(e)]	$ 23.75

If you own 5 percent of the fund's outstanding shares, what is the value of your investment?

SOLUTION

You own 50 shares (5% × 1,000 shares). The value of your investment is $1,187.50 ($23.75 × 50).

HOW DO YOU MAKE MONEY IN A MUTUAL FUND?

There are three ways to make money in mutual funds. NAV is only one of the three. You also receive dividends and capital gains.

DIVIDENDS

Mutual funds are closely regulated by federal and state laws. In order to retain their tax-exempt status, mutual funds ordinarily must distribute at least 90 percent of their income each year. *Remember:* The amount of income depends largely on the objective of the fund itself. For tax purposes, dividends from mutual funds are usually treated as corporate dividends.

CAPITAL GAINS DISTRIBUTION

When a mutual fund sells securities at higher prices than it paid for them, this gain will be distributed to the shareholders as a capital gain distribution. Some funds invest in small, fast growing companies and other speculative stocks in an attempt to achieve high returns from capital gains.

Most investors grew up on stocks and they are used to just looking at a price (NAV) in the paper. Keep in mind that for evaluating stock performance this is perfectly acceptable, but not for mutual funds. Do not just look at the NAV in the paper. It only indicates the current market value of the underlying portfolio. Be sure to know how many shares you have in order to figure out the total value of your holdings. Chances are, anyone in a fund for more than several months has more shares than when he/she started. This is because most funds pay dividends and capital gains distributions, which usually are reinvested automatically in the form of additional shares.

To get a good feel for how many shares are owned, look at the most recent statement from the fund company. By multiplying the number of shares by the net asset value per share, you can come up with a more accurate picture of how much money you have actually made.

To give you an idea, take a 6-year investment in T. Rowe Price's International Fund. $10,000 invested in 1982 is worth more than $32,000 for a 220 percent ($22,000/$10,000) total return at the end of 1988. But nearly half of those gains came from capital gains and dividends. Just looking at net asset value would have come up with only about a 120 percent return.

HOW DO YOU CALCULATE A RATE OF RETURN ON MUTUAL FUND INVESTMENTS?

Since the return on your investment in a mutual fund is distributed in three ways (dividends, capital gains distribution, and price appreciation), the annual rate of return, or the holding period return (HPR), in a mutual fund is calculated incorporating all these three, as follows:

$$HPR = \frac{\text{Dividends} + \text{Capital gain distributions} + (\text{Ending NAV} - \text{Beginning NAV})}{\text{Beginning NAV}}$$

where (Ending NAV − Beginning NAV) represents price appreciation.

SOLVED PROBLEM 17.3

Your mutual fund paid dividends of $.50 per share and capital gain distributions of $.35 per share over the course of the year, and had a price (NAV) at the beginning of the year of $6.50 that rose to $7.50 per share by the end of the year. What is the holding period return (HPR)?

SOLUTION

$$HPR = \frac{\$.50 + \$.35 + (\$7.50 - \$6.50)}{\$6.50} = \frac{\$1.85}{\$6.50} = 28.46\%$$

A more accurate way of calculating your personal rate of return in a mutual fund will be discussed in a future section ("Performance of Mutual Funds").

WHAT FEES ARE ASSOCIATED WITH MUTUAL FUNDS?

All mutual funds charge some type of fee. It is important that you know the associated fees in order to judge whether your investment is worth the cost of these fees. The fees associated with mutual funds can be categorized in the following ways: loads, management and expense fees, 12b-1 fees, redemption fees or exit fees, and deferred sales charges or back-end loads.

LOAD

A load is a sales commission charged to purchase shares in many mutual funds sold by brokers or other members of a sales force. Typically, the charge ranges from 2 percent to 8.5 percent of the initial investment. The charge is added to the net asset value per share when determining the offer price. Not all mutual funds have a load. It is important to note that the absence of a sales charge in no way affects the performance of the fund's management and ultimately the return on investment.

MANAGEMENT AND EXPENSE FEES

All funds, whether "no load" or "load," have management and expense fees—paid by the fund to the fund's advisor for managing its investments. They represent computer costs, salaries, and office expenses. These fees run in the range of .25 to 1.5 percent of the fund's assets on an annual basis. An unusually high management fee and/or expense fee might indicate poor management of fund costs.

12b-1 FEES

These fees cover advertising and marketing costs, but do nothing to improve the performance of the fund. Their main purpose is to bring new customers to the fund, and ultimately more money for the fund's management to invest.

REDEMPTION FEES OR EXIT FEES

When you sell your share of a fund, some funds charge a fee. These fees can range from a flat $5 to 2 percent of the amount withdrawn.

DEFERRED SALES CHARGES OR BACK-END LOADS

Similar to exit fees these fees are charged when you withdraw money from the fund. These charges are intended to discourage frequent trading in the fund. Deferred sales charges are usually on a scale which reduces them each year until it disappears after a predetermined period of time. An example of a mutual fund having a back-end load is Prudential-Bache.

WHAT ARE THE TYPES OF MUTUAL FUNDS?

Mutual funds may be classified into different types, according to organization, the fees charged, methods of trading funds, and their investment objectives.

In *open-end funds,* you buy from and sell shares back to the fund itself. This type of fund offers to sell and redeem shares on a continual basis for an indefinite time period. Shares are purchased at NAV plus commission, and redeemed at NAV less a service charge. On the other hand, *closed-end funds* operate with a fixed number of shares outstanding, which trade among individuals in secondary markets like common stocks. That is, if you wish to invest in a closed-end fund, you must purchase shares from someone willing to sell them. In the same manner, in order to sell shares you must locate a buyer. Transactions involving closed-end mutual funds are easy to arrange, however, since most of these funds are traded on the New York Stock Exchange, American Stock Exchange, or the over-the-counter market. All open- and closed-end funds charge management fees. A major point of closed-end funds is the size of discount or premium, which is the difference between their market prices and their NAVs. Many funds of this type sell at discounts, which enhance their investment appeal.

Funds that charge sales commissions are called *load funds. No-load funds* do not charge sales commissions. Sales strategy includes advertisements and (800) toll-free telephone orders. Load funds perform no better than no-loads. Many experts believe you should buy only no-load or low-load funds. You should have no trouble finding such funds that meet your investment requirements.

If you are interested in investing in mutual funds, obtain and study closely the *prospectus* in order to select a fund meeting your investment goals and tolerance for risk. The prospectus contains such information as the fund's investment objective, method of selecting securities, performance figures, sales charges, and other expenses.

Depending on their investment philosophies, mutual funds generally fall into 10 major categories:

1. *Money market funds.* Money market funds are mutual funds that invest exclusively in debt securities maturing within 1 year, such as government securities, commercial paper, and certificates of deposit. These funds provide a safety valve because the price never changes. They are known as dollar funds, which means you always buy and sell shares at $1.00 each. Money market funds are a good choice if you are looking for high interest income with no risk of losing your principal.

2. *Growth funds.* Growth funds seek to maximize their return through capital gains. They typically invest in the stocks of established companies which are expected to rise in value faster than inflation. These stocks are best if you desire steady growth over a long-term period but feel little need for income in the meantime.

3. *Aggressive growth funds.* Aggressive growth funds are willing to take greater risk in order to yield maximum appreciation (instead of current dividend income). They invest in the stocks of upstart, and high-tech oriented companies. Return can be great but so can risk. *Note:* These funds are suitable only if you are not particularly concerned with short-term fluctuations in return but with long-term gains. Aggressive investment strategies include leverage purchases, options, short sales, and even the purchase of junk stock. Aggressive growth funds are also called maximum capital gain, capital appreciation, and small-company growth funds.

4. *Income funds.* Income funds are best if you seek a high level of interest and dividend income. Income funds usually invest in high-quality bonds and blue-chip stocks with consistently high dividends.

5. *Growth and income funds.* Growth and income funds seek both current dividend income and capital gains. The goal of these funds is to provide long-term growth without much variation in share value.

6. *Balanced funds.* Balanced funds combine investments in common stock and bonds and often preferred stock, and attempt to provide income and some capital appreciation. Balanced funds tend to underperform all-stock funds in strong bull markets.

7. *Bond and preferred stock funds.* These funds invest in both bonds and preferred stock with the emphasis on income rather than growth. The funds that invest exclusively in bonds are called bond funds. There are two types of bond funds: bond funds that invest in corporate bonds, and municipal bond funds that provide tax-free income and a diversified portfolio of municipal securities. If you are in a high tax bracket, consider investing in tax-free municipal bond funds. In periods of volatile interest rates, bond funds are subject to price fluctuations. The value of the shares will fall when interest rates rise. Some municipal bond funds provide insurance on the amount invested.

8. *Index funds.* Index funds invest in a portfolio of corporate stocks, the composition of which is determined by the Standard & Poor's 500 or some other market index. Vanguard Index Trust invests exclusively in all the companies comprising the Standard and Poor's 500 Stock Index.

9. *Sector funds.* Sector funds are funds that invest in one or two fields or industries. These funds are risky in that they rise and fall depending on how the individual fields or industries do. They are also called specialized funds.

10. *International funds.* International funds invest in the stocks and bonds of corporations traded on foreign exchanges. Some international funds invest exclusively in one region such as Fidelity Europe Fund. These funds make significant gains when the dollar is falling and foreign stock prices are rising.

INVESTMENT PROGRAMS TIED WITH MUTUAL FUNDS

Not only are there many different types of mutual funds available to investors, there are many diverse ways of buying into them. The investment method should be based on your financial position and the ultimate goal of investing (extra income, retirement fund, education fund, etc.). Below are some of the more common investment programs available.

Withdrawal plan. As an investor in a mutual fund, you can receive monthly or quarterly payments of a specified amount.

Accumulation plan. The investor generally invests on a monthly basis. Minimum investments usually range between $25 and $50 a month. This plan is an excellent choice if you are a long-term investor.

Automatic dividend reinvestment.   Under this plan, all proceeds from the fund (dividends and capital gains) are automatically reinvested.

Individual Retirement Accounts (IRA).   IRA allows you to set aside up to $2,000 before-tax income annually. Withdrawals are made after retirement when it is assumed that you are in a lower tax bracket.

403(B) plan.   Employees of nonprofit organizations, hospitals, school districts, or municipalities can shelter before-tax income in plans of this type.

Payroll deduction plans.   Investment through payroll deduction allows companies to purchase mutual fund shares for employees with lower or no-load charges.

Life insurance–mutual fund plans.   Funds of this type combine life insurance with shares of a particular mutual fund. If the fund does well it will pay your life insurance premiums. If, however, the fund's share value drops significantly you may be required to pay the premium yourself.

MORE ABOUT MONEY MARKET FUNDS

Money market mutual funds invest in short-term government securities, commercial paper, and certificates of deposits. They provide more safety of principal than other mutual funds since net asset value never fluctuates. Each share has a net asset value of $1. The yield, however, fluctuates daily. The advantages are

Money market funds are no-load.

A minimum deposit in these funds can be as little as $1,000. If you want to buy short-term securities, a minimum purchase is at least $10,000.

The fund is a form of checking account, allowing you to write checks against your balance in the account. The usual minimum withdrawal is $500.

You earn interest daily.

You can use these funds as a "parking place" in which to put money while waiting to make another investment.

A disadvantage is your deposit in these funds is not insured as it is in a money market account or other federally insured deposit in banks.

WHAT DO YOU NEED TO KNOW ABOUT A BOND FUND?

There are three key facts about the bonds in any portfolio. If you cannot find them in the fund's annual report or prospectus, phone the fund and get the answers.

1. *Quality.*   Check the credit rating of the typical bond in the fund. Ratings by Standard & Poor's and Moody's show the relative danger that an issuer will default on interest or principal payments. AAA is the best grade. A rating of BB or lower signifies a junk bond.

2. *Maturity.*   The average maturity of your fund's bonds indicates how much you stand to lose if interest rates rise. The longer the term of the bonds, the more volatile is the price. For example, a 20-year bond may fluctuate in price four times as much as a 4-year issue.

3. *Premium or discount.*   Some funds with high current yields hold bonds that trade for more than their face value, or at a premium. Such funds are less vulnerable to losses if rates go up. Funds that hold bonds trading at a discount to face value can lose most.

You must keep in mind the following guidelines:

Rising interest rates drive down the value of all bond funds. For this reason, rather than focusing only on current yield, you should look primarily at total return (yield plus capital gains from falling interest rates or minus capital losses if rates climb).

All bond funds do not benefit equally from tumbling interest rates. If you think interest rates will decline and you want to increase your total return, buy funds that invest in U.S. Treasuries or top-rated corporate bonds. Consider high-yield corporate bonds (junk bonds) if you believe rates are stabilizing.

Unlike bonds, bond funds do not allow you to lock in a yield. A mutual fund with a constantly changing portfolio is not like an individual bond, which you can keep to maturity. If you want steady, secure income over several years or more, consider, as alternatives to funds, buying individual top-quality bonds or investing in a municipal bond unit trust, which maintains a fixed portfolio.

CONSIDERING UNIT INVESTMENT TRUSTS

Like a mutual fund, a unit investment trust offers to small investors the advantages of a large, professionally selected and diversified portfolio. Unlike a mutual fund, however, its portfolio is fixed; once structured, it is not actively managed. Unit investment trusts are available of tax-exempt bonds, money market securities, corporate bonds of different grades; mortgage-backed securities; preferred stocks; utility common stocks; and other investments. Unit trusts are most suitable for people who need a fixed income and a guaranteed return of capital. They disband and pay off investors after the majority of their investments have been redeemed.

HOW TO READ MUTUAL FUND QUOTATIONS

Below are quotations of mutual funds shown in a newspaper.

Funds	NAV	Offer Price	NAV Chg.
Acorn Fund	30.95	N.L.	+ .38
.	.	.	
.	.	.	
.	.	.	.
American Growth	8.52	9.31	+ .05

In a *load fund,* the price you pay for a share is called the offer price, and it is higher than net asset value (NAV), the difference being the commission. American Growth is a load fund. As shown above, American Growth has a load of $.79 ($9.31 − $8.52), or 8.49 percent ($.79/$9.31). Acorn Fund is a no-load fund, as "N.L." indicates. In a *no-load fund,* the price you pay is NAV.

In the case of a *closed-end fund,* the following is a typical listing shown in a newspaper.

Funds	NAV	Strike Price	% Diff.
Claremont	35.92	$29\frac{3}{8}$	−18.2
.	.	.	.
.	.	.	.
.	.	.	.
Nautilus	34.41	$34\frac{1}{2}$	+.2

In the "% Diff." column, negative difference means the shares sell at a discount; positive difference means they sell at a premium.

PERFORMANCE OF MUTUAL FUNDS

As discussed previously, mutual funds provide returns in the form of (1) dividend income, (2) capital gain distribution, and (3) change in capital (or NAV) of the fund. *Remember:* To calculate your personal rate of return, do not just look at the net asset value in the paper. Using the statement you receive from the fund company, fill out the form given in Fig. 17-1. The following example uses the data provided in Fig. 17-2 for ABC Mutual Company.

		EXAMPLE	**YOUR FUND**
1.	The number of months for which your fund's performance is being measured.	8	_____
2.	Your investment at the beginning of the period (multiply the total number of shares owned by the NAV) [(32.501 + 2.667) × $18.75]	$659.40	_____
3.	The ending value of your investment (multiply the number of shares you currently own by the current NAV) (57.508 × $20.15)	$1,158.79	_____
4.	Total dividends and capital gains received in cash ($10.40 + $13.60)	$24	_____
5.	All additional investments (any redemptions subtracted) ($100 + $100 + $150 + $50)	$400	_____
6.	Computation of your gain or loss		
	Step (a): Add line 2 to one-half of the total on line 5 [$659.40 + $\frac{1}{2}$ ($400)]	$859.40	_____
	Step (b): Add line 3 and line 4, then subtract one-half of the total on line 5 [($1,158.79 + $24) − $\frac{1}{2}$ ($400)]	$982.79	_____
	Step (c): Divide the step (b) sum by the step (a) sum ($982.79/$859.40)	1.144	_____
	Step (d): Subtract 1 from the result of step (c), then multiply by 100 [(1.144 − 1) × 100]	14.4%	_____
7.	Computation of your annualized return Divide the number of months on line 1 into 12; multiply the result by the step (d)% [($\frac{12}{8}$ × 14.4]	21.6%	_____

Fig. 17-1 Figuring your personal rate of return.

In assessing fund performance, you must also refer to the published *beta* of the fund to determine the amount of risk. Beta is based on the price swings of a fund compared with the market as a whole, measured by the Standard & Poor's 500-stock index. The higher the beta, the greater the risk.

Beta	What It Means
1.0	A fund moves up and down just as much as the market.
>1.0	The fund tends to climb higher in bull markets and dip lower in bear markets than the S&P index.
<1.0	The fund is less volatile (risky) than the market.

Betas for individual funds are widely available in many investment newsletters and directories. An example is *Value Line Investment Survey.*

Figure 17-2 below is an assumed mutual fund statement.

Date	Transaction	Dollar Amount		Share Price	Shares
	Beginning balance				32.501
7/01/19X1	Investment	$ 50.00		$18.75	2.667
9/7	Investment	100.00		20.63	4.847
9/25	Cash dividend at .26	10.40	(1)	—	—
10/02	Investment	100.00		21.53	4.645
11/30	Investment	150.00		19.55	7.673
12/31	Cash dividend at .26	13.60	(2)	—	—
12/31	Capital gain reinvestment at 1.03	53.90	(3)	20.01	2.694
2/27/19X2	Investment	50.00		20.15	2.481
	Total shares				57.508

(1) (32.501 + 2.667 + 4.847) shares × $.26 per share = 40.015 × .26 = $10.40

(2) (32.501 + 2.667 + 4.847 + 4.645 + 7.673) shares × $.26 per share = 52.333 × .26 = $13.60

(3) (32.501 + 2.667 + 4.847 + 4.645 + 7.673) shares × $1.03 per share = 52.333 × 1.03 = $53.90

Fig. 17-2   ABC Mutual Fund Inc.

MUTUAL FUND RATINGS

You can get help in selecting mutual funds from a number of sources, including investment advisory services that charge fees. More readily available sources, however, include *Money, Forbes, Barron's,* and *Personal Finance. Money* has a "Fund Watch" column appearing in each monthly issue. In addition, it ranks about 450 funds twice a year reporting each fund's 1-, 5-, and 10-year performances along with a risk rating. *Personal Finance* also rates mutual funds in terms of 3-month, 1-year, and 3-year performances and risk factor.

Forbes has an annual report covering each fund's performance in both up and down markets. *Value Line Investment Survey* shows the makeup of the fund's portfolio beta values. Information about no-load funds is contained in *The Individual Investor's Guide to No Load Mutual Funds* (American Association of Individual Investors, 612 N. Michigan Ave., Chicago, IL 60611). *Remember:* You should not choose a fund only on the basis of its performance rating. You should consider both performance and risk.

HOW TO CHOOSE A MUTUAL FUND?

What mutual fund to choose is not an easy question and there is no sure answer. It will be advisable to take the following steps:

1. Develop a list of funds that appear to meet your investment goals.

2. Obtain a prospectus. In the *prospectus,* you will find the fund's investment objectives. Read the statement of objectives as well as risk factors and investment limitations. Also request the Statement of Additional Information, which includes the details of fees and lists the investments, a copy of the annual report, and the most recent quarterly report.

3. Make sure the fund's investment objectives and investment policies meet your goals.

4. Analyze the fund's past performance in view of its objectives, in both good markets and bad markets. The quarterly and annual statements issued by the fund will show results for the previous year and probably a comparison with the S&P 500 stock average. Look at historical performance over a 5- or 10-year period. Look for risk measures (such as beta figures) in

investment newsletters and directories. Also, read the prospectus summary section of per-share and capital changes. *Note: Money, Forbes,* and other investment periodicals publish semi-annual or annual performance data on mutual funds.

5. From the prospectus, try to determine some clues to management's ability to accomplish the fund's investment objectives. Emphasize the record, experience, and capability of the management company.

6. Note what securities comprise the fund's portfolio to see how they look to you. Not all mutual funds are fully diversified. Not all mutual funds invest in high-quality companies.

7. Compare various fees (such as management and redemption fees), sales charges, if any, and various shareholder services offered by the funds being considered (such as the right of accumulation, any switch privilege within fund families, available investment plans, and a systematic withdrawal plan).

WHERE DO YOU BUY MUTUAL FUND SHARES?

You can buy shares in mutual funds in several ways: directly from the mutual fund company (in the case of no-load and load funds), or through a financial intermediary such as a broker, a financial planner, or an insurance company (in the case of load funds). Today, many banks are also making mutual funds available to customers. Some mutual fund companies have local offices where you can ask questions and purchase shares. *Suggestion:* Look in the financial pages of your newspaper for advertisements of mutual funds, or ask your local reference librarian for a book that lists mutual funds. *Warning:* The mutual fund your broker suggests may not be the best for several reasons. First, certain mutual funds cannot be sold through a broker. Second, the broker may be pushing a mutual fund that pays the broker the highest commission.

Some brokerage firms will let you use your margin account to buy mutual fund shares. For example, Charles Schwab lets you buy Fidelity Investor shares.

Review Questions

(1) A mutual fund is a(n) _____, run by professional managers, that pools the money of many people to purchase a diverse _____ of investments.

(2) Major advantages of investing in mutual funds are _____, small minimum investment, automatic reinvestment, automatic withdrawals, liquidity, and switching.

(3) There are three ways to make money in mutual funds: net asset value, dividends, and _____.

(4) The fees associated with mutual funds can be categorized in the following ways: _____, management and expense fees, 12b-1 fees, redemption fees or exit fees, and deferred sales charges or back-end loads.

(5) A _____ is a sales commission paid up front when you invest in a fund.

(6) A _____ operates with a fixed number of shares outstanding, which trades among individuals in secondary markets like common stocks.

(7) _____ are mutual funds that invest exclusively in debt securities maturing within 1 year, such as government securities, commercial paper, and certificates of deposit.

(8) _____ are funds that invest in one or two fields or industries.

(9) _____ is the one that employees of nonprofit organizations, hospitals, school districts, or municipalities can shelter before-tax income.

(10) There are three key facts you should know about the bonds in any portfolio: quality, _____, premium or discount.

(11) Unlike mutual funds, _____ are fixed portfolios.

(12) Beta is a measure of risk, the _____ the beta, the greater the risk.

(13) If beta is greater than 1, the fund is more _____ than the market.

(14) From the _____, we can determine some clues to management's ability to accomplish the fund's investment objectives.

(15) _____ cover advertising and marketing costs of a mutual fund.

(16) In _____ mutual funds, the investor buys from and sells shares back to the mutual fund itself.

Answers: (1) investment company, portfolio; (2) diversification; (3) capital gains; (4) loads; (5) load; (6) closed-end fund; (7) Money market funds; (8) Sector funds; (9) 403(b) Plan; (10) maturity; (11) unit investment trusts; (12) higher; (13) volatile (risky); (14) prospectus; (15) 12b-1 Fees; (16) closed-end.

Additional Solved Problems

17.1 ABC Mutual Fund owns the following:

STOCK	NUMBER OF SHARES
GM	100
Royal Dutch	100
IBM	100

What does a 5 percent investment in ABC Mutual Fund represent in terms of the number of shares of each stock?

SOLUTION

A 5 percent investment in ABC Fund would represent a 5 percent interest in each of the above (five shares of GM, five shares of Royal Dutch, and five shares of IBM).

17.2 In Problem 17.1, assume that on a particular day, the market values below existed:

(a)	GM ($80 per share × 100 shares)	$ 8,000
(b)	Royal Dutch ($50 per share × 100 shares)	5,000
(c)	IBM ($110 per share × 100 shares)	11,000
(d)	Value of the fund's portfolio	$24,000

Assuming the fund has no liabilities, calculate the net asset value (NAV) of the fund. Also, compute the value of your investment if you own 7 percent of the fund's outstanding shares.

SOLUTION

$$NAV = \frac{\text{Fund's total assets} - \text{Liabilities}}{\text{Number of shares outstanding in the fund}}$$

The NAV is calculated as follows:

(a)	GM ($80 per share × 100 shares)	$ 8,000
(b)	Royal Dutch ($50 per share × 100 shares)	5,000
(c)	IBM ($110 per share × 100 shares)	11,000
(d)	Value of the fund's portfolio	$24,000
(e)	Number of shares outstanding in the fund	1,000
(f)	Net asset value (NAV) per share [(d)/(e)]	$ 24

Since you own 70 shares (7% × 1,000 shares), then the value of your investment is $1,680 ($24 × 70 shares).

17.3 The market value of the holdings of Fidelity Mutual Fund are as follows:

Cash	$ 10,000
Shares in JGS Corp.	100,000
Shares in JKS Corp.	400,000
Total	$510,000

Fidelity has total liabilities of $30,000. It has 300,000 shares outstanding. Fidelity is a no-load fund. What is its net asset value (NAV)?

SOLUTION

$$NAV = \frac{\text{Fund's total assets} - \text{Liabilities}}{\text{Number of shares outstanding in the fund}}$$

$$= \frac{\$510,000 - \$30,000}{300,000} = \frac{\$480,000}{300,000} = \$1.60$$

17.4 In Problem 17.3, calculate Fidelity's offer price if it is a load fund charging 5 percent in sales commissions.

SOLUTION

Since the load is 5 percent, 95 percent (100% − 5%) of the funds are invested. Let x be the offer price. Then, $.95x = \$1.60$. Therefore, $x = \$1.60/.95 = \$1.68$, which is the offer price.

17.5 On October 11, the XYZ Mutual Fund had $12,500,000 market value of all securities held, $3,000,000 in liabilities, and 1,250,000 shares. On that day, *The Wall Street Journal* reported an offer price of $8.50.

(*a*) Calculate the net asset value for the XYZ Mutual Fund.

(*b*) Calculate the load charge per share for the fund.

SOLUTION

(*a*)

$$NAV = \frac{\text{Fund's total assets} - \text{Liabilities}}{\text{Number of shares outstanding in the fund}}$$

$$= \frac{\$12,500,000 - \$3,000,000}{1,250,000} = \frac{\$9,500,000}{1,250,000}$$

$$= \$7.60 \text{ per share}$$

(b)

$$\text{Load charge} = \text{Offer price} - \text{NAV} = \$8.50 - \$7.60 = \$.90$$

17.6 Guru Mutual Fund charges a 7.5 percent load. Its total assets equal $450,000, and total liabilities equal $25,000. It has 22,000 shares outstanding.

(a) What is its net asset value?

(b) What is the offer price per share of Guru Fund?

SOLUTION

(a)

Total assets	$450,000
Liabilities	25,000
Net assets	$425,000

$$\text{Net asset value} = \frac{\$425,000}{22,000} = \$19.32 \text{ per share}$$

(b) Let x = offer price:

$$\text{Offer price} - \text{Load} = \text{Net asset value}$$

$$x - .075x = \$19.32$$

$$(1 - .075)x = \$19.32$$

$$x = \frac{\$19.32}{1 - .075} = \$20.89$$

17.7 Assume that XYZ Mutual Fund paid dividends of $.50 and capital gain distributions of $.25 per share over the course of the year, and had a price (NAV) at the beginning of the year of $8.50 that rose to $9.50 per share by the end of the year. What is the holding period return (HPR)?

SOLUTION

The return is calculated as follows:

$$\text{HPR} = \frac{\text{Dividends} + \text{Capital gain distributions} + (\text{Ending NAV} - \text{Beginning NAV})}{\text{Beginning NAV}}$$

$$= \frac{\$.50 + \$.25 + (\$9.50 - \$8.50)}{\$8.50} = \frac{\$1.75}{\$8.50} = 20.59\%$$

17.8 You bought 100 shares of Goodyear Mutual Fund 1 year ago at $10 per share. You received a $.50-per-share dividend and capital gain distribution 6 months ago. If the fund's NAV was $12 per share at the end of the year, what is the holding period return?

SOLUTION

$$\text{HPR} = \frac{\$.50 + (\$12 - \$10)}{\$10} = \frac{\$2.50}{\$10} = 25\%$$

17.9 Calculate the holding period return (HPR) for the following no-load mutual funds:

Fund	Dividends	Capital Gains Distributions	Beginning Fund Price per Share	Ending Fund Price per Share
A	$1.50	.05	$12.00	$13.50
B	1.25	.65	13.50	14.50
C	.50	.10	5.00	6.00

SOLUTION

$$HPR = \frac{\text{Dividends} + \text{Capital gain distributions} + (\text{Ending NAV} - \text{Beginning NAV})}{\text{Beginning NAV}}$$

For Fund A:

$$HPR = \frac{\$1.50 + \$.05 + (\$13.50 - \$12.00)}{\$12.00} = \frac{\$3.05}{\$12.00} = 25.42\%$$

For Fund B:

$$HPR = \frac{\$1.25 + \$.65 + (\$14.50 - \$13.50)}{\$13.50} = \frac{\$2.90}{\$13.50} = 21.48\%$$

For Fund C:

$$HPR = \frac{\$.50 + \$.10 + (\$6.00 - \$5.00)}{\$5.00} = \frac{\$1.60}{\$5.00} = 32.00\%$$

17.10 Faith Baker is considering buying the following three mutual funds:

Mutual Fund	NAV	Offer Price	Closing Price on NYSE
A	$12.50	$13.90	
B	9.50	N.L.	
C	28.75	—	$25.65

Explain what these quotations mean.

SOLUTION

Fund A is a load fund that charges a commission on the purchase of its shares as indicated by the higher offer price. Fund B is a no-load fund (as indicated by the letters N.L.) and most likely an open-end fund because it is listed on the New York Stock Exchange (NYSE). Fund C does not specify a commission, but is certainly a closed-end mutual fund because it is listed with an organized exchange.

17.11 Given the mutual fund quotations:

Mutual Fund	NAV	Offer Price	NAV Change
X	$55.69	N.L.	−.08
Y	28.66	$29.24	+.04

Answer the following questions:

(*a*)   What was the NAV of Fund X at the close of the day?

(*b*)   How much did it cost to purchase 100 shares of Fund X on the day in question?

(*c*)   What sales commission as a dollar amount and as a percentage of the amount actually invested would you have paid to buy a share of Fund X?

(*d*)   What would your paper gain/loss have been had you held 100 shares of Fund X on the day of the quotation?

(*e*)   What was the NAV of Fund Y at the close of the day?

(*f*)   How much did it cost to purchase 100 shares of Fund Y on the day in question?

(*g*)   What sales commission as a dollar amount and as a percentage of the amount actually invested would you have paid to buy a share of Fund Y?

SOLUTION

(*a*) $55.69

(*b*) $55.69 × 100 shares = $5,569

(*c*)   None. Fund X is a no-load fund.

(*d*) $8.00 paper loss (100 shares × −$.08)

(*e*) $28.66

(*f*) $28.66 × 100 shares = $2,866

(*g*) $29.24 − $28.66 = $.58; $.58; $28.66 = 2.02%

17.12   You own shares of Los Alamitos Mutual Fund whose statement shows the following:

Los Alamitos Mutual Fund, Inc.

Date	Transaction	Dollar Amount	Share Price	Shares
	Beginning balance			82.435
1/4/19X1	Investment	$1,000	$53.46	18.706
2/6	Cash dividend at $.25	25.29	52.25	.484
2/6	Capital gain reinvest. at $.45	45.52		
4/1	Investment	2,000	55.37	36.121
6/4	Cash dividend at $.25	34.44	57.04	.604
9/10	Cash dividend at $.25	34.59	61.89	.559
12/17	Cash dividend at $.20	27.78	66.13	.420
2/3/19X2	Capital gain reinvest. at $.50	69.66		
2/3	Cash dividend at $.30	41.80	65.88	.635
	Total shares			139.964

Calculate your rate of return over the past 13 months, using the worksheet in Fig. 17-1 (Figuring Your Personal Rate of Return).

SOLUTION

1.   The number of months for which your fund's performance is being measured   13 months

2.   Your investment at the beginning of the period (multiply the total number of shares you owned by the NAV) [(82.435 + 18.706) × $53.46] $5,407

3.   The ending value of your investment (multiply the number of shares you currently own by the current NAV) (139.964 × $65.88) $9,221

4. Total dividends and capital gains received in cash
   ($45.52 + 69.66) $115

5. All additional investment (any redemptions
   subtracted) $2,000

6. Computation of your gain or loss

   Step (a): Add line 2 to one-half of the total on
              line 5 [$5,407 + $\frac{1}{2}$ ($2,000)] $6,407

   Step (b): Add line 3 and line 4, then subtract
              one-half of the total on line 5
              [($9,221 + $115) − $\frac{1}{2}$ ($2,000)] $8,336

   Step (c): Divide the step (b) sum by the step (a)
              sum ($8,336/$6,407)   1.30

   Step (d): Subtract 1 from the result of step (c),
              then multiply by 100 [(1.30 − 1) × 100]   30%

7. Computation of your annualized return

   Divide the number of months on line 1 into 12;
   multiply the result by the step (d) % [($\frac{12}{13}$) × 30]   27.7%

17.13 During a 5-year period, the relevant results for the aggregate market are that r (risk-free rate) is 8 percent and the r' (return on market) is 14 percent. For that period, the results of three mutual funds are as follows:

MUTUAL FUND	AVERAGE RETURN (%)	BETA
A	13	.80
B	14	1.05
C	17	1.25

(a) Calculate the expected (required) rate of return (R) for each fund and compare the actual results with the expected returns.

(b) Based on your calculations, select the fund with the best performance.

SOLUTION

(a) Using the equation $R = r + b(r' − r)$, the expected rates of return are as follows:

Mutual Fund	(1) Expected Return (%)	(2) Average Return (%)	Actual − Expected (2) − (1)
A	8% + .8(14% − 8%) = 12.8%	13	+ .2%
B	8% + 1.05(14% − 8%) = 14.3%	14	− .3
C	8% + 1.25(14% − 8%) = 15.5%	17	+1.5

(b) Mutual Funds A and C did better than expected, since A exceeded the expected return by 1.6 percent (.2%/12.8%) and C bettered the expected return by 9.68 percent (1.5%/15.5%). C showed the best performance. B showed the worst performance because the average return was below the expected return by 2.1% (−.3%/14.3%).

Chapter 18

Retirement Planning

Many people do not prepare for retirement even though it is a major event in their lives. Are you adequately planning for retirement? A financial advisor such as a financial planner, a CPA, or a life insurance agent may advise you on the type of retirement plan to meet your particular needs. However, you can do much retirement planning yourself. You may compute retirement contributions necessary to achieve your retirement goal as well as compute amounts to be received upon retirement. This chapter discusses

What retirement planning involves

How to estimate retirement needs

Types of pension and retirement plans

How to check your pension fund

Ways to put the retirement plan to work

How to buy annuities

WHAT DOES RETIREMENT PLANNING INVOLVE?

The first step in retirement planning is to develop retirement goals. Once they have been set, you should develop specific saving plans aimed at achieving them. You must take into account present versus future needs, and an examination of how present resources may be allocated to serve future needs. It is important to note that your financial situation at retirement hinges not only on your plans for retirement but also on your choice of career and lifestyle. It is essential to economic security in old age to devote some income toward retirement goals. Means of saving for retirement are social security, employer retirement and pension plans, annuities, and individual retirement and savings plans.

An easy way to plan for retirement is to state your retirement income objectives as a percent of your present earnings. For example, if you desire a retirement income of 70 percent of your final take-home pay, you, along with your life insurance agent or financial planner, can determine the amount necessary to fund this need.

HOW TO ESTIMATE RETIREMENT NEEDS?

Retirement planning basically involves two steps: first target your retirement needs and then estimate the annual savings necessary to meet that target. Figure 18-1 can be of help for this purpose.

A life expectancy table is given in Table 18-1. It may be difficult to accurately determine your future social security benefits, since these benefits are based on your highest 26 years of earnings. A helpful general rule is: The higher the income level, the more supplemental income needed to bridge the gap between current earnings and social security payouts. Social security benefits that have to be considered are indicated in Table 18-2.

IS IT GOING TO BE A DEFINED BENEFIT PLAN OR A DEFINED CONTRIBUTION PLAN?

All pension plans can be classified as defined benefit plans, defined contribution plans, or some combination of the two.

		SAMPLE
1.	Current salary	$ 50,000
2.	Percentage of current salary to be replaced	× .70
3.	Retirement income target	$ 35,000
4.	Minus: Vested defined benefits	(5,000)
5.	Minus: Social security benefits (assume 20% of current salary approximated from Table 18-2)	(10,000)
6.	Required annual income from investment fund	$ 20,000
7.	Life expectancy (from Table 18-1)	× 18.9
8.	Required target investment	$378,000
9.	Present target resources:	

IRA	$20,000	
Keogh	0	
Defined contribution plan	45,000	
Other investments	90,000	
Total		(155,000)

10.	Required additions to target fund	$223,000
11.	Years to retirement	÷ 25
12.	Current annual savings required to achieve target	$ 8,920

Fig. 18-1 Worksheet for retirement planning.

Table 18-1   Life Expectancy by Race, Age, and Sex (in years)

Age	Total	White Male	White Female	Black Male	Black Female
50	28.3	25.6	31.3	22.2	28.0
51	27.5	24.8	30.4	21.5	27.2
52	26.7	24.0	29.6	20.8	26.5
53	25.8	23.2	28.7	20.2	25.7
54	25.0	22.4	27.8	19.5	24.9
55	24.2	21.6	27.0	18.9	24.1
56	23.4	20.8	26.1	18.2	23.4
57	22.6	20.1	25.3	18.6	22.7
58	21.9	19.3	24.4	17.0	21.9
59	21.1	18.6	23.6	16.5	21.2
60	20.4	17.9	22.8	15.9	20.5
61	19.6	17.2	22.0	15.3	19.8
62	18.9	16.5	21.2	14.8	19.2
63	18.2	15.8	20.4	14.3	18.5
64	17.5	15.2	19.6	13.8	17.9
65	16.8	14.5	18.9	13.3	17.2
70	13.7	11.6	15.3	10.9	14.1
75	10.8	9.1	12.0	8.8	11.3
80	8.3	7.0	9.0	6.7	8.6
85 and over	6.3	5.3	6.7	4.8	6.5

Source: Adapted from *Statistical Abstract of the United States 1986,* Table 18, No. 108, p. 69 (U.S. Department of Commerce, Bureau of the Census).

Table 18-2 Social Security Benefits

Annual Earnings	Annual Social Security Amount (avg.)	Percentage of Earnings Replaced
$44,000 or more	$9,468	22% or less
33,000	9,144	28
24,000	8,496	35
17,000	6,672	39
12,000	5,304	44

DEFINED BENEFIT PLAN

A defined benefit plan specifies the monthly benefit at your retirement age. Each year, the employer contributes to a pension plan an amount necessary to pay for those future predetermined benefits. The present contribution is determined, based upon assumed investment returns and probabilities of survival. A typical benefit formula states that the eligible employee will receive for each year of service some percentage (usually between $\frac{1}{2}$ and 2 percent) of the average salary in the last 5 years of employment.

SOLVED PROBLEM 18.1

Under a 1.5 percent formula, if your salary for the 5 years prior to retirement averaged $3,000 a month and you had 20 years of service, how much would you receive each month?

SOLUTION

$900 a month (20 years × 1.5% × $3,000).

With this plan you know how much you will receive, but you do not know how much those monies will be worth. Inflation can be a discouraging factor.

DEFINED CONTRIBUTION PLAN

In this plan, you are not guaranteed a specified benefit at retirement. Your benefits will hinge on future contributions and the investment performance of the retirement plan you are in. The contribution to the pension fund is usually fixed as some percentage of the worker's salary. The defined contribution plan specifies the annual contribution to be paid each year to the pension plan.

SOLVED PROBLEM 18.2

You earn an average annual salary of $40,000 and make a 10 percent annual contribution to the fund—that is, $4,000 annually. If the contribution earns an 8 percent annual return, how much would be accumulated in the fund after 30 years?

SOLUTION

$4,000 × Appendix Table 2 factor = $4,000 × 113.283 = $453,132

Note: Many defined contribution plans permit you to make an additional voluntary contribution to the retirement account.

WHAT ARE THE TYPES OF PENSION AND RETIREMENT PLANS?

Two major sources of retirement income are company-sponsored pension plans and individual retirement plans. They are summarized below:

Company-sponsored pension plans
>   Qualified company retirement plans
>   Profit sharing plans
>   401(k) salary reduction plans
>   Tax-sheltered annuities (TSA)
>   Employee stock ownership plans (ESOP)
>   Simplified employee pension plan (SEP)

Individual retirement plans
>   Individual retirement accounts (IRAs)
>   Keoghs
>   Annuities

Company-sponsored plans are described below:

Qualified company retirement plans. The IRS permits a corporate employer to make contributions to a retirement plan that is qualified. Qualified means that it meets a number of specific criteria in order to deduct from taxable income contributions to the plan. The investment income of the plan is allowed to accumulate untaxed.

Profit sharing plans. A profit sharing plan is a type of defined contribution plan. Unlike other qualified plans, you may not have to wait until retirement to receive distributions. *Note:* Since the company must contribute only when it earns a profit, the amount of benefit at retirement is highly uncertain.

401(k) Salary reduction plans. In addition to, or in place of, a qualified pension plan or profit sharing plan, you may set up a 401(k) salary reduction plan, which defers a portion of your salary for retirement. This is like building a nest egg for the future by taking a cut in pay. Tax savings more than offset a "paper cut" since you end up with more take-home pay and more retirement income.

SOLVED PROBLEM 18.3

You save 10 percent of your $40,000-a-year salary in a 401(k) plan. You are married with two children, are the only wage earner in the family, and do not itemize deductions. See how you fare with a 401(k) plan and without one.

SOLUTION

	Take-Home Pay	
	With 401(k) Plan	Without 401(k) Plan
Base Pay	$40,000	$40,000
Salary reduction	4,000	None
Taxable income	$36,000	$40,000
Federal and FICA taxes	8,159	9,279
Savings after taxes	None	4,000
Take-home pay	$27,841	$26,721

Extra take-home pay under 401(k) is $1,120 ($27,841 − $26,721).

Note that your retirement income will grow faster inside a tax-sheltered plan, such as 401(k), than outside one. This is because the interest you are earning will go untaxed and therefore keep compounding.

Tax-sheltered annuities (TSA).   If you are an employee of a nonprofit institution, you are eligible for a TSA. A TSA is similar to the 401(k), but you may withdraw the funds at any age for any reason without tax penalty. *Note:* You must pay ordinary taxes on all withdrawals.

Employee stock ownership plans (ESOP).   ESOP is a stock-bonus plan. The contributions made by the employer are tax deductible.

Simplified employee pension (SEP).   SEP is a plan whereby an employer makes annual contributions on the employee's behalf to an individual retirement account set up by the employee.

MANAGING FOR RETIREMENT

Just how golden your golden days will be depends on how well you manage your IRA, 401(k), or other retirement plans now, while they are building up. This means staying on top of interest rates and being ready to move your money to get the best return.

A few percentage points can make all the difference. If you have, say, $20,000 in tax-free retirement funds earning 6 percent in a savings account, that will grow to $114,860 after 30 years. If you invested the same amount at 9 percent, you'd have $265,360 after 30 years.

SOLVED PROBLEM 18.4

If you invested $20,000 at 10 percent, 12 percent, or 15 percent, how much would you have after 30 years?

SOLUTION

	10%	12%	15%
Amount invested	$ 20,000	$ 20,000	$ 20,000
Future value of $1 (Appendix Table 1)	× 17.449	× 29.960	× 66.212
Compound amount after 30 years	$348,980	$599,200	$1,324,240

Even if your retirement funds are managed for you, you usually have a choice of investments, offering different yields and risks. Usually, you can divide your savings among them, with the option of switching periodically. If you manage your own funds, you have a broad choice that ranges from certificates of deposit (CDs) to mutual funds.

The key is to be aware of the interest on your investments. Be sure interest is ahead of current inflation. Understand the magical power of compound interest and tax-deferred growth.

WHAT ARE INDIVIDUAL RETIREMENT ACCOUNTS (IRAs)?

If you do not have a company retirement plan, or you would like to supplement a company plan through additional private savings, the benefits of tax deferral can also be attained through individual-oriented investments, such as IRAs, Keoghs, and annuities.

The IRA is a retirement savings plan that individuals set up themselves. The maximum contribution is $2,000 or the amount of compensation earned, whichever is less. A married couple may contribute up to $4,000 if each of them earns $2,000 (up to $2,250 if you have a nonworking spouse). The IRA is a qualified individual retirement plan whereby your contributions not only grow tax-free but are also either tax deductible or not included in your income.

It is important to remember that under the Tax Reform Act of 1986, however, a person who is covered by an employer's retirement plan, or who files a joint return with a spouse who is covered by such a plan, may be entitled to only a partial deduction or no deduction at all, depending on adjusted gross income (AGI). The deduction begins to decrease (that is, the allowable deductions are reduced $1 for each $5 increase in income) when the taxpayer's income rises above a certain level and is eliminated altogether when it reaches a higher level.

Specifically, the deduction is reduced or eliminated entirely depending on your filing status and income as follows:

If Filing Status Is	Deduction Is Reduced If AGI Is Within Range of	Deduction Is Eliminated If AGI Is
Single, or head of household	$25,000–$35,000	$35,000 or more
Married—joint return, or qualifying widow(er)	$40,000–$50,000	$50,000 or more
Married—separate return	$0–$10,000	$10,000 or more

SOLVED PROBLEM 18.5

How much would a single worker with an adjusted gross income of $30,000 be able to deduct in IRA contributions?

SOLUTION

$$\$2,000 - \left(\frac{\$30,000 - \$25,000}{\$5} \times \$1 \right) = \$1,000$$

If you are not covered by an employee retirement plan, you can still take a full IRA deduction of up to $2,000, or 100 percent of compensation, whichever is less. *Note:* If you are self-employed, you can set up a Keogh plan.

A Keogh pension plan is a tax-deferred retirement plan for self-employed individuals meeting certain requirements. It is also called an H.R.10 plan. Self-employed individuals can contribute to their plan up to 25 percent of earnings, up to a maximum of $30,000.

HOW TO PUT AN IRA TO WORK FOR YOU

Here are some ways to put your IRA to work:

Certificates of deposit (CDs).   If you are conservative, put money in CDs. Returns on CDs are not flashy, but you sleep well at night!

Money market funds.   Again, when you put safety first over anything else, you can put your IRA in a money market fund that specializes especially in Treasury securities.

Bond funds and gold funds.   This is a way to get secure income while hedging against inflation. *Warning:* With any hedge, you reduce risk but at the same time reduce return.

Ginnie Maes.   Many financial advisors recommend Government National Mortgage Association mutual funds. They pay monthly principal and interest.

Mutual funds of "blue-chip" stocks.   If you are investment-oriented but want professional management, you can invest in a mutual fund concentrating in large, established companies. Over time, dividends will compound. In case stock prices tumble, think long term. *Note:* By the time you retire, many more bull markets will have come to boost the value of those shares.

Fund of funds.   When using a family of funds, you pay no sales charge when switching.

United States gold and silver coins.   IRAs can include U.S. gold and silver coins. They have the potential for future appreciation.

HOW TO CHECK YOUR PENSION FUND

Every year, employees enrolled in hundreds of retirement plans are surprised to find that the "nest egg" they were counting on for their later years is not as secure as they once believed. Employers may have used pension assets to make questionable loans, to make bad investments, or simply "line their own pockets." *Tip:* Check your pension fund on a regular basis. You do not want to find out at retirement that the fund has been mismanaged. Here are some questions you might want to ask about your pension plan:

Are your pension plan's investments diversified enough?

What kind of investments have been made?

Is there evidence of financial losses or loans in default?

Have there been suspicious transactions with people that have connections with the fund?

Do the fees paid to the trustees or managers seem excessive?

Have CPAs given any "qualified" or negative opinions on the plans?

Warning: Most employer pension plans are built and funded on the assumption that many plan members will never receive benefits. It is also important to check out as early as possible what the rules are so you can guard against becoming one of those losers (nonqualifiers). For example, quitting a job a few months or even weeks or days before a certain pension deadline might result in a loss of pension rights. Here are some points to investigate:

Is your job covered by your company pension plan?

When will you become eligible for membership?

How long must you work before your benefits are vested?

How many hours must you work during the year to remain in the plan and accrue benefits?

What is the formula for determining benefits?

What is the earliest age or combination of age and years of service at which you may retire?

How much will your retirement benefits be reduced if you retire early?

How much will your retirement check be increased if you stay past age 65?

Will your pension amount be reduced by social security benefits and, if so, by how much?

What would happen to your pension status if you took a leave of absence?

WHAT ARE THE BASICS ABOUT ANNUITIES?

An annuity is a savings account with an insurance company or other investment company. You make either a lump-sum deposit or periodic payments to the company and at retirement, you "annuitize"—receive regular payments for a specified time period (usually a certain number of years or for the rest of your life). All your payments build up tax-free and are only taxed when withdrawn at retirement, a time when you are usually in a lower tax bracket. Although mostly sold by life insurance companies, annuities are really the opposite of life insurance: Annuities pay off when you retire; life insurance pays off when you die.

Annuities come in two basic varieties: fixed and variable.

1. *Fixed-rate annuities.* In a fixed-rate annuity, the insurance company guarantees your principal plus a minimum rate of interest. If you have little tolerance for risk, the fixed-rate annuity is an ideal investment. In buying a fixed-rate annuity, you should be aware of two interest rates. One is the minimum guaranteed rate which applies for the duration of the contract. The other is the "current" rate of interest, which reflects market conditions.

2. *Variable annuities.* In a variable annuity, the company does not provide the same guarantee as for fixed annuities. The company invests in common stocks, corporate bonds, or money

market instruments, and the investment value fluctuates with the performance of these investments. With a variable annuity, you bear the risk of the investment options. The good thing is that most companies allow you to switch to another fund within the variable variety.

Annuities can be for everybody. For young people, the vehicles are an excellent forced savings plan. For older people, they are tax-favored investments that can guarantee an income for life. Retirement annuities offer three main advantages:

Interest is not taxed until you collect those monthly checks at retirement, when your tax bracket should be lower.

Interest earned each year without a tax compounds your wealth quickly.

Unlike pension plans and IRAs, there are no limitations on the amount you may contribute to an annuity.

PITFALLS OF ANNUITIES

Limit your financial freedom. You cannot get your money back before age $59\frac{1}{2}$. There are penalties for early withdrawals imposed by the IRS and the insurance company.

The interest earned can be reduced by inflation or lag behind the return of other investments.

Surrender charges if you decide to cash in the contract early.

The so-called nonqualified annuities, which are annuities with the tax-deferral feature but which are paid for with after-tax dollars.

Qualified annuities, on the other hand, are used to fund such vehicles as Individual Retirement Accounts (IRAs) and pension plans. In a qualified annuity, the contributions not only grow tax-free but are also either tax deductible or not included in your income. If you qualify, you should always make contributions to programs like IRAs and pension plans first. It makes sense to invest first in a plan where contributions are made with before-tax dollars.

HOW TO PURCHASE ANNUITIES

Here are some tips for buying an annuity:

Deal with a firm that is financially sound and strong. There was an instance where Baldwin-United, a leading annuity seller, filed for bankruptcy.

Only buy annuities from companies which have an A+ rating (which you find in A.M. Best's publication, *Best's Insurance Reports*). For example, Equitable Life Insurance Company is financially secure.

Ask the sales representative about the company's investment performance. Make sure you see written documentation.

When considering variable annuities, select those that are well diversified.

Ask the sales representative for a detailed description in the contract of all charges (such as surrender, administrative, mortality, and investment advisory). List them and compare different annuities.

Closely read the sales literature and the annuity contract. For variable annuities, examine the prospectus just like you would do for a mutual fund. The company does not have to issue a prospectus for a fixed annuity since it is not considered a registered security.

Shop around. Annuity sellers are very competitive. Comparison shopping will pay off.

Recommendations: You should consider buying a retirement annuity if you

May not get other tax-free retirement plans such as Keoghs and company-sponsored savings plans.

Need a "pay-the-bill" approach to make you save.

Enjoy the security of that guaranteed check during retirement.

Do not want to manage individual investments such as stocks.

You might not want to consider them if you

Can obtain other tax-deferred savings programs.

Expect income and savings to be sufficient enough that you can afford the luxury of risk-taking in your retirement savings.

SOLVED PROBLEM 18.6

When you retire, you want to receive an annual annuity of $20,000 for your expected remaining life of 20 years. The interest rate is 10 percent. How much do you need in your pension plan to do that?

SOLUTION

$20,000 × present value of ordinary annuity for $n = 20$, $i = 10\%$ (Appendix Table 4)

$$\$20,000 \times 8.514 = \$170,280$$

Review Questions

(1) The first step in retirement planning is to _____.

(2) Means of saving for retirement are _____, employer retirement and pension plans, annuities, and individual retirement and savings plans.

(3) Retirement planning basically involves two steps: first target your retirement needs and second estimate _____ necessary to meet that target.

(4) All pension plans can be classified as defined benefit plans, _____, or some combination of the two.

(5) A _____ specifies the monthly benefit at your retirement age.

(6) The _____ specifies a fixed percentage of the worker's salary.

(7) Two major sources of retirement income are _____ and individual retirement plans.

(8) A Keogh is one type of _____.

(9) If you are an employee of a _____, you are eligible for tax-sheltered annuities.

(10) The _____ is a retirement savings plan that individuals set up themselves.

(11) An _____ is a savings account with an insurance company or other investment company.

(12) In a _____, the insurance company guarantees your principal plus a minimum rate of interest.

(13) With a _____, you bear the risk of the investment options.

(14) A _____ is a plan whereby the employer gives contributions for the employee to an individual retirement account established by the employee.

Answers: (1) develop retirement goals; (2) social security; (3) the annual savings; (4) defined contribution plans; (5) defined benefit plan; (6) defined contribution plan; (7) company-sponsored pension plans; (8) individual retirement plan (IRA); (9) nonprofit institution; (10) IRA (Individual Retirement Account); (11) annuity; (12) fixed annuity; (13) variable annuity; (14) simplified employee pension (SEP).

Additional Solved Problems

18.1 Nancy Degan is in the 28 percent marginal tax bracket. What would her tax savings be if she were to place $1,500 in a tax-sheltered retirement plan that qualified for using contributions up to $2,000 to reduce taxable income?

SOLUTION

$$\$1,500 \times .28 = \$420$$

18.2 Karen Singleton is in the 28 percent marginal tax bracket. What would her tax savings be if she were to place $1,800 in a tax-sheltered retirement plan that qualified for using contributions up to $2,000 to reduce taxable income?

SOLUTION

$$\$1,800 \times 28\% = \$504$$

18.3 John Mossman hopes to retire in 25 years and wants to deposit one lump sum that will grow to $300,000 at that time. If he can now invest at 8 percent, how much must he invest to realize the $300,000 when needed?

SOLUTION

The present value of $1 for 25 years at 8% (from Appendix Table 3) is .146.

$$\$300,000 \times .146 = \$43,800$$

18.4 Andy Messersmith plans to retire after 16 years. To provide for that retirement, he initiates a savings program of $5,000 per year in an investment yielding 8 percent. What will be the value of the retirement fund at the beginning of the seventeenth year?

SOLUTION

From Appendix Table 2, the future value of an annuity of $1 for 16 years and 8 percent is 30.324.

$$\$5,000 \times 30.324 = \$151,620$$

18.5 What will be the value of an investment if you put $1,500 into a retirement plan yielding 10 percent for 25 years?

SOLUTION

From Appendix Table 2, the future value factor is 98.347.

$$\$1,500 \times 98.347 = \$147,521$$

18.6 Melody is trying to decide between putting $4,000 or $5,000 annually for the next 20 years into an investment yielding 8 percent for retirement purposes. What is the difference in the value of investing the extra $1,000 for 20 years?

SOLUTION

The Appendix Table 2 factor is 45.762.

$$\$1,000 \times 45.762 = \$45,762$$

18.7 Bruce expects to have $300,000 available in a retirement plan upon retirement. If the amount invested yields 9 percent and he hopes to live an additional 20 years, how much can he withdraw each year so that the fund will just be liquidated after 20 years?

SOLUTION

The present value of an annuity of $1 for 20 years at 9 percent (from Appendix Table 4) is 9.129. Dividing $300,000 by 9.129 gives $32,862. He can withdraw $32,862 each year for 20 years.

18.8 Gary Otto has the option of using a 401(k) plan as a supplement to his company retirement plan. His salary is $45,000 per year and he is in the 28 percent marginal tax bracket. His employer's plan calls for a mandatory (if the plan is chosen) 10 percent contribution from employees to be matched by a 7.5 percent employer contribution.

(a) If Gary chooses the plan, how much will be contributed during the first year?

(b) What portion of the answer to part (a) would Gary be allowed to use to reduce his taxable income?

(c) If Gary is 35 years old, what would that first year's contribution grow to by age 65 if it earned a 6 percent return?

SOLUTION

(a) $7,875 = $45,000 × 17.5 percent

(b) The full amount, since it is less than 24 percent of his salary income.

(c) $45,226.12 = $7,875 × 5.743 (from Appendix Table 1 for 30 years and 6 percent)

18.9 Harriet, aged 35, estimates that, in addition to the amounts she has planned, she will require $4,800 a year at retirement to meet her spending needs. An annuity to provide the additional income would cost $60,000.

(a) Assume that Harriet retires at 65 and that she can earn a 10 percent annual return under a tax shelter, how much must she save annually to achieve her target income goal of $60,000 if she started immediately?

(b) How much must she save if she starts at age 45?

SOLUTION

(a) At age 35, Harriet has 30 years to save. The future value (compound amount) of an annuity of $1 for 30 years at 10 percent (Appendix Table 2) is 164.49. Dividing $60,000 by 164.49 gives the annual savings needed to produce $60,000. The answer is $364.76 ($60,000/164.49).

(b) At age 45, the savings period is 20 years. The Appendix Table 2 factor is 57.27. The answer is $1,047.67 ($60,000/57.27).

18.10 In Problem 18.9, if Harriet can earn 12 percent on her savings, how much should she save annually in parts (a) and (b)?

SOLUTION

(a) and (b)   The 12 percent factors from Appendix Table 2 are 241.33 and 72.05, respectively. Annual savings needed are $248.62 ($60,000/241.33) and $832.76 ($60,000/72.05), respectively.

18.11 How much must be saved annually for 10 years to accumulate $85,000 at

(*a*) 10 percent?

(*b*) 5 percent?

SOLUTION

(*a*) Get the Appendix Table 2 (future value of an annuity of $1) factor and divide it into $85,000. The table value is 15.937.

$$\frac{\$85,000}{15.937} = \$5,333.50$$

So, equal annual installments of $5,333.50 at 10 percent for 10 years will be sufficient to provide the required sum of $85,000.

(*b*) At 5 percent, the table value is 12.578.

$$\frac{\$85,000}{12.578} = \$6,757.83$$

At a lower rate of return, you have to put aside more money each year.

18.12 Peter Slusser is almost 62 years old. Based on his social security contributions, if he were to retire at age 65, he would receive $570 in monthly benefits. He would prefer to continue working on a part-time basis after retirement, earning about $9,000 annually. Assume that these earnings are tax-free.

(*a*) What would Peter's social security benefits be if he were to retire at age 65?

(*b*) What would Peter's retirement benefits be if he retires at age 62? (Assume that benefits will be reduced by 20 percent.)

(*c*) What advice do you have for Peter about retiring at age 62 or 65?

SOLUTION

(*a*) If Peter retires at age 65, he would receive $570 per month in benefits before adjustments. Peter would lose ($9,000 − $8,160)/2 = $420 in annual benefits because he works. $420 annually is $420/12 = $35 monthly. Thus, Peter would receive $570 − $35 = $535 per month.

(*b*) Peter would receive $570 × .8 = $456 per month in benefits if he retires at age 62. The earnings limitations would reduce his benefits by ($9,000 − $6,000)/2 = $1,500 annually, or $1,500/12 = $125 monthly. He would receive $456 − $125 = $331 monthly.

(*c*) Peter should delay his retirement until age 65.

18.13 Pam Shriver has $160,000 with which to cover her retirement living expenses. She is evaluating two options. She can invest the money in money market mutual funds that will pay her 16 percent annually or she can buy a straight-life fixed annuity. The insurer, based on her life expectancy of 5 years and rate of return of 13 percent, will pay her an annuity of $40,257 each year.

(*a*) Prepare a table to show that this annuity amount of $40,257 is correct.

(*b*) Which option is desirable for Ms. Shriver?

SOLUTION

(*a*) At a 16 percent rate of return, she will receive $160,000 × .16 = $25,600 annually. The table for the annuity is given below:

Period	Begin. Balance	Payment	Balance	Return	End. Balance
1	$160,000	$40,257	$119,743	$15,567	$135,310
2	135,310	40,257	95,053	12,357	107,410
3	107,410	40,257	67,153	8,730	75,883
4	75,883	40,257	35,626	4,631	40,257
5	40,257	40,257			

For year 1, the return is $119,743 \times .13 = \$15,567$.

(*b*) If Ms. Shriver wants to leave an estate, then she should opt for the money market fund. If she has no desire to leave an estate, then she should go with the annuity.

18.14 David Climi has recently started working for a company that has a defined benefit retirement plan. David's contribution to the retirement plan of 8 percent of his salary is matched by his employer. The retirement benefits are 2 percent of David's average salary for the 5 years prior to retirement for each year of service. David has 30 more years to work before retiring. Thus, this plan would pay him 60 percent of his average salary for the 5 years before retiring. His friend, Laura Basset, is enrolled in a defined contribution retirement plan. She also contributes 8 percent of her salary to the plan, and her employer matches this contribution. Although her retirement benefits cannot be guaranteed, her employer believes that the plan will pay about $11 in monthly retirement benefits for each $1,000 of retirement principal contributed. Laura is also eligible for retirement after 30 years.

Which plan is better? What is your analysis?

SOLUTION

Assume that both David and Laura make $20,000 annually, and this amount will remain constant until retirement. David is contributing $20,000 \times .08 = \$1,600$ annually. When he retires, he will receive .6 \times \$20,000 = \$12,000$ annually, or $1,000 monthly.

Laura also contributes $1,600 annually. Over 30 years, Laura will contribute $1,600 \times 30 = \$48,000$. Her contributions are matched by her employer. Thus, her account will have $48,000 \times 2 = \$96,000$ in principal. She will receive $96 \times 11 = \$1,056$ in monthly benefits.

Laura's plan appears to be better than David's.

18.15 James Nelson plans to take early retirement at age 62. If he were to retire at age 65, he would receive $550 per month in social security retirement benefits. If he were to retire at age 62, he would receive 80 percent of $550. James has an IRA that will have $50,000 in it by the time he turns 62. He plans to roll over the IRA amount in a life insurance annuity that would pay him a fixed amount annually for his remaining life. Based on his life expectancy and a certain rate of return, the insurance company has used a present value factor of 5.747 to calculate the annual annuity payment that it would make to James. His current living expenses are $1,750 per month. He estimates that at retirement at age 62, he would need about 80 percent of his current living expenses to maintain his present life-style. Based on the information provided, perform a retirement analysis for Mr. Nelson. Does he have sufficient funds to meet his retirement needs?

SOLUTION

Eighty percent of $1,750 is $1,400, which is the monthly amount that James would need for retirement purposes. At age 62, James would receive only $550 \times .8 = \$440$ per month in social security retirement benefits because of his early retirement.

James would receive $50,000/5.747 = $8,700 annually, or $725 monthly in benefits from the annuity. All together, James would receive $440 + $725 = $1,165 in monthly income. This leaves him with an earnings deficit of $1,400 − $1,165 = $235 per month.

As it stands right now, it appears that Mr. Nelson does not have sufficient funds to provide for his retirement at age 62. If he has other assets that can provide him with a monthly income of $235, then retirement at age 62 is feasible. However, in the absence of other income-producing assets, James will not have sufficient retirement income at age 62. He may want to delay retirement until age 65. He would receive higher social security benefits then. Also, his life insurance annuity payments would be higher then because he would have a shorter life expectancy at age 65. Also, his IRA funds would have grown larger than $50,000 by the time he is 65. All factors indicate that Mr. Nelson should defer retiring until age 65.

18.16 Norman and Julie make about $50,000 a year combined and would like to have a similar level of income when they retire. Norman and Julie are both 25 years old. They hope to retire when they both are 65. They feel that they could maintain their current level of living if their retirement income represented 75 percent of their current income.

(a)   Assuming a 5 percent inflation rate, what would Norman and Julie's income need to be during the first year of retirement?

(b)   Both Norman and Julie are covered by a defined contribution plan at work. Norman's and Julie's employers each contributes $2,000 per year. Assuming an 8 percent rate of return, what would their nest egg be at retirement 25 years from now?

(c)   For how many years would the nest egg provide the amount of income indicated in part (a)? Assume a 5 percent rate of return.

SOLUTION

(a)   75% × $50,000 = $37,500. From Appendix Table 1 (future value of $1 for 40 years at 5 percent), we get 7.040.

$$\$37,500 \times 7.040 = \$264,000$$

(b)   Using Appendix Table 2, the future value of an annuity of $1 for 40 years at 8 percent, factor is 259.1. For both Norman and Julie: ($2,000 + $2,000) × 259.1 = $1,036,400.

(c)   The nest egg will provide the retirement income needed for about 4 years ($1,036,000/$264,000 = 3.924); see the 5 percent column in Appendix Table 4 (present value of an annuity of $1).

18.17 In Problem 18.16, what would the answers to questions (a), (b), and (c) have been if Norman and Julie were to retire at 55?

SOLUTION

(a)   75% × $50,000 = $37,500. From Appendix Table 1 (future value of $1 for 30 years at 5 percent), we get 4.322.

$$\$37,500 \times 4.322 = \$162,075$$

(b)   Using Appendix Table 2, the future value of an annuity of $1 for 30 years at 8 percent, factor is 113.34. For both Norman and Julie: ($2,000 + $2,000) × 113.34 = $453,360.

(c)   The nest egg will provide the retirement income needed for about 3 years ($453,360/$162,075 = 2.797); see the 5 percent column in Appendix Table 4 (present value of an annuity of $1).

18.18 Given the retirement planning worksheet for Natalie and Bruce:

Worksheet for Retirement Planning

	NATALIE	BRUCE
1. Current salary	$ 30,000	$ 42,000
2. Percentage of current salary to be replaced	× .80	× .60
3. Retirement income target	_____	_____
4. Minus: Vested defined benefits	$ (4,000)	$ (6,000)
5. Minus: Social security benefits (assumed)	(16,020)	(17,280)
6. Required annual income from investment fund	_____	_____
7. Life expectancy	× 16.7	× 16.7
8. Required target investment	_____	_____
9. Present target resources:	$(12,500)	$(16,000)
10. Required additions to target fund	_____	_____
11. Years to retirement	÷ 20	÷ 15
12. Current annual savings required to achieve target	_____	_____

Complete the worksheet.

SOLUTION

Worksheet for Retirement Planning

	NATALIE	BRUCE
1. Current salary	$ 30,000	$ 42,000
2. Percentage of current salary to be replaced	× .80	× .60
3. Retirement income target	$ 24,000	$ 25,200
4. Minus: Vested defined benefits	$ (4,000)	$ (6,000)
5. Minus: Social security benefits (assumed)	(16,020)	(17,280)
6. Required annual income from investment fund [(3) − (4) − (5)]	$ 3,980	$ 1,920
7. Life expectancy	× 16.7	× 16.7
8. Required target investment [(6) × (7)]	$ 66,466	$ 32,064
9. Present target resources:	$(12,500)	$(16,000)
10. Required additions to target fund [(8) − (9)]	$ 53,966	16,064
11. Years to retirement	÷ 20	÷ 15
12. Current annual savings required to achieve target [(10)/(11)]	$ 2,698	$ 1,071

18.19 Ronald Jackson has developed a retirement budget totaling $50,000 a year. He is 45 years old and expects to retire at 65. Relevant data follow:

1.   Social security income expected, $9,000
2.   Expected income from employer benefit plan, $16,000
3.   Inflation rate, 5 percent
4.   Anticipated return on assets held in the retirement fund, 8 percent
5.   Expected return on investments prior to retirement, 12 percent

Calculate:

(a)   Additional required income (or shortfall)
(b)   Inflation-adjusted annual required income (or shortfall)
(c)   Amount of retirement funds required—size of nest egg
(d)   Annual savings required to fund retirement nest egg

SOLUTION

(a)

$$\$50,000 - (\$9,000 + \$16,000) = \$25,000$$

(b)   Using Appendix Table 1, the compound amount of $1 for 20 years at 5 percent factor is 2.653.

$$\$25,000 \times 2.653 = \$66,325$$

(c)   The nest egg is obtained by dividing the amount of inflation-adjusted annual income (or shortfall) by the anticipated return after retirement.

$$\frac{\$66,325}{8\%} = \$829,063$$

(d)   Dividing the nest egg by the Appendix Table 2 factor gives the amount of annual savings required to fund retirement nest egg. The Appendix Table 2 value for 20 years at 12 percent factor is 72.052.

$$\frac{\$829,063}{72.052} = \$11,506$$

Chapter 19

How Can You Make Use of Tax Planning to Lower Taxes?

You want to make a personal financial planning decision that will result in lower taxes consistent with your overall objectives. For many, income taxes are the largest expense so why not find legally allowable ways of reducing them? You have to analyze the tax consequences of alternative approaches in your decision making. You have to shift income and expenses into tax years that will be best for you. Are you missing any tax-saving opportunities? You should develop a long-term tax planning strategy that takes into account your age, income, liquidity, family status, estate planning preferences, etc.

You have to keep up-to-date with the basic changes in the tax law as it affects you. You should also consult with a competent tax practitioner who preferably should be a certified public accountant (CPA) and/or tax attorney. There are many comprehensive tax publications that you may refer to, such as those published by McGraw-Hill.

HOW DO YOU POSTPONE YOUR TAXES?

You may wish to defer taxes when

You will be in a lower tax bracket in a future year.

You lack the funds to meet the present tax requirement.

You can earn a return on the funds that you would have had to pay the federal and local taxing authorities.

By deferring payment of taxes, you will be paying in cheaper dollars because of the inflationary effect.

You may possibly avoid the tax payment.

Properly time the receipt of income and the payment of expenses to minimize the tax payment, particularly if your income is on the border line between two tax brackets. A good tax strategy is to receive income in a year in which it will be taxed at a lower rate. Try to convert income to less taxed sources. Also, pay tax-deductible expenses in a year in which you will receive the most benefit. In other words, accelerate deductible expenses into years when the tax rates are higher. Further, accelerate expenses which will no longer be deductible or will be restricted in the future. Finally, try to convert nondeductible expenses to deductible ones.

EXAMPLE 19.1 You are in a high tax bracket this year but expect to be in a lower one next year. You should increase tax-deductible expenses in the high tax year (for example, making a thirteenth mortgage payment). You should delay receiving income in the high tax year (for example, have your employer pay you a bonus next year for the services rendered in the prior year).

It may be advantageous to defer the receipt of your salaries, commissions, and professional fees to the following year so that the tax may be postponed until the filing of next year's tax return. (This assumes that tax rates will be the same or decline the following year.) Also, money has a time value since it could be invested with the expectation of a return.

You may take advantage of a deferred compensation agreement representing a contract for payments of current services to be made in the future. As a result, there are tax savings in the current year. You may wish to postpone the receipt of income on the expectation that lower tax rates will exist, later year gross income will be less, or deductions will be higher.

WHAT SOURCES OF TAX-EXEMPT INCOME ARE THERE?

Search out income that you do not have to pay tax on. Table 19-1 lists some sources of tax-exempt income.

Table 19-1   Sources of Tax-Exempt Income

Child support
Payments received by matriculated students for fellowships
    and grants if the proceeds are used for educational purposes
Casualty insurance proceeds not exceeding the cost of the
    destroyed property
Personal injury damages
Life insurance proceeds
Relocation payments

There is a tax-free buildup for certain types of life insurance and deferred annuity policies. Taxes may be postponed on the interest earned until the policy matures.

A single-premium whole life insurance policy (one lump-sum immediate payment) provides a good tax shelter. It offers tax-deferred income accumulations and tax-free cash potential. The minimum investment is $5,000 and the maximum amount is $1 million or more. The policy normally has borrowing privileges allowing loans slightly in excess of 90 percent of the built-up cash value. Thus, almost all the earnings may be borrowed without generating taxable income. Interest earned on the policy is not subject to tax unless the policy is surrendered during the insured's life. If the policy is in effect at the death of the insured, accumulated earnings go to the insured's beneficiaries free of tax. Single-premium policies are especially helpful if (1) you want to fund your child's education (borrowed funds from the policy may be used to pay for college without incurring taxes) and (2) you are near retirement age and already have a sizable portfolio of taxable fixed-income securities. Table 19-2 indicates the tax benefits of single-premium whole life insurance.

**Table 19.2   Tax Benefits of Single-Premium
Whole Life Insurance**

Tax-deferred accumulation of cash value
Tax-free loans from principal
Tax-free withdrawals of interest
Tax-free benefits to named beneficiaries

Funds received from a life insurance contract paid to beneficiaries when the insured dies are generally not taxable. Also, disability benefits and health insurance benefits are excludable when attributable to premiums paid by the holders.

Try to obtain tax-exempt income! You receive the full benefit of that income since you do not have to pay tax on it. You can determine the equivalent taxable return as follows:

$$\text{Equivalent taxable return} = \frac{\text{Tax-free return}}{1 - \text{Marginal tax rate}}$$

Interest earned on municipal bonds is not subject to federal tax and is exempt from tax of the state in which the bond was issued. Of course, the market value of the bond changes with changes in the "going" interest rate. *Recommendation:* To reduce the risk of price fluctuation, you can buy short-term bonds. However, short-term bonds will have a lower interest rate than long-term bonds.

SOLVED PROBLEM 19.1

You own a municipal bond that pays an interest rate of 6 percent. Your tax rate is 28 percent. What is the equivalent rate on a taxable instrument?

SOLUTION

$$\frac{.06}{1 - .28} = \frac{.06}{.72} = 8.3\%$$

Table 19-3 shows what return you would have to obtain in a taxable investment to yield the same return in a nontaxable investment.

Table 19-3   Tax-Free Return Equivalent to Taxable Return in Various Income Tax Brackets

	Income Tax Brackets	
	15%	28%
6%	7.01%	8.3%
8	9.41	11.1
10	11.76	13.89

Interest on U.S. government bonds are fully taxed by the federal government but exempt from state and local taxes.

You must disclose on your tax return the amount of tax-exempt income received.

Some items such as sick pay are excludable in a limited amount. Prizes, awards, and gambling winnings are includable in gross income. Gambling losses may only be deducted to the extent of gambling winnings. The deduction may only be claimed if the taxpayer itemizes deductions. Also, unemployment compensation benefits are includable in gross income. It is also possible that social security received may be tax-free. In any event, at most one-half may be taxable.

SOLVED PROBLEM 19.2

You have the following sources of income: gross wages, $40,000; interest income, $3,000; child support, $5,000; relocation payments, $3,000; casualty insurance net proceeds, $8,000; capital gain on sale of real estate, $6,000; interest on a municipal bond, $2,000; prizes, $1,000; and unemployment compensation, $400. How much is your taxable gross income?

SOLUTION

Taxable gross income equals

Gross wages	$40,000
Interest income	3,000
Capital gain	6,000
Prizes	1,000
Total	$50,000

HOW YOU CAN DELAY PAYING TAX ON INTEREST

You can defer reporting interest as income if you keep U.S. Savings Bonds after their maturity date or have a tax-free exchange of the U.S. bonds for another nontransferable U.S. obligation.

You can postpone taxes by buying a U.S. Series EE Savings Bond. The bonds are issued on a discount basis with interest represented by yearly increases in the redemption value. Tax on the interest may be postponed until the maturity date of the bond or when redeemed. The difference between the maturity value and the purchase price represents interest that is taxable in the year the obligation matures. Further, taxes may still be postponed by converting the Series EE bond to a Series HH bond at maturity.

Defer interest income by purchasing financial instruments (for example, Certificates of Deposit, Treasury Bills, U.S. Savings Bonds), maturing in a later year. Taxes are not due on the interest until the investment matures and the interest income is made available.

Be careful: Interest on zero-coupon bonds is taxable each year when the interest is accrued even though not received.

SOLVED PROBLEM 19.3

You own a $50,000 zero-coupon bond you bought on January 1, 19X4, for $40,000. The bond is due on January 1, 19X9. What is the interest you will have to pay tax on in 19X9?

SOLUTION

$$\frac{\$10,000}{5} = \$2,000$$

SCHOLARSHIPS AND FELLOWSHIPS

If you are going for a degree, you can exclude from taxable income the value of scholarships or fellowships limited to tuition, fees, books, supplies, and equipment. You cannot exclude living expense awards. If you are not a degree candidate, you are unable to exclude from income the scholarship or reimbursement of incidental expenses.

Compensation received for services such as teaching and research is includable taxable income.

ARE THERE ANY TAX STRATEGIES IF YOU HAVE CHILDREN?

You can engage in several income-shifting strategies to your children. You can give a child money to buy U.S. Savings Bonds or to purchase an annuity from an insurance company. You can give appreciating assets (for example, growth stocks) to young children. Caution must be exercised since there may be a gift tax consequence if the value of the gift is in excess of $10,000 ($20,000 where the taxpayer and spouse make a joint election). There may be no tax until the asset is sold or the annuity payments start. If the sale takes place after the child is 14, the capital gain is taxed at the child's *lower* tax rate.

Net unearned income is taxed at the parent's rate if the child is under age 14. However, in general, the first $1,000 of net unearned income is taxed at the child's lower rate. *Recommendation:* Structure your child's investments so the child recognizes only $1,000 of net unearned income in a particular year, with the excess deferred until the child is 14.

It pays to shift income to children over 14, such as through a savings account in your child's name, say for a college education. In 1990, the child may use the $3,100 standard deduction indexed for inflation to shelter income.

Series EE savings bonds provide an opportunity to maximize funds for your child's education. Bond interest is paid at maturity and is exempt from state and local taxation. The bonds guarantee a minimum yield of $7\frac{1}{2}$ percent. If held for a minimum of 5 years, the bonds will pay 85 percent of the average yield on a 5-year Treasury note. You can give a Series EE bond to your child under age 14 and have the interest taxed at the child's lower rate. However, the bonds have to mature after the child has reached age 14.

Another approach is to use deferred annuity contracts issued by insurance companies. There is a deferment of payment of interest until withdrawals begin. Actual yield is based on market interest rates over the term of the annuity. To be taxed at the child's rate, withdrawals have to start after the child's 14th birthday.

WHAT DEDUCTIONS ARE YOU ENTITLED TO?

Itemized deductions are subtracted from adjusted gross income. Adjusted gross income equals gross income less adjustments to gross income. Gross income includes wages, interest, dividends, state and city tax refunds, alimony received, gains on the sale of capital assets (including securities), royalties, rental income, all or part of pension income, and under certain conditions, part of Social Security benefits. Adjustments to gross income include deductions for Individual Retirement Accounts, contributions to self-employed (Keogh) retirement plans, alimony paid, and forfeiture penalties paid to banks for premature withdrawals from certificates of deposit.

SOLVED PROBLEM 19.4

You have the following financial information: gross wages, $50,000; interest income, $7,000; business income, $15,000; contribution to Keogh pension plan, $2,000; royalty income, $5,000; interest on municipal bonds, $500; alimony paid, $6,000; and rental income, $7,000. What is your adjusted gross income?

SOLUTION

Gross income:		
Gross wages	$50,000	
Interest income	7,000	
Business income	15,000	
Royalty income	5,000	
Rental income	7,000	
Total gross income		$84,000
Deductions from gross income:		
Contribution to Keogh pension plan	$ 2,000	
Alimony paid	6,000	
Total deductions from gross income		8,000
Adjusted gross income		$76,000

SOLVED PROBLEM 19.5

What is the distinction between deductions and tax credits?

SOLUTION

Deductions reduce adjusted gross income, which is then used to compute the tax. Credits are applied to the tax itself to determine your actual liability.

SOLVED PROBLEM 19.6

What do itemized deductions include?

SOLUTION

Itemized deductions include deductions for medical expenses, interest, state and local income taxes, real estate taxes, charitable contributions, casualty and theft losses, and miscellaneous expenses.

You must save canceled checks and receipts to support the deductions you claim!
An overall picture of items affecting your tax appears in Table 19-4.

Table 19-4   Tax Computation Items

Gross taxable income
Less: Adjustments (e.g., IRA, Keogh, alimony payments,
    business expenses, capital losses)
Adjusted gross income
Less: Itemized deductions (or the standard deduction)
     Exemptions
Net taxable income
Less: Tax expense
     Tax credits
Tax liability

MEDICAL EXPENSES

Physician's fees and prescription drugs net of insurance reimbursement are deductible only if they exceed 7.5 percent of adjusted gross income. Some less obvious medical items you should not overlook are given in Table 19-5.

Table 19-5   Medical Items Not to Be Overlooked

Cosmetic surgery
Meal and lodging expenses incurred enroute to medical treatment
Medical portion of life insurance
Medically prescribed items, such as hot tubs
Parking fees and tolls
Prescribed diet foods
Transportation to and from the doctor's office
Prescribed vitamins

SOLVED PROBLEM 19.7

Your adjusted gross income is $40,000. The medical fees incurred are $3,400. How much is deductible on your tax return?

SOLUTION

Medical fees	$3,400
Needed amount (7.5% × $40,000)	3,000
Deductible amount	$ 400

INTEREST DEDUCTION

Mortgage interest is deductible on your first and second homes (for example, vacation home). You cannot deduct interest on that portion of a mortgage loan that exceeds the cost of the property including improvements. However, you can deduct the interest on loan proceeds in excess of the cost (plus improvements) of your property but limited to its fair market value if the funds are used to pay educational or medical expenses. Excess mortgage proceeds not used for medical or education expenses will be treated in a manner similar to personal interest. Points paid to obtain a *new* mortgage are tax deductible. *Beware:* Points incurred on the refinancing of a mortgage are only deductible over the life of the loan, unless the proceeds of the refinanced mortgage are used for home improvements.

EXAMPLE 19.2 You paid $100,000 for a home and made capital improvements of $10,000. You can borrow up to $110,000 and the interest will be entirely deductible. You may use the available funds to meet payments on credit card balances and auto loans.

Interest on personal loans (for example, auto loans, credit cards, and interest on tax deficiencies) is being phased out. Allowable interest deductions for personal loans in 1990 is 10 percent of interest incurred.

SOLVED PROBLEM 19.8

Your interest on an auto loan in 1990 is $1,800. How much are you allowed to deduct for interest?

SOLUTION

$$\$1,800 \times 10\% = \$180$$

Tax strategy: Take out a mortgage loan and use the proceeds to buy personal items (for example, an auto) so that you may get a tax deduction for the interest.

If you use credit cards for expenses just prior to year-end, you still can claim a current-year deduction even though you do not pay the bill until next year.

Interest on debt incurred for investment purposes may be partially or totally deductible. However, interest is disallowed on debt used to acquire securities that generate tax-free income.

Interest incurred on a prepayment penalty is deductible.

TAX DEDUCTION

State and local income taxes paid are deductible. This includes amounts withheld, estimated payments, and deficiencies attributable to prior years. Real and personal property taxes are also deductible. However, sales taxes are not deductible.

SOLVED PROBLEM 19.9

You incurred the following taxes: real estate, $4,000; sales tax, $2,000; state tax, $6,000; and city tax, $1,000. How much is your itemized deduction for taxes?

SOLUTION

$$\$4,000 + \$6,000 + \$1,000 = \$11,000$$

CHARITABLE CONTRIBUTIONS

Charitable contributions are deductible only by those who itemize their deductions. Charitable contributions are not deductible by those claiming the standard deduction. However, the itemized deduction is limited to 50 percent of adjusted gross income.

A charitable donation of property (other than cash or securities) requires a qualified written appraisal if you claim it has a value in excess of $5,000.

SOLVED PROBLEM 19.10

You made cash contributions of $3,000 and gave property to charities having an appraised value of $10,000. Your adjusted gross income is $25,000. How much can you deduct as a charitable contribution?

SOLUTION

Cash contribution	$ 3,000
Appraised value of property	10,000
Total	$13,000
Limitation: 50% × adjusted gross income (50% × $25,000)	$12,500

You are limited to $12,500.

THEFT AND CASUALTY LOSSES

Theft and casualty losses are deductible as itemized deductions if they exceed 10 percent of adjusted gross income plus $100. Included are legal costs applicable to settling an insurance claim. Because of this low amount of tax deductibility, you may wish to lower your insurance deductibles on property and automobile insurance.

SOLVED PROBLEM 19.11

Your adjusted gross income is $50,000. You can deduct a casualty loss only if it exceeds how much?

SOLUTION

$$(\$50,000 \times 10\%) + \$100 = \$5,100$$

MISCELLANEOUS EXPENSES

Total miscellaneous expenses are deductible only to the extent they exceed 2 percent of adjusted gross income. Table 19-6 lists miscellaneous deductions.

Table 19-6   Miscellaneous Deductions

Investment counseling and magazine subscriptions
Safe deposit box rental used for investment or other income-producing property
Tax preparation fees
Subscription to professional journals
Administrative expenses charged by a mutual fund
Unreimbursed employee expenses
Expenses incurred in seeking a new job in present field
Continuing education course
Malpractice insurance premiums incurred as an employee
Professional and union dues, except for voluntary assessments
Specialized work clothes
Business use of personal residence
Pocket calculator and computer bought for business or investment purposes
Video tape recorder to tape programs needed for business
Attache case for business
Calls to your stockbroker

You may deduct education expenses if the education is necessary to

Maintain or improve skills required in your current work

Meet employer or regulatory requirements to keep your status or job

Moving expenses of an employee or self-employed individual are generally allowed as an itemized deduction but are *not* subject to the 2 percent floor. You can deduct moving expenses if the move puts you significantly closer to a new job or place of work.

Business meals and entertainment are limited to 80 percent of the cost, before the application of the 2 percent of adjusted gross income limitation.

SOLVED PROBLEM 19.12

Your adjusted gross income is $100,000 and your miscellaneous expenses are $3,500. How much is deductible as a miscellaneous expense?

SOLUTION

$$\$3,500 - (2\% \times \$100,000) = \$3,500 - \$2,000 = \$1,500$$

ARE YOU SELF-EMPLOYED?

You must make a profit in your business in three out of the most recent five consecutive years. Otherwise, the losses will be attributable to a hobby, and the loss will be nondeductible. Hobby expenses may be deducted only to the extent of hobby income.

A home office deduction is limited to the net income arising from the trade or business. The home office deduction in excess of net income may be carried forward to future years.

In general, you can immediately expense up to $10,000 of equipment acquired in a particular year.

HOW MUCH IN PERSONAL EXEMPTIONS ARE YOU ENTITLED TO?

You can take an exemption on your tax return for each dependent. The number of exemptions multiplied by the amount of the exemptions is subtracted from adjusted gross income to derive taxable income. To claim an exemption, you must provide more than 50 percent of the dependent's total support for the year. *Be careful:* If you give money to a multimember household (for example, parents) and that aid when divided equally among members of the household does not satisfy the 50 percent support test for any one member, you cannot claim that exemption on your tax return. *Recommendation:* Give the support directly to one person so that the support test can be met. The personal exemption in 1990 is $2,050.

SOLVED PROBLEM 19.13

You are married with three children. In addition, you provide 60 percent of the support of your mother and 30 percent of the support of your father. The personal exemption is $2,050. Your adjusted gross income is $70,000.

(*a*)   How many personal exemptions are you entitled to?

(*b*)   What is your deduction for personal exemptions?

(*c*)   What is your taxable income?

SOLUTION

(*a*)   6

(*b*) $2,050 × 6 = $12,300

(*c*) $70,000 − $12,300 = $57,700

WHAT IF YOU TAKE THE STANDARD DEDUCTION?

The standard deduction is available if you do not itemize deductions. The standard deduction in 1990 is

Married, joint return	$5,450
Head of household	4,750
Single	3,250

Taxpayers over the age of 65 and blind taxpayers may increase their standard deductions by $650 for each married person. The increase is $800 if the elderly or blind taxpayer is single.

SOLVED PROBLEM 19.14

You are married filing a joint return. How much of a standard deduction are you entitled to?

SOLUTION

$5,450

SOLVED PROBLEM 19.15

A single person is over the age of 65. How much of a standard deduction is he/she entitled to?

SOLUTION

$$\$3,250 + \$800 = \$4,050$$

WHAT ARE THE TAX IMPLICATIONS OF YOUR PENSION PLAN?

There are various types of pension plans. You may set up an Individual Retirement Account (IRA) and/or Keogh plan. There are also employer-sponsored pension and profit sharing plans. You are not usually taxed on pension monies until you begin to make withdrawals from the plans. If you withdraw money from a pension plan, you can avoid taxes by rolling it over into another qualified pension plan within 60 days. You are not taxed until you take the funds out.

INDIVIDUAL RETIREMENT ACCOUNT

If you are working and not covered by (that is, not an active participant in) another retirement plan, you may deduct an annual IRA contribution up to $2,000 ($4,000 if both husband and wife are working). The deduction is treated as an adjustment to gross income in arriving at adjusted gross income. If you are working and are an active participant in another retirement plan, you may deduct IRA contributions (up to $2,000) if your adjusted gross income is below $25,000 a year ($40,000 for a married couple filing a joint return). However, if you are an active participant in another retirement plan, you may not make deductible IRA contributions if your adjusted gross income is in excess of $35,000 a year ($50,000 for a joint return). The deduction will be disallowed proportionately as adjusted gross income increases within the phase-out range (that is, $25,000–$35,000 for single taxpayers and $40,000–$50,000 for married taxpayers filing a joint return). *Warning:* If one spouse is an active participant in another retirement plan, then both spouses will be subject to the phase-out rules.

SOLVED PROBLEM 19.16

You are single and not covered by a pension plan at work. Your salary is $80,000.

(*a*)   How much of an IRA deduction are you entitled to?

(*b*)   If you were covered by a pension plan, how much of an IRA deduction could you take?

SOLUTION

(*a*) $2,000

(*b*)   0

Even if the IRA contribution is not deductible, you do not have to pay tax now on the return earned from the IRA investment. The interest earned on the account is tax-deferred until withdrawn. Probably, at retirement, the taxable income will be lower and will result in less tax. Even if the lower retirement tax rate is not expected, the tax-deferred aspect is desirable so as to spread taxable income over several years or to lower taxable income in any one particular year.

If an IRA distribution is received it is taxable to the recipient unless such distribution is rolled over into another IRA account. This rollover is sometimes done to change the investment goal of the tax-payer. If you use this exception, payments have to be made at a yearly minimum. The payments must continue for at least 5 years or until you reach age $59\frac{1}{2}$.

Warning: Early withdrawals (before age $59\frac{1}{2}$) are subject to a 10 percent penalty in addition to the tax (unless there is a disability). IRA withdrawals taken after 1986 as a life annuity are not subject to the early withdrawal penalty.

KEOGH PLAN

Keogh pension plans are for self-employed individuals who may contribute up to 20 percent of the net self-employed income (before considering the deduction) up to a maximum of $30,000 per year. The monies earn interest without being currently taxed. You can have a Keogh even though you have an IRA. You may also have a Keogh plan for your self-employed income even though you belong to an employer's retirement plan. You cannot withdraw Keogh funds without penalty until age $59\frac{1}{2}$ and withdrawals must commence by age $70\frac{1}{2}$. Under certain circumstances, you can with stringent limitations borrow against the funds in the plan.

A distribution from a retirement plan that equals 50 percent or more of your balance in the plan may be rolled over into an IRA or Keogh without being taxed as current income. The rollover must occur within 60 days of distribution, and the distribution will be taxable when it is withdrawn at a later date.

401(k) PLANS

Your employer may offer a contributory employee pension plan allowing you to voluntarily put in some of your current income together with the employer's contribution. The employee's money is deducted from current income.

401(k) Plans are salary-reduction plans permitting you to deposit part of your income to a retirement account through your company. The plan enables the deferral of taxes on part of your salary. The limitation on compensation that can be deferred was $7,000 in 1987. This amount is indexed for inflation using the Consumer Price Index today. Money may be withdrawn with minimal or no penalty in the event of financial hardship. Loans are allowed from 401(k) plans but not from IRAs. FICA tax is not deducted on contributions to salary-reduction plans.

WHAT ABOUT REAL ESTATE TRANSACTIONS?

You can avoid *current* tax on a sale of a home if the selling price of the former residence is used to purchase a new home. Further, if a homeowner is 55 or older, there is available a one-time exclusion on the first $125,000 of the profit on the sale of the home.

The profit on the sale of your home equals the net selling price less the adjusted cost basis. The basis of your property is the price paid plus settlement and closing costs (title insurance, sales commissions, transfer taxes) plus capital improvements (for example, roof, driveway, new wiring, central air conditioning) less claimed depreciation and casualty losses. Careful property records must be kept.

SOLVED PROBLEM 19.17

You originally paid $130,000 for your house including attorney and closing costs. While in the house, you made capital improvements of $80,000. At age 50, you sold the home for $350,000 but will have to give the real estate agent 4 percent of the selling price. You will move into an apartment.

(*a*) What is the taxable gain or loss?

(*b*) Assuming a 28 percent tax bracket, how much will you have to pay in taxes, if any?

(*c*) What is your net gain or loss after tax?

SOLUTION

(*a*) Real estate agent fee = $350,000 × 4% = $14,000

Selling price ($350,000 − $14,000)	$336,000
Adjusted cost basis ($130,000 + $80,000)	210,000
Gain	$126,000

(*b*) $126,000 × .28 = $35,280

(*c*) $126,000 − $35,280 = $90,720

SOLVED PROBLEM 19.18

At age 45, you sell your primary residence for $160,000. The original purchase price was $140,000. You buy a new home for $200,000 six months later.

(a)   What is the capital gain or loss?

(b)   Is the capital gain from the sale of the house deferred, taxed, or qualified for the one-time exclusion?

SOLUTION

(a) $160,000 − $140,000 = $20,000

(b)   Deferred

If you rent out part of your residence, you have to include the rental income in gross income but may deduct rental expenses against it.

If you rent out a vacation home for less than 15 days during the year, the rental income is not taxable. But if you rent the home for 15 days or more, all rental income is reportable.

Deductible real estate rental losses are capped at $25,000, but are reduced for taxpayers with adjusted gross incomes between $100,000 and $150,000. Losses are not deductible within the $25,000 cap unless you actively participate in managing the property and own at least 10 percent of the property for the entire year. The $25,000 cap is to be reduced by 50 percent of the amount by which the taxpayer's adjusted gross income is in excess of $100,000. Active participation mandates that you be involved in the operations on a regular, continuous, and substantial basis. Losses over $25,000 may only be applied against gains from other passive investments. *Recommendation:* If you have tax-sheltered losses, you should invest in a profitable general partnership or an "S" corporation.

Losses on real estate investments (for example, Real Estate Investment Trusts) that you do not manage cannot exceed the amount for which you are "at-risk." "At-risk" means that you cannot deduct a loss that exceeds the adjusted cost basis (cost and improvements) of your property. However, there is a phase-in period for the rules related to real estate in that you can deduct 10 percent of the losses from passive rental properties in 1990 provided the investment was made before the enactment of the Tax Reform Act of 1986 (October 22, 1986).

Losses from investments made subsequent to enactment are disallowed in the current year completely to the extent that they exceed passive income.

Since the maximum tax rate is 28 percent, there is much less of an incentive to invest in real estate tax shelters. Income from the sale of tax shelter assets is subject to the ordinary income tax rates.

Residential rental properties are depreciated over 27.5 years while nonresidential rental properties are depreciated over 31.5 years.

Note: Working interest in oil and gas properties are still allowable as a tax shelter.

CAN YOU TAKE CREDIT FOR YOUR CHILDREN?

You may be entitled to claim a child-care credit. In general, to obtain the credit, the child must be your dependent and be under the age of 15. The child-care credit ranges from a low of 20 percent to a high of 30 percent of qualifying expenses incurred during the year. The expenses must be incurred to enable you to be gainfully employed.

IS YOUR ESTIMATED TAX OK?

To avoid an estimated-tax penalty, you must pay in for taxes during the year 90 percent or more of the determined tax liability or 100 percent of the tax liability from last year.

SOLVED PROBLEM 19.19

Your tax for the current year is $20,000 of which you paid in estimated tax of $15,000.

(a) Are you subject to an estimated-tax penalty?

(b) If so, what is the tax penalty based on?

SOLUTION

(a) Yes

(b)

$20,000 × 90%	$18,000
Paid in	15,000
Deficiency	$ 3,000

WHAT ABOUT GIFTS?

Gifts are not included in the taxable income of the recipient. They may be taxed to the donor. Nonliquid holiday gifts or bonuses received from an employer are also tax-free. You can make a gift to another person which is exempt up to $10,000 per year ($20,000 if an election is made by a taxpayer and his or her spouse).

All gifts between spouses are tax-free without limitations. Gifts are also unlimited if they are made for education and medical reasons.

The gift tax return is filed on Form 709 and is typically due on or before April 15 of the year following the gift.

HOW ABOUT EMPLOYEE DISCOUNTS?

Employee discounts are not taxable as long as the discount does not go below the employer's cost.

HOW DO YOU FIGURE YOUR TAX?

Your tax is computed using the federal income tax schedules. Table 19-7 shows the tax schedules for 1990.

Table 19-7   Tax Schedules for 1990

Tax Rate	Married/Joint	Single	Married/Separate	Head of Household
15%	First $32,450	First $19,450	First $16,225	First $26,050
28%	Over 32,450	Over 19,450	Over 16,225	Over 26,050

SOLVED PROBLEM 19.20

You are single and have taxable income of $35,000.

(a) What is your tax?

(b) What is your average (effective) tax rate?

SOLUTION

(a)

On the first $19,450	$2,918
Balance [($35,000 − $19,450)	
= $15,550 × .28]	4,354
Total tax	$7,272

You are in the 28 percent marginal tax bracket, meaning that for every $1 earned above $19,450 until $47,050, you have to pay 28 percent in tax.

(b)
$$\frac{\text{Tax}}{\text{Taxable income}} = \frac{\$7,272}{\$35,000} = 20.8\%$$

The average (effective) tax rate is below the marginal tax rate because the first $19,450 of taxable income was taxed at a lower rate.

SOLVED PROBLEM 19.21

You are single and have no dependents. Relevant financial information in preparing your tax return follow: (1) gross wages, $25,000; (2) interest paid on mortgage, $3,000; (3) charitable donation, $500; (4) allowable medical deduction, $1,000; (5) interest earned, $8,000; (6) dividends earned, $4,000; (7) state and local income taxes, $4,000; (8) property taxes, $3,500; (9) inheritance from parent, $42,000; (10) alimony paid, $8,000; (11) penalty on early withdrawal of savings, $500; and (12) interest on municipal bonds, $300.

(a) Determine in which of the following categories each item belongs: gross income (GI), gross income deduction (GID), itemized deduction (ID), standard deduction (SD), or tax-exempt (TE).

(b) Determine the taxable income (assume the personal exemption is $2,050).

(c) If the tax rate is 15 percent, what is the tax?

(d) If the tax withheld during the year was $1,500, what is the additional tax owed or the tax refund?

(e) Assume the same facts as part (d) except you made estimated tax payments of $1,000. What is the additional tax owed or tax refund?

SOLUTION

(a) (1) GI;   (2) ID;   (3) ID;   (4) ID;   (5) GI;   (6) GI;   (7) ID;   (8) ID;   (9) TE;
(10) GID;   (11) GID;   (12) TE

(b)

Gross income		
Gross wages	$25,000	
Interest earned	8,000	
Dividends earned	4,000	
Total gross income		$37,000
Less: Deductions from gross income		
Alimony paid	$ 8,000	
Penalty on early withdrawal of savings	500	
Total deductions from gross income		8,500
Adjusted gross income		$28,500
Less: Itemized deductions		
Interest on mortgage	$ 3,000	
Charitable donation	500	
Medical	1,000	

	State and local income taxes	4,000	
	Property taxes	3,500	
	Total itemized deductions		12,000
	Balance		$16,500
	Less: Personal exemption		2,050
	Taxable income		$14,450
(c)	Tax ($14,450 × 15%)		$ 2,168
	Less: Tax withheld		1,500
(d)	Amount you owe		$ 668
(e)	Taxes		$ 2,168
	Less: Tax withheld	$ 1,500	
	Estimated tax	1,000	2,500
	Tax refund		$ 332

WHAT KIND OF ESTATE PLANNING DO YOU NEED?

You should be familiar with some of the very basic points in estate planning. However, consult a tax lawyer and/or CPA for estate planning advice because of the complicated tax and legal ramifications.

Estate planning is concerned mostly with planning the disposition of your property to heirs during your lifetime as well as at death so that the amount transferred is maximized. A will is usually adequate to settle a small estate. However, will substitutes and trusts may be needed for larger estates.

Good estate planning enables the transfer of assets to designated heirs (prior to or after death), preserves assets during lifetime by lowering taxes, minimizes administrative confusion occurring at death, and reduces tax and legal expenses. A will indicates how the decedent's assets are to be divided. A will is needed to minimize costs, disruptions, and other disadvantages of probate.

Related parties should have separate, individual wills because joint wills (husband and wife) may cause problems (for example, the husband or wife may change the will without the consent of the other).

A trust can shift the tax burden to lower-tax-bracket beneficiaries to lower the total tax assessment and/or assist the grantor in avoiding estate taxes altogether.

You can give property to future heirs during your lifetime and receive gift tax exemptions. Gifts to relatives go tax-free up to $10,000 per beneficiary per year. If a married couple files a joint election, $20,000 can be given tax-free (for example, husband and wife to a child).

Spouses enjoy tax-free spousal estate transfers. A spouse can pass his or her entire estate to the other without paying tax.

SOLVED PROBLEM 19.22

You have five children that you and your spouse would like to give a gift to. How much can you give in total that will pass tax-free to your children?

SOLUTION

$$\$20,000 \times 5 = \$100,000$$

SOLVED PROBLEM 19.23

You received a $10,000 gift from your grandmother. By the end of the year, the funds had earned $800 in interest. You are in the 15 percent tax bracket. How much tax do you owe?

SOLUTION

$$\$800 \times 15\% = \$120$$

SOLVED PROBLEM 19.24

What is the dollar amount of an estate that can be passed to a surviving spouse free of estate tax?

SOLUTION

Unlimited

You should calculate the estate's estimated net value as

Total assets

Less: Funeral costs
       Compensation to executors
       Debt payments

Estimated net value

The gross estate includes all assets owned (for example, stocks, bonds, real estate, cash accounts, insurance policies). Jointly held marital property is divided equally between spouses. The valuation of the assets is at the date of death or 6 months later at the option of the estate's executor.

The allowable deductions include administrative expenses, debts, and, of course, the *marital deduction*.

SOLVED PROBLEM 19.25

You are single. When you die your funeral costs are estimated at $1,000. Your house is projected to have a fair market value of $300,000. There will be an outstanding mortgage of $50,000. Your personal property is estimated at $100,000. Debts are estimated at $60,000. Your IRA will be valued at $95,000. You are also entitled to a pension benefit from your employer projected at $150,000. There is also a life insurance policy of $200,000. In your will there is a provision for a $5,000 gift to a charity. Administration expenses will be $6,000. What is your estimated net estate?

SOLUTION

The estimated net estate is

Gross estate		
Home	$300,000	
Personal property	100,000	
Pension plans	245,000	
Life insurance	200,000	
Total		$845,000
Less: Allowable deductions		
Funeral expense	$ 1,000	
Administration expense	6,000	
Mortgage and debts	110,000	
Charitable contribution	5,000	
Total deductions		122,000
Net estate		$723,000

SOLVED PROBLEM 19.26

Mr. B's gross estate was valued at $1,500,000. He left $500,000 to his wife and another $100,000 to a charity. The remainder was distributed to other relatives. Expenses of settling the estate were $10,000.

(a)   What was the adjusted gross estate?

(b)   How much was the marital deduction?

(c)   What is the net taxable estate?

SOLUTION

(a) $1,500,000 − $100,000 − $10,000 = $1,390,000

(b) $500,000

(c) $1,390,000 − $500,000 = $890,000

Estate tax is on a graduated basis on the value of transferred property. *Warning:* Do not confuse estate taxes with inheritance taxes. Inheritance taxes are levied by the states and are payable by the heirs and not by the estate of the deceased.

The federal estate tax exemption limit is currently $600,000. *Recommendation:* To settle an estate of $600,000 or below, you should have a joint ownership agreement between spouses along with a will. Use a trust if minor children or other dependents are involved.

If the estate is above the federal estate tax exemption, make a combination of lifetime gifts to lower the estate value to the exemption limit. For example, by transferring real property and gifts 25 years prior to death, the donor transfers tax-free 25 years' worth of appreciating value.

SOLVED PROBLEM 19.27

In the event there are children, how can the husband and wife minimize estate taxes?

SOLUTION

The husband and wife can minimize estate taxes by having the spouse that dies first give children $600,000 which is exempt. The remainder should go to the surviving spouse which passes tax-free. When the other spouse dies, $600,000 of that spouse's estate is exempt to the children. In this manner, $1,200,000 of the estate passes to the children without tax. If the first spouse had given everything to the other spouse upon death, the initial $600,000 exemption would have been lost. Thus, the only exemption would have been the $600,000 passing to the children upon the death of the second spouse.

Property may be passed tax-free between spouses in several ways including:

Outright transfer.   The will provides transfer of property by right of survivorship.

General power trust.   A trust is established for the surviving spouse. In this arrangement, all the income from the trust's investments must be distributed to the spouse. The surviving spouse must also have control over the property.

Qualified terminable interest property (Q-tip) trust.   You may choose the ultimate disposition of the property. Income is paid out to your spouse for life. When your spouse dies, the trust interest terminates and the assets pass as you direct. In this way, you can assume that your children eventually receive the money. If you set up a bypass trust properly, you can give $1.2 million to the children without paying tax.

In 1990, the maximum estate tax rate is 50 percent. Federal estate taxes are paid with the filing of Form 706 (U.S. Estate Tax Return). The form is due 9 months after the date of death. The state estate tax rate varies among states.

Consult an expert regarding such complicated issues as probate and setting up a trust (for example, irrevocable, revocable).

Your executor will need certain information which you should make available to him or her including documents and their location, list of assets and liabilities, and name and address of accountant, stockbroker, and insurance agent.

TAX PLANNING SOFTWARE

Tax planning software involves looking at the different tax options to minimize the tax liability in current and future years. For example, projections may be made for real estate shelters and the timing of the sale of securities.

Tax planning programs are basically just fancy spreadsheet programs that are already set up and require you only to plug in real and hypothetical (projection) numbers in the rows and columns. All current tax rates and regulations are already in the program.

Function keys show the automatic increase or decrease of tax input for each estate strategy at specified incremental amounts, increase or decrease of subsequent strategies by a compound percentage whereby each entry's increment is based upon the prior entry, increase or decrease of subsequent strategies by a fixed percentage over the first or last entry, and the ability to alter one variable while holding constant subsequent values derived from that variable.

An example of tax planning software is Arthur Andersen's "A-Plus Tax" which performs "what-if" analysis. It can forecast tax strategies and investments.

Customized estate and tax planning software may be written using macros and predefined formula formats for handling a particular practitioner's clientele. The advantages here are that they can easily be updated in conformity with tax law developments as well as have usefulness in preparing customized reports and presentations.

Many applications exist showing how microcomputers can be utilized in the estate planning process.

EXAMPLE 19.3   Mr. Smith wants to estimate his future estate tax if he starts shifting property and making gifts starting now. Spreadsheets provide "what-if" analysis of the estate tax based on the expected value of the estate making different assumptions of when, who, and how much is the property shifted to or gifts given to. Electronic worksheets enable us to look at the effect of tax due to timing and amounts given to others prior to death. What is the tax effect of making X dollars in gifts for X years to X persons? Varying alternatives can be considered. What will the estate be, given certain types of investments? Are risk or risk-adverse investments best? What dollar effect will tax shelter investments have? Factors such as current and projected market value of assets, current and estimated future tax rates, tax-deferred investments, etc., can be included in the spreadsheet formula. Alternative scenarios can be developed of when to and how much to invest in tax shelters. Assumptions as to the effect of buying or selling varying types of securities of the estate may be considered.

Specialized estate tax planning programs exist. You should engage in tax planning as much as possible.

SOLVED PROBLEM 19.28

What are some tax planning tips?

SOLUTION

Tips to save on taxes include:

Use your charge cards for deductible purchases. You can deduct items charged in the current year even though they are paid for in the following year.

Donate appreciated property instead of cash. If you donate appreciated property to a charity, you can deduct the full market value and avoid paying tax on the gain.

Put away the most you can to a retirement plan. Even if the contribution is not deductible, interest earned is tax-deferred. *Recommendation:* Contribute at the beginning of the year to maximize the tax deferral on the interest.

Offset gains with losses. You can avoid paying taxes on gains by selling securities having losses. You can use tax swaps (selling an investment and replacing it immediately with a similar investment) to establish a gain or loss and still maintain your investment decision.

Transfer savings to members of the family in lower tax brackets (for example, children).

Review Questions

(1) A _____ whole life insurance policy provides a good tax shelter.

(2) Interest on _____ bonds is tax-free for federal and state tax purposes.

(3) Interest on _____ bonds is taxed by the federal government but exempt from state taxes.

(4) Interest on _____ bonds is taxable each year when the interest is accrued even though not received.

(5) Net unearned income above $1,000 is taxed at the parent's rate if the child is under age _____.

(6) In 1990, interest on personal loans is only allowable up to _____ percent.

(7) Miscellaneous expenses are only deductible exceeding _____ percent of adjusted gross income.

(8) An individual working but not covered by the company's pension plan may contribute to an _____ account.

(9) Self-employed individuals may contribute to a _____ pension plan.

(10) You cannot withdraw pension monies from an IRA or Keogh pension plan before age _____ without incurring a penalty unless you are disabled.

(11) A rollover of pension monies to another plan may be made within _____ days of distribution to avoid tax.

(12) A contributory pension plan is referred to as a _____ plan.

(13) If you rent out a vacation home for _____ days or more, the rental income is taxable.

(14) Losses on real estate investments that you do not manage cannot exceed the amount for which you are _____.

(15) Residential rental properties are depreciated over _____ years.

(16) A child-care credit can only be obtained if the child is under the age of _____.

(17) To avoid an estimated tax penalty, you must pay in for taxes during the year _____ percent or more of the tax liability or _____ percent of the tax liability from last year.

(18) You can give a gift to another person which is exempt up to $_____ per year.

(19) A gift made for _____ or _____ reasons is unlimited.

(20) Form _____ is the gift tax return.

(21) The federal estate tax exemption limit is $_____.

(22) Form _____ is the estate tax return.

Answers: (1) single-premium; (2) municipal; (3) U.S. government; (4) zero-coupon; (5) 14; (6) 10; (7) 2; (8) IRA; (9) Keogh; (10) $59\frac{1}{2}$; (11) 60; (12) 401(k); (13) 15; (14) "at-risk"; (15) 27.5; (16) 15; (17) 90, 100; (18) $10,000; (19) education, medical; (20) 709; (21) $600,000; (22) 706.

Additional Solved Problems

19.1 You own a municipal bond that pays 5 percent interest. Your tax rate is 28 percent. What is the equivalent rate on a taxable instrument?

SOLUTION

$$\frac{.05}{1 - .28} = \frac{.05}{.72} = 6.94\%$$

19.2 Your adjusted gross income is $35,000. The medical fees incurred are $3,000. What is the amount of the allowable medical deduction?

SOLUTION

Medical fees	$3,000
Needed amount (7.5% × $35,000)	2,625
Deductible amount	$ 375

19.3 If your interest on an auto loan in 1990 was $1,600, how much interest can you deduct on your tax return?

SOLUTION

$$\$1,600 \times .10 = \$160$$

19.4 Your adjusted gross income is $42,000. In order to deduct a casualty loss, it must exceed how much?

SOLUTION

$$(\$42,000 \times 10\%) + \$100 = \$4,300$$

19.5 Your adjusted gross income is $75,000 and your miscellaneous expenses are $2,800. How much of your miscellaneous expenses are deductible?

SOLUTION

Miscellaneous expenses	$2,800
Limitation (2% × $75,000)	1,500
Deductible amount	$1,300

19.6 You received a $6,000 gift from your father. At year-end, you earned $500 in dividend income from the funds. If you are in the 28 percent tax bracket, how much tax do you have to pay because of this gift?

SOLUTION

$$\$500 \times .28 = \$140$$

19.7 You are married with one child. In addition, you are providing more than 50 percent of the support of your parents. The personal exemption is $2,050. Your adjusted gross income is $50,000.

(*a*)   How much personal exemptions are you entitled to?

(*b*)   What is your deduction for personal exemptions?

(*c*)   What is your taxable income?

SOLUTION

(*a*) 5

(*b*) $2,050 × 5 = $10,250

(*c*) $50,000 − $10,250 = $39,750

19.8 During the year, you made cash contributions of $1,000 and donated property to a charity having a fair market value of $10,000. Your adjusted gross income is $80,000.

(*a*)   If you are taking a standard deduction, how much can you deduct as a charitable contribution?

(*b*)   If you are itemizing your deductions, how much can you deduct for charitable contributions?

SOLUTION

(*a*) 0

(*b*)

Cash contribution	$ 1,000
Fair market value of donated property	10,000
	$11,000
Limitation: 50% of adjusted gross income (50% × $80,000)	$40,000

You can deduct $11,000 since it is less than the limitation.

19.9 You have the following sources of income: gross wages, $60,000; dividend income, $4,000; personal injury damages, $5,000; life insurance proceeds, $20,000; business income, $10,000; net gambling winnings, $1,000; and scholarship for tuition, $3,000. How much is your taxable gross income?

SOLUTION

Taxable gross income	
Gross wages	$60,000
Dividend income	4,000
Business income	10,000
Gambling winnings	1,000
Total	$75,000

19.10 You are single and have no dependents. Relevant financial information in preparing your tax return follows: (1) gross wages, $50,000; (2) penalty on early withdrawal of savings, $500; (3) interest earned, $4,000; (4) interest on municipal bonds, $1,800; (5) taxable refund of state and local taxes, $3,000; (6) real estate tax, $12,000; (7) alimony received, $10,000; (8) allowable miscellaneous expenses, $11,000; (9) capital gain on sale of stock, $6,000; and (10) interest on mortgage on primary residence, $13,000. The tax withheld was $5,000.

(*a*) Determine in which of the following categories each item belongs: gross income (GI), gross income deduction (GID), itemized deduction (ID), standard deduction (SD), or tax-exempt (TE).

(*b*) Determine the taxable income (assume the personal exemption is $2,050).

(*c*) Determine your tax.

(*d*) Determine the amount you owe or refund you are entitled to.

SOLUTION

(*a*)   (1) GI;   (2) GID;   (3) GI;   (4) TE;   (5) GI;   (6) ID;   (7) GI;   (8) ID;   (9) GI; and (10) ID.

(*b*)

Gross income		
Gross wages	$50,000	
Interest earned	4,000	
Tax refund of state and local taxes	3,000	
Alimony received	10,000	
Capital gain	6,000	
Total gross income		$73,000
Less: Deductions from gross income		
Penalty on early withdrawal of savings		500
Adjusted gross income		$72,500
Less: Itemized deductions		
Real estate taxes	$12,000	
Interest on mortgage	13,000	
Allowable miscellaneous expenses	11,000	
Total itemized deductions		36,000
Balance		$36,500
Less: Personal exemptions		2,050
Taxable income		$34,450

(*c*)

Tax		
15% × $19,450	$ 2,918	
28% × $15,000	4,200	$ 7,118
Less: Tax withheld		5,000

(*d*)

Amount you owe		$ 2,118

19.11 Mr. A's gross estate was valued at $1,300,000. He left $400,000 to his wife and another $200,000 to a charity. The remainder was distributed to other relatives. Expenses of settling the estate were $8,000.

(*a*)   What was the adjusted gross estate?

(*b*)   How much was the marital deduction?

(*c*) . What is the net taxable estate?

SOLUTION

(*a*) $1,300,000 − $200,000 − $8,000 = $1,092,000

(*b*) $400,000

(*c*) $1,092,000 − $400,000 = $692,000

19.12 You are single. When you die your funeral costs are estimated at $2,000. Your house is estimated to have a fair market value of $400,000. There will be an outstanding mortgage of $60,000. Your personal property is estimated at $120,000. Your stocks and bonds are worth $150,000. Debts are projected at $70,000. Your Keogh pension plan will be worth $700,000. You have a life insurance policy for $300,000. You have provided in your will to give a gift to charity of $10,000. Administrative expenses will be $7,000. What is your estimated net estate?

SOLUTION

Gross estate		
Home	$400,000	
Personal property	120,000	
Stocks and bonds	150,000	
Pension plans	700,000	
Life insurance	300,000	
Total		$1,670,000
Less: Allowable deductions		
Funeral expense	$ 2,000	
Administrative expense	7,000	
Mortgage and debts	130,000	
Charitable contribution	10,000	
Total deductions		149,000
Net estate		$1,521,000

Appendix A

Tables

Table 1 Future Value of $1.00

(n) Periods	2%	2½%	3%	4%	5%	6%
1	1.02000	1.02500	1.03000	1.04000	1.05000	1.06000
2	1.04040	1.05063	1.06090	1.08160	1.10250	1.12360
3	1.06121	1.07689	1.09273	1.12486	1.15763	1.19102
4	1.08243	1.10381	1.12551	1.16986	1.21551	1.26248
5	1.10408	1.13141	1.15927	1.21665	1.27628	1.33823
6	1.12616	1.15969	1.19405	1.26532	1.34010	1.41852
7	1.14869	1.18869	1.22987	1.31593	1.40710	1.50363
8	1.17166	1.21840	1.26677	1.36857	1.47746	1.59385
9	1.19509	1.24886	1.30477	1.42331	1.55133	1.68948
10	1.21899	1.28008	1.34392	1.48024	1.62889	1.79085
11	1.24337	1.31209	1.38423	1.53945	1.71034	1.89830
12	1.26824	1.34489	1.42576	1.60103	1.79586	2.01220
13	1.29361	1.37851	1.46853	1.66507	1.88565	2.13293
14	1.31948	1.41297	1.51259	1.73168	1.97993	2.26090
15	1.34587	1.44830	1.55797	1.80094	2.07893	2.39656
16	1.37279	1.48451	1.60471	1.87298	2.18287	2.54035
17	1.40024	1.52162	1.65285	1.94790	2.29202	2.69277
18	1.42825	1.55966	1.70243	2.02582	2.40662	2.85434
19	1.45681	1.59865	1.75351	2.10685	2.52695	3.02560
20	1.48595	1.63862	1.80611	2.19112	2.65330	3.20714
21	1.51567	1.67958	1.86029	2.27877	2.78596	3.39956
22	1.54598	1.72157	1.91610	2.36992	2.92526	3.60354
23	1.57690	1.76461	1.97359	2.46472	3.07152	3.81975
24	1.60844	1.80873	2.03279	2.56330	3.22510	4.04893
25	1.64061	1.85394	2.09378	2.66584	3.38635	4.29187
26	1.67342	1.90029	2.15659	2.77247	3.55567	4.54938
27	1.70689	1.94780	2.22129	2.88337	3.73346	4.82235
28	1.74102	1.99650	2.28793	2.99870	3.92013	5.11169
29	1.77584	2.04641	2.35657	3.11865	4.11614	5.41839
30	1.81136	2.09757	2.42726	3.24340	4.32194	5.74349
31	1.84759	2.15001	2.50008	3.37313	4.53804	6.08810
32	1.88454	2.20376	2.57508	3.50806	4.76494	6.45339
33	1.92223	2.25885	2.65234	3.64838	5.00319	6.84059
34	1.96068	2.31532	2.73191	3.79432	5.25335	7.25103
35	1.99989	2.37321	2.81386	3.94609	5.51602	7.68609
36	2.03989	2.43254	2.89828	4.10393	5.79182	8.14725
37	2.08069	2.49335	2.98523	4.26809	6.08141	8.63609
38	2.12230	2.55568	3.07478	4.43881	6.38548	9.15425
39	2.16474	2.61957	3.16703	4.61637	6.70475	9.70351
40	2.20804	2.68506	3.26204	4.80102	7.03999	10.28572

Table 1 (*continued*)

8%	9%	10%	11%	12%	15%	(*n*) Periods
1.08000	1.09000	1.10000	1.11000	1.12000	1.15000	1
1.16640	1.18810	1.21000	1.23210	1.25440	1.32250	2
1.25971	1.29503	1.33100	1.36763	1.40493	1.52088	3
1.36049	1.41158	1.46410	1.51807	1.57352	1.74901	4
1.46933	1.53862	1.61051	1.68506	1.76234	2.01136	5
1.58687	1.67710	1.77156	1.87041	1.97382	2.31306	6
1.71382	1.82804	1.94872	2.07616	2.21068	2.66002	7
1.85093	1.99256	2.14359	2.30454	2.47596	3.05902	8
1.99900	2.17189	2.35795	2.55803	2.77308	3.51788	9
2.15892	2.36736	2.59374	2.83942	3.10585	4.04556	10
2.33164	2.58043	2.85312	3.15176	3.47855	4.65239	11
2.51817	2.81267	3.13843	3.49845	3.89598	5.35025	12
2.71962	3.06581	3.45227	3.88328	4.36349	6.15279	13
2.93719	3.34173	3.79750	4.31044	4.88711	7.07571	14
3.17217	3.64248	4.17725	4.78459	5.47357	8.13706	15
3.42594	3.97031	4.59497	5.31089	6.13039	9.35762	16
3.70002	4.32763	5.05447	5.89509	6.86604	10.76126	17
3.99602	4.71712	5.55992	6.54355	7.68997	12.37545	18
4.31570	5.14166	6.11591	7.26334	8.61276	14.23177	19
4.66096	5.60441	6.72750	8.06231	9.64629	16.36654	20
5.03383	6.10881	7.40025	8.94917	10.80385	18.82152	21
5.43654	6.65860	8.14028	9.93357	12.10031	21.64475	22
5.87146	7.25787	8.95430	11.02627	13.55235	24.89146	23
6.34118	7.91108	9.84973	12.23916	15.17863	28.62518	24
6.84847	8.62308	10.83471	13.58546	17.00000	32.91895	25
7.39635	9.39916	11.91818	15.07986	19.04007	37.85680	26
7.98806	10.24508	13.10999	16.73865	21.32488	43.53532	27
8.62711	11.16714	14.42099	18.57990	23.88387	50.06561	28
9.31727	12.17218	15.86309	20.62369	26.74993	57.57545	29
10.06266	13.26768	17.44940	22.89230	29.95992	66.21177	30
10.86767	14.46177	19.19434	25.41045	33.55511	76.14354	31
11.73708	15.76333	21.11378	28.20560	37.58173	87.56507	32
12.67605	17.18203	23.22515	31.30821	42.09153	100.69983	33
13.69013	18.72841	25.54767	34.75212	47.14252	115.80480	34
14.78534	20.41397	28.10244	38.57485	52.79962	133.17552	35
15.96817	22.25123	30.91268	42.81808	59.13557	153.15185	36
17.24563	24.25384	34.00395	47.52807	66.23184	176.12463	37
18.62528	26.43668	37.40434	52.75616	74.17966	202.54332	38
20.11530	28.81598	41.14479	58.55934	83.08122	232.92482	39
21.72452	31.40942	45.25926	65.00087	93.05097	267.86355	40

Table 2   Future Value of Annuity of $1.00

(n) Periods	2%	2½%	3%	4%	5%	6%
1	1.00000	1.00000	1.00000	1.00000	1.00000	1.00000
2	2.02000	2.02500	2.03000	2.04000	2.05000	2.06000
3	3.06040	3.07563	3.09090	3.12160	3.15250	3.18360
4	4.12161	4.15252	4.18363	4.24646	4.31013	4.37462
5	5.20404	5.25633	5.30914	5.41632	5.52563	5.63709
6	6.30812	6.38774	6.46841	6.63298	6.80191	6.97532
7	7.43428	7.54743	7.66246	7.89829	8.14201	8.39384
8	8.58297	8.73612	8.89234	9.21423	9.54911	9.89747
9	9.75463	9.95452	10.15911	10.58280	11.02656	11.49132
10	10.94972	11.20338	11.46338	12.00611	12.57789	13.18079
11	12.16872	12.48347	12.80780	13.48635	14.20679	14.97164
12	13.41209	13.79555	14.19203	15.02581	15.91713	16.86994
13	14.68033	15.14044	15.61779	16.62684	17.71298	18.88214
14	15.97394	16.51895	17.08632	18.29191	19.59863	21.01507
15	17.29342	17.93193	18.59891	20.02359	21.57856	23.27597
16	18.63929	19.38022	20.15688	21.82453	23.65749	25.67253
17	20.01207	20.86473	21.76159	23.69751	25.84037	28.21288
18	21.41231	22.38635	23.41444	25.64541	28.13238	30.90565
19	22.84056	23.94601	25.11687	27.67123	30.53900	33.75999
20	24.29737	25.54466	26.87037	29.77808	33.06595	36.78559
21	25.78332	27.18327	28.67649	31.96920	35.71925	39.99273
22	27.29898	28.86286	30.53678	34.24797	38.50521	43.39229
23	28.84496	30.58443	32.45288	36.61789	41.43048	46.99583
24	30.42186	32.34904	34.42647	39.08260	44.50200	50.81558
25	32.03030	34.15776	36.45926	41.64591	47.72710	54.86451
26	33.67091	36.01171	38.55304	44.31174	51.11345	59.15638
27	35.34432	37.91200	40.70963	47.08421	54.66913	63.70577
28	37.05121	39.85980	42.93092	49.96758	58.40258	68.52811
29	38.79223	41.85630	45.21885	52.96629	62.32271	73.63980
30	40.56808	43.90270	47.57542	56.08494	66.43885	79.05819
31	42.37944	46.00027	50.00268	59.32834	70.76079	84.80168
32	44.22703	48.15028	52.50276	62.70147	75.29883	90.88978
33	46.11157	50.35403	55.07784	66.20953	80.06377	97.34316
34	48.03380	52.61289	57.73018	69.85791	85.06696	104.18376
35	49.99448	54.92821	60.46208	73.65222	90.32031	111.43478
36	51.99437	57.30141	63.27594	77.59831	95.83632	119.12087
37	54.03425	59.73395	66.17422	81.70225	101.62814	127.26812
38	56.11494	62.22730	69.15945	85.97034	107.70955	135.90421
39	58.23724	64.78298	72.23423	90.40915	114.09502	145.05846
40	60.40198	67.40255	75.40126	95.02552	120.79977	154.76197

Table 2 (*continued*)

8%	9%	10%	11%	12%	15%	(n) Periods
1.00000	1.00000	1.00000	1.00000	1.00000	1.00000	1
2.08000	2.09000	2.10000	2.11000	2.12000	2.15000	2
3.24640	3.27810	3.31000	3.34210	3.37440	3.47250	3
4.50611	4.57313	4.64100	4.70973	4.77933	4.99338	4
5.86660	5.98471	6.10510	6.22780	6.35285	6.74238	5
7.33592	7.52334	7.71561	7.91286	8.11519	8.75374	6
8.92280	9.20044	9.48717	9.78327	10.08901	11.06680	7
10.63663	11.02847	11.43589	11.85943	12.29969	13.72682	8
12.48756	13.02104	13.57948	14.16397	14.77566	16.78584	9
14.48656	15.19293	15.93743	16.72201	17.54874	20.30372	10
16.64549	17.56029	18.53117	19.56143	20.65458	24.34928	11
18.97713	20.14072	21.38428	22.71319	24.13313	29.00167	12
21.49530	22.95339	24.52271	26.21164	28.02911	34.35192	13
24.21492	26.01919	27.97498	30.09492	32.39260	40.50471	14
27.15211	29.36092	31.77248	34.40536	37.27972	47.58041	15
30.32428	33.00340	35.94973	39.18995	42.75328	55.71747	16
33.75023	36.97371	40.54470	44.50084	48.88367	65.07509	17
37.45024	41.30134	45.59917	50.39593	55.74972	75.83636	18
41.44626	46.01846	51.15909	56.93949	63.43968	88.21181	19
45.76196	51.16012	57.27500	64.20283	72.05244	102.44358	20
50.42292	56.76453	64.00250	72.26514	81.69874	118.81012	21
55.45676	62.87334	71.40275	81.21431	92.50258	137.63164	22
60.89330	69.53194	79.54302	91.14788	104.60289	159.27638	23
66.76476	76.78981	88.49733	102.17415	118.15524	184.16784	24
73.10594	84.70090	98.34706	114.41331	133.33387	212.79302	25
79.95442	93.32398	109.18177	127.99877	150.33393	245.71197	26
87.35077	102.72314	121.09994	143.07864	169.37401	283.56877	27
95.33883	112.96822	134.20994	159.81729	190.69889	327.10408	28
103.96594	124.13536	148.63093	178.39719	214.58275	377.16969	29
113.28321	136.30754	164.49402	199.02088	241.33268	434.74515	30
123.34587	149.57522	181.94343	221.91317	271.29261	500.95692	31
134.21354	164.03699	201.13777	247.32362	304.84772	577.10046	32
145.95062	179.80032	222.25154	275.52922	342.42945	644.66553	33
158.62667	196.98234	245.47670	306.83744	384.52098	765.36535	34
172.31680	215.71076	271.02437	341.58955	431.66350	881.17016	35
187.10215	236.12472	299.12681	380.16441	484.46312	1014.34568	36
203.07032	258.37595	330.03949	422.98249	543.59869	1167.49753	37
220.31595	282.62978	364.04343	470.51056	609.83053	1343.62216	38
238.94122	309.06646	401.44778	523.26673	684.01020	1546.16549	39
259.05652	337.88245	442.59256	581.82607	767.09142	1779.09031	40

APPENDIX A

Table 3 Present Value of $1.00

(n) Periods	2%	2½%	3%	4%	5%	6%
1	.98039	.97561	.97087	.96154	.95238	.94340
2	.96117	.95181	.94260	.92456	.90703	.89000
3	.94232	.92860	.91514	.88900	.86384	.83962
4	.92385	.90595	.88849	.85480	.82270	.79209
5	.90573	.88385	.86261	.82193	.78353	.74726
6	.88797	.86230	.83748	.79031	.74622	.70496
7	.87056	.84127	.81309	.75992	.71068	.66506
8	.85349	.82075	.78941	.73069	.67684	.62741
9	.83676	.80073	.76642	.70259	.64461	.59190
10	.82035	.78120	.74409	.67556	.61391	.55839
11	.80426	.76214	.72242	.64958	.58468	.52679
12	.78849	.74356	.70138	.62460	.55684	.49697
13	.77303	.72542	.68095	.60057	.53032	.46884
14	.75788	.70773	.66112	.57748	.50507	.44230
15	.74301	.69047	.64186	.55526	.48102	.41727
16	.72845	.67362	.62317	.53391	.45811	.39365
17	.71416	.65720	.60502	.51337	.43630	.37136
18	.70016	.64117	.58739	.49363	.41552	.35034
19	.68643	.62553	.57029	.47464	.39573	.33051
20	.67297	.61027	.55368	.45639	.37689	.31180
21	.65978	.59539	.53755	.43883	.35894	.29416
22	.64684	.58086	.52189	.42196	.34185	.27751
23	.63416	.56670	.50669	.40573	.32557	.26180
24	.62172	.55288	.49193	.39012	.31007	.24698
25	.60953	.53939	.47761	.37512	.29530	.23300
26	.59758	.52623	.46369	.36069	.28124	.21981
27	.58586	.51340	.45019	.34682	.26785	.20737
28	.57437	.50088	.43708	.33348	.25509	.19563
29	.56311	.48866	.42435	.32065	.24295	.18456
30	.55207	.47674	.41199	.30832	.23138	.17411
31	.54125	.46511	.39999	.29646	.22036	.16425
32	.53063	.45377	.38834	.28506	.20987	.15496
33	.52023	.44270	.37703	.27409	.19987	.14619
34	.51003	.43191	.36604	.26355	.19035	.13791
35	.50003	.42137	.35538	.25342	.18129	.13011
36	.49022	.41109	.34503	.24367	.17266	.12274
37	.48061	.40107	.33498	.23430	.16444	.11579
38	.47119	.39128	.32523	.22529	.15661	.10924
39	.46195	.38174	.31575	.21662	.14915	.10306
40	.45289	.37243	.30656	.20829	.14205	.09722

Table 3 (*continued*)

8%	9%	10%	11%	12%	15%	(*n*) Periods
.92593	.91743	.90909	.90090	.89286	.86957	1
.85734	.84168	.82645	.81162	.79719	.75614	2
.79383	.77218	.75132	.73119	.71178	.65752	3
.73503	.70843	.68301	.65873	.63552	.57175	4
.68058	.64993	.62092	.59345	.56743	.49718	5
.63017	.59627	.56447	.53464	.50663	.43233	6
.58349	.54703	.51316	.48166	.45235	.37594	7
.54027	.50187	.46651	.43393	.40388	.32690	8
.50025	.46043	.42410	.39092	.36061	.28426	9
.46319	.42241	.38554	.35218	.32197	.24719	10
.42888	.38753	.35049	.31728	.28748	.21494	11
.39711	.35554	.31863	.28584	.25668	.18691	12
.36770	.32618	.28966	.25751	.22917	.16253	13
.34046	.29925	.26333	.23199	.20462	.14133	14
.31524	.27454	.23939	.20900	.18270	.12289	15
.29189	.25187	.21763	.18829	.16312	.10687	16
.27027	.23107	.19785	.16963	.14564	.09293	17
.25025	.21199	.17986	.15282	.13004	.08081	18
.23171	.19449	.16351	.13768	.11611	.07027	19
.21455	.17843	.14864	.12403	.10367	.06110	20
.19866	.16370	.13513	.11174	.09256	.05313	21
.18394	.15018	.12285	.10067	.08264	.04620	22
.17032	.13778	.11168	.09069	.07379	.04017	23
.15770	.12641	.10153	.08170	.06588	.03493	24
.14602	.11597	.09230	.07361	.05882	.03038	25
.13520	.10639	.08391	.06631	.05252	.02642	26
.12519	.09761	.07628	.05974	.04689	.02297	27
.11591	.08955	.06934	.05382	.04187	.01997	28
.10733	.08216	.06304	.04849	.03738	.01737	29
.09938	.07537	.05731	.04368	.03338	.01510	30
.09202	.06915	.05210	.03935	.02980	.01313	31
.08520	.06344	.04736	.03545	.02661	.01142	32
.07889	.05820	.04306	.03194	.02376	.00993	33
.07305	.05340	.03914	.02878	.02121	.00864	34
.06763	.04899	.03558	.02592	.01894	.00751	35
.06262	.04494	.03235	.02335	.01691	.00653	36
.05799	.04123	.02941	.02104	.01510	.00568	37
.05369	.03783	.02674	.01896	.01348	.00494	38
.04971	.03470	.02430	.01708	.01204	.00429	39
.04603	.03184	.02210	.01538	.01075	.00373	40

Table 4 Present Value of Annuity of $1.00

(n) Periods	2%	2½%	3%	4%	5%	6%
1	.98039	.97561	.97087	.96154	.95238	.94340
2	1.94156	1.92742	1.91347	1.88609	1.85941	1.83339
3	2.88388	2.85602	2.82861	2.77509	2.72325	2.67301
4	3.80773	3.76197	3.71710	3.62990	3.54595	3.46511
5	4.71346	4.64583	4.57971	4.45182	4.32948	4.21236
6	5.60143	5.50813	5.41719	5.24214	5.07569	4.91732
7	6.47199	6.34939	6.23028	6.00205	5.78637	5.58238
8	7.32548	7.17014	7.01969	6.73274	6.46321	6.20979
9	8.16224	7.97087	7.78611	7.43533	7.10782	6.80169
10	8.98259	8.75206	8.53020	8.11090	7.72173	7.36009
11	9.78685	9.51421	9.25262	8.76048	8.30641	7.88687
12	10.57534	10.25776	9.95400	9.38507	8.86325	8.38384
13	11.34837	10.98319	10.63496	9.98565	9.39357	8.85268
14	12.10625	11.69091	11.29607	10.56312	9.89864	9.29498
15	12.84926	12.38138	11.93794	11.11839	10.37966	9.71225
16	13.57771	13.05500	12.56110	11.65230	10.83777	10.10590
17	14.29187	13.71220	13.16612	12.16567	11.27407	10.47726
18	14.99203	14.35336	13.75351	12.65930	11.68959	10.82760
19	15.67846	14.97889	14.32380	13.13394	12.08532	11.15812
20	16.35143	15.58916	14.87747	13.59033	12.46221	11.46992
21	17.01121	16.18455	15.41502	14.02916	12.82115	11.76408
22	17.65805	16.76541	15.93692	14.45112	13.16300	12.04158
23	18.29220	17.33211	16.44361	14.85684	13.48857	12.30338
24	18.91393	17.88499	16.93554	15.24696	13.79864	12.55036
25	19.52346	18.42438	17.41315	15.62208	14.09394	12.78336
26	20.12104	18.95061	17.87684	15.98277	14.37519	13.00317
27	20.70690	19.46401	18.32703	16.32959	14.64303	13.21053
28	21.28127	19.96489	18.76411	16.66306	14.89813	13.40616
29	21.84438	20.45355	19.18845	16.98371	15.14107	13.59072
30	22.39646	20.93029	19.60044	17.29203	15.37245	13.76483
31	22.93770	21.39541	20.00043	17.58849	15.59281	13.92909
32	23.46833	21.84918	20.38877	17.87355	15.80268	14.08404
33	23.98856	22.29188	20.76579	18.14765	16.00255	14.23023
34	24.49859	22.72379	21.13184	18.41120	16.19290	14.36814
35	24.99862	23.14516	21.48722	18.66461	16.37419	14.49825
36	25.48884	23.55625	21.83225	18.90828	16.54685	14.62099
37	25.96945	23.95732	22.16724	19.14258	16.71129	14.73678
38	26.44064	24.34860	22.49246	19.36786	16.86789	14.84602
39	26.90259	24.73034	22.80822	19.58448	17.01704	14.94907
40	27.35548	25.10278	23.11477	19.79277	17.15909	15.04630

Table 4 (*continued*)

8%	9%	10%	11%	12%	15%	(*n*) Periods
.92593	.91743	.90909	.90090	.89286	.86957	1
1.78326	1.75911	1.73554	1.71252	1.69005	1.62571	2
2.57710	2.53130	2.48685	2.44371	2.40183	2.28323	3
3.31213	3.23972	3.16986	3.10245	3.03735	2.85498	4
3.99271	3.88965	3.79079	3.69590	3.60478	3.35216	5
4.62288	4.48592	4.35526	4.23054	4.11141	3.78448	6
5.20637	5.03295	4.86842	4.71220	4.56376	4.16042	7
5.74664	5.53482	5.33493	5.14612	4.96764	4.48732	8
6.24689	5.99525	5.75902	5.53705	5.32825	4.77158	9
6.71008	6.41766	6.14457	5.88923	5.65022	5.01877	10
7.13896	6.80519	6.49506	6.20652	5.93770	5.23371	11
7.53608	7.16073	6.81369	6.49236	6.19437	5.42062	12
7.90378	7.48690	7.10336	6.74987	6.42355	5.58315	13
8.24424	7.78615	7.36669	6.98187	6.62817	5.72448	14
8.55948	8.06069	7.60608	7.19087	6.81086	5.84737	15
8.85137	8.31256	7.82371	7.37916	6.97399	5.95424	16
9.12164	8.54363	8.02155	7.54879	7.11963	6.04716	17
9.37189	8.75563	8.20141	7.70162	7.24967	6.12797	18
9.60360	8.95012	8.36492	7.83929	7.36578	6.19823	19
9.81815	9.12855	8.51356	7.96333	7.46944	6.25933	20
10.01680	9.29224	8.64869	8.07507	7.56200	6.31246	21
10.20074	9.44243	8.77154	8.17574	7.64465	6.35866	22
10.37106	9.58021	8.88322	8.26643	7.71843	6.39884	23
10.52876	9.70661	8.98474	8.34814	7.78432	6.43377	24
10.67478	9.82258	9.07704	8.42174	7.84314	6.46415	25
10.80998	9.92897	9.16095	8.48806	7.89566	6.49056	26
10.93516	10.02658	9.23722	8.54780	7.94255	6.51353	27
11.05108	10.11613	9.30657	8.60162	7.98442	6.53351	28
11.15841	10.19828	9.36961	8.65011	8.02181	6.55088	29
11.25778	10.27365	9.42691	8.69379	8.05518	6.56598	30
11.34980	10.34280	9.47901	8.73315	8.08499	6.57911	31
11.43500	10.40624	9.52638	8.76860	8.11159	6.59053	32
11.51389	10.46444	9.56943	8.80054	8.13535	6.60046	33
11.58693	10.51784	9.60858	8.82932	8.15656	6.60910	34
11.65457	10.56682	9.64416	8.85524	8.17550	6.61661	35
11.71719	10.61176	9.67651	8.87859	8.19241	6.62314	36
11.77518	10.65299	9.70592	8.89963	8.20751	6.62882	37
11.82887	10.69082	9.73265	8.91859	8.22099	6.63375	38
11.87858	10.72552	9.75697	8.93567	8.23303	6.63805	39
11.92461	10.75736	9.77905	8.95105	8.24378	6.64178	40

TABLE 5   A Table of Monthly Mortgage Payments (Monthly payments necessary to repay a $10,000 loan)

Rate of Interest	Loan Term				
	10 years	15 years	20 years	25 years	30 years
7½%	$118.71	$ 92.71	$ 80.56	$ 73.90	$ 69.93
8%	121.33	95.57	83.65	77.19	73.38
8½%	123.99	98.48	86.79	80.53	76.90
9%	126.68	101.43	89.98	83.92	80.47
9½%	129.40	104.43	93.22	87.37	84.09
10%	132.16	107.47	96.51	90.88	87.76
10½%	134.94	110.54	99.84	94.42	91.48
11%	137.76	113.66	103.22	98.02	95.24
11½%	140.60	116.82	106.65	101.65	99.03
12%	143.48	120.02	110.11	105.33	102.86
12½%	146.38	123.26	113.62	109.04	106.73
13%	149.32	126.53	117.16	112.79	110.62
13½%	152.28	129.84	120.74	116.57	114.55
14%	155.27	133.18	124.36	120.38	118.49
14½%	158.29	136.56	128.00	124.22	122.46
15%	161.34	139.96	131.68	128.09	126.45

TABLE 6   A Table of Monthly Installment Loan Payments (to Repay a $1,000 Simple Interest Loan)

Rate of Interest	Loan Term						
	6 Months	12 Months	18 Months	24 Months	36 Months	48 Months	60 Months
7½%	$170.33	$86.76	$58.92	$45.00	$31.11	$24.18	$20.05
8	170.58	86.99	59.15	45.23	31.34	24.42	20.28
8½	170.82	87.22	59.37	45.46	31.57	24.65	20.52
9	171.07	87.46	59.60	45.69	31.80	24.89	20.76
9½	171.32	87.69	59.83	45.92	32.04	25.13	21.01
10	171.56	87.92	60.06	46.15	32.27	25.37	21.25
10½	171.81	88.15	60.29	46.38	32.51	25.61	21.50
11	172.05	88.50	60.64	46.73	32.86	25.97	21.87
11½	172.30	88.62	60.76	46.85	32.98	26.09	22.00
12	172.55	88.85	60.99	47.08	33.22	26.34	22.25
12½	172.80	89.09	61.22	47.31	33.46	26.58	22.50
13	173.04	89.32	61.45	47.55	33.70	26.83	22.76
14	173.54	89.79	61.92	48.02	34.18	27.33	23.27
15	174.03	90.26	62.39	48.49	34.67	27.84	23.79
16	174.53	90.74	62.86	48.97	35.16	28.35	24.32
17	175.03	91.21	63.34	49.45	35.66	28.86	24.86
18	175.53	91.68	63.81	49.93	36.16	29.38	25.40

Appendix B

PERSONAL FINANCE COMPUTER SOFTWARE

MONEY MANAGEMENT SOFTWARE

Dollars and Sense
Monogram
8295 South La Cienega Blvd.
Inglewood, CA 90301
(213) 215-0355

Andrew Tobias Managing Your Money
MECA Software
285 Riverside Ave.
Westport, CT 06880
(800) 962-5583 (Outside Conn.)
(203) 222-9087 (Conn. only)

Financial Independence
Charles Schwab & Co.
101 Montgomery St.
San Francisco, CA 94104
(800) 334-4455
(415) 627-7197

Personal Financial Planner
Lumen Systems
P.O. Box 9893
Englewood, NJ 07631
(201) 592-1121

Sylvia Porter's Your Personal Financial Planner
Timeworks Inc.
444 Lake Cook Rd.
Deerfield, IL 60015
(800) 323-9755
(312) 948-9200

J. K. Lasser's Your Money Manager
Simon & Schuster Electronic Publishing
Gulf & Western Building
One Gulf & Western Plaza
New York, NY 10023
(800) 624-0023
(212) 333-3397

PC/PFP II
Best Programs
5134 Leesburg Pike
Alexandria, VA 22302
(800) 368-2405
(703) 931-1300

The Home Accountant Plus
Continental Software
6711 Valjean Ave.
Van Nuys, CA 91406
(800) 468-4222
(818) 989-5822

Financier II
Financial Software Inc.
P.O. Box 558
Hudson, MA 01749
(617) 568-0374

INVESTMENT SOFTWARE

Value/Screen Plus
Value Line Inc.
711 Third Ave.
New York, NY 10017
(212) 687-3965

Stockpak II
Standard & Poor's Corp.
Micro Services Dept.
25 Broadway
New York, NY 10004
(800) 852-5200
(212) 208-8581

Dow Jones Market Microscope
Dow Jones & Company
P.O. Box 300
Princeton, NJ 08540
(800) 257-5114
(609) 452-2000

COMPUTERIZED DATA BASES FOR INVESTORS

CompuServe
5000 Arlington Center Blvd.
P.O. Box 20212
Columbus, OH 43220
(800) 848-8990
(614) 457-0802

Dow Jones News/Retrieval (DJN/R)
Dow Jones & Company
P.O. Box 300
Princeton, NJ 08540
(800) 257-5114
(609) 452-1511

The Equalizer
Charles Schwab & Co.
101 Montgomery St.
San Francisco, CA 94104
(800) 334-4455
(415) 627-7197

The Source
Source Telecomputing Corp.
1616 Anderson Rd.
McLean, VA 22102
(800) 336-3366
(703) 734-7500

TAX SOFTWARE

J. K. Lasser's Your Income Tax
Simon & Schuster Electronic Publishing
Gulf & Western Building
One Gulf & Western Plaza
New York, NY 10023
(800) 624-0023
(212) 333-3397

PC/TaxCut
Best Programs
5134 Leesburg Pike
Alexandria, VA 22302
(800) 368-2405 (outside Virginia)
(703) 931-1300 (Virginia only)

The Tax Series
Financial Software Inc.
P.O. Box 558
Hudson, MA 01749
(617) 568-0374

Forecast
Monogram
8295 South La Cienega Blvd.
Inglewood, CA 90301
(213) 215-0355

Swiftax
Timeworks Inc.
444 Lake Cook Rd.
Deerfield, IL 60015
(800) 323-9755
(312) 948-9200

The Tax Advantage
Continental Software
6711 Valjean Ave.
Van Nuys, CA 91406
(800) 468-4222
(818) 989-5822

Professional Tax Planner
Ardvark McGraw-Hill
1020 Broadway
Milwaukee, WI 53202
(414) 225-7500

Turbo Tax
Chipsoft
5045 Shoreham Place
San Diego, CA 92122-3954
(800) 782-1120
(619) 453-8722

Glossary

Acceleration clause   a clause in a credit contract or mortgage that states that if the borrower does not meet the payment schedule, all remaining payments may become immediately due.

Actual cash value (ACV)   replacement cost less depreciation.

Actuarial method   a method which uses one-twelfth of the annual percentage rate (APR) to figure the amount of interest to credit to a borrower when a loan is retired early.

Add-on method   a method for calculating loan payments in which the interest is figured on and then added to the amount to be financed.

Adjustable rate mortgage (ARM)   a mortgage on which the interest rate can change prior to maturity, depending on the changes of a particular fund cost index.

Adjustment   on the federal tax return, an expenditure that reduces gross income to arrive at adjusted gross income including items such as IRA and Keogh pension contributions.

Administrator   the individual appointed by the court to handle an estate.

Advisory letters   specialized newsletters on various investment media that are typically high in cost.

Aggressive growth fund   a mutual fund that aims for a greater return by accepting greater investment risk, either by investing in new or small companies or by using speculative techniques in its investment strategy.

Amended return   a second income tax return filed if, after filing the original return, the taxpayer finds additional income, deductions, or credits that should have been reported.

Annual percentage rate (APR)   a measure of the total cost of the loan, expressed as a yearly percentage rate. This method of calculating interest rates is required by the Federal Consumer Protection Act (Truth-in-Lending Act).

Annual percentage yield   the true (effective) rate of interest earned on an account that reflects the frequency of compounding; also called *effective annual yield*.

Annuitant   a person who receives regular annuity benefits.

Annuity   a contract that guarantees a fixed income to the annuitant and other beneficiaries of the annuity for life, or for a specified period of years.

Appraisal   the estimate of the fair market value of a piece of property.

Assessed value   the value assigned property for tax purposes, generally a percentage of the appraised value.

Assets   the items of value that a person owns, such as cash, auto, and stocks.

Assumption   the ability of a new buyer to take over the seller's old mortgage, typically at the original rate.

Average daily balance   a method for determining the balance on which interest is to be paid. The figure is calculated by averaging the daily balance throughout the month.

Automobile insurance   insurance purchased to pay for the loss to individuals or to property, resulting from an automobile accident, theft, or other perils specified in the insurance contract.

Balanced fund   a mutual fund that stresses income over growth.

Balloon clause   a final payment specified in a loan agreement.

Balloon-note mortgage   a mortgage that carries a fixed rate of interest and is written like a conventional mortgage but for a short period of time, for example, 3 to 5 years.

Balloon payment   *see* Balloon clause.

Bankruptcy   a court action that involves taking some of a debtor's assets, selling them, and dividing the proceeds among the creditors.

Basic disability   a definition in a disability insurance policy that describes the insured as unable to perform the duties of his or her regular occupation.

Bearer (coupon) certificate   a certificate that does not have the name of the owner on it. Payment of interest is made to whomever presents the coupon.

Beneficiaries   those who are to receive the proceeds from a policy or estate at the time of an individual's death.

Better Business Bureau (BBB)   a local agency supported by business organizations that helps to resolve problems between businesses and customers.

Blank endorsement   the signature of only the payee's name on the back of the check.

Blue-chip stocks   stocks of major companies that are leaders in their industry and have a proven track record of earnings and dividend payments.

Bond funds   mutual funds that invest primarily in bonds in order to emphasize current income.

Budget   detailed guideline for spending over a short period of time.

Bullion coins   gold coins that are legal tender in the countries that issue them.

Call option   the right to buy a fixed number of shares of a stock at a predetermined price over a stated period of time.

Call provision   a provision of a security issue that allows the issuer to redeem the outstanding securities for a predetermined value before maturity.

Capital gain   the profit received from the sale of a capital asset at a price higher than the original cost.

Capital loss   the loss resulting from the sale or exchange of a capital asset at a price below the original cost.

Cash flow statement   compilation of cash receipts and disbursements used to develop the monthly budget.

Cash value   the accumulated portion of life insurance premiums as a savings feature that can be borrowed against or obtained as cash if the policy is canceled.

Cash value insurance   life insurance protection that provides death benefits and a savings feature.

Cashier's check   a check from a depository institution made out to a specified person for a specified amount.

Certificate of deposit (CD)   a term account paying a slightly higher rate of interest than passbook or other savings, with a penalty for early withdrawal.

Certified check   a check from an individual's own checking account that has been completely filled out and certified by the depository institution. The certification guarantees the validity of the signature and the amount of the check.

Chapter 7   *see* Straight bankruptcy.

Chapter 13   a court approved and coordinated plan that pays off an individual's debts over a period of 3 years; also known as the *wage earner plan*.

Check truncation   the procedure whereby depository institutions keep the canceled checks and send only a listing of the month's activities to the account holder, thus saving on processing and mailing of checks.

Checking account   an account that allows the depositor to transfer funds to another party through a written order, a demand deposit, or a check.

Chicago Board Options Exchange (CBOE)   the exchange formed to deal exclusively in options.

Cleaning deposit   a nonrefundable fee paid to cover the painting and cleaning of a rental unit after a tenant moves out.

Closed-end account   a credit account that allows the customer to use the extended credit only once, usually to make a specific purchase.

Closed-end investment company   an investment company that issues a limited number of shares.

Closed-end lease   a lease that entails monthly payments over a specified period of time. At the end of the leasing period, the lessor sells the leased item and bears any gain or loss from the entire transaction.

Closing costs   costs resulting from the financing and transfer of property ownership in a real estate sale.

Codicil   a document amending a will

Coinsurance factor   the percentage of medical expenses covered by the insured over and above the deductible amount.

Collateral   an asset that is used to secure a loan.

Collectible   an item collected for its value or enjoyment.

Collision insurance   insurance purchased to pay for damages to one's own car in case of an accident.

Commercial bank   a depository institution commonly referred to as a bank, with stockholders as owners and an elected board of directors. Depositors are creditors of the bank.

Commodities   wheat, eggs, soybeans, silver, pork bellies, and other economic goods.

Common stock   a security that represents ownership in a corporation, and typically having voting rights.

Community property   property held jointly by husband and wife. If acquired after the marriage it is considered to be owned equally by both spouses, no matter who contributes the earnings to pay for the property.

Compounding the process of earning interest on the interest already earned on an investment. Compound interest is earned when the interest is left to accumulate.

Comprehensive insurance insurance purchased to cover losses resulting from a stolen car, or from repairs if the car is hit by a falling object, or damaged by fire, flood, or vandals.

Condominium a form of home ownership in which each individual owns the interior living space in a planned community.

Conforming loans loans that adhere to national guidelines by Fannie Mae and Freddie Mac, who buy the loans on the secondary market.

Consolidated liability plan liability coverage in automobile insurance that sets a specific dollar amount as the maximum that would be paid for all losses resulting from a liability claim.

Consumer credit counseling service a nonprofit organization that provides several inexpensive services to assist consumers with financial difficulties in getting back on their feet.

Consumer Credit Protection Act a federal act that includes the Fair Credit Billing, Equal Credit Opportunity, Fair Credit Reporting, Consumer Leasing Acts, and the Truth-in-Lending Act.

Consumer Price Index (CPI) a price index that measures the changes in the cost of a specific "market basket" of goods and services. The CPI measures the cost of living.

Consumer Product Safety Commission (CPSC) the federal agency that deals specifically with the risks of injury resulting from a wide range of consumer products.

Conventional mortgage a mortgage that requires a large down payment, is typically only available to good credit risks, and has fixed monthly payments, including principal and interest for the life of the loan.

Convertibility a term life insurance feature that allows the policyholder to convert to a whole life policy without a medical examination or proof of insurability.

Convertible bonds bonds that may be converted into a predesigned number of shares of common stock.

Convertible stock preferred stock that may be converted into common stock.

Cooling off ruling a federal rule that provides a buyer with 3 business days in which to cancel a door-to-door sales contract.

Cooperative a form of home ownership that entails issuing stock and then leasing dwelling units to each stockholder.

Corporate bond a debt instrument of a corporation. It is a corporate IOU. It represents an agreement that the face value of the loan will be repaid at maturity and that interest will be paid at regular intervals.

Cosigner someone who agrees to accept responsibility for a loan if the original borrower defaults.

Coupon rate the interest rate of a bond as a percent of the face value.

Credit loans extended to businesses, individuals, or the government.

Credit bureau an organization that supplies credit information to creditors and to others who demonstrate an acceptable need for the information.

Credit health and accident insurance insurance purchased as payment protection for a loan in case the borrower is unable to meet the payments due to a disability or illness.

Credit life insurance insurance that will retire a loan if the borrower dies.

Credit or consumer report a report from a credit bureau describing an individual's credit history and providing other information such as name, address, length of time at an address, occupation (past and present), public record, and similar background material.

Credit property insurance insurance purchased to compensate the lender if property placed as security for a loan is destroyed.

Credit record an individual's credit history.

Credit scoring an objective method for evaluating whether an individual should be extended credit.

Credit union a depository institution formed as a cooperative. Individuals interested in membership may have to meet specific credit union requirements.

Creditor the person or institution to whom money is owed.

Cumulative dividends preferred dividends which if not paid as scheduled must be paid before any common stock dividends can be paid.

Current yield the measurement of return that relates investment income to the market price.

Custodian   the individual who retains control of and manages property.

Cyclical stock   stock that fluctuates with changes in business conditions, improving its position when the economy is on an upswing and falling during times of decline.

Damage deposit   a fee paid to cover any physical damage beyond normal wear and tear, or any economic damage beyond normal wear and tear, or any economic damage such as failure to pay rent, caused by a tenant or a tenant's guests.

Day-of-deposit-to-day-of-withdrawal (DDDW)   a method of calculating the account balance on which interest is earned. Interest is calculated on the actual number of days the money is deposited in the account.

Dead days   days appearing at the end of an interest period during which the bank will allow funds to earn interest even though they are not actually on deposit (typically a maximum of 10 days).

Debentures   unsecured bonds that carry no claim against any specified assets.

Debit card   a card issued for making electronic transfers of funds in stores, depository institutions, and other businesses.

Debt consolidation loans   loans that combine all of a person's debts into one loan with small monthly payments. The tremendously high rate of interest for the new loan greatly increases the total cost of the credit although the monthly payment may be lower than the sum of all the former payments.

Decreasing term insurance   term insurance that provides decreasing death benefits while maintaining a stable premium.

Deductible   the amount that an individual must pay on any insured loss before payment by the insurance company begins.

Deduction   an expenditure listed on the federal tax return that reduces adjusted gross income in order to arrive at taxable income.

Deed   a detailed description of a piece of property that formally transfers the title of the property over to the buyer.

Default   failure to meet the conditions of a loan. It generally refers to the failure to meet the loan payments as scheduled.

Defensive stock   a stock that has relatively stable prices during business downturns and market declines.

Deferred annuity   an annuity that begins fixed payments after a period of years.

Defined benefit plan   a pension plan that promises to pay a specified benefit to qualified employees at retirement.

Defined contribution plan   a pension plan that specifies a certain plan contribution but not future benefits.

Dental insurance   insurance to pay for dental care, typically including preventive expense.

Deposit insurance   insurance on certain depository institution accounts provided by either a federal or a state agency.

Depreciation   in real estate appraisal, the decrease in value of property due to use, deterioration, or the passing of time. The cost of wear and tear.

Disability insurance   insurance to provide income to the insured in the event of disability.

Discount   a reduction in the amount paid for an item. As for investments, it is a security that sells for less than its face value.

Discount house   a brokerage house that provides few investor services but offers low transaction costs, especially on larger orders.

Discount interest   a method for calculating the interest charged on a loan wherein the lender subtracts the interest from the principal amount and lends the borrower the difference, to be repaid in installments.

Discount rate   the interest rate charged to financial institutions for loans by the Federal Reserve Bank.

Disposable income   income left after deducting taxes from gross income.

Diversification   the spreading of investment money among many investment vehicles in order to reduce overall risk.

Dividend   the portion of a corporation's profits paid to stockholders.

Dividend reinvestment   dividends that an investor reinvests in the company or mutual fund through the purchase of additional shares. A mutual fund does not charge a sales commission on reinvested dividends.

Dollar cost averaging   the regular investment of a specified amount in a stock or mutual fund.

Double or triple indemnity   a life insurance rider that pays the beneficiary two or three times the policy's face value if the death of the insured is due to an accident.

Dow Jones Industrial Average (DJIA)   a price-weighted average of 30 stocks that attempts to show the general movement of the stock market.

Down payment   the cash a borrower puts toward a purchase, with the remainder of the purchase price borrowed from a creditor.

Dread disease insurance   a health insurance policy that provides protection against medical expenses resulting from a certain dreaded disease such as cancer.

Due-on-sale clause   a clause permitting the lender to raise the interest rate or require full payment of the mortgage at the time of assumption.

Duplexes   two living units placed side by side in one building.

Durable power of attorney   a legal device that allows individuals to grant to other persons general or specific powers for managing their finances.

Earnest money   a specified deposit to secure an agreement.

Earnings per share (EPS)   the earnings figure divided by the number of outstanding shares of common stock.

Easy money   an increase in the amount of money available for business and individual spending as a result of economic conditions.

Economic risk   the chance of loss due to economic conditions.

Effective annual yield   *see* Annual percentage yield.

Electronic fund transfer   the transfer of funds through a computerized banking system. It will eliminate much of paper handling involved with cash, checking account, and credit card systems.

Elimination period   the period of time before insurance begins.

Emergency fund   money kept at maximum liquidity in order to have access to cash for unexpected situations.

Employee Retirement Income Security Act   Federal legislation that provides protection to workers who are covered by private retirement plans.

Endowment policy   a cash value life insurance policy that assesses premiums over a specified period of time. At the end of that time, the cash value equals the face value, the policy endows, and is redeemed.

Energy labels   labels attached to certain appliances that give operation costs and energy information.

Equal Credit Opportunity Act   a federal act prohibiting discrimination in lending.

Equity   The ownership value of a business. In reference to real estate, the portion of a property owned by an individual, that is, the market value of the property less any amount owed on the property.

Equity REIT   a type of REIT whose investment money is directed toward the purchase of a portfolio of identified properties to be managed for the purpose of producing investment return through current income as well as capital gains.

Escrow account   an account to which payment is made for a specified expense to ensure that funds will be available.

Estate planning   the creation of wealth and conservation of assets so that an individual will reap the greatest benefit from their use.

Eviction   the action taken by a landlord to remove a tenant from leased property.

Excess major medical policy   medical insurance that provides coverage over and above the benefits of a major medical policy.

Exclusive listing   an agreement with a real estate agent that pays commission to the agent even if the property is sold to a buyer found by the owner.

Executor   a person appointed in a will to handle the disposition of the estate according to the will's directives.

Exemption   when filing a tax return the amount deductible from income that each taxpayer is allowed for oneself, a spouse, and each dependent, plus an additional deduction for each person who is blind and over 65.

Face value   1. a security's value at maturity.   2. the maximum coverage available on an insurance policy.

Fair Credit Billing Act   a federal law providing credit card holders certain rights in case of billing errors.

Fair Credit Reporting Act (FCRA)   a federal law passed to control the use of credit and investigative reports.

Fair Debt Collection Practices Act   a federal act regulating professional bill collectors and their actions.

FAIR program   an insurance program sponsored by the federal government for individuals who are unable to obtain insurance through the marketplace.

Family of funds   a group of mutual funds, all with different investment objectives, that are under the same management company.

Farmers Home Administration   a federal agency that offers home financing to qualified individuals in low-income rural areas.

Federal agency securities   debt investments issued by federal government agencies that are backed either by the full faith and credit of the agency or by the federal government itself.

Federal Deposit Insurance Corporation (FDIC)   the federal agency that insures depository institution accounts.

Federal estate tax   the federal tax that must be paid by a decedent's estate.

Federal Housing Administration (FHA)   a federal agency that provides financing opportunities for home buyers, especially those with little down payment funds or with a need for smaller monthly payments.

Federal Insurance Administration   a federal agency that sponsors crime insurance for families living in high crime areas.

Federal Reserve System   the central bank of the United States. Its primary function is to control the money supply and financial markets.

Federal Savings and Loan Insurance Corporation (FSLIC)   the federal agency that provides deposit insurance to savings and loan associations.

Federal Trade Commission (FTC)   a federal agency responsible for policing unfair trade practices.

Filing status   indicated on the tax return to show whether the taxpayer is filing a return as a single, married (filing jointly or separately), or head of household taxpayer.

Finance charge   the total dollar amount paid when obtaining a loan or charging a purchase.

Finance companies   companies that primarily make smaller loans at higher interest rates than competitive institutions because they will accept individuals with lower than average credit ratings.

Financial advisor   a business person who sells a particular product and financial advice or one who sells only financial advice.

Financial needs approach   a method for calculating life insurance needs, which bases the amount of insurance protection on the goals, net worth, and projected income and expense figures of the insured.

Financial risk   the chance of loss resulting from business difficulties of the issuer.

Financial tables   tables found in most daily newspapers, to provide price yield and volume information on secondary markets. Extensive listings appear in *The Wall Street Journal*.

First-in, first-out (FIFO)   a method for calculating the account balance on which interest is earned. In this case, interest is earned on any balance remaining after deducting all withdrawals from the deposits available at the beginning of the interest period.

Fiscal policies   an economic policy that employs government spending and taxation programs.

Fixed-income investment   an investment that promises to pay a specified amount of income on a periodic basis, such as a bond.

Fixed rate of interest   certificates of deposit (CDs) issued for periods ranging from 3 months to 8 years or more. These CDs have minimum deposit requirements that are established by each institution and interest rate ceilings that are set by the federal government's Regulation Q.

Floater endorsement   an addition to a policy that itemizes specific item(s) for insurance protection under the endorsement.

Freddie Macs   nickname for Federal Home Loan Mortgage Corporation (FHLMC) securities. The FHLMC buys mortgages, pools them, and then sells the packages to individual investors.

Fringe benefits   legislated or employer-provided benefits that exceed wages.

Full replacement policy   a homeowner's policy that will replace, rebuild, or repair damaged property for up to the maximum of the policy, which is set at a value equal to what is estimated as the cost of replacing the property.

Full service brokerage house   a brokerage house that provides research reports, investment advice, and a broker to act as a sounding board for ideas.

Full warranty   the term used to describe warranties that meet certain requirements of the Magnusson-Woss Warranty Act and offer the best warranty protection available.

Fundamental analysis   a system for evaluating stocks by first analyzing industry conditions and then picking the companies within selected industries that are likely to perform most successfully.

Futures contract   a contract to buy or sell a given commodity on a future date for a predetermined price.

Futures market   the market that handles futures contracts.

General obligation bond   a municipal bond that has the payment of the bond interest and principal backed up by the full faith and credit of the issuing government.

General partner   a member of a partnership who can be held liable for all of the partnership debts.

Ginnie Maes   nickname for Government National Mortgage Association (GNMA) securities, which are issued by approved organizations who pool their FHA or VA backed mortgages and then sell them as a package to investors.

Goals   specific objectives for which a person aims and that are based on the person's values.

Gold bars   bars of varying sizes and quality of gold.

Grace days   days appearing at the beginning of an interest period during which a depository institution will allow its funds to earn interest even though the funds are not actually on deposit.

Grace period   the 30-day period allowed on life and health insurance policies, which maintains the policy coverage although the premium has not yet been paid.

Graduated payment mortgage   a mortgage that carries a fixed rate of interest for the life of the mortgage; however, the payments are not fixed but instead slowly increase to a fixed amount that is maintained until the end of the loan period.

Grantor   the person setting up a trust.

Growth   the investment objective that aims at producing a capital gain at the time of sale.

Growth fund   a mutual fund whose primary objective is long-term capital appreciation by investing in companies' common stocks that are expected to show increased earnings.

Growth and income fund   a mutual fund that attempts to provide regular dividends along with capital gains by investing in bonds and quality stocks.

Guaranteed insurability   a cash value life insurance feature that allows the policyholder to purchase additional cash value insurance at predesignated intervals and standard rates without passing a medical examination.

Guaranteed renewable policy   a policy that is always renewable as long as the premiums are paid, although the company can raise the policy's rates.

Guardian   the individual appointed to take care of minors.

Hazard   a condition that affects the probability of loss.

Health Maintenance Organizations (HMOs)   health insurance agencies that offer group health insurance for a fixed, prepaid premium and stress preventive health care.

Holographic will   will that does not meet all the formal requirements of a valid will.

Homeowners insurance   an insurance policy designed for a variety of risks of homeowners.

Homeowners Warranty (HOW) Program   a program in which builders guarantee their workmanship, materials, and construction defects.

"House poor"   purchasing more house than one can afford.

Implied warranty   warranty stating that a product is capable of doing what it is supposed to do.

Income stocks   stocks of companies with relatively large and stable dividends.

Incontestable clause   a clause in life insurance policies providing that the insurer cannot question the validity of the information provided by the insured after the policy has been in force for 2 years.

Indemnity   a legal principle that determines the amount of the economic loss reimbursed for destroyed property.

Indenture   a formal contract between a bond issuer and a bond buyer that establishes the terms of a bond.

Individual retirement account (IRA)   a retirement plan for an individual.

Inflation   a general rise in the prices of goods and services.

Inflation risk   the risk that the value of investments do not rise due to inflation.

Inheritance tax   a state tax levied on individuals who inherit property.

Insider trading   trading of securities by insiders such as corporate officers or others who have inside knowledge about a company that is unavailable to other investors.

Installment loans   loans that are repaid by making a series of fixed payments.

Installment sales   the sale of property on installment terms.

Insurance   a legal contract transferring the risk of the insured loss to the insurance company.

Interest-adjusted cost index   a method of determining the cost of life insurance which takes into account the cost to the policyholder of lost interest on premium paid for coverage.

Interest rate risk   changes in the value of fixed-income securities such as bonds and preferred stocks due to changes in market interest rates.

Intestacy   the situation created when an individual dies without leaving a valid will.

Investment banker   a person who provides financial advice and who underwrites and distributes new investment securities.

Investment club   a club of members who pool their funds to buy and sell securities.

Irrevocable trust   a trust in which the grantor has no control over the trust.

Joint account   a bank account in the names of two or more persons.

Joint tenancy   a form of ownership of property in which more than one person shares an undivided interest in the property.

Joint tenancy with right of survivorship   a special form of joint tenancy where if one person dies, the surviving owner automatically becomes the sole owner of the property.

Jumbo loans   loans that differ from *conforming loans* in that they are above the maximum conforming amount and reflect each lender's own guidelines.

Junior bonds   bonds whose priority of claims are lower than that of senior bonds.

Junk bond   a bond with a speculative credit rating of BB or lower by the major rating agencies such as Standard & Poor's or Moody's.

Keogh plan   a plan that allows self-employed persons to establish tax-sheltered retirement programs themselves.

Kelly Blue Book   a source that lists the wholesale and retail value of used cars. Available at depository institutions and libraries.

Kugerrand   bullion coin from South Africa.

Lease agreement   a rental contract intended to protect the lessor from nonpayment or some adverse action of the lessee.

Ledger   the financial record book which should contain separate sections for assets, liabilities, sources of income, and expenditure items.

Letter of last instructions   an informal memorandum containing suggestions or recommendations for carrying out the provisions of a will.

Leverage   the use of borrowed funds or other people's money (OPM) to magnify returns.

Liabilities   a person's debts. Examples are department store charges, bank card charges, installment loans, or mortgages on real estate.

Liability exposures   risk incurred by an individual who might negligently cause property damage or bodily injury to someone else.

Liability insurance   a type of insurance coverage that pays for damages the insured has accidentally caused another and for the insured's defense against another who is seeking compensation arising out of a covered occurrence.

Licensing fees   means by which state and local governments obtain revenue by licensing certain professions and from the sale of automobile licenses.

Lien   legal claim that permits the lender to liquidate the items that serve as collateral in the event of a default.

Life annuity, period certain   type of guaranteed minimum annuity in which the annuitant is guaranteed a stated amount of monthly income for life and the insurer agrees to pay for at least a minimum number of years, regardless of whether the annuitant survives.

Life annuity with no refund (straight life)   annuitant receives a specified amount of income for life, regardless of whether the period over which income is distributed is 1 year or 50 years.

Life expectancy   mean number of years of life remaining at a given age.

Life goals   goals, not necessarily financial, which most individuals wish to achieve during their lives. The ability to achieve them often depends on realizing a certain level of financial success.

Limit order   an order to either buy a security at a specified price or lower or sell a security at or above a specified price.

Limited liability   the concept under which an investor in a business cannot lose more than the amount of his or her investment.

Limited partnership   a type of partnership in which the limited partner is legally liable only for the amount of his or her initial investment.

Limited payment whole life   whole life insurance policy that offers coverage for the entire life of the insured but schedules the premium payments to end after a limited period.

Line of credit   an arrangement by which a credit customer can borrow up to a specified maximum amount of funds.

Liquid assets   includes cash, money in checking and savings accounts, certificates of deposit (CDs), and other investments that can readily be converted into cash.

Liquidity ratio   ratio of liquid assets divided by total current debt.

Listed securities   securities that trade on organized markets.

Living trust   trust created while the grantor is still alive.

Load fund   a mutual fund that charges a commission on the purchase or sale of its stock.

Loan amortization   the systematic repayment of the loan principal and interest.

Loan-to-value (LTV) ratio   the percentage of the property's value the lender is willing to make a loan on.

Long-term gains (losses)   the sale of a capital asset held for more than 1 year at a higher (lower) price than the original cost.

Loss prevention   any activity that reduces the probability that a loss will occur.

Lump-sum payments   payments under workers' compensation of a specific amount for specific types of losses.

Magnetic Ink Character Recognition (MICR)   a magnetic coding imprinted on checks and deposit slips to speed up the check and deposit clearing process.

Maintenance margin   the minimum percentage equity an investor must maintain in a stock purchased using borrowed funds.

Major medical plan   an insurance plan designed to supplement the basic coverages of hospital, surgical, and physicians expenses, which are designed to cover smaller health care costs. Major medical is used to finance medical costs of a more catastrophic or long-term nature.

Margin purchases (buying)   the buying of securities using some borrowed funds. The percentage of borrowed funds is limited by both law and brokerage firms.

Margin requirement   provision which specifies what proportion of each dollar used to purchase a security must be provided by the investor.

Marital deduction   a deduction allowed to married persons for gift tax purposes by which one spouse may make a tax-deductible gift to another.

Market maker   person who specializes in creating markets for certain securities in the over-the-counter market by offering to buy or sell a given security at specified bid and ask prices.

Market order   an order to buy or sell stock at the best price available at the time the order is placed.

Market rate of interest   the rate of interest paid on instruments with similar types of risk in the marketplace.

Market risk   factors, such as changes in political, economic and social conditions, as well as changes in investor tastes and preferences, which may cause the market price of a security to change.

Marriage penalty   under the U.S. tax code, the increased taxes paid under certain circumstances by a two-income married couple filing a joint return compared with taxes paid by a two-income couple filing as "separate" persons.

Medicaid   A public assistance program under Social Security that is designed to provide medical benefits for those persons who are unable to pay their own health care costs.

Medical payments insurance (automobile)   insurance that provides for payment to eligible insureds of an amount no greater than the policy limit for all reasonable and necessary medical expenses incurred within 1 year after an automobile accident.

Medicare   A health care plan administered by the federal government designed to help persons over age 65 and others who receive monthly Social Security disability benefits.

Minimum payment (charge account)   the minimum payment required on a charge account; usually represents a specified percentage of new account balance.

Money market   the marketplace in which short-term securities are traded.

Money market certificate (MMC)   type of certificate of deposit issued by banks, savings and loan associations, mutual savings banks, and credit unions. They have 6-month maturities and pay interest at a maximum rate set equal to the rate paid on the most recently issued 6-month Treasury bills.

Money Market Deposit Account (MMDA)   offered as of December 1982 by federally insured financial institutions; basically the same as a money market mutual fund.

Money market fund   mutual fund that pools the deposits of many investors and invests in short-term debt securities offered by the U.S. Treasury, major corporations, and commercial banks.

Monthly investment plan (MIP)   an arrangement that allows investors to invest specified amounts, typically in the range of $50 to $1,000, in securities listed on the New York Stock Exchange every month or every 3 months.

Mortality rate   the number of deaths per 1,000 that will occur at specified ages each year.

Mortgage   a document conveying legal interest in a property to a lender as security for payment of a debt.

Mortgage bonds   secured bonds that have real property such as land, buildings, or equipment pledged against them as collateral.

Mortgage life insurance   an insurance policy on the life of the borrower in which the lender is the beneficiary. If the borrower dies, the mortgage is automatically paid off.

Mortgage loan   borrowing to finance the purchase of a piece of property.

Mortgage points   fees charged by a lender in a mortgage loan.

Mortgage REITs   REITs that invest in long-term mortgage bonds.

Multiple earnings approach   a method of multiplying annual gross earnings by some arbitrary multiplier to determine life insurance needs.

Municipal bonds   bonds issued by state and local governments and other public institutions.

Mutual fund   an investment company that invests in a diversified portfolio of securities.

Mutual savings banks   financial institutions similar to savings and loan associations whose depositors are their owners.

Named peril policy   an insurance policy which names the perils covered individually.

National Association of Securities Dealers (NASD)   a self-regulatory agency made up of all brokers and dealers in over-the-counter securities. It regulates the OTC securities market.

National Credit Union Administration (NCUA)   an organization of federal credit unions that insures deposits in all federal and many state-chartered credit unions.

National Foundation for Consumer Credit   an organization which sponsors nonprofit credit counseling centers in many communities.

National health insurance   a much discussed form of insurance coverage under which the government would assume all or part of the costs of health care services.

Needs approach   method of determining life insurance needs which considers the financial resources available in addition to life insurance and the specific financial obligations a person may have.

Negligent action   an action inconsistent with the "reasonable man doctrine"—the doctrine that if a person fails to act as would one with normal intelligence, perceptions, and experiences common to the community, he or she is negligent.

Negotiable Order of Withdrawal (NOW)   account similar in appearance and behavior to a checking account that can be viewed as an interest-earning checking account or as a savings account against which checks can be issued. While interest is paid at the passbook rate on regular NOW accounts, no interest rate ceiling exists on Super NOW accounts.

Net asset value (NAV)   the price at which a mutual fund will buy back its own shares based upon the current value of the securities which it owns.

Net cost method   a method by which the relative cost of life insurance can be assessed. It is calculated by totaling the premiums paid over a given period, subtracting from it the total dividends and cash values projected for the period, and dividing the remainder by the number of years in the period.

Net earnings   the amount of earnings an employee takes home after the employer has made all required as well as requested deductions.

Net federal estate tax payable   amount of estate tax payable to the federal government after all credits are subtracted.

Net payment cost index   measure of cost of an insurance policy exclusive of its cash value.

Net worth   often considered the amount of personal or family wealth, it is determined by subtracting total liabilities from total assets.

New York Stock Exchange (NYSE)   the largest and most prestigious organized securities exchange; it handles a majority of the dollar volume of securities transactions and a high percentage of the total annual share volume on organized securities exchanges. Also called "Big Board."

Night depository   a protected type of mail slot on the exterior of a bank or other financial institution. Deposits can be submitted in special envelopes provided for after-hour deposits.

No-fault   a concept of automobile insurance that favors reimbursement without regard to negligence.

No-load fund   a mutual fund that does not charge transaction costs.

Nominal rate of interest   stated rate of interest on a loan or savings deposit; this rate does not necessarily represent the true rate of interest being paid on the funds.

Noncatastrophic loss   a loss that is not the result of catastrophic occurrences such as war, nuclear explosion, and large-scale flooding; generally speaking, losses from catastrophes cannot be safely insured by private insurance companies.

Noncumulative preferred stock   preferred stock on which dividends do not accumulate. The current dividend must be paid prior to earnings being distributed to common stockholders.

Nonforfeiture right   an option that gives the life insurance policyholder the portion of those assets that had been set aside to provide payment for the death claim that was not made. The amount, often called cash value, is given to the policyholder when the policy is canceled.

Nonparticipating preferred stock   preferred stock on which only the stated amount of dividends is owed to the shareholder.

Nonqualified deferred compensation plan   an arrangement between an employer and employee to defer payment for services rendered by the employee. Such an agreement is most useful when an employee's future needs for funds exceeds his or her present requirements.

Note   the formal promise on the part of the borrower to repay the lender as specified in a sales contract.

N-ratio method   a formula for estimating the annual percentage rate on an add-on loan.

Odd lot   a quantity of fewer than 100 shares of a security.

Old age, survivor's, disability, and health insurance (OASDHI)   commonly referred to as Social Security, a U.S. government program established in 1935 and providing not only retirement benefits but also payments for survivors, disability income for workers and their dependents, and health care benefits for low-income and elderly families and individuals.

Open account credit   form of credit extended to a consumer in advance of any transaction. It is often referred to as a charge account.

Open-end investment company   investment company that will sell or buy back its own shares at a price that is based on the current value of the securities the fund owns. It is commonly called a mutual fund.

Operating in the red   state when an individual or a business has total expenditures in excess of total income.

Option   a contract that permits one to either purchase or sell a specified security at a predetermined price within a certain period of time.

Option charge account   a type of revolving charge account.

Organized securities exchange   institution where listed financial securities are traded by exchange members on a floor organized according to different types of securities. The largest and most prestigious example is the New York Stock Exchange.

Over-the-counter market (OTC)   the market in which the securities of smaller, less well-known firms are generally traded.

Overdraft   a check written for an amount greater than the current account balance.

Overdraft protection   special arrangement between bank and account holder whereby the bank automatically advances money to cover an overdrawn check. The account holder is charged interest on the advance.

Overspending   consumers spend more money or incur more obligations for future payment than they have income to cover.

Par value   the stated or face value of a stock or bond.

Participating policy   the life insurance policy that pays dividends which reflect the difference between the premiums that are charged and the amount of premium necessary to fund the actual mortality experience of the company.

Participating preferred stock   preferred stock on which the shareholder is allowed to share in the distribution of dividends once the common stockholder has received a specified dividend.

Participation or coinsurance clause   a provision in many health insurance policies stipulating that the company will pay some portion of the amount of the covered loss in excess of the deductible.

Partnership   a business owned by more than one person. Its income is normally taxed as the personal income of the owners, and their liability is not limited to their investment in the business.

Passbook account   a regular savings account at a financial institution.

Past due balance method   method of computing finance charges whereby customers who pay their account in full within a specified period of time, such as 30 days from the billing date, are relieved of finance charges.

Pawnshop   a loan source which accepts certain types of goods such as jewelry, guns, and stereos against which it lends 25 to 75 percent of their established market value.

Pay-as-you-go basis   method of paying income taxes whereby the employer deducts a portion of income every pay period and sends it to the IRS.

Payoff (on a loan)   amount required to terminate a loan.

Pecuniary legacy   type of clause in a will which passes money to a specified party.

Pension   a fixed sum paid to a person following retirement.

Pension Benefit Guarantee Corporation   established by a provision of the Employee Retirement Income Security Act of 1974, organization that guarantees to eligible workers certain benefits payable to them even if their employer's pension plan has insufficient assets to fulfill its commitments.

People planning   estate planning that places primary emphasis on satisfaction of human needs, anticipating psychological and financial needs of others, especially dependents with special problems or gifts and others who cannot, or do not want to, manage financial resources themselves.

Performance (go-go) fund   an investment company portfolio that emphasizes performance as measured by the total return earned on the shareholders' investments; the investment strategies are speculative.

Peril   cause of a loss.

Personal article floater (PAF) policy   insurance policy that provides for comprehensive coverage on a blanket basis for virtually all personal property of the insured.

Physicians expense insurance   insurance that can provide coverage for costs of such services as physicians' fees for nonsurgical care in a hospital, at home, in a clinic, or in a doctor's office.

Pocket money   all currency and coin under the control of an individual or family. This includes cash on the person or in the home.

Policy limits   the benefit limits described in an insurance policy.

Policy loan   an advance made by a life insurance company to a policyholder secured by the cash value of the life insurance policy.

Portfolio   a combination of stocks and bonds owned by an investor.

Preauthorized payment   mechanism that allows a savings institution to make payments from the customer's account at the customer's directions.

Precious minerals   minerals, such as gold, silver, and diamonds, that are used for investment purposes.

Preferred stock   hybrid stock that has a legal right to a fixed amount of dividend.

Prepayment penalty   a penalty charged by a lender for advance payment of a loan.

Previous balance method   a method of computing finance charges by which interest is computed on the outstanding balance at the beginning of the billing period.

Price-earnings (P/E) ratio   the ratio of current stock price to the earnings per share. Also called earnings multiplier.

Primary market   a market in which new securities are traded.

Prime rate   the interest rate charged by banks to their best customers.

Principal (on an annuity)   amount paid by the annuitant or person buying the annuity during the accumulation period.

Principal amount   the amount being borrowed on which interest is paid.

Principle of indemnity   an insurance principle that states an insured may not be compensated by his or her insurance company in an amount exceeding the amount of economic loss.

Private Mortgage Insurance (PMI) program   insurance plan for lenders that insures them against loss on certain mortgages, usually those with a low down payment.

Probate   a process of liquidation that occurs when a person dies. The deceased's debts are collected or paid, and the remaining assets are distributed to the appropriate individuals or organizations.

Probate estate   the real and personal property a person owns in his or her own name that can be transferred according to the terms of that person's will.

Professional corporation   corporation established by groups of lawyers, doctors, architects, dentists, and other professionals in part to allow them to set up pension and retirement plans.

Professional liability insurance   policies designed to protect such professionals as doctors, lawyers, architects, professors, and engineers in the event that they are sued for malpractice.

Profit sharing plan   an arrangement whereby the employees of a firm participate in the earnings of the firm. Such an arrangement may qualify as a pension plan.

Progressive tax   a tax schedule in which the larger the amount of taxable income, the higher the rate at which the income is taxed.

Property damage liability losses   losses caused by an insured to the property of another as a result of an accident in which the insured is legally obligated to pay such property damages.

Property insurance   insurance that provides coverage for physical damage to or destruction of property.

Property inventory   a prepared schedule of property with corresponding values noted.

Property owner association agreement   rules and regulations for owners of condominiums and other developments in which owners share use of a property or facilities.

Property tax   a tax levied on the value of various items of property, such as real estate, automobiles, and boats, owned by the taxpayer.

Prospectus   a document made available to prospective security purchasers by the issuer describing the new security being offered.

Proxy   a written statement used to assign a stockholder's voting rights to another person, typically the existing directors.

Purchasing power risk   a risk resulting from possible changes in price levels in the economy that can have a significant effect on the prices of securities.

Put option   an option to sell a specified number of shares of a stock at or before a specified future date for a stated "strike" price.

Qualified pension plan   a retirement plan that meets specified criteria established by the Internal Revenue Code.

Real estate investment company   a corporation that sells its shares and uses the proceeds to make real estate investments.

Real Estate Investment Trust (REIT)   an investment company that accumulates money for investment in real estate ventures by selling shares to investors.

Real Estate Settlement Procedures Act (RESPA)   law which requires mortgage lenders to clearly disclose settlement costs, closing costs, and the annual percentage rate to loan applicants and borrowers.

Real estate tax   the dominant form of property taxes, it is typically collected by the county and distributed among other governmental bodies to finance schools and other services.

Reasonable man doctrine   doctrine stating that if a person fails to act in a reasonable manner, he or she is said to be negligent.

Recession   the phase of the economic cycle during which both the level of employment and the overall level of economic activity are slowing down.

Regional stock exchanges   organized markets other than the NYSE and AMEX.

Registered bond   bond registered in the name of the bond purchaser.

Regulation Z   a regulation (Consumer Credit Protection Act) issued by the Federal Reserve Board.

Renewable term   a type of term insurance which may be renewed at its expiration for another term of equal length.

Renewal   right of the insured to continue coverage upon the expiration of the policy period.

Rent controls   controls imposed by a local government which limit annual rent increases to a "reasonable" level.

Rental contract   a legal device intended to protect the lessor from nonpayment or some adverse action of the lessee. It specifies the amount of the monthly payment, the payment date, penalties for late payments, length of the lease agreement, any deposit requirements, distribution of expenses, renewal options, and any other restrictions.

Replacement cost   the amount necessary to repair, rebuild, or replace an asset at today's prices.

Repossession   the act of seizing collateral when the borrower defaults on an installment loan.

Restrictive endorsement   this check endorsement, by adding the word "only" after the third party's name, prevents the check from being endorsed over to a fourth party.

Retirement goals   goals aimed for by individuals at retirement.

Revocable living trust   trust in which grantor reserves the right to revoke the trust and regain the trust property.

Revolving charge account   type of credit which allows customers to continue to purchase goods as long as they do not exceed the credit limit established or let their account become delinquent by not making specified minimum payments.

Right   an instrument that gives the holder an opportunity to purchase a specified number of shares of common stock at a specified price over a designated period of time.

Right of election   the right of a surviving spouse to take a specified portion of the probate estate regardless of what the will provides.

Rights offering   an offering of new shares of corporate stock to existing shareholders on a proportional basis relative to their current ownership.

Risk   uncertainty regarding economic loss or the outcome from an investment.

Risk avoidance   avoidance of the act that creates the risk.

Rollover mortgage   a mortgage in which the rate of interest is fixed but the whole loan is negotiated, or rolled over, at stated intervals, usually every 5 years.

Round lot   securities sold in 100-share lots or some multiple thereof.

Rule of 78 (sum of the digits)   a rule that is used to determine the portion of the total finance charges the lender receives when a loan is paid off prior to its maturity.

Safe deposit box drawer in a bank's vault that can be rented. It is used as a storage place for jewelry, contracts, stock certificates, titles, and other special documents.

Salary-reduction plan agreement under which a portion of a covered employee's pay is withheld tax-free and invested in an annuity or other eligible form of investment.

Sales contract a formal agreement to purchase a house, automobile, or other major item which states the offering price and all conditions—including repairs, inspections, closing date, and so on—required by buyer and seller. It is a contractually binding agreement.

Sales finance company a company that purchases notes drawn up by sellers of certain types of merchandise—typically more expensive items, such as automobiles, furniture, and appliances.

Sales tax tax levied by many state governments on the purchase price of an item or service. Some states exempt items viewed as necessities, such as food and drugs.

Savings money that has been set aside, commonly in an interest-earning form, in order to achieve any of a number of savings or investment goals.

Savings accumulation plan an arrangement under which an investor makes scheduled purchases of a given dollar amount of shares in a mutual fund.

Savings and loan association financial institution that channels the savings of its depositors primarily into mortgage and home improvement loans.

Savings ratio ratio of savings to income after taxes (disposable income).

Second mortgage mortgage that is next to a first mortgage.

Secondary market market in which old securities are sold and bought. Equivalent to a used car market.

Secured (and unsecured) loans if collateral is named for a loan, the loan is secured; if none is given, it is unsecured.

Securities obligations of issuers that provide purchasers with an expected or stated return on the amount invested. The two basic types of securities are stocks and bonds.

Securities and Exchange Commission (SEC) the agency of the federal government that has the responsibility of enforcing the Securities Exchange Acts of 1933 and 1934. This agency regulates the disclosure of information about the securities exchanges and markets in general.

Securities exchanges marketplaces—either organized or over-the-counter—in which buyers and sellers of securities can be brought together to make transactions.

Securities Investor Protection Corporation (SIPC) an agency of the federal government that insures brokerage customers' accounts.

Securities markets the marketplace in which stocks, bonds, and other financial instruments are traded.

Security agreement a legal agreement which gives the installment lender control over the item being purchased.

Security interest the legal claim of an installment lender providing control over the item being financed.

Self-Employment Individuals Tax Retirement Act (1962) HR-10 or Keogh Act, which gives self-employed persons the right to establish retirement plans for themselves and their employees that provide them the same tax advantages available to corporate employees covered by qualified pension plans.

Self-employment tax a tax that must be paid to the federal government by self-employed persons. The proceeds of this tax are used to provide self-employed persons with the same benefits regularly employed persons receive through the FICA tax.

Sell order an order to sell a specified number of shares of a given security.

Senior debts debts or bonds to which debentures are subordinated; these debts have a senior claim on both the income and assets of the issuer.

Settlement options the various ways in which the death proceeds of a life insurance policy may be paid, such as interest only, payments for a stated period, payments of a stated amount, or income for life.

Share draft account checking account offered by credit unions. They are similar to the negotiable order of withdrawal (NOW) account offered by other financial institutions.

Shared-appreciation mortgage a mortgage on which the rate of interest is set lower than market in exchange for giving the lender a partial—about one-third-interest in any gain in the property's value.

Short-run financial goals goals set for 1 or 2 years only.

Short sale a transaction made in anticipation of a decline in the price of a security. It is the practice of selling borrowed securities with the expectation that they can be replaced at a lower price at some future date.

Short-term capital gain   gain from sale of a capital asset owned for 1 year or less at a higher price than its original cost that is taxed as ordinary income.

Short-term municipal bond fund   a type of money market fund investing in short-term municipal bonds offering liquidity and interest free of federal income taxes.

Sickness policies   insurance policies which cover a named disease such as cancer.

Signature card   card containing account number, name, address, phone number, and signature kept on file in a financial institution and used to confirm validity of signatures on checks drawn on the account.

Simple interest method   the method by which interest is charged only on the actual loan balance outstanding.

Simplified Employee Pension (SEP)   account that can be used to either supplement or replace an employee's self-selected and controlled IRA. Through employer participation, this plan can substantially increase the amount that can be credited each year to an IRA.

Single limit automobile liability   an automobile liability policy that specifies the maximum amount paid per accident as a single lump sum rather than in terms of separate per-individual and per-accident limits for bodily injury and property damage.

Single-payment loan   a loan made for a specified period of time at the end of which full payment is due.

Single-premium annuity contract   annuity purchased with a lump-sum payment, often just prior to retirement.

Single-premium whole life   a whole life insurance policy that is purchased on a cash basis by making a single premium payment.

Small loan company   another name for a consumer finance company. The company makes secured and unsecured loans to qualified individuals. These companies do not accept deposits but rather obtain funds from their stockholders and through borrowing.

Sole proprietorship   a business owned by one person and operated on his or her own behalf. Its income is taxed as personal income, and the owner's liability is unlimited.

Solvency ratio   ratio of net worth (assets minus liabilities) divided by total assets.

Spec home   new homes constructed by builders on speculation that a buyer will be found. They vary in price, size, and other features and can be found in various stages of construction.

Special endorsement   check endorsement that includes a notation indicating specifically to whom the check is to be paid.

Special savings account   a savings account that offers slightly higher interest rates than a passbook account but in exchange requires the saver to maintain a specified minimum balance and/or to maintain that balance for a specified period of time. Certificates of deposit are an example.

Specialist   an exchange member who specializes in making transactions in certain securities traded on an organized securities exchange.

Specialty fund   a common stock fund that invests in the shares of firms within a specific industry.

Speculative stock   risky stocks that are purchased in the hope that their price per share will increase.

Speculative (day) traders   traders who purchase stocks with the intention of gaining from their day-to-day fluctuations in price.

Split-funded pension plan   qualified pension plan in which both a trust fund and an insurance contract is used to fund the plan.

Standard deduction   called the zero bracket amount, it is the level of a taxpayer's income to which zero tax rate applies. A taxpayer can use this blanket deduction instead of itemizing personal expenses.

State taxes   taxes levied by state governments to finance their operating costs. Sources include sales tax, income tax, property tax, and licensing fees.

Step-up trust   type of living trust in which the trustee steps up to take the grantor's place in decision making and day-to-day management.

Stock average (or index)   an average or index of a group of stocks that is believed to reflect the behavior of a given industry or the entire securities market. These averages are used to gauge the behavior of the securities market.

Stock company   an insurance company that is owned by stockholders.

Stock dividend   new shares of stock distributed to existing stockholders as a supplement to or in place of cash dividends.

Stock purchase option (plans) an option given to employees of a corporation that allows them to purchase a specified number of shares of its stock at a price set above the prevailing market price when the option is granted.

Stock split a trade of old shares for new shares typically initiated by management in order to either increase or reduce the price of stock.

Stockbroker sometimes called an "account executive." The stockbroker purchases and sells securities on behalf of clients, to whom he or she provides advice and information.

Stockholders' report sometimes called an annual report, a report that includes a variety of financial and descriptive information about a firm's operations during the year.

Stop-loss order an order an investor gives his/her broker to sell a security if the market price reaches a certain level, which is lower than its current price.

Stop payment an order to the bank not to make payment on a check that has been written.

Store charges a type of open account credit which is offered by various types of retail merchants.

Straight bankruptcy legal proceeding that results in "wiping the slate clean and starting anew."

Straight term a term insurance policy that is written for a given number of years. Coverage remains unchanged throughout the period of the policy.

Striking price the price at which an option (call or put) can be exercised, normally at a price set close to the market price of the stock at the time the option is issued.

Subordinated debenture an unsecured bond that carries only a secondary claim (with respect to both income and assets) to that of other bondholders or lenders.

Suicide clause life insurance clause which voids the contract if an insured commits suicide within a specified period of time after its inception.

Super NOW account a negotiable order of withdrawal (NOW) account issued by financial institutions that may pay interest without restrictions and offer unlimited check-writing privileges. Minimum balances are required.

Surgical expense insurance health insurance coverage for the cost of surgery.

Survivorship benefit (on an annuity) that portion of the premiums and interest that has not been returned to the annuitant prior to his or her death.

Syndicate (real estate) a limited partnership that invests in various types of real estate and is professionally managed. There are various types of real estate syndicates—such as single property and blind pool—involved in specific kinds of real estate acquisitions.

Systematic withdrawal plan a plan that allows the mutual fund shareholder to be paid specified amounts each period.

Take-home pay the amount of earnings an employee takes home after the employer has made all required as well as requested deductions.

Tangible property tangible items of real and personal property that generally have a long life, such as housing and other real estate, automobiles, jewelry, and other physical assets.

Tax avoidance the minimizing of tax payments in which the taxpayer accurately reports all items of income and expenditure but utilizes legitimate deductions and computational procedures.

Tax credits a deduction from a taxpayer's tax liability, such as the child-care credit.

Tax-deferred annuity an annuity that is exempted from current income taxes.

Tax evasion failure to accurately report income, expenditures, and tax liabilities; failure to pay taxes. Persons found guilty of this illegal act are subject to severe financial penalties and prison terms.

Tax-exempt income certain types of income, such as child support payments and disability payments, that do not have to be claimed as part of the taxpayer's gross income for tax purposes.

Tax-exempt securities bonds paying interest that is exempt from federal, and in many cases, state income taxes. These securities are issued by various state and local governments and are often called municipal.

Tax liability actual amount of taxes owed.

Tax preparation services professionals trained in the preparation of taxes, including national services, local services, attorneys with tax training, or CPAs.

Tax refund amount of money due an individual taxpayer from the IRS as a result of withholding and/or estimated tax payments exceeding the actual tax liability.

Tax shelter   certain types of investments that provide tax write-offs (deductions). Tax shelters often involve real estate and oil-related investments.

Tax-sheltered college education fund   fund in which money can be accumulated tax-free and used to pay future college education expenses of a child.

Tax write-off   in accounting terminology, depreciation, amortization, and depletion, used as a means to lower tax liability.

Taxable gift   money or property that is subject to a gift tax.

Taxable income   amount of income that is subject to taxes. It is calculated by subtracting itemized deductions and exemptions from adjusted gross income.

Technical theory   belief that security prices are solely the result of the forces of supply and demand.

Temporary life annuity   annuity in which benefits continue for the specified period only if the annuitant survives.

Tenancy by the entirety   form of ownership by husband and wife, recognized in certain states, in which the rights of the deceased spouse automatically pass to the survivor.

Tenancy in common   title to property under which each tenant who owns an interest is free to dispose of that interest without the consent of other tenants.

Term life insurance   insurance that covers the insured only for a specified period, most often 5 years, and does not provide for the accumulation of any cash values.

Testamentary trust   trust created in a will.

Testator   person whose will directs the disposition of property at his or her death.

30-Day charge account   charge account which requires the customer to pay the full amount billed within 30 days after the billing.

Thrift and savings plan   plan established by employers to supplement pension and other insurance fringe benefits. The employer generally makes contributions to a savings plan in an amount contributed by the employee.

Time deposit   the term used in the banking and financial industry to refer to a savings account.

Time-sharing   in real estate, arrangement under which buyers purchase rights to a resort condominium or hotel unit for a specified time each year; also called *interval ownership*.

Title check   research of legal documents and records—usually performed by an attorney or title insurance company—to verify ownership and interest in a title to real estate.

Total return   the return received on a security investment over a specified period of time. It is made up of two basic components—the dividend (or interest) yield and capital gains.

Travel and entertainment credit card   credit cards, such as American Express, Diners Club, and Carte Blanche, that enable the holder to charge purchases at a variety of locations. The holder is charged an annual fee to use the card.

Traveler's check   a check which can be purchased at commercial banks and other financial institutions in denominations ranging from $10 to $1,000. When properly endorsed, they are accepted by most U.S. businesses and can be exchanged for local currencies in most parts of the world.

Treasury bill   a short-term (91- to 360-day) debt instrument issued by the federal government. It is considered to be a safe and marketable investment.

Treasury bond   a federal government obligation, ordinarily payable to the bearer, that is issued at par, with maturities of more than 5 years and interest payable semiannually.

Treasury note   an obligation of the federal government, usually issued payable to the bearer, with a fixed maturity of not less than 1 year or more than 7 years; issued at par, with a specified interest return paid semiannually.

Trust   a relationship created when one party (the grantor) transfers property to a second party (the trustee) for the benefit of a third party (the beneficiary).

Trust fund pension plan   a pension plan in which the employer places its contributions with a trustee, who is then responsible for the investment of contributions and the payments of benefits.

Trustee   someone appointed to enforce the indenture and protect the interest of a bondholder, or (in the case of estate planning) a person or corporation that manages a grantor's property for the benefit of his or her beneficiaries.

Truth-in-Lending Act   a wide-ranging law designed to protect credit purchasers. The most important provision is the requirement that both the dollar amount of finance charges and the annual percentage rate (APR) charged must be disclosed prior to extending credit. It was formally called Consumer Credit Protection Act (1969).

Umbrella personal liability policy a policy that provides excess liability coverage for both homeowner's and automobile insurance, as well as coverage in some areas not provided for in either of these policies.

Underwriting (insurance) the process of deciding who can be insured and determining the applicable rates.

Underwriting (securities) the process of selling a new security issue, a task normally carried out by an investment banking firm.

Underwriting syndicate a group of underwriting firms (that is, investment banking firms) who accept the responsibility for selling a new security issue.

Unfunded pension plan pension plan which allows the employer to make payments to retirees from current income.

Unified rate schedule the graduated table of rates used for both federal gift and estate tax purposes; these rates are applied to all taxable gifts.

Uninsured motorists coverage insurance designed to meet the needs of innocent accident victims when involved in an accident in which an uninsured or underinsured motorist is at fault.

Universal life insurance insurance contract that combines investment features with term life insurance.

Unlimited liability liability that can extend beyond the amount of money an investor has put into a business (for example, the liability of owners of a sole proprietorship or partnership).

Usury laws state laws that prohibit the charging of interest above a certain limit.

U.S. Savings Bond bond issued in various denominations and maturities by the U.S. Treasury to assist in financing federal government operations.

Utility the amount of satisfaction a person receives from purchasing certain types or quantities of goods and services.

VA loan guarantee guarantee of a mortgage loan by the U.S. Veterans Administration to lenders who make qualified mortgage loans to eligible veterans.

Valued approach under health insurance, payment to an insured of amounts specified in a policy. Such payments may not necessarily bear a direct relationship to actual costs incurred.

Variable annuity annuity in which the monthly income provided can be adjusted according to the actual investment experience of the insurer.

Variable life insurance insurance in which the benefits payable to the insured are related to the value of the company's assets that support its payment obligation.

Vesting the right of employees to benefits in a retirement plan based on their own and their employer's contributions.

Wage earner plan arrangement that schedules debt repayment over future years that is an alternative to straight bankruptcy when a person has a steady source of income and there is a reasonable chance of repayment within 3 to 5 years.

Waiting period a provision of some disability income insurance policies that requires that the insured wait a specified length of time after the disability before payment begins.

Waiver of premium a clause that provides for automatic payment of premiums should an insurance policyholder be unable through disability to make the payments.

Warrant an instrument that gives the holder an opportunity to purchase a specified number of shares of common stock at a specified price, normally set above the market price at time of issue, over a designated period of time.

Warranty for automobiles and other products, contract stating responsibilities for repair and maintenance of a vehicle or product, offered by manufacturers and dealers.

Whole life insurance life insurance designed to offer financial protection for the entire life of the individual. Cash values are accumulated under this type of insurance.

Will a written document that allows a person, called a testator, to determine the disposition of property at his or her death.

Workers' compensation insurance a type of insurance paid for by the employer and designed to compensate the worker for job-related injuries or illness.

Writer (of options) in an option transaction, an individual who writes the options to be purchased or sold by the option buyer.

Yield   the return on an investment.

Yield to maturity (YTM)   the annual rate of return that a bondholder purchasing a bond today and holding it to maturity would receive on his or her investment.

Zero bracket amount (ZBA)   a specified amount of a taxpayer's income to which a zero tax rate applies. A taxpayer can use this blanket deduction instead of itemizing personal expenses.

Zero-coupon bond   bond, sold at a deep discount, that accrues interest semiannually.

Zoning laws   laws that govern permissible uses of property. They may also control factors such as building size and appearance and site placement.

Index

Notes

Notes

Notes

Notes

Notes

Notes

Notes

Notes

Notes

Notes

Notes

Notes

Notes

Notes